HEGEL
AND LEGAL
THEORY

HEGEL AND LEGAL THEORY

Edited by

Drucilla Cornell

Michel Rosenfeld

David Gray Carlson

1991

ROUTLEDGE

New York •
London

Published in 1991 by

Routledge
An imprint of Routledge, Chapman and Hall, Inc.
29 West 35 Street
New York, NY 10001

Published in Great Britain by

Routledge
11 New Fetter Lane
London EC4P 4EE

Library of Congress Cataloging-in-Publication Data

Hegel and legal theory / Drucilla Cornell, Michel Rosenfeld, David
Carlson, editors.
  p. cm.
  Proceedings from a conference held in March 1988 and sponsored by
the Benjamin N. Cardozo School of Law.
  Includes bibliographical references and index.
  ISBN 0-415-90162-6 (HB).   ISBN 0-415-90163-4 (PB)
  1. Hegel, Georg Wilhelm Friedrich, 1770–1831—Congresses. 2. Law—
Philosophy—Congresses. I. Cornell, Drucilla. II. Rosenfeld,
Michel, 1948–   . III. Carlson, David (David Gray) IV. Benjamin N.
Cardozo School of Law.
K230.H432H44   1991
340'.1—dc20   90-25928
                                                                        CIP

British Library Cataloguing in Publication Data

Hegel & legal theory.
  1. Jurisprudence /
  I. Cornell, Drucilla   II. Rosenfeld, Michel   III.
  Carlson, David
  340

  ISBN 0-415-90162-6
  ISBN 0-415-90163-4 pbk

Contents

Acknowledgments

Although sporadic citations to Hegels' *Philosophy of Right* can be found in legal scholarship, the birth of Hegelian studies within American legal scholarship can be traced to a conference held on March 27–29, 1988, at the Benjamin N. Cardozo School of Law, Yeshiva University, New York, N.Y. This conference, entitled *Hegel and Legal Theory,* inspired the title of this volume. Some of the essays in this volume were presented at that conference, and some others are outgrowths of different papers presented there. The proceedings of this conference are published in volume 10 of the *Cardozo Law Review,* pp. 847–1931 (1989). We gratefully acknowledge the permission of the *Cardozo Law Review* to reprint portions of some of the papers here.

This extraordinary conference was made possible by a generous gift by Jacob Burns and the Jacob Burns Institute. Through his generosity toward the Hegel project and, since then, several other projects which have explored deconstruction and legal theory, Mr. Burns has assured himself an important role in the recent unfolding of new energy and new/old ideas within American legal studies. It is to him that the editors are honored to dedicate this volume.

Introduction

The recent surge of interest in Hegel's writings on law among scholars spanning the broad range of disciplines represented in this volume of essays—namely, law, philosophy, political science and sociology—seems in significant measure linked to a paradox that strikes at the heart of our present relationship to law. That paradox is that ever greater numbers of people are turning (or returning) to the rule of law, at the very same time that frustration and dissatisfaction with law are on a steep increase. On the one hand, as attested by the dramatic changes over the last couple of years in Eastern Europe and by the series of transitions from authoritarian regimes to constitutional democracies in other parts of the globe, there appears to be a sweeping worldwide mobilization in support of the rule of law. On the other hand, in the United States, where respect for the rule of law has been a centerpiece of the national ideology for over two hundred years, there is a serious crisis of confidence concerning the law's objectivity as well as fractious debate and stiffening polarization concerning the proper function and legitimacy of law.[1] In view of these developments, moreover, it is not surprising that Hegel scholars should focus with particular interest on his writings on law or that those troubled by the fragmentation and apparent delegitimation of much contemporary legal discourse should turn to Hegel's systematic approach to law for possible alternatives.

The current importance of Hegel to legal theory is clearly underscored by the concurrent retreat of Marxism and the increasingly evident failure of liberalism cogently to integrate the legitimate needs and concerns of the individual with those of the community.[2] The retreat of Marxism in the face of the return of formerly socialist societies to the rule of law evinces a broad based rejection of the conception of law as a mere instrument for the advancement of the interests of the ruling class.[3] Indeed, there now seems to be irrefutable proof that systematic departures from the rule of law are much more prone to lead to intolerable affronts against human dignity than to any genuine emancipation. Accordingly, Hegel's vision of the legal sphere as necessary to the development of relationships of mutual recognition and respect among autonomous social actors looms as superior to Marx's one-sided grasp of law.

If Marxism has tended to underestimate the worth of the rule of law, liberalism has often erred in the opposite direction. Under some prevalent conceptions of liberalism, the legitimate role of the state is reduced to that of neutral and impartial enforcer of generally applicable legal rules. These rules are primarily concerned with securing the legal enforceability of certain fundamental individual rights in the belief that respect for such rights triggers the operation of some invisible hand mechanism that automatically harmonizes individual interests with the common good.[4]

The various proponents of liberalism may disagree as to which particular rights deserve the greatest legal protection. For example, liberals who believe that a free market economy supplies the desired invisible hand mechanism stress negative freedom over equality rights whereas Neo-Kantian liberals insist that rights to equal concern and respect are paramount.[5] But all proponents of liberalism tend to purge history and politics from the arena of social interaction. Liberalism thus enhances law's importance at the expense of politics and historically grounded collective norms and customs, but in so doing it impoverishes the realm of social relations by reducing it to an arena of formal rights attaching to largely a historical an unduly abstract individual subjects.

In contrast to liberalism, Hegel neither decontextualizes legal relationships nor does he overvalue the role of the rule of law. In his *Philosophy of Right*, Hegel situates legal relationships in the broader context of the sphere of Objective Spirit—that is, the sphere of social relationships broadly conceived as encompassing moral and political relationships as well as legal ones, and as requiring an active state openly devoted to the pursuit of the common good as concretely shaped by historically evolved communal norms. Under Hegel's analysis, moreover, adherence to the rule of law designed to uphold individual rights cannot alone bring about the common good. Significantly, Hegel rejects the proposition that we can rely on invisible hand mechanisms to turn our individual-regarding pursuits into communal goods.[6] Consistent with Hegel's dialectical method, however, law is not merely discarded, but rather subsumed in a comprehensive intersubjective scheme that also encompasses individual morality (*Mioralität*) and the ethical life of the community (*Sittlichkeit*). In short, to the extent that invisible hand explanations leave much to be desired in contemporary settings, Hegel's conception of the rule of law as necessary but circumscribed by the positive role of the state in the quest for the common good offers an attractive alternative to the rigid formal structures of liberalism. Furthermore, because he insists that the modern state must pursue collective aims in a way that leaves room for the expression of individuality (§ 261A), Hegel's theory appears to lack the deficiencies of collectivist or communitarian theories that fail to offer safeguards for individual autonomy.

Hegel's legal theory also appears to afford fruitful and attractive alternatives from the standpoint of the search for coherence in contemporary legal doctrine.[7] In both private and public law there has been— at least in the North American context—a progressive erosion of confidence in the legitimacy and intelligibility of prevailing legal doctrine. As the seemingly self-enclosed legal formalism of the 19th century, with its clear cut regime of abstract rights operating in apparent utter disregard of considerations of welfare, has given way to a more flexible approach designed to delineate legal rights in ways that accommodate diverse welfare concerns, legal doctrine has loomed as both increasingly opaque and ever more unprincipled.[8] Whereas legal formalism conveyed the impression that law could remain separate from politics and that legal interpretation could be objective, the injection of explicit welfare concerns into the process of formulating legal rules and rights often appears to efface the boundary between law and politics and to render all legal interpretation merely subjective.

Legal theorists have grappled with the problems posed by the retreat of formalist legal doctrine, but their analyses and proposed solutions so far leave much to be desired. In the broadest terms, contemporary American legal theory is comprised of three different approaches to law. At one end of the spectrum is the Critical Legal Studies Movement (CLS), a loose aggregation of diverse scholars who have variously claimed that law is thoroughly permeated by politics, that laws advance class-interests and that legal doctrine tends to be inconsistent or incoherent.[9] At the other end of the spectrum, one finds the law and economics approach according to which the purpose of legal rules and legal doctrine is to promote wealth maximization.[10] Accordingly, the principal purpose of law is to safeguard the unimpeded functioning of the free market economy, and to supplement or reinforce the invisible hand mechanisms designed to regulate that market to the extent that these mechanisms are subject to malfunction or failure. Finally, between these two ends of the spectrum, there is a third position, namely a Neo-Kantian liberal one that evaluates law and legal doctrine in terms of the principle of equal concern and respect.[11]

Although CLS has accomplished much that is valuable in demystifying inflated claims regarding the benefits to be derived from adherence to the rule of law, it remains unsatisfactory to the extent that it overstates the importance of legal indeterminacy and of doctrinal inconsistencies and that it severely underestimates the importance of basic legally enforceable civil and political rights. Similarly, law and economics is fundamentally flawed, for it legitimates a wealth maximizing legal regime by arbitrarily reducing the multifaceted legal person to the abstract and undimensional image of *homo economics*. Furthermore, Neo-Kantian liberalism also falls short of the mark because of its failure to provide the law giver and the law interpreter with workable means to implement the kind of neutrality required to vindicate the fundamental equal respect rights of all persons. Indeed, either principles of neutrality are articulated at such high levels of abstraction that they provide no determinate guidance in the actual allocation of legal rights and duties, or such principles, if rendered sufficiently concrete to affect the outcomes of actual legal controversies, seem doomed to remain neutral only in appearance, while in fact privileging some legal actors—usually those who already occupy dominant positions—over others.[12]

In contrast to the three principal contemporary American approaches to law discussed above, Hegel's legal theory is not reductionist. In particular, Hegel neither ignores nor enshrines the legal formalism of abstract right. Instead, he provides us with a rich and sharply focused image of the inner workings of legal relationships in the context of abstract right, while also stressing the limitations of abstract right, by situating it in the much broader landscape of which it is but a part. Not only does Hegel present abstract right in relation to individual morality and the ethical life of the community but he also indicates how legal relationships are delimited through interplay with the respective institutional frameworks of civil society and the state. Thus, although Hegel's integration of the individual, abstract right, civil society and the collective processes of the state raises many vexing problems of its own, it furnishes a useful and in many respects attractive holistic alternative to the three reductionist approaches that have dominated recent American jurisprudence.

The essays collected in this volume are divided into three parts. The three essays in Part One examine Hegel's writings on law in relation to broader systemic concerns. In his essay, Michael Theunissen draws upon Hegel's logic to interpret Hegel's *Philosophy of Right* as being animated by a repressed intersubjectivity that casts a critical gloss upon abstract right. According to Theunissen's interpretation, moreover, Hegel's treatment of abstract right evinces his intent to provide a critical portrayal of modern thinking on natural rights. Unlike the proponents of natural rights, Hegel maintains, in Theunissen's view, that freedom cannot be achieved through abstract right, but only through the kind of intersubjective interaction made possible by commonly partaking in the ethical substance.

Charles Taylor focuses on Hegel's ambivalent contribution to modern liberalism and to the relation between law and politics. According to Taylor, Hegel sides with the anti-liberalist position of the civic humanists, and rejects the invisible hand theory of the regulation of society. Stressing that civic humanism requires a common understanding regarding what constitutes the good life, Taylor indicates how Hegel's theory supplies weighty arguments against the type of liberalism advanced by Ronald Dworkin. Taylor also notes, however, that Hegel's theory is not without its own weaknesses to the extent that it leaves too little room for competition or difference. Taylor concludes that Hegel's communitarianism provides a useful antidote to the distortions of liberalism, but that it should be used with great care.

Robert Bernansconi turns to Hegel's *Phenomenology of Mind* in search of what governs law. Noting that the *Phenomenology* presents many laws—human and divine, moral and natural—Bernansconi asks whether there is a law of laws. Emphasizing certain differences between Hegel's treatment of law in the *Phenomenology* and in the *Philosophy of Right*—for example in the former in contrast to the latter *Sittlichheit* precedes *Moralität*—Bernansconi traces Hegel's use of the transition between the Greek ethical community and the abstract and impoverished legalistic world of Rome as a means to illustrate how the replacement of the ethical substance by abstract right leads to a soulless and disconnected existence.

The essays gathered in Part Two all deal with Hegel's *Philosophy of Right*, and in particular with his treatment of abstract right in the context of private law. Arthur Jacobson advances the thesis that an adequate understanding of the theoretical underpinnings of the common law requires reference to Hegel's jurisprudence. Hegel had little use for the common law, but Jacobson maintains that this was because Hegel misunderstood the thrust of the common law system. In fact, Jacobson argues that Hegel's jurisprudence, like the common law, is a correlation breaking dynamic jurisprudence which must be contrasted

with positivism and naturalism, the predominant contemporary jurisprudences, which are based on a static order sustained by the maintenance of a strict "Hohfeldian" correlation between rights and duties.
Moreover, not only is Hegel's jurisprudence non-Hohfeldian, but its
correlation breaking nature makes possible, according to Jacobson, the
growth of the person through a process of mutual recognition.

Alan Brudner sets Hegel's systematic account of law against the
modern trend towards denying private law's autonomy and towards
asserting an unbridgeable gap between individualism and the public
good. According to Brudner, Hegel is the only philosopher to offer an
immanent account of private law from the standpoint of the common
good. Brudner further emphasizes that abstract right is a necessary
but one-sided aspect of the internal synthesis between rights and the
common good envisaged by Hegel's theory. Finally, Brudner maintains
that this synthesis reveals the inner unity that binds together various
phases of the common law.

Peter Benson takes the view that Hegel's approach is constructivist
and that abstract right in the *Philosophy of Right* represents lexically
the first step in the normative order. Abstract right, Benson points out,
supplies the minimum necessary for the expression of positive freedom
by requiring that subjects be respected as persons having a juridical
capacity to possess property. But because abstract right ties respect of
personhood to the *fact* of possession rather than to the *nature* of the
property possessed, Benson argues that abstract right is purely nondistributive and fully compatible with great disparities in wealth. Abstract right always involves external relations between formally equal
persons. As Benson indicates, distributive considerations are important
within Hegel's normative scheme, but such considerations can only be
properly introduced by going beyond the stage of abstract right.

Peter Stillman concentrates on Hegel's account of property in the first
part of the *Philosophy of Right*. Stillman notes that Hegel's account of
property relations bears various similarities to modern liberal, neoconservative and market-oriented visions of society. Because of Hegel's
rejection of monological thinking, however, he is led, according to
Stillman, to a fundamentally different conception of property. On
this account, property is essential for the setting of intersubjective
relationships, but it must be transcended (*Aufgehoben*) in the process
of education and culturation (*Bildung*) of the individual which prepares
the latter for the achievement of genuine freedom in the context of the
institutional framework generated by the ethical life rooted in the
community. Consistent with Stillman's interpretation, Hegel's theory

teaches us that property rights must be protected but only to the extent that they do not contravene basic welfare requirements.

Michel Rosenfeld examines Hegel's conception of contract in the context of both legally binding contractual relationships and contractarian justifications for political institutions. Linking Hegel's analysis of contract in the first part of the *Philosophy of Right* to his account of the celebrated dialectic of lord and bondsman in the *Phenomenology of Mind*, Rosenfeld argues that Hegel's systematic analysis of contractual relationships provides a superior alternative to that of Hobbes. Extracting from Hegel's account the paradigm of contract as "reciprocal recognition," Rosenfeld elaborates a Hegelian framework for the reconciliation of individual-regarding and community-regarding values in contemporary contractual relationships. Moreover, relying on Hegel's subordination of the realm of abstract right, which includes contract, to the ethical life of the community, Rosenfeld argues that the legitimacy of contractual relationship is always ultimately dependent on substantive collective norms.

Ernest Weinrib appeals to Hegel's conception of abstract right to resolve an important controversy regarding contemporary tort jurisprudence. According to Weinrib, Hegel's account of abstract right in the *Philosophy of Right* amounts to the purest and most uncompromising treatment of private law from the perspective of rights. Because of this, Weinrib maintains, recourse to Hegel's abstract right is very helpful to sort out, in the context of torts, the dichotomy between right and advantage. Weinrib points out that modern scholars are confused about the relationship between rights and advantages, and that even as explicitly a rights based approach as Nozick's is insufficiently separated from an advantage based model. Rejecting the law and economic approach to torts as being incapable of coherently sustaining rights, Weinrib argues that tort law should be confined to redressing wrongs rather than also providing compensation for disadvantages. Weinrib further specifies that it is only by concentrating on rights to the exclusion of advantages that tort law can remain cogent and intelligible.

The essays contained in Part Three all relate to Hegel's discussion of the ethical life in the last part of the *Philosophy of Right*. The ethical life, which circumscribes the proper scope of legal relationships, is divided by Hegel into three different dialectically consecutive stages. The first of these is the stage of the family, the second that of civil society, and the third that of the state.

David Krell looks at the role of women in Hegel's system. Krell argues that the place of the family in Hegel's dialectics of the ethical life turns on the role of the three women protagonists found in the *Philosophy of Right*. These women are Aphrodite, Antigone and Lucinde. It is on Lucinde, a romantic heroine, that Krell concentrates; she represents a necessary yet disruptive force that amounts to a law that unsettles all laws and undermines marriage and religion. Thus, in Krell's view, Lucinde puts Hegel's system as a whole into jeopardy.

Andrew Arato assesses Hegel's conception of the role of civil society in the realization of the ethical life of the community. Drawing on contemporary social and political theory, Arato discusses the deficiencies in Hegel's account, which Arato believes are due to Hegel's étatist tendencies and to his failure to fully appreciate the complex interaction between the private and public spheres. On the other hand, Arato credits Hegel with developing a theory of social integration that prefigures the contributions of Durkheim, Parsons and Habermas. Specifically, Arato argues that, in framing the ethical life in terms of communally shared substantive norms, Hegel failed to account for a new form of *Sittlichkeit* containing a plurality of forms of life and making consensus possible only on the level of procedures. Furthermore, Arato is of the view that modern civil society is the locus of a struggle between *Sittlichkeit* and *Anti-Sittlilchkeit* as the principal domain for the confrontation between individual-regarding and communal norms.

Fred Dallmayr sets out to reexamine Hegel's theory of the state in light of post World War Two doubts concerning the positive ethical character of the state, and of the postmodernist tendency towards antifoundationlism. Finding it still captivating, Dallmayr seeks to reinvigorate *Sittlichkeit* in the radically different context of a postmetaphysical and poststatist approach to democracy. Taking into account Karl Popper's criticism of Hegel as an enemy of the open society, and Jean François Lyotard's charge that Hegel's totalizing approach is incompatible with the postmodern experience of disjunction and fragmentation, Dallmayr searches for ways to recreate the public spirit but not the letter of the Hegelian state. Dallmayr proposes that *Sittlichkeit* can be given new life in our contemporary world through the embodiment of the public spirit in a plurality of open-ended and shifting collective alliances such as "rainbow coalitions," ecology oriented groups and "ashrams."

In the last essay of this volume, Bernhard Schlink looks at the contemporary implications of Hegel's theory of the state from the standpoint of a constitutional scholar. Schlink argues that the state is an even stronger presence today than it was in Hegel's time. In fact, Schlink maintains that the state has become the predominant political

formation of our society, but that, from the perspective of a constitu-
tionalist, the contemporary state must be understood as being inherently rational. Without the state observes Schlink, it is impossible to
achieve a satisfactory reconciliation of the individual and the community. Such reconciliation, however, becomes feasible through constitutional government. Finally, Schlink emphasizes that Hegel proceeds
meticulously, from level to level, starting with abstract right and passing through subjective morality the family and civil society before
reaching the state. This consititues proof, according to Schlink, that in
Hegel's theory the state is in no way totalitarian.

Drucilla Cornell
Michel Rosenfeld
David Gray Carlson
—August 1990

NOTES

1. Compare, e.g., R. Posner, Economic Analysis of Law (2d Ed. 1977) with R.
   Dworkin, A Matter of Principle (1985); R. Dorkin, Taking Rights Seriously
   (1977); Unger, The Critical Legal Studies Movement, 96 Harv. L. Rev. 561
   (1983).
2. See, e.g., M. Sandel, Liberalism and the Limits of Justice (1982).
3. See 3 K. Marx, Capital 793 (1972); K. Marx, Gundisse 469–70 (1969); K. Marx
   & F. Engels, The German Ideology, in 5 K. Marx & F. Engels, Collected Works
   90–92 (1976).
4. For a contemporary example of such liberal conception, see R. Nozick, Anarchy,
   State and Utopia (1974).
5. Among liberals who concentrate on the virtues of the market economy are Nozick
   and Posner. See R. Nozick, supra note 4; R. Posner, supra note 1. Included among
   neo-Kantian liberals, on the other hand, are Rawls and Dworkin. See J. Rawls,
   A Theory of Justice (1971); R. Dworkin, Liberalism, in Public and Private Morality (S. Hampshire, ed. 1978).
6. See G. Hegel, Philosophy of Right § 243–45 (T. Knox trans. 1952). All further
   references in the text to section numbers are citations to the *Philosophy of Right.*
7. For a more extended discussion of the current crisis in legal interpretation in the
   United States, see Rosenfeld, Deconstruction and Legal Interpretation: Conflict,
   Indeterminacy and The Temptations of the New Legal Formalism, 11 Cardozo
   L. Rev. 1211 (1990).
8. See, e.g., G. Gilmore, The Death of Contract (1974).
9. See, e.g., Dalton, An Essay in the Deconstruction of Contract
   Doctrine, 94 Yale L. J. 1007 (1987): Feinman, Critical Approaches to Contract
   Law, 30 UCLA L. Rev. 829 (1983); Abel, Torts, in The Politics of Law 185 (D.

Kairys, ed. 1982); Freeman, Legitimizing Racial Discrimination Through Autidis-crimination of Law: A Critical Review of Supreme Court Doctrine, 62 Minn. L. Rev. 1049 (1978).

10. See, e.g., R. Posner, supra note 1.

11. See, e.g., R. Dworkin, Law's Empire (1986); R. Dworkin, supra note 1.

12. For a more extended discussion of this point in the context of a Rawlsian con-tractarian approach, see M. Rosenfeld, Affirmative Action and Justice: A Philo-sophical and Constitutional Inquiry 233–38 (1991).

Part One

Being, Person, Community
and the
Ethical Foundation of Law

1

The Repressed Intersubjectivity in Hegel's Philosophy of Right

Michael Theunissen

INTRODUCTION

The previous discussions of the *Philosophy of Right* from 1821 centered primarily on the question whether Hegel renews premodern philosophy of order such that he relapses behind the Enlightenment's ethic of autonomous individuals or whether he succeeds in integrating the modern freedom of the individual into his conceptual scheme guided by Greek and Roman role models.* In such discussions it is agreed that if the spirit of the Restoration, which sacrifices the present to the past, is not itself present in Hegel's *Philosophy of Right* from Berlin, his philosophy of right at least remains within the confines of a liberal conservatism that strives to reconcile the present with the past. It is ruled out that Hegel is on the way to a new future that posits a new principle against the metaphysics of order and the Enlightenment's ethic. We who live later know that the new principle arises in Marx's theory. It bases phenomena that are the object of Hegel's philosophy of right neither in isolated individuals nor in a whole that contains them, but rather in social relationships through which the individuals first become themselves. The following considerations are to explain the thesis that already Hegel makes this third element the basis of right.

On the one hand, the thesis seems to be superfluous since it only retains what Hegel clearly and distinctly says. He defines right as "the existence of the free will" (§ 29), that is, as an existence that gives freedom to itself. But "the proper and true ground upon which freedom is existent" is, he assures us, the "relation of will to will" (§ 71). On the other hand, it appears as if this thesis were completely untenable. Hegel affirms the metaphysical order to which classical politics commits the citizen in the name of substantiality, which he overtakes in

(RIEDEL)

Translated by Eric Watkins in consultation with Fred Dallmayr the concluding part of his philosophy of right, in the theory of ethical life (Sittlichkeitslehre).[1] "In dealing with ethical life," he explains, however, to his listeners, "only two views are possible: either we start from the substantiality of the ethical order, or else we proceed atomistically and build on the basis of individuality" (§ 156 A). This alternative describes the predominant features of the condition in which this discordant book finds us. My thesis, in contrast, concerns an intention that is only partially fulfilled in the text. It does not attempt to characterize "the" intention of Hegelian philosophy of right but rather only what I like about it. Its flip side is the claim that the correctly held intention is partially obscured in its actual realization and partially reversed into its opposite. I need not proliferate as to the alleged motive for the fall from it.[2] One must assume that the deformation is also politically motivated.

The only place to be mentioned here is the one at which the "good" intention occurs despite its insufficient realization. I assume that Hegel's philosophy of right is a critical portrayal in its approach and not merely on the periphery, a critical portrayal of modern thinking on natural rights and, through this, of a social reality that the tradition from Hobbes to Fichte projects, to speak with Marx, into the eternal natural necessity of the heavens.[3] This assumption will not be left as such, but rather will itself need to be justified. Accordingly, I look at the extended line of Hegel's criticism for his intention of primitive social relations. The intention can be made tangible in the standard that Hegel uses to measure modern thinking on natural rights. As we will see, the criticism is developed in both of the first parts of the book from 1821, in the theories of abstract right and morality. But Hegel already circumscribes the target of this criticism in the introduction. It turns against "the view, especially widely held since *Rousseau*, according to which what is fundamental, substantive, and primary is supposed to be the will of an individual in its characteristic arbitrariness, not the rational will, existent in and for itself, and the spirit as a *particular* individual, not as *true spirit*" (§ 29 F; see § 258 F). In order to be able to perceive the object of criticism sharply and also so that the position taken here becomes identifiable, one must read this passage carefully: Hegel does not oppose the will in and for itself, which, according to his conception, is the principle of legally composed reality, with the will of the individual; rather he contrasts it with the will of the particular individual or the will of the individual *in its characteristic arbitrariness* (Wilkür). Accordingly, his criticism is directed at the opinion that one can start with freedom in the sense of individual arbitrariness. Moreover, it covers a concept of right that—like the

Kantian, according to Hegel—justifies the social capacity of an individual's arbitrariness in its "restriction" by the arbitrariness of others (§ 29 F). In the perspective of this criticism, according to my thesis, there arises, in contrast to freedom in the above sense, a freedom that Marx confronts civil freedom with: a freedom for which the other is ꜰᴜʀꜰʟɪᴄʜᴇ not a "*barrier*" but rather "*realization*."[4] That individuals must form the origin is in a sense self-evident. The question is only whether the freedom of the individuals is what it is independent of the relations into which they enter, or whether it is only realized in interactions. The subject of discussion is thus whether freedom is initially individual or mediated intersubjectively from the start. It may be that Hegel overshoots the goal of his criticism and denies the naturality of the individuals themselves when he polemicizes against the prejudice that "a merely atomistic *agglomeration* of individuals" (§ 273 F) is given. But his criticism serves as a guide here only insofar as it destroys the modern natural right tradition's presocial concept of freedom. And it exercises a function of orientation in the form of a divining rod that I use in my search for Hegel's alternative concept of freedom and that serves as a guideline of the criticism that turns against Hegel when this criticism reveals the aberration from the intention that resides in it. (ɪɴ ʜɪꜱ ᴄᴏɴᴄᴇᴘᴛ ᴏꜰ ꜰʀᴇᴇᴅᴏᴍ)

The title of the present study subsumes under the concept of intersubjectivity those relations that constitute freedom or the social relations through which the individuals first become themselves. Its range extends beyond the class of primitive relations. But it also covers a manifold of forms within this class. One need only consider the differing strengths of the claim that freedom is "intersubjectively mediated." That freedom "is first realized in institutions" can mean, at one extreme, that it only originates in them, whereas, at the other extreme, it can mean that it exists prior to them and persists in them as well. It is impossible to analyze the whole gamut of forms of relations at this point. Only the main difference that is directly relevant to the interpretation of the *Philosophy of Right* is to be named.

A sufficient understanding of this work depends essentially on one seeing enough of the breadth of what Hegel calls "right." The subject of his philosophy of right is not at all exhausted in the relations of strictly legal form that are defined by being subject to prosecution.[5] ʀᴇᴄʜᴛʟɪᴄʜ? His philosophy of right deals with such relations only in the realm of abstract right, which Hegel also calls strict right (see § 94 N). Already his theory of morality extends beyond right "as such" (E § 487). Ethical relations are characterized precisely by the fact that no "merely legal ʀᴇᴄʜᴛʟɪᴄʜᴇꜱ positive bond" (§ 176) conjoins their elements. Hegel does not only reach ethics[6] with his comprehensive concept of right, which also fixes the sense in which his work is to be philosophy of right; he also reformulates with it early Greek theology. Thus, it is to be taken seriously when he calls right[7] "holy" (§ 30). A comment from the margin of the paragraph that contrasts "pardon" with right in its usual sense (§ 132) remarks on distichs 76 and 77 from Goethe's *Jahreszeiten* with the words: "What is the holy?—what holds human beings together. . . . What is the holiest? what unifies the spirits eternally." Accordingly, right is the reason for and the whole of relations and precisely those through which human beings first become free and themselves. The main difference in what is intended by the concept "intersubjectivity" corresponds exactly with the difference between strict and nonstrict relations of legal forms. It is only in relations that transcend "limited legal right" (E § 486) that an emphatic sense of intersubjectively mediated freedom is conceivable. On the basis of positive right, conversely, all intersubjective relations can contribute in only certain particular ways to the realization of freedom and to the development of the person.

The given explanations of the program also adumbrate the outline of this study. It is apparent that the theory of ethical life constitutes a privileged test case for the thesis. First, because it appears most expressly to disclaim the thesis; Hegel states with respect to ethical life that there is no third approach other than those from substantiality and individuality. Second, because it and only it appears to subsume under it those relations that are candidates for verifying the strong claim involved in the thesis, namely that Hegel starts with social relations through which individuals first become themselves. For these reasons we must first examine the thesis with material from his theory of ethical life. The result of the examination will force us to go back to the foundation of his theory of ethical life in the introduction. From what has already been said, however, a further motive favors starting with ethical life. It is concealed in the distinction between a criticism and an affirmative standard. The philosophy of ethical life fixes Hegel's affirmative standpoint. For this reason it forms the actual beginning for Hegel himself as well. Abstract right and morality are, in contrast, the addressees of the criticism. We shall have to ask to what extent, on the one hand, Hegel's affirmative and, on the other hand, his critical approach are involved in the disclosure of intersubjectivity. In pursuit of this question I want to illuminate to a presently not yet sufficiently clear extent the criticism that is involved in Hegel's portrayal of right and morality—and with respect to this assumption I concur with an extended, if not oppositionless research tradition. This illumination will proceed by means of an analysis of the logic that preconstructs the

connection between these two subordinate spheres and ethical life.
Only after this analysis can it be shown to what extent and in which
problem horizon the criticism is directed at asociality. The last two
sections are to then work out Hegel's actual productive contribution
to the theory of intersubjectivity. A turning point lies between these
sections and all of what precedes. Namely, one perceives the contribution only if one uncovers a dimension of the criticism that does not fit
the distinction between itself and its affirmative standard. In the face
of this dimension, we shall have to go deeper into the thesis in a way
that cannot yet be anticipated.

THE REPRESSION OF INTERSUBJECTIVITY OUT OF
ETHICAL LIFE: FAMILY, SPIRIT AND
SELF-CONSCIOUSNESS OF SUBSTANCE

That the family at any rate, with which Hegel's theory of ethical life
begins, encompasses constitutive relations in a strong sense is obvious.
For this reason it interests us the least. It appears expedient, however,
to advance from the unproblematic to the problematic. We perceive
most clearly the point still deserving of interest in this respect when we
get clear about the question of why the theory of ethical life begins
with the family. That this is a real question is shown by Hegel's
orientation towards those individuals that were already persons "for
themselves" before they became members of a family (see § 158). This
implies two things. First, Hegel is not oriented to the life story of the
individual; he does not follow the personality development of a child
raised in a family. Rather he takes the perspective of adults who decide
to marry and found a family. Second, he assumes the mates belong to
civil society and live in a state (see § 256 F). Thus, he is concerned not
with the traditional family, but rather with the civil family. Objectively,
the family he thematizes is accordingly based on civil society.[8] All
the same, it initiates the portrayal because only it satisfies all three
conditions that are to be made at the beginning of the theory of ethical
life, namely being (a) unity, (b) immediate unity, and (c) simultaneously
a unity of the spirit, that is, an institution that can be known and
desired as an end in itself. That the family is a unity in the form of a
totality ("Totalität") qualifies it for the beginning. Because ethical life
is always a totality (see E § 515), the individuals circumscribed by it
are also always determined as members, not only in the family, but
also in civil society and in the state. However, the family-specific unity,

as an immediate or natural one that is still open to the spirit, is "life in its Totality" (§ 161).

"Unity" functions in this manner as the guiding concept in Hegel's theory of the family. The concept is exposed in § 158 and developed in the paragraphs up to 163 in such a way that the spirituality of the initially merely immediate unity comes to light. It becomes apparent along with this: the "unity of family" (§ 159) is a communal unity. That is to say, the individual has "his life in this unity itself" and only in it (§ 159.) The human beings who decide to marry accede "to constitute *one* person" (§ 162). This person is neither the one that every individual already was for itself, nor the one that the family forms in the legal sense; for the family first becomes a legal person only by dissolving into a plurality upon the transition into civil society (§ 181). What the person signifies into whom the marriage partners unite, in contrast, is indicated by the familial unity being a unity of "love" (§ 158). Hegel describes love from the perspective of each of the mates as a unity of self-renunciation and self-acquisition, that is, of renunciation of the "natural and individual personality" and of acquisition of "substantial self-consciousness" (§ 162).[9] The resulting "unity of myself with the other and the other with myself" (§ 158 A) is, however, simultaneously *freedom*, an equally *communal* freedom.[10] By helping the mates to substantial self-consciousness, it effects "their liberation" (§ 162). This freedom is also to be distinguished from the one the mates must already have in order to be able to give their "free accession" to a union. The latter can, as Hegel's diagnosis of civil society will teach us, only be an abstract or formal freedom. Hegel had it in mind when he claimed in the *Differenzschrift* from 1802 that the individual who enters into "a truly free community of living relations" relinquishes his own freedom. For this freedom was only an "indeterminacy" (GW 4, 55). The freedom enabled by the loving community is, in contrast, determinate and concrete. Already in the explanation of his theory of will as it was developed in the *Philosophy of Right* Hegel points toward "friendship and love" in order to demonstrate to his listeners how "the concrete concept of freedom" is to be understood (§ 7 A).

Now the theory of ethical life as a whole must rest upon a foundation that can carry such a communal unity and freedom. But the primitive position of a union through which individuals become themselves must also be taken into consideration by the approach of the theory of ethical life because there is concern for such a union even still in the theory of the state. Hegel does emphasize that the unity of love is replaced by the unity of the law in the state (see § 158 A). However, that does not deter him from the explanation, which is certainly intended for the state: "The union as such is itself the true content and end [of the individual], and the destiny of individuals is to live a universal life" (§ 258 F). At the conclusion of the study I will have reason to return to this sentence, which I feel is the most engaging and contemporary in all of Hegel's philosophy of right, but under a point of view that relativizes it essentially. Prior to all else, what lies in the connection between union and universal life should be appreciated: the sentence commits the individuals to a universal life that is, at any rate, also a communal one. In the process Hegel consciously drives at—initially familial—life. He does not actually remove love itself from the state, but rather its sensual moment. What remains of love is what is further developed into the life of the spirit. Even if one were to suppose that communal life forms did not fall into the core area of ethical life, its basic principles would still have to measure out the area in which intersubjective relations in general are to be planted. For all forms of ethical life—family, civil society and state—are forms of communal living. In the introduction to the theory of ethical life Hegel himself prognosticates "that in the following the determinations of ethical life turn up as necessary relations" (§ 148 F).

I want to make room for intersubjectivity in the foundation of the theory of ethical life by dividing the approach into three levels. The lowest level of the foundation is formed by "the living good" in § 142. In contrast to the abstract idea of the good at which—in a way yet to be explained—moral philosophy arrives (§ 131), the living good assumes a position corresponding to the absolute spirit. It does not stand opposed to the finite subject any more but rather covers self-consciousness and world as their common ground (see also § 33). It is *"the absolute final end of the world"* and thus "the *idea*" simpliciter (§ 129) as the Platonic idea *tou agathou* and, at the same time, as the good for which, according to the first sentence of the *Nichomachean Ethics*, everything strives.[11] The directedness of the philosophy of the objective spirit toward that of the absolute spirit is entirely in agreement with his system. For Hegel always understood, already in the Jena years, ethical life such that it transgresses religion. But the topology of the living good is objectively justified as well. It has the same argument in favor of it that supports the attribute "living": the living good is the good life in a Platonic and Aristotelian sense along with the absolute standard towards which it orients itself.

The approach from the living good is not all unproblematic. From it follow questionable consequences insofar as Hegel universalizes the good as he rises to the niveau of ethical life. Evil has been taken care of in his criticism of morality and does not come into view any more, which is why "the private conscience of the individual" (§ 152) becomes superfluous. The universalization of the good rests on a premise taken from the philosophy of history, namely that reality has turned out essentially good. The living good is living as the historical emergence of good in modern states as well. For this reason Hegel feels exonerated from the task of subjecting the state to a normative examination; and for this reason virtue is reduced for him to "the simple conformity of the individual to the duties of the relationships to which it belongs" (§ 150).[12] However, this problematic lies in an area different from the question about intersubjectivity. The approach of the theory of ethical life from the living good does not yet thematize intersubjectivity. But it does disclose the conditions for its possibility. It thus limits itself, completely convincingly, to the function that the philosophy is not itself communal life but rather the source of its life (Lebendigkeit).

The approach of the theory of ethical life in § 144 attains the second level with the turn to "objective ethical life." As *objective* ethical life is not the absolute any more; as the nature of the historically "*present world*" (§ 142) it stands opposite the finite subject. It is first with this move that Hegel brings the concept of substance into the game.[13] Objective ethical life proves to be substance by becoming experienceable to the individuals as a power that penetrates everything, not only in the play of "*ethical powers* which regulate the life of the individuals" (§ 145), but also, on the one hand, in the recognition of persistent independence that it has as an "object of knowledge" (§ 146), and on the other hand, in its internalization in which the subject encounters it as "*its very own essence*" (§ 146); for the recognition of its existence-for-itself and the identification with it are only opposite modes of submission. However, this substance has a peculiar "*ethical*" substantiality (§ 152). Hegel reveals its specifically ethical character by developing it into the spirit. Objective ethical life is "the *spirit* living and present as a world" (§ 151). But Hegel also thinks of the spirit here in a determinate sense. The movement presented in the remarks on the foundation of ethical life culminates in the sentence: "The ethical substance . . . is the *real spirit* of a family and people." (§ 156). This concept of spirit that Hegel develops subsequent to Montesquieu whom he appreciates so much (see § 3 F).[14] And he works into his early conception Montesquieu's historical concrete *Esprit* according to which spirit is the all-comprehensive medium of interaction.[15] Only in this manner can it be explained that and how the theory of family can, in a similar recourse to Hegel's early period, cash out spirit as love. If the approach from the living spirit, as the governor of the absolute spirit, reveals the conditions of the possibility of intersubjectivity, then the turn to the objective spirit leads to intersubjectivity itself. This turn adumbrates, for the first time, the profile of Hegel's theory of ethical life. One can say with good reason that the concept of spirit designates Hegel's *promium* when contrasted with other representatives of German Idealism. Hegel's understanding of spirit extends beyond Fichte's "Ego" as well as Schilling's "Absolute." But such a statement is only correct if it is driving at the fact that Hegel intends "spirit" to mean the room for interaction that his idea of ethical life demarcates most exactly.

We thus arrive at the perhaps unexpected result that the substantialism of the theory of ethical life, instead of precluding, precisely includes the acceptance of primitive social relations. Hegel is correct insofar as he claims that the approach from substantiality and the origin from the individuality of the particular individual form an exhaustive disjunction for ethical life. Yet Hegel undertakes still a third step in the course of laying the foundation of ethical relations. He ascribes "*self-consciousness*" to substance.[16] When he says in § 142 that the living good has "in its self-consciousness knowledge, desire and, through its actions, actuality," he still has the self-consciousness of the individual in mind; he is describing at that point the realization of the good in the good life of the finite subject. In § 146, on the contrary, he speaks of substance and "its" self-consciousness. Accordingly, he creates the prerequisite for the personification of the state criticized by Marx that, as the ethical spirit, is the substantial will, which "thinks and knows itself, and accomplishes what it knows and insofar as it knows it" (§ 257). Hereafter Hegel will determine the connection of the individuals with the ethical substance, in a reversal of the manner of speaking of § 142, such that the individuals "have their essential self-consciousness" (§ 264) in the institutions in which the ethical substance becomes concrete (see § 144). This new way of talking is, however, only a disguised expression for the delegation of the individual self-consciousness to substance. The delegation is divulged when Hegel recourses to the individuals as soon as he must empirically authenticate how the substantial will is "accomplished." He is already forced into this in the theory of family. There he projects the entirety of the development, which the "ethical substantiality" takes along its path from the family to the state, onto the level of the relation between the marriage partners. Whereas the wife remains at the standpoint of the family, it is the husband who runs through this development (see § 166). The man becomes in this matter the surrogate for the self-consciousness of substance.

The second and third steps of the approach ᵀᵒ of the theory of ethical life are for Hegel of course aspects of one and the same thing. For him, both follow from the first step, the starting point of the absolute spirit. The justification of ethical life in the philosophy of the absolute spirit is not at all to be deplored. The objection that plagues the foundation of the theory of ethical life is directed rather at the razing of the difference between the absolute and the objective spirit. Or it is directed against Hegel's transfer of the self-consciousness that is ascribed to the absolute spirit onto the objective spirit. It is this transfer that removes all intersubjectivity from the basis of ethical reality. For it destroys the communal constitution of the spirit in which individuals come together for the construction of their world.

The destruction of the intersubjective approach, for which the original situation of the theory of ethical life is at least open, can be read off precisely from the thought that is to mediate intersubjective relations with the self-consciousness of substance. Hegel understands substance there as the *relation* of substantiality as he determines it in the final chapter of the logic of essences. Substance is "essentially the relation to itself of accidents" (§ 163 F). The stylistic unevenness of the sentence already intimates the violence of the procedure that Hegel applies in connecting intersubjective relations with the self-consciousness of substance. The connection proceeds in two stages: Initially Hegel transfers every relation between persons into a relation of substance to these persons; he then interprets the allegedly primitive relation as a relation of substance to itself. Accordingly, the independence of the persons disappear, which persons Hegel consistently accidentalizes. In the textual passage of the Heidelberg *Encyclopedia* which he refers to in the footnote to § 163, the "necessary," into which the *Philosophy of Right* translates the "objective ethical" (see § 145), as a "relation of *substantiality* and *Accidentality*," sublates itself into the "absolute identity of this relation with itself" (HE § 98). The incompatibility of this identity with the communal *unity*, as which Hegel conceives of the family as a consequence of the original situation of his theory of ethical life, testifies not least to the way in which he forces both of them together into the definition of substance in his philosophy of right: No communal unity results from the "identification of personalities through which the family is *one* person and the members of the family are accidents of it" (§ 163 F), because the accidentalization of the related members deny communal *freedom*.

Intersubjectivity is not completely eliminated from the state-theoretical actualization of the program of the theory of ethical life. However it is retained in a form that only strengthens the departure from it. It emigrates namely from the region of relations between human persons in order to settle into their relation to the state. The relation to the state is, in Hegel's view, itself a social relation. Hegel does remark in the foundations to the theory of ethical life that the individuals would gain through the internalization of substance a relation that is "even more identical" than "*trust*" (§ 147). He then characterizes the political attitude, however, as "*trust*" in the state (§ 268). He certainly has in mind that one can only have trust in a person. He expressly assigns the state the role of "an other." Whereas he does not find "trust" completely adequate as a name for the relation to substance, where he has substance only as the objective ethical in front of himself, he chooses the name as soon as its personality has stepped forward. The limiting explanation that the state "is immediately no other for me" is only supposed to protect him from the suspicion of foreignness. I am aware, claims Hegel, of it as "an other" such that I "am free in this consciousness." Into the trust flows, accordingly, that "*free love*" with which the *Science of Logic* is concerned, freedom as being-in-the-other-with-one-*self*, love as being-with-oneself in the *other*. However, substance accompanied with self-consciousness allows at most a quasi-personal relation to itself. Trust is no truly free consent, but rather a trust that the person of the state knows what he wants and also "accomplishes" it.

(2) THE REASON FOR THE REPRESSION: PROBLEMS WITH THE APPROACH FROM INDIVIDUALITY

Insofar as self-consciousness is to be attributed to the ethical substance, one may also, in Hegel's opinion, speak of the latter's *individuality*. The "*immediate*" individuality of spatio-temporal existents is not suited for it (E § 481; see HE § 390). For this reason the state, in which the ethical substance completes itself, "has" a "mediate existence" (§ 257) "in" the self-consciousness of human individuals. However, Hegel claims, the "individuality of the concept" (L II 261), which the *Science of Logic* distinguishes from the former, can be attributed to it. The assurance that one can begin only with either substantiality or individuality is thus also misleading to this extent. However, the logical distinction between immediate individuality and the individuality of the concept initially only leads deeper into the labyrinth. It counts as one of Hegel's most peculiar and darkest thoughts. Still we must turn to it in order to be able to clarify how and why intersubjectivity is eliminated from the approach of the theory of ethical life. Hegel brings the distinction up in the introduction to the *Philosophy of Right* (see § 7 F). Therefore, it is necessary to return to the introduction.

The topic of the introduction is the will, from which Hegel develops what defines the concept of right, namely "that any existence is the existence of the free will." The preliminary decisions that are most portentous are made in § 1 when Hegel substitutes the concept *simpliciter* for the concept of *right*. He does not define right, but rather explicates its concept with the structure of the concept. Correspondingly, he raises the determinate concept of the will to the concept as well. The determinations of the concept, existent for itself, are universality (Allgemeinheit), particularity (Besonderheit) and individuality (Einzelheit). He dissects the will into these determinations, from which it can be explained in what manner the philosophy of right, which presupposes the logic in every respect, extracts from it the principle that determines the division (§ 33 F). It is true that its three parts correspond to the three parts of his logic so that abstract right, morality and ethical life have the logical constitution of existence, essence and concept, respectively. However, the whole thing rests on the foundation of the concept existent for itself: the foundation of abstract right is thus a conceptual-logically derivative existence, and the foundation of morality a conceptual-logically derivative essence. Since the conceptual logic reformulates being as universality and essence as particularity, this means that abstract right is the sphere of universality, and morality the sphere of particularity. The concept, however, as unity of universality, particularity and individuality, is to be characterized essentially by individuality; it is "really nothing other than the concept itself" (§ 7 F). Accordingly, the philosophy of right deals *in toto* with individuality. Viewed more closely, the logical principle of abstract right is individuality as unity of universality, particularity and individuality in the determinacy of universality, the logical principle of morality is individuality as the unity of these three determinations of the concept in the form of particularity and the logical principle of ethical life is the individuality that contains the universal and particular in the form in which they emerge as such. According to this logic the mystery of individuality that is the origin and the whole is revealed through the self-consciousness of the ethical substance that manifests itself at the end.[17]

I would like to demonstrate with the first sentences of § 13 how obscure this mystery initially is. The sentence reads: "By resolving, the will posits itself as the will of a certain individual and as separating oneself off from an other." The will becomes a resolving one by giving itself the form of individuality (§ 12; see E § 469). With this, it distinguishes itself from otherness because the resolve acts exclusively; it enters into a negative relation to the other due to its "excluding and resolving individuality" (§ 24). But what does it mean for the will to posit itself as the will of a certain individual? The phrase is ambiguous. On the one hand, it means that the will is posited in the analysis of its individuality as the individual will that it always already was "in itself." The will with which the philosophy of right begins is the will, dealt with in encyclopaedic theory of the subjective spirit, of the human individual that is found as itself a natural essence in the midst of nature (see HE § 389). Even when observing the will whose individuality is not yet posited, Hegel attends to the natural drives, desires and inclinations (see § 11). On the other hand, the above phrase indicates that the will that posits itself as the will of a certain individual is not itself an individual will. Hegel who emphasizes that the will that forms the ground for abstract right "is *in itself an individual* will of a *subject*" (§ 34) defends in the introduction against understanding the will in question here "as a previously presupposed *subject* or *substrate*" (§ 7 F). Due to this ambiguity, the expression "individuality" becomes ambiguous as well, and in a twofold manner. First, one must demarcate the thematic individuality from an almost completely unthematic individuality, from the in the most precise sense "immediate" individuality that can be ascribed to the individual as an Aristotelian conceived substance.[18] From this immediate individuality is distinguished the thematic individuality as a "individuality of the concept" that arises when the individual mediates its particularity with universality.[19] Understood in this manner, it is individual as well. Second, one must further distinguish from this individuality an individuality of the concept that the concept "gives itself" by coming into existence in the individual that accomplishes the achievement of reflection of its particularity. This thought uses the assumption that individuality forms "the side of existence or reality" of the concept (HE § 388). It sketches the movement of right. If the concept has existence at the beginning of the *Philosophy of Right* only in the self-consciousness of the individual, then it is shown at the end that it exists for itself as a self-conscious substance.

If one retains the presented ambiguity in mind, the problematic of the beginning of the *Philosophy of Right* can be divided into three problems. First, the question naturally arises whether it is legitimate to presuppose a supra-individual will, prior to the individuals. Second, the introduction appears questionable in describing the will of the subject without giving any important consideration to intersubjectivity. Third, it calls forth doubts insofar as it projects the asocial, or deficiently social, condition of the individual will onto a supra-individual will. The discussion in the literature on the "individualistically" oriented starting point[20] of the 1821 book that also differs in that respect from Hegel's other pertinent texts,[21] is fixated on the relative asociality of the will of human subjects. But the real problematic point is the projection that creates the will of the concept from the concept of the will. This project forces us to answer the first question with no. It lets on that the presupposition of a will separate from the individuals rests upon a hypostatization. But it is also this projection that causes the loss of intersubjectivity in the foundation of the theory of ethical life. This is not only the case insofar as the concept inherits the asociality from the individuals. The projection represses social relations much more from the foundation of ethical life by personalizing ethical substance.

Now the claims about the directly relevant questionable points must still be substantiated. Their support is all the more necessary since most interpreters that speak of the social deficiency of the individual will, so fundamental for Hegel, do not have the introduction in front of them, but rather the first part of the book and the comments that introduce it. But the individual will upon which the introduction constructs the *entire* philosophy of right is certainly also deficient. Hegel remarks in a handwritten note that "*the Other*"[22] does not belong here (§ 29 N). To what extent this is the case is shown initially by the sentence quoted from § 13. First, the other is debated only at a place where the Other is normally situated. Second, the Other could only come into view as an excluded Other. Third, the exclusion, as we saw, is based on resolving. The Other is thus, if at all, merely mediate and present *modo negativo*.

But why must one say that the Other could only be the topic of the introduction as an excluded Other, and why is it not also in fact thematized as such? The question refers to the actual weighty deficiency. It lies in the concept of freedom. If one were permitted to take the statement "free is the will *that wills the free will*" (§ 27) only with respect to itself, it could be interpreted socio-philosophically. However, such an interpretation is impossible because Hegel understands his statement such that "the will has itself as an object" (§ 10). Thus, Hegel also prescribes the path to which the understanding of his definition of right, according to which right is the existence of the free will, is to remain true. The definition, taken in itself, demands of the will only that its object is freedom. However, Hegel adds the further requirement of the will "that its freedom is the object" (§ 27). But this is to be understood, in turn, such that the will "refers to nothing other than itself" (§ 23). Whereas in the introduction Hegel sets in with his genuine concept of freedom according to which freedom means being-with-oneself-*in-the-other* (*Im-Anderen*-bei-sich-sich-selbst-Sein), his thought here drives him to the idea that freedom is pure being-with-oneself (Bei-sich-Sein). The Other could thus only be the topic of the introduction as an excluded Other because it is more completely eliminated as *in*cluded Other. However, it is not thematized as excluded either because Hegel construes the pure being-with-oneself according to the model of affirmative infinity that, as the first and still abstract form of reflection, contains the other neither inside nor outside itself. Thus free will, as the "*real-infinite*", is the object of itself in that there is for it "neither an *other* nor *barrier*" (§ 22) and "all relation of *dependency* upon some thing other recedes" (§ 23).[23]

At this point, the further question naturally arises how Hegel can think of the will without considering its autarky nor as "separating SELBSTÄNDIGKEIT? itself off from an other," or how he can grasp an individuality that excludes, if not the Other, at least the other. The suspicion arises that he projects, in a reversed order, the absolute onto the finite subject. However, a different answer emerges up close. At the same time, it provides a contribution to an even deeper problematization of the freedom proffered by Hegel. The introduction does not really develop determinations of a consistent concept of freedom, but rather different concepts of freedom. Apart from the communal freedom that is only presented in oral remarks and even there only in traces, we encounter in the text, on the one hand, as an element of the definition of right, a freedom that is realized only in institutions, and on the other hand, a freedom that activates itself in thought. Beyond the unity of desire and thought that resulted from the theory of the subjective spirit, Hegel makes two claims: first, the will is "*thinking getting its own way* in the will" (§ 21 F), second,—less explicitly stated but implied in it—freedom is essentially the freedom of such thought (see § 4 F).[24] The change in reflection taking place in the course of the introduction from being-with-oneself in the other to pure being-with-oneself expresses the attempt to create a logical foundation for distinguishing the intellectualistic concept of freedom. The cashing out of the will according to the model of affirmative infinity does not result immediately from a projection of the absolute spirit onto the finite subject but rather from the tendency to let it arise in thought, which stands, however, Aristotelian as participation in the absolute.[25] This might also answer the question why at the start Hegel detaches the individual from its social relations so much. Rolf Peter Horstmann showed with great plausibility that the freedom of the finite subject, which Hegel affirms on the basis of his theory of ethical life oriented towards self-consciousness, is only the formal freedom conceived as being-with-oneself of the *knowing* subject that remains unfree, however, as an agent.[26] Presumably, Hegel delimits the only space in which he can recognize the finite subject as free through the intellectualization of freedom, through which he also detaches it from the context of social action.

The consequence is that he runs into the same criticism that he raises against the rational rights of modernity. He speaks himself in support of a freedom that realizes itself without others and prior to forming a community with them. Perhaps this conception of freedom alleviates for Hegel the projection of the constitution of the individual will onto the supra-individual will. But the projection fails precisely due to the individuality that it is to establish. The concept of individuality, due to which it is in effect the individuality of the concept, reformulates Aristotelian theology, which was faced with the problem of how the absolute can be both the all-comprehensive as the divine cosmos and a separate as god. Hegel attempts to solve the problem in the *Science of Logic* by attributing to the absolute conceived of as concept, an individuality that does not exclude otherness, but rather includes it or excludes it only in the form of enclosure. In the *Philosophy of Right*, on the contrary, he necessarily attributes to the supra-individual will, insofar as he views the will as resolving or acting, a strictly exclusive individuality. The same thing, however, that causes the projection to fail testifies to it as well.

(3) THE FORM OF CRITICAL PORTRAYAL OF RIGHT AND
     MORALITY; THE LOGIC OF DISSAPEARANCE

Our investigation of the fate of intersubjectivity in Hegel's philosophy of right relies upon the hypothesis that the third element, beyond the substantialistic metaphysics of order and the atomistic ethic of freedom, to which this philosophy is under way, arises in the perspective of the criticism in which it is formed. In this respect, the study has so far disappointed this expectation. The intersubjectivity initially aimed at is quickly removed from the approach from ethical life, the Hegelian alternative to starting with the individual freedom of the individual, so that the substantialism of the theory on ethical life in fact relapses into the restoration of Greek and Roman philosophy of order. The individuality of the concept that is allegedly from the individuality of the particular individual and is to be the reason for and the whole of it reveals itself as the projection of an individual's presocial free will so that it is hard to see how Hegel's philosophy of right can elude the atomism of modern natural rights.

In light of the preliminary result, we should ask if we might not differentiate the guiding hypothesis. We could check what it means in detail for the sought-after third element to arise in the perspective, or "extended line," of his criticism. It seemed to be saying that Hegel intends intersubjectivity in an affirmative standpoint that he holds in opposition to modern natural rights. He raises the criticism in the portrayal of abstract right and morality, whereas he posits the affirmative standpoint in the theory on ethical life. Thus, the connection between abstract right and morality, on the one hand, and ethical life, on the other, is under scrutiny. It is to be shown in this connection that and how Hegel gives a *critical* portrayal of abstract right and morality; and it is to be stated more precisely in which way he liberates truth by doing so.

Morality and formal right are "both abstractions whose truth is only ethical life" (§ 33 A). They are mere constructs that proceed from the anticipation of certain formations of a completely ethically constituted reality. It is first upon the basis of this similarity that morality rises above formal right. The reality that ethical life and only ethical life describes is, as we have ascertained, historical reality. Abstract right is in a distinguished sense abstract because it lies completely beyond history.[27] Morality, conversely, as the "right of subjective *freedom*" (§ 124 F; see § 121), forms an extrahistorical enclave within the historical process itself. The moral philosophy outlined in the second part of the *Philosophy of Right* turns out so meager because its topic is not really moral action as such but rather the borders of moral action[28]; and its borders are already prescribed by morality's limited meaning for history. Moral consciousness is actually only legitimate insofar as the individual has the right to satisfy its own particular interest in addition to following the universal end that it wants to accomplish in the historical process. Hegel goes so far in a handwritten note as to claim that moral interests are "only remnants" (§ 126 N).

One preliminary question important for the clarification of the question at hand is, *in what sense* is ethical life the truth of the abstractions of formal right and morality? Besides the approach of the theory of ethical life and the forms of the ethical spirit we have only taken the family and state into consideration, and not civil society. But the theory of civil society that constitutes superficially merely one part of the theory of ethical life really reflects its entirety. We have already seen that the family Hegel examines is the civil family. That this society also provides the basis upon which Hegel will plant the state has often been noted in secondary literature.[29] Not only is the condition illuminated by Marx to be considered, namely that civil relations continue into the political state, but also that, in a reversed direction, civil society draws the state into it. In order to delimit the political state immanent to civil society, Hegel calls the latter *"external"* (§183), but that he anticipates the state itself under this title, just as under that of corporations, betrays his analysis of civil society by already presupposing the "universal power" (§ 141).

Both subordinate spheres also result from the anticipation of formations of ethical reality insofar as they picture certain regions of civil society. The membership of abstract right and morality to civil society can be taken from either the portrayal that Hegel provides of this society or his theories of right and morality. In a remark in a margin of the theory of right he expressly notes that property, which yields the foundation, is to be thematized under the assumption of societal relations in which everything belongs to someone (see § 58 N). That these relations are civil, is clear from, among other passages, the section on the sale of property, to which the intermittent sale of labor for a restricted period belongs (see § 67).[30] Similarly, Hegel characterizes the standpoint that fixes his moral philosophy in its context as that of civil morality (see § 125 N). In this manner he expresses that moral consciousness, this extrahistorical enclave of history, is itself an historical result, a result of a process in which civil society forms itself. One can extract the civility of right and morality from the middle section of the theory of ethical life just as easily. With initial respect to abstract right, it reaches universal validity only in civil society. People are citizens as legal people, and they are legal people as owners, as which people in general were defined in the theory of right. Correspondingly, Hegel's theory of civil society confirms that morality too has its place in civil society's domain. Morality especially mediates love that is thinned into charitable activity and that acts temporarily in the empty spaces of civil society (see § 242). Whereas love does not have any immediate access to civil society due to love's familial character, morality can penetrate into civil society's pores precisely because it is equally private without familiarity.

Civil society is distinguished from the state and family, from Hegel's viewpoint, precisely due to the "loss" of ethical life (§ 181). Thus, if the integration of abstract right and morality into ethically constituted reality implies that these subordinate spheres are layers of civil society, then ethical life is also their truth and especially so as lost ethical life. That ethical life is the truth of abstract right and morality apparently means initially that civil society unveils, due to its own untruthfulness, the truth about the abstractions. Accordingly, the theory of civil society does not separate off from the criticism that Hegel presents in his theories on abstract right and morality. Rather, the criticism is completed in it. It is completed in it, however, in a way that simultaneously saves the productive approaches that the theories of abstract right and morality work out. If we are directed not by Hegel's intentions as such, but rather by the actual condition of the philosophy of right that resulted from an insufficient fulfillment of the intention followed here, then we may only understand the hypothesis, according to which primitive intersubjectivity arises only in the extended line of criticism, in a limited way such that the affirmative position points at it behind the criticism. We must then tune our hopes down to the expectation that the sought after third element appears along with the criticism itself. In the section after next, I will reveal the truth that is generated in abstract right and morality and virtually hidden by the theory of civil society. Before this and prior to the exhaustion of substantial criticism that Hegel presents in the theories of abstract right and morality, the formal movement of the subordinate spheres is to be outlined with respect to the manner in which it makes the portrayal of these spheres critical.

The movement that leads from abstract right to morality and then ethical life cannot be a *development*, insofar as the subordinate spheres are untrue, in the sense that "the concept" becomes progressively richer and continually develops an initially one-sided truth in all directions. When abstract right reverses itself in wrong (literally "unright") at the end and morality changes into evil, both become, as it were, lost in themselves. Both subordinate spheres are not capable of finding a way out of themselves. For this reason, Hegel must entrust their sublation into a higher realm to anticipated forms of ethical life. The good plays this role for morality and punishing justice plays it for abstract right.

One need only compare § 129, with which the last section of the part on morality begins, with the already interpreted initial paragraph of the theory of ethical substance and its explication in § 143 in order to confirm that the concept of good that is used in the second part of the *Philosophy of Right* extends beyond reality. According to § 129, the good is the *idea*," according to § 142, "the *idea of freedom.*" For the former it appears as "realized freedom," for the latter as "the *concept of freedom developed into the existing world and the nature of self-consciousness*;" initially it is for Hegel "*the absolute final end of the world,*" and then he characterizes it as the "motivating end;" and just as he initially conceives of it as "unity of the *concept* of the will and of the *particular* will," he then presents it also in § 143 once

again as "unity of the *concept* of the will and its existence." Without
being guilty of exaggeration, one may say that the portrayal of the
morally good only begins with the second sentence of § 131. In § 130
Hegel continues the anticipation of ethical life on morality's ground
by bending morality, as the sphere of the finite subject that is concerned
with its welfare, as well as abstract right, as the moral constitution of
the objective world, under the ethical spirit as the absolute spirit in
whose horizon he will explicate ethical life. Accordingly, the good has
an "*absolute right* over the abstract right of property and the particular
ends of welfare." Thus, the first sentence of §131 explains the position
of the subjective will toward the good with the same expression that
gives an account of the position of the subject in general to the absolute
spirit in the concluding section of the *Encyclopaedia*: the subjective
will has value and dignity only insofar as it is "in accordance with"
the good. When the second sentence sets the "*abstract idea* of the
good" off against the good that the theory of ethical life will qualify
as living, he is not merely exposing a lack of reality; rather he is saying
that morality contradicts the good. For, according to his inquiries, "the
subjective will has not yet been taken up into the good and posited in
accordance with it." The published text provides as a reason that the
subjective will to the good still stands in a relation and the good is still
only an ought. However, Hegel changed the justification in his own
handwriting such that the good "is supposed to be a possession of
the subjective will." He thus makes clear: the contradiction is a self-
contradiction of moral consciousness. Because the subjective will does
not only stand in relation to the good, instead of standing *in* it, but
rather appropriates the good as its own, he turns the truly existing
subordination relation around in a contradictory manner.[31]

The reversion-into-themselves of the subordinate spheres, which are
not capable of connecting directly with ethical life and whose overpow-
ering requires ethical life, can be described even more clearly for abstract right. In the transition from right to morality Hegel distinguishes
the respective "formation" from the "conceptual determination of the
will" attained in each stage (§ 104). By relying on this distinction, I
would like to sketch the movement, characteristic for the critical function of the theory of right, first in a description of the form that
abstract right takes on at the conclusion and then in an analysis of the
appropriate conceptual determination or logic of perishing right.

GESTALT   The "*form* of the development of the will" that we must take into
consideration, is "crime" (§ 104). As a form of *abstract* right crime
could not injure the existence of freedom "in its *concrete* sense" (§ 95).
The philosophy of right from 1821 refers it to an aspect according to

which it originates from the subjective will, into the realm of morality (see § 113 F), without the philosophy of right having taken it into consideration more than peripherally (see §§ 132 F, 140 F); he only returns to it in a relevant way in his diagnosis of civil society (see §§ 218, 220). Thus, he in effect only strengthens the ascertainment of the logic of 1816 that crime falls in the domain of ethical life (L II, 285). Accordingly, already with crime perishing right protrudes into ethical life, which had provided the framework for Hegel's early theory of crime as well.

The only side of crime that is immanent to the sphere of abstract right is that of force, and "a force against the *existence* of my freedom   DASEIN
in an *external* affair" (§ 94). In this lies its power to unfold this whole   SACHE
sphere. With it, it becomes apparent that abstract right simpliciter rests on force and is, as for Fichte, the *"right to coerce"* (§ 94). Force against things forms the basis for abstract right. I acquire property, according to Hegel, by bringing a thing under my control (see § 45), and, accordingly, I retain it by exercising unlimited rule over a thing that is "an unfree and nonpersonal thing without rights" (§ 42). But then I am exposed to the force of others and run the danger of being coerced by them, that is, to be forced into actions (see § 90). Under the conditions of abstract right force continually spreads out, insofar as force against persons joins force against things. Also the uprooting of wrong can only proceed under these conditions such *"that coercion is sublated by coercion"* (§ 93). *Revengeful* justice, which is in accordance with the basic principles of abstract right, attaches a new link onto the chain of force; with it force posits itself "into the unlimited" (§ 102). *Punishing* justice, however, remains a mere "demand" on this ground, a demand, Hegel claims, that can only be satisfied morally (§ 102). The genuine end of abstract right thus consists of the endless repetition of the same. It unmasks the whole sphere as an infinite connection of force in the sense of bad infinity.

Hegel attempts to capture the same movement that he derives from the dynamic of the concluding form of right through the fixation of the correlative conceptual determination. We can put it to the test by examining the phenomenal data with the proper logic of the elementary sphere. Hegel copies the movement of abstract right from the logic of existential judgment. Even in this logical dimension of depth the partial movement of property prescribes the path upon which wrongful action completes the whole movement in itself. The three determinations of property—acquisition, use, and alienation—express "the will's *positive, negative* and *infinite* judgment about a thing" (§ 53). Of the three forms of wrong, nonmalicious wrong corresponds to the simply negative judgment (see § 85), fraud corresponds to the infinite judgment "in its positive sense" (§ 88) and crime corresponds to the negative-infinite judgment "in its complete sense" (§ 95). Hegel believes this analogy to be justified, because nonmalicious wrong merely negates the particular under the recognition of the universal (of right), because fraud—as does the infinite judgment in its positive expression or its "identical meaning"—becomes a tautology, insofar as false information's deception deprives the controversial object of its objective meaning, or "the side of the absolute existing *in itself* is absent" (§ 88), and finally because crime together with the particular negates simultaneously, and above all, the universal itself.

But what the assignment of abstract right to the existential judgment says in principle is only illuminated by the way in which the property determinations are repeated in the forms of wrong. While the wrong runs through the path taken in the sequence of property determinations from the positive to the infinite judgment, it displays the infinite judgment as the logical figure of abstract right. However, this produces a double negative from which no positive result emerges (see L II 284 ff.).[32] Insofar as the assignment of abstract right to the existential judgment gets its orientation towards the infinite judgment, it retains its affirmationless negativity. Already the alienation of property, interpreted as infinite judgment, lacks any affirmation, excepting the anticipatory value determination; it is a return, but as a step back, no being-with-oneself *in* a thing, rather "the reflection of the will in itself from the thing" (§ 53). A double negation without any positive result is ultimately also the punishment of crime, namely only "the injury of injury" (§ 101). Hegel does counterpoint this purely destructive annihilation of the void by a "sublation of crime" that is supposed to lead to a "restoration of right" (§ 99). However, it is not without reason that the concept of crime only reaches explication after the movement of force against force. For it makes evident that a return of right to itself, mediated by the negation of negation, can only be the sublation of crime insofar as crime itself is settled beyond abstract right. Within 'he borders that define right as abstract, the falsehood posited with its abstractness bears no truth.

Hegel characterizes this type of falsehood, which is not a one-sidedness capable of being completed, with a certain concept of appearance ("Schein"), the concept of that kind of appearance whose "truth" lies alone in "that it is void" (§ 82). He also cashes out wrong in terms of such an appearance, which is simultaneously intensified in the increments of wrong through the three forms of nonmalicious wrong, fraud and crime according to his view (see § 83). This interpretation is supported by right, the universal in itself, becoming in wrong a right that particular subjects assume for themselves and by thus reversing itself into "a *particular*" (§ 83). The appearance that attaches to the wrong rests on the contradiction into which right involves itself. However, abstract right was contradictory from the beginning, because its formal universality was merely particularity from the beginning. Wrong brings to light what abstract right is in itself by revealing the falsehood of the abstract as the falsehood of the false.

The indicated end of abstract right, which is not an actualization, repeats itself, however, *mutatis mutandis* in the perishing of morality. In the transition from morality to ethical life both morality and right pass into a higher sphere. Only both final determinations of morality, the abstract good and the subjectivity that insists upon itself in conscience, enter into the transition directly. But Hegel can refer the abstract good back to abstract right, because it, as the universal in itself, which becomes a particular as a contrast to conscience, is the same contradiction as this one is. Due to this, the transition of morality into ethical life does not have the structure of a positive sublation while in the negative, but rather the structure of a resolution of the contradiction (see L II 51 ff.). The independent reflection determinations, according to the *Science of Logic*, achieve a contradiction that is resolved in the same manner. Each of the members of the relation is "heightened for itself into a Totality" such that each contains otherness in itself while denying otherness (§ 141). Such reflection determinations are independent in the sense that they seem to be independent. Thus, morality also terminates in appearance. For this reason, its transition into ethical life, if taken precisely, can only be, just as that of abstract right, a *downfall*. As, according to the *Science of Logic*, the contradiction is resolved when the independent reflection determinations perish and the lost essence rises from their ashes, ethical life also triumphs in the self-destruction of the moral final moral determinations "as its essence, existent in itself" (§ 141 F). The genesis of ethical life occurs as little here as it does in the domain of abstract right. Like the theory of right, morality terminates with a demand that cannot be satisfied on its own soil. That the reciprocal mediation of the abstract good and conscience is only "*demanded*" (§ 141) corresponds to the "demand of the will, which as a particular *subjective* will desires the universal as such" (§ 103). Because right and morality dissolve into nothing, ethical life can only be generated out of them, or better yet, in them, such that ethical life presupposes itself.

The formal connection of the subordinate spheres with the sphere of ethical life teaches more impressively than all substantial objections that Hegel's abstract right and morality express a critical attitude. For he proves that criticism does not flow in at merely certain places, but rather places its stamp on the entire theory.[33] A consequence of this omnipresence is that even its standard is barely thematized at all. Still Hegel gives the standard of his criticism a name: life.[34] The unexplicatedness of the concept of life, which is invested in the philosophy of right of 1821, stands in an inverse proportional relationship to its significance. Against the abstract idea of good to which moral consciousness directs itself, Hegel will bring the "living" good to bear whose concealed intersubjectivity finally reveals itself as "universal life." Accordingly, the concept of life in the theories of abstract right and morality function as a code for the reality that excludes these spheres. In the correction of all particularizations and false totalizations it refers to the real "Totality" (§§ 70, 127) and the individual that works towards it, in which the universal presently exists as such" (§ 119 F).

(4) THE CONTENT OF THE CRITICAL PORTRAYAL OF RIGHT AND MORALITY: SOCIAL DEFICIENCY OF THE SUBJECT

Many have noticed and raised several times the social deficiency of Hegel's theories, especially that of abstract right. Likewise the critical intent has often already been noted with which Hegel portrays both subordinate spheres. Moreover, there is especially extensive consensus that the portrayal of abstract right contains a criticism of modern natural right. However, it has not yet become sufficiently clear in the discussion *how* this portrayal criticizes natural right thinking of the modern age. Due to this, it has also remained obscure in what manner the social deficiency that is so noticeable in Hegel's concepts of property and contract is connected with the criticism. Although it seems plausible to grasp the criticism as one of social deficiency, it is not obvious why the criticism is directed precisely at it. I would like to advance the thesis: Hegel's criticism of abstract right reveals the meagerness of the subjects that are presupposed by rational natural right, and his moral criticism drives at the lack of determinacy of the individuals that conceive of themselves as moral beings. The lack consists of the social underdevelopment of the legal entities.

This thesis can, by the way, also be seen as contributing support to the interpretation proposed by Ilting.[35] Ilting interprets the philosophy of right from 1821 as a "phenomenology of the consciousness of freedom" in the sense that of its comprehensive object, i.e., freedom in itself or for us completely differentiated from the beginning, it (in its different stages) only thematizes what the involved individuals can be aware of. He observes here Hegel's theory of abstract right with rational natural right in the background.[36] But he does not expressly show how the debate with the modern tradition of natural right is related to the phenomenological feature of the whole undertaking. The presented thesis procures the requisite intermediary link: Hegel criticizes rational natural right by presenting the limited consciousness—and beyond that the incomplete existential constitution—of the subjects that are to be responsible for the institutions devised from Hobbes to Fichte.

The theory of crime provides preliminary support *ex post* for this thesis. The criminal is the first human being in Hegel's philosophy of right. All individuals that precede him are in Marx's sense "masks of characters," thus persons in the original sense of the word. The first real human being is the criminal precisely because he "injures right as right" (§ 95). He is namely the first one who knows right as right and places himself in relation to universality that makes human beings into human beings. Of course he refers to right as right *modo negativo*, in a manner that negates it. But it is exceedingly characteristic for Hegel's philosophy of right that it begins with a negative constitution of right as such. When Hegel says that the concept of morality is not *only* "something demanded" in the goal of the movement of abstract right, "but rather emerges in this movement itself" (§ 103; see § 141), he intends to make clear that the will, which defines that concept, exercises punishing justice and desires "the universal as such," is only called onto the scene by the criminal. The universal must be known as such before it can also be desired as such. That right determines itself by the "sublation of crime *that would otherwise be the case*" (§ 99) "as *real* and *valid*, because it was initially only *in itself* and something *immediate*" (§ 82; see § 104) means: it is only after the criminal has breached right as right that it is constituted such that it becomes the object of the particular will in its real universality.[37]

Property and contract are precursed by wrong, which pinnacles in crime. It must appear strange that Hegel limits contract to the sphere of property and then, on the basis of such a concept of contract, criticizes the theories of rational natural right which base the state upon a contract (see § 75). Yet the criticism initially just lies in the swearing in of the contract on the conditions dictated by property. It objects to the contractualistic tradition that it surrenders the state to a contract that is in fact bound to these conditions and thus involves the state in "relations of private property" (§ 75 F).[38] Hegel is certainly hitting on something with this. Hobbes, whose "covenant of every man with every man" he expressly mentions, defines contract, in the broad sense of "contract" as well as in the narrow sense of "covenant" so important for the justification of the state, as the reciprocal transmission of rights to *things* than can be bought, sold or otherwise exchanged.[39] One only gets a direct view of the mode of criticism, when one realizes that Hegel is interested in the question of what follows from the dependency of the contract on private property for the niveau of the subjects that consent to the contract. Then the extent and limits of contractually realized intersubjectivity also come into view.

Hegel's ascertainment introducing the present study that the proper and true ground upon which freedom is existent is the "relation of will to will" stands in the context of § 71 that leads from property to contract; the ascertainment circumscribes directly the sphere of the contract. In a later review of this sphere, Hegel even reminds the reader of "the *essential* relation that is to the will of the other" (§ 113 F). The relation is essential (so it would seem at any rate, if one takes the contract for itself (1) due to the identity that arises in it (§ 73), (2) because of the commonality that emerges in it (see § 75) and (3) thanks to the reciprocity, that the so-called real contract—the contract of exchange that is paradigmatic for Hegel—still implies (see § 76).) For the present, we can conceive of the identity, along with Siep, as the identity of the content of the contract, of the commonality as *"correspondence"* (§ 113 F) of the particular wills of the contracting parties;[40] the following attempt at tracing the intersubjective constitution of universality will have to start with a deeper interpretation of identity. One must take into consideration the reciprocity that arises in the contract as well, if one wishes to clarify the problem (debated by Ilting and Siep, which cannot be taken up here *in extenso*), whether and how the "recognition" that is thematized for the first time at the culmination of the contract is to already be presupposed for property.[41] Hegel expressly emphasizes in a remark in the margin that property, apparently even noncontractually regulated property, is already acquired "within and due to this recognition" (§ 72 N). However, the recognition is reciprocal for the first time in the real contract. What was always my interest was the recognition of my property by possible others. This interest made it appear prudent to respect foreign property; but insofar as the recognition of other's property by me was only a prudential rule, the recognition of my property by the other is nothing other than an ought. On the precontractual level it is not a necessary, but rather a contingent, condition for the acquisition of property. When, in contrast, the recognition becomes reciprocal in the real contract, it is also revealed as a necessary condition for the contract's coming into existence. It is only from this that it becomes sufficiently comprehensible why Hegel notes its being assumed for the first time in the transition to the contract.

The statement about the essentiality of the contractual relation and the fact that Hegel accordingly gets the relation, constitutive of right in general, of will to will from the contract contrast in an odd way with the explanation: "The *existence* that the will gives itself in formal right . . . has for itself initially no . . . *positive* relation to the will of others" (§ 113 F). The explanation is also aimed at the contract; in the context it is *expressis verbis* that the relation in the contract is negative as well. That seems all the more odd since a handwritten note takes the identity emerging in the contract precisely as a "positive relation" (§ 40 N). The apparent contradiction results out of the connection between contract and property. Hegel localizes the contract so much in the sphere of property that he can characterize it as property's *"real existence"* (§ 71 N). The contractual relation to the foreign will is negative as the exclusive relation of an owner of private property to other owners of private property. This negativity does not contradict the fact that the relation of will to will from the contract becomes for the first time constitutive for an institution of right. The relation of the will to another in the contract is constitutive insofar as it mediates property. It characterizes me as a subject that enters into contracts "to have property not any more due to the thing and my subjective will, but rather just as much due to another will" (§ 71); the contractually governed property thus contains "the moment" of foreign will (§ 72). The negativity does not contradict the essentiality either. Where Hegel observes the contract from the distance of the review upon the broad background of the "relations of private property," he interprets the essential relation that is to distinguish contractually governed property from a pure property relation as itself a negative relation; "the *essential* relation that is to the will of another is, as legal, the negative, of retaining my property (according to its value) and to let the other retain his" (§ 113 F).

Of course with this a fundamental tension is expressed. Insofar as I retain my property and let the Other have his own, I stand in the relationless relation of indifference. However, the contract certainly includes "involvement with Others" which means that I must be "considerate to others" and "may not simply let them go" (§ 38 N), thus excluding indifference. The specifying characterization of the essential relation as "legal" indicates how Hegel attempts to resolve the tension. The contract is a legally relevant institution, according to his estimate, only as a dependent function of private property. Hegel dissects the contract into the side of its source and the side of what begins with it. The latter side is to be further differentiated into a positive or constructive and a negative or destructive movement. The positive movement, which is to be sketched in the following section, begins with that part of the contract that extends beyond it. Its *terminus a quo* is identity and the positive relation to others that is implied in it. The negative movement, in contrast, develops what constitutes the contract as such, the proper form that appears with it. It brings to light what the commonality and the reciprocity of the contract involve. It reveals that commonality, as one that can be dissolved at any time by either party of the contract, rests upon arbitrariness and that the reciprocity is undermined by fraud. Hegel only reminds us of it when he recapitulates from the standpoint of morality: "The contract and wrong begin to have a relation to the will of Others,—but *correspondence* that arises in the former is based on arbitrariness" (§ 113 F). On this side lie the consequences that follow from the "involvement with Others." The other side, conversely, that of the source of the contract from property, is the negative, exclusive relation that even as essential is an indifferent relation. The indifferent relation of partners to a contract, who are no real partners at all due to their indifference towards one another, is essentially the relation of owners of private property. The relation that runs together with relationlessness and that owners of private property have to one another influences the being and consciousness of the subjects who enter into the contract. Thus, in order to state the specific manner in which Hegel criticizes the contractual tradition of natural right, we must turn from the contract to property as such.

One usually claims that the beginning the philosophy of right from 1821 takes is "individualistic" with a view towards the concept of property developed in it. However, the book conceives of property not merely as individualistic, but also as solipsistic. According to the common robinsonades it presents the owner as someone who lives alone in his world. There is not yet a distinction between "*several persons*" (§ 49 F). In spite of the fact that almost everything has long since been divided up, the thing which the *solus ipse* takes into possession appears "masterless;"[42] and even the private reference to fellow human beings that lies in this characteristic is only an external reflection of the anticipated relation to Others (§ 51).

If we proceed even further back from the section on property to the preceding §§ 34–40 that are dedicated to the special introduction to the theory of abstract right, we discover that Hegel simply projects the asociality of the world of property onto the sphere of abstract right. He describes this sphere, as a whole, as that of a "directly encountered nature" (§ 39), as "an immediately given world" (§ 34), in which other subjects do not arise. The comment, made in the margin of the general introduction, that the relation to others does not belong here is encountered again in the introduction to abstract right in a new form; for we read there as well that the relation to others does belong to "reality that is further determined," but "not yet here" (§ 38 N). The note makes clear that the asocial world of abstract right is a construct that rests upon an abstraction from reality. It may remain open as to how we so hit upon certain features of such a construct in the general introduction that does have to do with reality. The suspicion is not far off that Hegel continues the backward projection even further and that he sees himself forced into it because he must imagine a freedom that occurs presocially in thought due to his orientation towards his picture of owners.[43] Although such a projection would be wrongful, the transmission of property's asocial determinations to the whole sphere of abstract right is legitimate under Hegel's premises. The argument upon which it rests is the membership of the contract and its deformed successors to the sphere of property.

It is another question, however, what justifies Hegel in presuming asociality for property itself and, thus, for the entire sphere. The person of the owner, "as an *exclusive individuality*," has a world empty of people and reduced to external nature, in front of himself (§ 34; see § 39). However, the intended exclusion cannot be thought without thinking other subjects as well. Hegel could abstract from this in the general introduction, if necessary, insofar as the other, which the individuality conceived of there primarily excludes, contains the Other indifferently. Private property, on the contrary, is exclusive with respect to the Others as themselves exclusive owners of private property. If one does not want to charge Hegel with a blatant conceptual mistake, one can give only *one* answer to the question: he stylizes the negative, exclusive and indifferent relation of owners of private property to each other into a complete relationlessness, in order to work out as sharply as possible that the parties to a contract do not even possess the premises for grounding a state. He wants to belie contractualism by stripping the individuals, who are supposed to come together in the contract that founds the state, of their sociality that, however, they need in order to do so. In this manner it is the uninterrupted tendency of the introduction to abstract right, that accordingly points out the existential and conscious constitution of the subjects of this sphere, to expose these subjects' abstractness, correlative to their domain of objects. It does define "*personality*," that is, the essence of the "*person*" that I am as the subject of abstract right, in such a manner that I am cognizant of myself in finitude "as the *infinite, universal* and *free*" (§ 35). But this universality and freedom are not, as one would expect after such a description, a concrete freedom that is saturated with the particular or the finite, but rather an abstract one; it is the constitution of consciousness "of itself as a completely abstract I" (§ 35). And the individuality of the person in the owner, whose particularity is not interesting (see § 37), is also, as resolving, the "*immediate* individuality" (§ 39), not that of the concept; "it is the individuality of freedom in pure being-for-itself" (§ 35 A).

The direct addressee of this criticism is, as we said above, the modern *thinking* of natural right. Indirectly, throughout the critical portrayal of the contractualistic theory, the criticism certainly refers to reality. If one takes it in its direct function as a criticism of modern natural right thinking, it is not difficult to coordinate it with the criticism that Hegel presents in his philosophy of right's theory of morality. The unity of both criticisms is designated by the name Kant. Hegel has most directly in front of him the theory of rational natural right in the form that Kant and Fichte have given it, and, similarly, the theory of morality presented in his philosophy of right is a debate with Kant.[44] However, both first sections of the book can be discerned in their solidarity as a critical portrayal of reality as well. As the construct "morality" has its real foundation in civil morality, the special construct "contract" has its real foundation in the social relations that reflect this morality. "Property now rests on *contract*" (§ 217)—is how it goes in the diagnosis of *civil society*. Along with the legal governing of property, the reciprocal, but in formal right merely formal, recognition of persons (see § 72 N), in the form of "being recognized . . . in the existent universal will and knowledge" (§ 217; see § 192), is also a reality only in civil society.[45] Hegel maintains in accordance with this the position that whoever founds the state on a contract "confuses it with civil society" (§ 258 F).

It is thus not surprising that Hegel's criticism of morality complains in a manner similar to his criticism of the contractual theories of state about the meagerness and social deficiency of the moral subject. Both criticisms stand in a comparable context as well. Similar to the criticism of contract, the criticism of moral consciousness is articulated equally in the portrayal of a story of degeneracy. Not only an "essential" (§ 113) but also "a *positive* relation to the will of Others" (§ 112) belongs to the original constitution of the consciousness analyzed in the second section of Hegel's philosophy of right; it is in this that the progress over the consciousness of the parties to the contract lies with respect to intersubjectivity. I will go into this relation in the following section. Corresponding to it is that for the consciousness of the agent, which the *Philosophy of Right* explicates at the beginning of its second section, the "*present world*," which as the sphere of formal right is the material world, has the primary determinacy of a socially shared world.[46] The positive relation to the will of Others disappears, however, in the further process of moral consciousness because the infinite relation of the particular will to itself disintegrates into a relation *only* to itself. Hegel characterizes the progress aimed for in the transition from abstract right to morality such that "the concept of freedom develops itself from the initially abstract to the self-relational determinacy of the will" (§ 104 F). In contrast to this, he maintains in the final part of the section on morality as the essential element in moral self-consciousness that it "only relates to itself within itself" (§ 135). The small word "only" expresses the whole degeneracy that has taken place in the meantime. The degeneration repeats, under changed conditions, the occurrence of wrong, in which the contractual commonality dissolves into particularity.

The degeneracy is, however, foreshadowed by a distinction that Hegel draws already in the transition from abstract right to morality. Hegel distinguishes there the concept of morality from the moral standpoint. The "principle of the *moral standpoint*" is a "subjectivity, infinite *for itself*" (§ 104), that owes its infinity to its self-relation (see § 33); the concept of morality is that the subjective will desires "the universal as such" (§ 103). This concept is at least open for an intersubjective interpretation. However, Hegel does not only neglect to explicate the relationship of the moral concept to the moral standpoint at that place; he does not capture the concept in the course of his moral theory either. Morality's process of degeneration can be conceived of as the movement in which moral consciousness becomes increasingly fixated on its own standpoint. The *concept* of morality, however, can only, if at all, be realized in the sphere of ethical life—in accordance with the fact that the crime-initiated movement, from which the concept results, anticipates ethical life.

So far, only Hegel's thesis about the "conceptual determinacy" of morality has been outlined and it has not yet been shown whether, and if so how, he may substantiate this thesis in his phenomenology of the forms of moral consciousness. In search of material that can support this thesis we will refer to the middle section on intention and welfare. The concluding section on the good and conscience does not provide anything else because intersubjectivity has already been completely eliminated in the final stage of the degeneration that it is reporting. The abstract good of morality is also abstract simultaneously and, above all, due to the abstraction of the community from whose life the actual, the ethical good receives its life. The moral good that is to consist, in the Kantian sense, of doing *"duty for the sake of duty"* (§ 133)) has a relation to the others only insofar as the duty, empty for itself, is reliant upon the content that the middle section supplies with its concept of welfare (see § 134).

With respect to the position of this section within the whole of morality, the question ought to be considered, whether Hegel is already describing *moral* consciousness at all in the preceding, thus the first, part of the second section of his philosophy of right. He drafts there a general theory of action under the title "Purpose and Responsibility." The action with which this theory is concerned is ethically qualified, certainly, namely as an action that stands in a historical context and that the subject attributes to itself (see § 117).[47] One could apparently understand this act as specifically moral, however, only in a sense of morality different from the one that the following sections develop. A circumstance becomes noticeable that we shall soon hit upon once again: Hegel's concept of morality is not unified. We must primarily distinguish morality as an historical enclave of the realm of subjective freedom from civil morality, which Kant reproduces in thought. If we limit the moral standpoint to the practical and theoretical manifestations of civil morality, the degeneration process of moral consciousness is presented as a story of degeneration *into* moral consciousness. However that may be, the subjectivity that is always also particular sinks down to *mere* particularity. The will that defines the original concept of morality and, as a "particular *subjective* will," desires the universal as such, draws back into its particularity in being-reflected-only-in-itself.

This particularity influences welfare. Welfare is the content of the action, taken "as *my* particular end of my particular subjective existence" (§ 114). But Hegel does not want to say merely that the moral individual is concerned among other things about his own welfare as well. Rather he increasingly identifies the moral standpoint with the standpoint of welfare in the course of his theory. The welfare that characterizes morality simpliciter is to be distinguished with respect to its particularity from what one calls *"general* welfare" (§ 130), "the so-called *universal* best" (§ 126 F).[48] The more decisively Hegel turns morality into mere particularity, the sharper he posits it, in the form of welfare, in contrast to the abstract universality of right. Welfare in the moral sense is welfare without right, right as abstract is right without welfare (see § 128). A *"general* welfare" can only arise, accordingly, on the condition that both the particular welfare and the abstract-universal right are sublated in the absolute good by each taking up the other into itself (see § 130). It has of course not remained hidden from the moral critic that the concern about one's own welfare is, as a rule, only viewed as a *"moral"* intention, if it also takes the "welfare of others" into consideration (§126). He attempts to do this justice with a logical construction that we will encounter again in his critical portrayal of civil society: the "subjective with the *particular* content of *welfare* stands as reflected in itself, infinite simultaneously in relation to the universal," and in a manner such that the universal is "posited in this particularity itself" as a moment (§ 125). I will examine the principles and the individual elements of the construction where it arises as that basic figure of civil society. I would only like to show here that Hegel uses it to completely subsume a manifold of social modes of behavior that appear to submit only partially to his moral concept.

Hegel states extraordinarily differing attitudes to other persons especially in his handwritten remarks to § 126. They can be classified into three types. Only one of these types fits without further ado the description that Hegel gives of the moral standpoint. It is the type of subject that *only* looks after the welfare of others when they culpably neglect it or for other reasons cannot perceive it, and *only* when this subject has provided for his own welfare first. Such a *"generosity* that has something extra" fits Hegel's description insofar as it points out that the welfare of others is added to one's own in a moral way of life, and accordingly, need not be added. In the sentence, the moment of the universal, posited in the particularity itself, is "the *welfare of others as well"* (§ 125), the "as well" means the accidental character of moral sociality. But the moral individual—that is the second behavioral type—has equally to do with the others insofar as his own welfare "cannot subsist" without the foreign welfare. This connection is elevated over the related reciprocal dependency of the subjects in the real basis of civil society because for the individual that conceives itself as truly moral the "universality of welfare itself is an end for itself." In a third type of social mode of behavior I even look after the welfare of others "by slighting, sacrificing" my own. Thus Hegel admits, on the one hand—and this in a published text—that the satisfaction of foreign interests is an "essential end" (§ 125) whereas, on the other hand, he persists in claiming that foreign welfare is not "determined absolutely as an end" for me (§ 126 N).

He believed it permissible to disregard all these differences. The permission for this is given to him, in his opinion, by the fixation of moral consciousness on particularity. On the path through particularity he captures the directedness of this consciousness to the universal in two steps. First, he advances that the others that I am taking moral care of are also intended as particular individuals. Their being is "particularity different from me, other particularity," but still "*particularity*" (§ 126 N). Even where foreign welfare, "in exhaustive, yet completely empty determination" is to be "the welfare of *all*," it is really the "welfare of *many* other particulars" (§ 125). Hegel then brings forth the argument—more or less unstated—that my particularity covers the foreign particularity. My welfare "widens" to the welfare of Others (§ 126 N). The universal is posited in particularity such that it is *reduced* to particularity. The reduction of the universal to the particular, that Hegel in principle accomplishes in the reduction of totality ("Allheit") to plurality, becomes completely apparent, according to his judgment, through the subsumption of the foreign welfare under one's own. The preceding definition, according to which welfare is the content of action as "*my particular*" end, even retains its validity.

In reality the definition certainly does not even cover sufficiently the cases of moral sociality that he himself raises. But precisely the violence with which Hegel forces morality into particularity testifies to his critical tendency. A closer look reveals that in his theory of morality the practical morality of civil society is also separated off from its theoretical reflection in Kant's moral philosophy. The latter is above all the topic of the final section that presents the good as a mere ought, the former is the subject matter of the middle section taken into account here, that commits the individual to the completely unkantian care for his welfare. The moments of welfare that Hegel perceives he would prefer not to correspond exactly to the aspects of civil society of which we will see that he shields them off or at least under-illuminates them in his diagnosis of the reality of this society. The only thing he aims for is the standpoint of an egoistical morality of altruism—which is also certainly characteristic for civil society. His portrayal of this standpoint is the criticism of the normative action pattern of a subject who atrophies increasingly in its relation only to itself and whose "subjectivity, floating for itself in its vanity," ultimately becomes so abstract as it initially was as the subject of abstract right.

(5) THE INTERSUBJECTIVE GENESIS OF THE
UNIVERSAL WILL: IDENTITY THROUGH ALTERATION

The disclosure of the formal structure, which intimates the critical function of Hegel's theory of mere right and mere welfare, and the passage through the substantial criticism of the deficient sociality of these subordinate spheres of right enable a final answer to the question, what it means that in the *Philosophy of Right* from 1821 primitive intersubjectivity appears essentially only in the perspective of the criticism. I already put the hypothesis, thus formulated, more precisely such that primitive intersubjectivity, if one prescinds from the familial domain, from barely developed seeds in the foundation of the theory of ethical life and from a few traces within the right of state, does not enter into the affirmative approach that Hegel works out independently of his criticism, but rather only becomes visible in the criticism itself. But what this in turn means can be circumscribed more exactly as follows: there exists for the Hegel of the *Philosophy of Right* a relation to other individuals that co-constitutes the individual in its existence and sparks the living freedom of the individual for the first time, a relation that is neither banished nor exiled in idylls, but rather that exists only in the underground of the disfigurements of the human beings that his criticism reveals.

The roots on which *communal* life feeds do not reach down into a sociality that remains unscathed by the criticized deficiency and that lies, at the same time on the soil of asociality. Excluded from it is every community that at all rests upon the *reciprocity* of giving and taking, as it is embodied most purely in the dialogical I-thou relation. Independent of the fact that the process that destroys reciprocity belongs to the subject matter of Hegel's theory, this theory itself destroys reciprocity. Hegel has no organ for it. This becomes clear in a paradigmatic way in the text with whose interpretation the reconstruction of intersubjectivity, disfigured in the disfigurements, has to begin. Hegel cuts off from property simpliciter contractually governed property as that "whose external side, its side as an existent, is no longer a mere thing, but contains the moment of a will (and consequently the will of a second person also)" (§ 72). It is evident from the objectivity ascribed to external existence that Hegel also understands an objective correlate by "side." In this he observes the other will and thus the Other all the more as an object, not as a natural thing, but still as an object.[49] And this means negatively that Hegel does not perceive the Other as the addressee whom the early phenomenologist Reinach assumes in his attempt (as a successor of Hobbes) at founding the contract in promises.[50] For as an addressee the Other would be neither subject nor object. Hegel's incapacity to see the Other as such follows from his not recognizing a third element in addition to subjectivity and objectivity, unless it be their mediation.

The space for all of the following considerations is hereby measured out. The stations of the path we have to take are the exposition of the contract, the theoretical foundation of morality and the fundamental thoughts on civil society. For abstract right and morality I would like to reveal in this section, with the help of paragraphs 72, 73 and 112, the genesis of what, according to Hegel, is completely developed reality in civil society. In content I need only pick up where the study last ended. The intersubjectivity, hidden in the underground of the disfigurements of human beings, from which Hegel draws a productive aspect, is to be sought after within the field of the problem of universality, with which moral consciousness had to deal in spite of its fixation with particularity. For universality is, within Hegel's system, the battle ground upon which truth and falsehood fight with one another. On its ground the loss that human being inflicts upon human being is supposed to break into victory. In civil society the war will break out in the form in which it also latently rules the relation of moral subjects to one another: as an explicit debate between universality and particularity. Universality is, however, the comprehensive topic of the following considerations, but it is so even already in this section. The genesis of civil reality to be revealed in it is the genesis of universality. Already the transition from property to contract is produced—according to at least one set of lecture notes—by "the interest of reason, that the subjective will become more universal" (§ 71 A). Even in Hegel's own notes the "transition to the contract" means: "I am subjectively determined as a *universal* will" (§ 55 N).

In order to reassure oneself of the systematic connection that the seemingly arbitrarily chosen quotes of the following considerations form, one must keep present the similarity that subsists between contract, morality and civil society. It is expressed formally in the reflection-logical constitution that the moral philosophy has as a second part, and the theories of contract and civil society as the second parts, respectively, of the first and third sections of the *Philosophy of Right*. As always with Hegel, the second moment, insofar as it goes over into the third moment through its reflection, with the exception of morality that contains "only cases of a highly limited sphere" (§ 126 N), is in reality the first moment.[51] In the *Philosophy of Right* from 1821 precontractual property only has the status of a thought experiment that Hegel undertakes analytically starting with the contract, just as the family has its place in civil society, whose practical morality reflects the consciousness that is concerned with its welfare. This assignment corresponds to the consequence that is to be drawn from the given explanation of Hegel's philosophy of right is nothing other than a theory of civil society. Its critical portrayal already initiates with the criticism of contractual right and continues, as we have seen, in the criticism of moral consciousness. With respect to the primitive intersubjectivity that this criticism reveals in addition, it too—for reasons that will be mentioned in the explication of his concept of universality—is indigenous in the spheres of reflection. The fundamental position of the spheres of reflection already testifies in a sense to its primitive character in the whole of Hegel's philosophy of right.

The reflection-logical predecessor of universality is called "identity." The process of the universalization of the will takes its starting point, accordingly, in the formation of identity. In § 72 Hegel approaches the "identity existent *in itself*" (§ 40) that he separates from commonality as subjectively "*posited*" (§ 75). Hegel characterizes the contract here as the "process in which the contradiction is presented and mediated that I *am* and *remain* an owner, existent for myself exclusive of the other will, insofar as I *cease* being an owner in a will, identical to the will of another" (§ 72). What kind of process Hegel means there and to what extent he sees a contradiction in it only become comprehensible with a twofold anticipation. In § 74 he completes the description of the process such "that each *ceases* being an owner with his own will and the will of another, yet *remains* and *becomes* an owner." This is the description a little later (§ 76) for the explicitly named exchange contract, or more precisely: the exchange as one that proceeds in "*purchase*" and "*sale*" (§ 80). In purchase and sale I cease being a property owner insofar as I give up a certain thing, continue to be a property owner insofar as I retain its value in monetary form, and become a property owner insofar as I receive a certain other thing for it. Thus, in § 72 Hegel anticipates the exchange contract in the form of purchase and sale. But that is not all that he anticipates. In this contract the contradiction is only presented, but such that it mediates itself. It mediates itself by dissolving into distinguishable aspects. The aspects become distinguishable because the exchanged things can be contrasted against one another. However, Hegel speaks straightaway of contradiction, that is of contradiction simpliciter or of a "posited" contradiction, because underlying the surface manifestation is the state of affairs that the same thing both is and is not in the same respect. In the depth of the occurrence, one apparently has to interpret in this manner the use of the concept of contradiction, that includes the claim of indiscernibility of aspects: I am and remain such a property owner in general that I simultaneously cease being a property owner in general, and not just being a property owner of a certain thing. Hegel thus anticipates a second thing, namely the identity, explicated for the first time in § 73, "*the unity* of different wills, in which its distinguishability and characteristics are relinquished." The unity is for him the condition of the possibility of the contract, particular for itself, and, thus, of the commonality produced in it.

In order to comprehend this identity, we must demarcate the objectification, that, according to Hegel, justifies the necessity of property from a further objectification due to which an *alienation* of property becomes necessary as well. According to the dimension of depth in which Hegel settles it, the necessary alienation, is not the alienation of particular property, dealt with much earlier (§ 65), that is contingent, but rather an alienation of property in general: "I *can* alienate myself from property not only (§ 65) as an external thing, rather I *must* alienate myself from property as such through the concept so that *my* will, as *existent*, is objective to me" (§ 73). But what does it mean that my will, as existent, is objective to me? The meaning of this dark phrase is illuminated upon the background of the former, original objectification. The state of affairs that justifies the necessity of property, "that I, as a free will, am in possession of myself objectively" (§ 45) is not to be understood such that I am in possession of myself as a free will; "a free will" is a subject, not an object. Conversely, my will itself is now to become objective so that it, as *my* will, becomes *existent*. "Mine-ness" is to receive the determinacy of existence. It may not cease to be what it is. Both—my will as mine and as existent—can only be conceived of together such that I become *one among others*. As one among others I am myself another and at the same time just myself. The alienation of property in general leads to self-alienation and must lead to it, because I am nothing other than a property owner. It possesses as self-alienation the character of an *alteration* (*Veranderung*).[52] "My will as alienated is simultaneously an Other" (§ 73) through alienation of property in general. My will is identical to the will of others only due to such an alteration. That I am and remain a property owner so that I cease being a property owner coincides in alteration with a contradictory unity, whose contradictoriness cannot be resolved by a differentiation of aspects. For I give up myself, as the property owner that I am, precisely insofar as I integrate myself into the community of property owners. That identity first enables contractual commonality means that I can only exchange things because I have already made myself exchangeable, that is, vanished into an abstract person, indiscernible from others.

This identity certainly also characterizes, as a condition of its possibility, the contract as such. According to the *Philosophy of Right*, the "identical will" that comes into existence through the contract is, insofar as it is "only a *common*" will in the manifestation's surface of existence, not yet a will, "universal in and for itself" (§ 75). Hegel is aiming at the same state of affairs when he ascertains retrospectively that the existence that the will gives itself in the contract does not only not have a "*positive* relation to the will of Others," but also does not have, "for itself initially, an *express* relation to the concept that is not yet contrasted with the subjective will and not distinguished from it" (§ 113 F). Hegel himself concedes with both formulations what Ilting works out so clearly: the contract is based, regardless of the reciprocal recognition of its partners, on the recognition of a normative order of right just as little as precontractual property does.[53] But when Hegel denies the contract simply an *express* relation to the concept, he makes known that the normative order of right, as "concept" or will, "universal in and for itself," is *implicitly* recognized in contractual agreements, in a manner different from precontractual property. The implicit recognition that therefore does not lie in the consciousness of the parties to the contract arises in the formation of the explained identity. Insofar as I become one among others, I transgress commonality in the direction of universality in the sense of totality. As one among others I am one among *all* others, not just the particular person any more who enters into a commitment toward another particular person. At the same time the implicitness of the recognition of norms designates an essential limit of the contract. The process of the universalization of the will extends beyond this limit for the first time in the transition to "*action*" as its "*subjective* or *moral*" expression. The action does not only have, according to Hegel's thesis, "a positive relation to the will of Others;" it also has an "essential relation to the concept" (§ 113). However, the concept here is at first only "an ought" (§ 113), that is, a norm not inherent to the action or a "*demand*" in the sense that the action can either be appropriate or not for the "*objectivity of the concept*" (§ 111).

   In this context lies the second passage upon which we must call for support in understanding the genesis of universality.[54] Paragraphs 110–112 develop three characteristics of the end of action: the obtainment of my subjectivity in external objectivity (§ 110), the correspondence or noncorrespondence with the objectivity of the concept (§ 111), and the "*positive* relation to the will of Others"—as the "identity of my will and other wills." Hegel describes this identity with express consideration for his explication of contract: "When I *obtain* my subjectivity in the accomplishment of my ends (§ 110), I sublate therein as in the objectification of these ends this subjectivity *simultaneously* as *immediate*, thus as my individual subjectivity. But the external subjectivity thus identical with me is the *will* of Others (§ 73)" (§ 112). The connection with contract lies more precisely in the return of alteration from which the identity arises. Although the subjectivity that is to be identical with the will of Others also remains one identical to me, "the will of others is at the same time an existence other than mine that I give to my end." The alteration has changed, however, insofar as the moments contradictorily combined in it have grown out of their substantial unity and entered into a reflected difference. This corresponds to the moral standpoint. With respect to it, the I is also abstract, but not any more how the person of the property owner was, but rather as an individual, withdrawn into itself, that takes care of itself in the "pure inwardness of the will" (§ 139). The will of such an individual can only become an other (will) such that it stands opposite itself as an other. Alteration is thus a doubling here of the I, and according to the "opposition of subjectivity and objectivity" (§ 109) that is characteristic of the moral standpoint, in a subject-will and an object-will. I obtain my subjectivity in the accomplishment of my ends insofar as I, in my inwardness, know the result of the action as mine, and I sublate it as immediate insofar as this just means that I have myself in front of me in external form.

Without a doubt, this thought presupposes Hegel's concept of action as alienation.[55] But Hegel does not at all take alienation, generally called such by him, for granted already as alteration. It is true that the alteration to be thought of here is as much an alienation as the one which underlies the contract, but also a specific one whose condition is alienation in its usual sense. It is conditioned by an alienation in the usual sense of elementary objectification, only not as the alteration underlying the contract is conditioned by my objectification into material objects, but rather by objectification in accomplished ends. For this reason Hegel believes himself justified in saying in § 112: "The ground of the *existence* of the will is now *subjectivity*. . . ." The altered alienation itself is still different from it. The otherness of the existence other than myself, that I give to my end, does not arise in the objectivity of that as which I, for myself, am an other, but rather is defined in its characteristic by my being an *Other* to myself. However, as an agent I am, at the same time, an other to myself in a manner different from that of the contract. In what manner this is so can be revealed from the genesis of the contract. Hegel made this clear in the transition from property to contract: just as existence *in general* is being for otherness, that is, "Something as conceived of in external influence and relations" (L I 111), the existence of will is being for another, that itself is for

ENTÄUßERUNG

SEIN FÜR ANDERES

Others and only for Others (see § 71). The existence that I give my freedom is only realized, excepting myself, by other persons as what it is, as the existence of freedom. If it does not materialize in sensual things any more, then they may even know their own will in it. The Others look at themselves in the ends accomplished by me. For this reason the existence other than myself, that I give to my end, *is* the will of Others. I am, as agent, regardless of my being-reflected-into-myself, the Other who I am for the others.

The interpretation suggested here explains, I think why and how the alterations presented in § 73 and § 112 are also different according to their negative side. For the former as well as the latter alteration, turned into the negative, means self-renunciation. But in the latter case the accent lies on the extinction of subjectivity, in the former on the sublation of this-ness: I do not give up my subjectivity as such, but rather "as my individual subjectivity." The mine-ness does not change yet one more time such that it receives the determinacy of existence and solidifies as it were in existence; it endures a new metamorphosis by becoming "own-ness" (Jameinigkeit). The action that I know to be mine is viewed by the Others as each one's own.

The action's relation to the will of Others being positive as well as, according to Hegel, the essential relation to the concept are both justified in this purification of mine-ness to own-ness. For own-ness includes the others in a positive manner, and such that it simultaneously raises itself above my and their individuality. However, the concept never in fact gets beyond an "ought." This is not the case for the first time insofar as it remains open whether the Others can view their will in the accomplished end of my action or not. The appropriateness of my will to the concept is, according to Hegel's criteria of "ought," already a mere "ought" because the identity of my will with the will of Others is only formed in the element of intuition foreign to the action. I admit that the talk of intuition is a construct of interpretation. It can, however, be translated back into the language of the text. Hegel expresses its content by elucidating the "identity of my will and other wills" as the unity of external objectivity emphasized in § 110 and the objectivity of the concept underlined in § 111. That it is formed in the element of intuition foreign to action, is said by the text as follows: the objectivity of the concept is simultaneously a mere external one. The identity formed in the action is, for this reason, exactly as contradictory as the identity that underlies the contract; the objectivity of the concept and the external objectivity are "only combined into a *contradiction*" (§ 112 F).

In the footnote to § 112, Hegel summarizes the determinations developed in this and the two preceding paragraphs: "The *objectivity* of the accomplished ends encloses the three meanings in itself or rather contains the three moments in one: (a) *External* immediate existence . . . (b) appropriate for the *concept* . . ., (g) being *universal* subjectivity."[56] The expression "*universal* subjectivity," a comprehensive title for the interpreted content of § 112, is not coincidentally one of the distinguished terms of the *Heidelberger Encyclopaedia* (see HE § 390), the immediate precursor for the anthropological and logical sections of the philosophy of right. The expression fixes the goal of the movement that begins with the identity, existent in itself, in the contract. The universal subjectivity is universal due to a constitutive achievement of intersubjective relations; it is, in a sense, intersubjectivity itself. On the other hand, it does not result from commonality as such. The paths that lead from abstract right and morality to civil society coincide in that both reveal particularity as the truth about commonality. What Hegel told his listeners about the development from contract to wrong, that revealed the lability of the common will of the contract partners, can be carried over to the degeneration of morality's care about the welfare of others as well to conscience circling in itself: "The path in general is to purify the will of its immediacy and thus to call forth from the commonality of the will a particularity that opposes it" (§ 81 A). In this becomes manifest Hegel's pejorative concept of commonality that, judging from his use of the concept, is not capable of freeing itself from its source, the egoism of the private property owners. Commonality—that is almost always for Hegel "only" commonality and is so relevant today once again—implies that narrow-mindedness of a communal life that closes off the universal life. For this reason it was one of his deepest convictions that no true universality can result directly from it, not the universality that is the truth. And still a partisanship *for* it can be found in the strategy of a provocation of particularity that acts *against* commonality. Hegel speaks up in favor of commonality insofar as universality, in spite of everything, is to be expected from it. Only he searches for universality not in the process of commonality that, as stepping forward for itself, disintegrates into its particular elements, but rather in the return to its foundation, identity. This procedure reproduces in theory his practical demands on the subject: to become universal not through a scattering into a plurality, that is, through mere extension of its particularity, but rather to complete itself in its universal subjectivity through reflection of the quality that is posited in its existence by the others. He readies the real foundation for such a demand in his theory of civil society. This theory must open up to us the concept of universality that defines the subjectivity that has come into view as universal.

(b) THE RESULT OF THE GENESIS: UNIVERSALITY IN CIVIL SOCIETY

In order to see how universality is determined in the sphere of civil society, one must envisage the dividedness that, from Hegel's viewpoint, runs through this society into its foundation. It already arises in the transition from the family into civil society (§ 181). The goal of this transition is, on the one hand, a *"difference"* into which the concept dissects itself and that remains contained in the concept, and, on the other hand, a *"plurality"* that, as a conceptless manifold, has the status of the difference into which identity, according to the *Science of Logic, "decays"* (L II 34). Hegel connects these sentences, in which he contrasts the two sides of the transition against one another, with an "or" that awakens the impression, as if they formulated one and the same state of affairs. But in reality the two sides diverge. For, first, the "identity of the family," from which the difference arises, is distinct from the only numerically one family that multiplies, namely as the "family unity," that can be experienced only from the inner perspective of familial life and that arises from the previously independent persons becoming *"one* person;" and, second, in the transition into difference, the members of the same family in the former case are "released to independent reality," whereas in the latter case, in the transition into plurality, the many families themselves take on the character of independent persons that relate externally to one another. The expression "release" points to the fact that Hegel can only connect the sides cryptotheologically. Analogous to the world into which the idea *"releases"* itself (L II 505), he interprets civil society as "the *world of manifestations* of the ethical." Such a world is civil society according to the plurality spreading out in it. But at the same time Hegel is taking its conceptless manifold for granted as the *other* in which the idea is with itself, when he substitutes for the family, the source of plurality, the concept that is to release the family members to independent reality.[57]

Corresponding to this dividedness of civil society itself, the universality correlated to civil society is also deeply divided. The civil society's *position* toward universality is already divided. Viewed logically or "expressed abstractly," this society, similar to the moral consciousness of the subject directed toward its welfare, has a determination of

particularity that only "relates" to universality (§ 181). Although Hegel names particularity "*one*" and universality the "*other*" principle,
he only wants the former to be understood as the principle of civil
society (§ 182). What all this means concretely can only be said when
one has defined the intended universality. This too is divided *in itself*,
and in several respects. That it only comes into consideration as such,
to which the particularity characteristic of civil society refers, reads
according to § 181: it is "in a formal and merely *appearing* manner in
the particular." Whatever the appearing may be—which we shall have
to look into later—at any rate the universality to be conceived of here
divides into one that appears equally in civil society from the outside
and another that is itself present in it. With this Hegel picks up a
distinction, basic to his conception of philosophy of right, that he has
already drawn in the introduction: one between universality, "existent
in and for itself," and "formal," or also "abstract," universality (see
§§ 15 F, 20, 21, 24 F). Universality existent in and for itself, is mediated
by particularity into individuality; the formal universality, conversely,
is formal insofar as it only subsumes content under it in a manner
such that form and content remain separate. The universality that is
transcendent of civil society is the "objective" universality (§ 263) as
which substantial universality, or universality, existent in and for itself,
gains worldly reality. We can oppose the formal universality with a
universality that is immanent to the thematic sphere: civil society is
"a connection of links as *independent individuals* in a, thus, *formal
universality*" (§ 157).

However, the universality to which civil society refers does not
only decay into transcendent and immanent universality, objective and
formal universality. Objective universality itself divides into that of the
family and that of the state. Hegel has in view the state, the "reality of
the substantial universal" (§ 157), when in § 263 he characterizes the
spirit, to which he raises the state, as "objective universality that
appears" in civil society. Yet, that he is also thinking of the family is
supported by the phrase used in § 181, universality forms a basis for
civil society that is "only" internal "any more."[58]

The formal universality, immanent to civil society, also fans out
into two universalities. On the one hand, it means an intersubjective
universality, the entirety of the members of civil society; Hegel is
occasionally aiming at it when he simply mentions "the universal"
(§§ 187, 199). On the other hand, the civil-formal universality means
the "formal *universality of knowledge and desire*" (§ 187) that Hegel
characterizes more precisely as the *form* of universality (see §§ 182,
186). A difference that was also already mentioned in the introduction

returns. For already at that point Hegel understands by formal universality the one that the I has in itself as "pure *thought* of itself" (§ 5) as well as "*communality*" or "*totality*" (§ 24 F). In the transmission of the universality of the subject to intersubjectivity lies the whole dubiousness of his social philosophy, which in general tends to hide the characteristic of its topic by projecting the terms read off the individual subjectivity onto intersubjective relations. Nonetheless Hegel can refer to a feature, common to abstract self-consciousness and totality, that at least partially justifies their subsumption under one concept of formal universality. The subjective-formal and the intersubjective-formal universality share with one another the distinction between form and content that defined this concept. Just as the formal universality of the individual for itself is unmediated by its particular contents, the universality that collects many individuals together remains as external to these individuals as the genus does to its exemplars in nature. One can clarify the difference that rests upon the soil of such similarity with the help of Hegel's logic and by realizing that he characterizes formal universality as one of "reflection" (§ 15 F): abstract self-consciousness is "pure" reflection, the collection of many individuals into a totality is an "external" reflection.

As complex as the universality that is relevant to civil society is, the founding relations that subsist between their forms are just as multilayered. The connection of constitution between subjective-formal and intersubjective-formal universality is especially difficult to grasp. If one unravels this connection, still further types of universality appear. Initially, intersubjectivity is justified by the formal universality of knowledge and desire. This line is covered by § 182 with whose help the question can be answered as to what we can concretely conceive of under particularity, which is to be the abstract logical expression of civil society. The answer reads: at least in the primitive realm of civil society, in the economical "system of desires," every person is "a *particular* end to itself," and such that, in contrast to the moral sphere, neither objective nor subjective universality is the end. In order to be able to be a particular end, however, every person must make every other person a means. To such an extent the person stands "essentially in *relation* to other such particularity." The person is mediated through the Others. Now Hegel distinguishes its mediation through the form of universality from its intersubjective mediation. And he remarks that the former is more original than the latter: every person is mediated "simpliciter" through the form of universality. To what extent the mediation through the form of universality also mediates it through other persons must be extrapolated, but one can do it without difficulty.

That one makes others into means to one's ends is only possible if one has raised oneself to the standpoint of abstract thought, which alone can produce means-ends relationships. Civil relations are based in the formal university of knowledge and desire insofar as they presuppose instrumental rationality.

What Hegel bases on subjective-formal universality in this manner, is, it should be noted, only intersubjectivity, not yet intersubjective universality. However, if we place intersubjectivity as totality in view, it becomes evident that it constitutes universality. The universality that it constitutes is not immediately the formal universality of knowledge and desire. Still, it coincides with this universality in that it influences the individual subject for itself. It even results from the subject's self-determination. The realization of selfish ends is namely also tied in civil society (and above all) to the condition that the individuals "themselves determine their knowledge, desire and action in a universal manner" (§ 187). Still, the individuals have the universality spoken of here as an objective quality in itself, as a property of their being, in which, in addition to their action, their knowledge and desire is embedded. The individuals give this determinacy to themselves, "from their own determination" (§ 207), but through their incorporation into the inter-subjective connection. They determine their knowledge, desire and action in a universal manner by, as it reads in § 187, making themselves "into a *link* in the chain of this *connection.*" Making-oneself-into-a-link is a new form of alteration. How important such an alteration is in the framework of the theory of civil society is testified to not only by the passage from § 187 that concludes the exposition of the theory, but also by the circumstance that Hegel draws the figure into the context of his theory of classes, which demands from the individuals that they "make themselves into a link of one of the moments of civil society" (§ 207). The new alteration is so important because the universality that emerges from it qualifies the subject as a specifically civil subject. Just as Hegel understands the whole of civil society reflection-logically, he also conceives of the independence that the individuals have in civil society as peculiarly reflection-logical independence that is to be distinguished from existential constitution-for-itself and that results from the dependency of the individuals upon each other. It is a dependency of all upon all, civil society as the combination of independent individuals is a "system of all-around dependency" (§ 183).[59] The objective universality of the civil subject thus arises from intersubjective universality. It is inherent to alteration, whose result is the new type of "universal subjectivity," that the individual assimilate with *all* others in civil society.

On the way through the determinacy of the civil subject, the intersubjective-formal universality now also constitutes the subjective-formal universality, the formal universality of knowledge and desire. To raise oneself to this universality means for Hegel to *"educate"* oneself (§ 187). The knowledge and desire to which Hegel ascribes this universality is theoretical and practical education, an education that the subject acquires in work itself (see § 197).[60] Education, however, as "the consciousness of the individual in the form of universality," presupposes "that I am grasped as a *universal* person in which *all* are identical" (§ 209 F). Hegel attributes this universality, so essential for his concept of I,[61] to civil society, as the product of the movement, in which the bourgeoisie makes itself into a link in the chain of a universal ᴮᵁᴿᵍᴱᴿ connection.

However, the intersubjective-formal universality only constitutes the subjective-formal universality of education in a mediated way. The constitution is not only mediated insofar as it proceeds via the determinacy of the civil subject. It also belongs to its mediacy that the universality in which the determinacy of the civil subject lies is not an *exclusively* intersubjectively constituted universality. In civil society the individuals are also determined by the "universal" that arises in their work (§ 198). This universality is that of an *"abstraction"* (§ 198). The abstraction characterizes directly the wants and means to satisfying these wants (see § 192). It arises from the fact that the wants and the means to their satisfaction are, on the one hand, multiplied and, on the other hand, dissected (see § 190). The opposite processes of pluralization and particularization have namely in common that they dissolve the concrete. However, pluralization and particularization are, in turn, forced in that the satisfaction of my wants and the satisfaction of other's wants are reciprocally conditioned in civil society (§ 192). I can only satisfy my wants *and* the wants of others through work, and the others can only satisfy their wants *and* my wants, when my wants and their wants become indiscernible due to the dissolution of their concreteness. Thus, *the* side of the civil subject's universality that consists directly in the abstractness of its wants and means also depends mediately on its relations to others.

The constitutional connection forms a functional circle in all of this. For the abstraction rooted in the relation to others retaliates against this relation. Originally "a quality of wants and means," it also becomes "a determination of the reciprocal relation of the individuals to one another" (§ 192). It is a determination of this relation in the same sense that it determines the individuals themselves, as objective determinacy. Hegel's later talk about the *"universalization* of the connection between human beings through their wants and the ways of readying and bringing forth the means for these" (§ 243) is aimed at it or at least also at it. The phrase of "doubled universality," used following this passage, can hardly be classified unambiguously. Presumably, the doubled universality means, on the one hand, the universalization of the connection between human beings and, on the other hand, the universalization of the modes of satisfaction of wants. But it is also possible that the difference contained in the first universalization is being expressed by it. The universalization of the connection between human beings would then be understood initially qualitatively as an abstraction and then quantitatively as the emergence of a social totality. Such an understanding is not excluded because in the neighborhood of this passage Hegel shows why civil society, extending beyond "*this specific one*," that is, of a certain people, tends to become a world-society. The universalization of the connection between human beings would then mean both at once: the abstraction as a determination of intersubjective relations and the intersubjective universality from which it is generated.

All of this goes on within the realm of the *formal* universality, which is a reality in civil society. How the universality, *existent in and for itself*, which merely appears in civil society, is related to it has not yet been shown. It is only when we bring it into view that we will also see in what Hegel relocates the division, that runs through this society and that he points out in the transition from the family into it. But the formal universality of knowledge and desire is already a new expression for the dividedness of civil society. Namely, it is, on the one hand, only a characteristic particularity. Hegel interprets education as an education of particularity. The educated particularity, as "its own particularity of knowledge and desire" (§ 208), coincides with its formal universality, because education is nothing other than the process by which particularity "fancies itself the universal" (§ 200 F), "the driving forth of the universality of thinking" (§ 20). On the other hand, the formal universality of knowledge and desire has in itself "the universality, existent *in and for itself*," but "only *abstractly*," yet still as existent in and for itself (§ 208). That the principle of the system of wants, according to the quoted concluding paragraph in his portrayal, as its own particularity of knowledge and desire has the universality, existent in and for itself, only abstractly, says in principle the same as the ascertainment, found in the transition from the family to civil society, according to which the universality (existent in and for itself) is for this society "the—that is only *internal* any more—basis and, thus, in a formal and merely *appearing* manner in the particular" (§ 181). The division worked out here reveals itself in the principle of the system of wants as its inner contradiction. The tension between the universality, existent in and for itself, and the formal or abstract universality is so strong, from Hegel's viewpoint, that the combination of the two can only be contradictory. Hegel sharpens the contradiction even more when he reduces the formal or abstract universality to particularity. We shall see upon what the contradiction depends, when we turn back to the description of the dividedness in § 181.

To what extent does the universality, existent in and for itself, under the conditions of domination, that set up the particularity in civil society exist in a "merely *appearing* manner in the particular"? Hegel locates the distinction between understanding and reason in the difference between abstract universality and concrete universality, existent in and for itself (see § 24 F). The complete, speculative dialectic construct of his philosophy stands and falls with the assumption that the understanding is, although an opponent of reason, simultaneously its organ. Guided by this conviction, Hegel identifies the appearing of the universality, existent in and for itself, in civil society with the "appearance of reasonability in this sphere of finitude," with an appearance that is "*the understanding*" (§ 189). The passage in the logic, which he alludes to with this, characterizes the understanding more precisely as "the *beginning*" of the manifestation of reason (L II 252). The passage gives us the right to interpret appearing as anticipating. Hegel takes appearing as anticipation to the extent that he posits the objective universality into the state that is still expected. To this extent he presents an eschatological conception of civil society. Not without reason does he call the understanding in § 189 "the side which is decisive in observation and which is the reconciliation within this sphere." Hegel's understanding takes the representation of the son into itself, who is called reconciliation and in whose promise it already starts dawning.

Now the universality, existent in and for itself, is in a formal and merely *showing* manner in the particular, because the foundation that ᔕᴄ ʜ ᴇ ɪ ɴ ᴇ ɴ ᵱ it forms is "only *internal* any more" in civil society. The "idea" is lost into particularity in civil society and "separated into the division of internal and external" (§ 229). The concepts of internal and external are not mere determinations that have their place in the reflection logic, but rather the basic determinations of the reflection logic itself, insofar as, namely, the essence, conceived of as reflection, as "the internal," is affected by being as something "external" to it (L I 44). The dividedness of civil society is also expressed logically according to § 181 such that universality and particularity, in themselves determinations of the concept existent for itself, enter into a "reflection relationship." This relationship develops into a relationship of independent reflection determinations that concur, apparently as equally original, such that universality itself in contrast to particularity sinks into particularity (see § 184). As the essence that divides into two independent reflection determinations "is lost into its negation" (L II 63, see 22), so civil society, already as a system, analogous to a "system of reflection determinations" (L I 44), is "the system of ethical life lost into its extremes" (§ 184). The "loss of ethical life" that § 181 notes also enters where the reflection relationship is initially only a relationship between internal foundation and external events, between a dimension of depth and the surface of the manifestation.

The dividedness that attaches to civil society, "expressed abstractly," already lies in the fact that the concept, determined as ethical life, remains, on the one hand, concept, but, on the other hand, as an essence sinks into the reflection-logical constellation. This dividedness is manifest concretely in the reciprocity of the processes that occur in the dimension of depth and on the surface of the manifestations. One of these processes is a self-negating movement of civil society, the other an affirming movement through which civil society is driven beyond itself. In contrast to Marx, who reduces a superficial unity to a contradiction deeply hidden,[62] Hegel plants, in the tradition of Adam Smith, the destructive movement on the surface and the constructive movement in the internal workings. That he understands the "world of manifestation of the ethical" as the world of consciousness and the internal foundation as a being that is economically determined points toward Marx. The contradiction that the concluding portrayal makes known in the system of wants consists, from the beginning, of the *resistance* that consciousness pits against being. A tension prevails between superficial consciousness and substantial being, insofar as the individual only aims at the satisfaction of his "subjective *particularity*," "but *universality* asserts itself in the relation to the wants and the free arbitrariness of others" (§ 189). That this universality "asserts itself" is to be taken precisely. This is supposed to mean that universality asserts itself *against* particularity. It must get its own way against the particularity in which consciousness is caught up. In this it is confirmed: Hegel's conception of civil society possesses eschatological features. Universality, existent in and for itself, breaks into the atheism of the ethical-unethical world like the kingdom of God. It is present in the mode of absence in civil society not thanks to a subjective anticipation but rather due to an objective prolepsis, that is, due to the fact that it nevertheless occurs in a world that denies it.

The decisive question is now: through what can universality assert itself? Hegel wants to express with this phrase that universality must battle against a hostile element. But he also lets one know with the phrase that it possesses the "power" (§ 184) that helps it to victory. In what is its power shown? Starting with superficial consciousness, Hegel answers the question initially in a superficial manner with Adam Smith. The "dialectical movement," which, as the "mediation of the particular through the universal," mediates the opposing movements, is supposed to be the one according to which the satisfaction of individual's wants, by in fact satisfying the wants of all others, produces a balance behind the back of consciousness (§ 199). But regardless of the fact that Hegel himself denies the "invisible hand",[63] by calling the state against the destructive forces of civil society, this is no answer to the question posed. How universality, existent *in and for itself*, is to put itself forward, and not the intersubjective universality to which the universal refers was to be explained.

Hegel's portrayal of the opposing movements in § 194 and § 195 point in the direction in which we must turn in our search for a binding answer. Hegel describes there the dividedness of civil society as the freedom that enables society. We can hope for an indication of what we are searching for in this description, because universality, existent in and for itself, which has the principle of the system of wants only abstractly, is a "universality of *freedom*" (§ 208; see § 188). The self-contradictoriness of an abstract present of a universality existent in and for itself is attested to in the system of wants itself according to §§ 194–95 in a "*liberation*" that is only "*formal;*" § 194 works out the liberation as such and § 195 describes its formal character. Civil society liberates its members from natural necessity, but only formally, because it fixes them to particular ends.[64] Due to this division education is not only one's own particularity of knowledge and desire, as which it participates in the universality of freedom, but rather the "natural" particularity with which a "remainder of the state of nature" remains in it (§ 200 F). The power of civil society to push forward lies for Hegel in the liberation from nature that takes place all the same. Accordingly, one must follow the trail of this liberation, if one wants to find the tracks of the "reconciliation." The goal, however, is not described previously in the text. In order to understand to any extent how objective universality can put itself forward under the conditions of its loss, one must develop a thought that, although it is one of Hegel's own, influences his theory of civil society at most implicitly.

One is to start precisely at the point that lies farthest away from objective universality. This is the point at which the alteration revealed in the theory of civil society extends beyond contractual right and

ENTFREMDUNG?

ENTFREMDET

moral alterations. If contractual right and moral alterations were characteristic types of alienation, then manifestly civil alteration is an alienation, an alienation of the individuals from themselves and each other. Civil society "alienates" the individuals "from one another" (§ 238) by alienating them from themselves. Clarifying this alienation also means: to grasp for the first time what it means that abstraction becomes a quality of inter-human relations. On the one hand, it shows that the alteration achieved by the individual by making itself into a link in the chain is an abstraction: and, on the other side, it becomes evident that the abstraction that lies in work contains alteration in it. For civil society influences onto work the determination of abstraction by awarding a bonus solely to the activity that I exercise for indeterminate others and indeterminately many others. Every other is there for me as one among others. Similarly, for the others I am just one among many for whom they carry out their work. That civil society submits the reciprocal relation of the individuals to one another to abstraction, thus says: already in the world of work, civil society creates relationships in which each one is there for each other in an only indeterminate, unindividuated manner. It alienates the individuals from each other. The others can only be present to me as such, for whom I am one among others, if I conceive of myself as one among others. Thus, civil society especially forces the individuals into self-alienation as well.

One must draw the conclusion here that what Hegel calls "formal universality," even independently of this social context, only gains complete reality in civil society. For formal universality is formal insofar as it does not let the individuals be themselves, but rather subsumes them under itself as exchangeable exemplars (see L II 290 ff.). To this extent it forms the most extreme contrast to universality existent in and for itself. According to the principles of Hegelian dialectic the point furthest away from truth is at the same time the *"turning point"* (L II 496) at which falsehood changes into truth. If one believes Hegel's general schema of dialectic, the "negative" reaches the turning point by reflecting itself in itself and in this manner becoming self-referring negativity. The formal universality that is realized in civil society assumes the position of such a negative. Hegel remarks in the sketch of that schema that the negative determination is *"as the contradiction the posited dialectic of itself"* (ibid.). He characterizes the understanding correspondingly where he explains it at the beginning of the manifestation of reason as the enspirited form in which the finite "arouses itself in itself" through universality and is "posited as dialectic" (L II 252). The application to the theory of civil society does not provide too many difficulties. Through the formal universality the universality, existent in and for itself, shines into the particular insofar as the links of the relation that has become abstract do not retain anything more for themselves. When abstraction dissolves the particularity of the individuals in their relations, it overcomes itself, that is the abstract or formal universality. For it is only what it is as long as it is composed out of many particularities. For this reason and only for this reason could Hegel reduce it to particularity. To the same degree that the particular disappears, the contrast of formal universality and universality, existent in and for itself, is sublated. The formal universality does not turn into universality, existent in and for itself, but through the loss of what resisted universality existent in and for itself, it opens itself up for it all the same. It is not concerned with a total opening only because particularity is also retained, because the liberation from natural necessity is not capable of soaking up the remains of the state of nature.

The three greatest of the great philosophers of the 19th century—Hegel, Marx and Kierkegaard—all play the motif through, each in their own manner, that stems from the Homeric cycle of legends, pervades later Greek tragedy and, turned critically, is also reminiscent of a Christian tradition: the spear that inflicts the wound also heals it. In contrast to Marx and Kierkegaard, Hegel identified the motif as the matrix of his dialectical theory of knowledge: "Knowledge heals the wound that it is itself."[65] However, knowledge is wounding from his viewpoint as abstraction, and extending beyond knowledge he saw, as Schiller and the whole German Rouseauism, the wounding and simultaneously healing spear ultimately in abstraction, causing sickness and the source of health. There is no doubt that such an interpretation of abstraction explains essentials of civil society. One can assure oneself of its explanatory power, when one observes upon a familial background Hegel's thesis about the universality realized in civil society. The family grants "safety, fortification, duration of the satisfaction of wants" to the relations of the individuals to one another. These qualities are also "nothing other than forms of universality" (§ 203 F). However, in order for them to enter into "the universal of freedom," which is the truth of the objective universal, abstraction must initially cut the individuals off from the return into idylls by devouring the enduring persistent, to which the universal is still attached in those forms. Having recognized this as the world-historical achievement of civil society, is not the least of Hegel's merits. However, the interpretation that he gives of it picks the myth that it works through up into itself. Its explanatory power has something of the "magical power" in itself that "reverses negativity into being" (PhS 30).

But even if the interpretation were free of mythology, a misgiving would still remain. Hegel does not really operate with it in the theory of civil society. That he keeps the basic thought of his dialectic at a distance from this theory seems to be motivated by his tendency to repress intersubjectivity. We find ourselves at the junction at which intersubjective universality is finally excluded from the process in which universality, existent in and for itself, is generated. This becomes apparent in the transition to the administration of justice. Hegel cuts off the possibility of an intersubjective constitution of universality, existent in and for itself, by relocating the whole sphere of education, in which the described occurrences took place, outside of civil society and by surrendering it to abstract right (see § 209). His understanding of education as the "pushing forth of the universality of thinking" provides him evidence for this. This thinking, especially conceived as consciousness of the I of itself as a universal person, "in which *all* are identical," now shrinks down to knowledge of the universality of abstract right. This shortens the constellation, rich in tension, in which the particular refers to universality, existent in and for itself, through the formal universality, to a unity of particularity and "the universal, merely existent in itself" (§ 229).

The relocation of education outside of civil society prescribes the manner in which Hegel continues to eliminate all intersubjectively mediated approaches to an objective universality from this society. In the corporation, "the universal that is contained in the particularity of civil society" is finally to be the end of persons who only had themselves as particular ends (§ 249); in it allegedly those moments "that are initially split in civil society into a particularity of wants and pleasures, *reflected in itself*, and into *abstract* legal universality, are unified in an internal manner" (§ 255). But when Hegel attributes to the state the universal end in and for itself, as in the theory of the administration of justice the universality of education is attributed to abstract right, the end only remains for the corporation itself "as limited and finite" (§ 256). The corporation, according to the systematic of Hegelean philosophy of right "the reconciliation," reveals itself as the administration of misery, as which Hegel presented it already in the overview of the construction of civil society in § 188.[66] This certainly belongs with the fact that the sphere of administration of justice, as the stadium of the difference in itself condemned to impotence, appears there reversed like the anticipated reconciliation. For the reconciliation dissolves in appearance due to the regression into abstract right.

The same happens to the universal end in and for itself, which Hegel delegates to the state, that happened to the universal of freedom which was entrusted to the administration of justice: the theory of state erases every trace of intersubjectivity in it. It is true that it commits, as we have heard, the individuals to "lead a universal life" for which *"unification* as such" is the true end. However, the demand can only be an empty ideal, because intersubjective universality is not the problem any more with which the theory of state is concerned. The only theoretical and practical task left is the mediation of the particularity of the individual with an objective universal that is to be objective precisely insofar as it is beyond all intersubjective relationships. But the problem of the relation of intersubjective universality and universality existent in and for itself remains unsolved. It is *the* unsolved problem of Hegel's philosophy of right.

NOTES

* NOTE ON TEXT: I have almost completely rewritten and partially modified the content of the paper that formed the basis of my talk at the conference on Hegel's philosophy of right at Fontenay-aux-Roses. The present study ties in with the "outlook" given in my book *Sein und Schein* 472–86 (1978). The state, which stood in the limelight of the concluding remark's perspective, receives very little consideration here—for reasons to be made evident and for which Hegel is to be held responsible.

  With respect to the mode of quotation, all of the section markings without preceding letters refer to Hegel's *Philosophy of Right* (1821). F = footnote, A = addendum and N = personal note of Hegel. E = Encyclopaedia of the Philosophical Sciences, HE = Heidelberger Encyclopaedia of the Philosophical Sciences, L = The Science of Logic, PhS = Phenomenology of Spirit, JS = Early Theological Works.

1. Translator's footnote: Hegel's term "Sittlichkeitslehre" will be translated as "theory of ethical life." Moreover, "Sittlichkeit" will be translated as "ethical life." In general, as with the latter case, Knox's English translation of terms that indicate Hegel's titles of books, sections, paragraphs, etc., will be used for easy reference.

2. For such a discussion, see my book *Sein und Schein*, supra note *, at 472 ff.

3. See H. Flickinger: Neben der Macht: Begriff und krise des buergerlichen Rechts 19 ff (1980); E. Angehrn: Freiheit und System bei Hegel 178 ff (1977).

4. 1 K. Marx, A World Without Jews (1959).

5. See A. Wildt: Autonomie und Anerkennung: Hegels Moralitaetskritik im Lichte seiner Fichte-Rezeption (1982).

6. See the remark, communicated by J. Hoffmeister: "So I take Logic and Metaphysics one semester and natural law and the science of state or the philosophy of right, in the sense that ethics or teachings of duty are contained in it, the other semester of the same year" (Nuremberg Works). See also Peprzak, Zur Hegelschen Ethik, in Hegels Philosophie des Rechts, Die Theorie der Rechtsformen und ihre Logik 103 ff (D. Henrich & R. Horstmann eds. 1982).

7. Liebrucks distinguishes comprehensive right from limited right with this notation.

See Liebruks, Recht, Moralitaet und Sittlichkeit bei Hegel, in 2 Materialien zu Hegels Rechtsphilosophie 13–51 (M. Riedel ed. 1975).

8. See G. Ahrweiler, Hegels Gesellschaftslehre, 72 ff., 93 ff (1976). A noticeable, and considering the theme of the present study, remarkable feature of Hegel's analysis of the family is that he downplays the influence of civil society on the family extensively. He describes familial life, in accordance with the civil ideology of family of the 19th century, as the intact world with which the "loss of ethical life" in civil society is to contrast. See also S. Blasche, Natürliche Sittlichkeit and bürgerliche Gesellschaft: Hegels Konstruktion der Familie als sittliche Intimität im entsittlichten Leben, in 2 Materialien zu Hegels Rechtsphilosophie 312–37 (M. Riedel ed. 1975).

9. For this concept of love which Hegel assimilates his early concept, see also §§ 40 F, 158 A, 167, 168. In the text Hegel follows this up immediately with the metamorphosis of sexuality into eros, but he observes sensual love simultaneously in the horizon of the new testamental αΥαπη.

10. In *Sein und Schein*, supra note *, at 37 ff, 433 ff, I spoke of "communicative" freedom. In the present study I use the expression "communal freedom" in order to prevent the misunderstanding that language is constitutive for this freedom. This does not yet, of course, determine the concept of freedom itself sufficiently. Pothast's objections against its uncritical use in the philosophy of the 20th century are very weighty. See U. Pothast, Die Unzulänglichkeit der Freiheitsbeweise: Zu einigen Lehrstücken aus der neueren Geschichte von Philosophie und Recht (1980).

11. See K. Ilting, Die Struktur der Hegelschen Rechtsphilosophie, in 2 Materialien zu Hegel Rechtsphilosophie 52–78, esp. 61, 64 (M Riedel ed. 1975).

12. See K. Ilting, Sitte, Sittlichkeit, Moral, in 5 Geschichtliche Grundbegriffe: Historisches Lexicon zur politisch-sozialen Sprache in Deutschland (O. Brunner, W. Conze, R. Kosselleck eds.) (forthcoming). I thank the compositors for the friendly transmission of the manuscript.

13. Through which he retroactively overhauls in Spinozistic fashion his Platonic-Aristotelian approach from the good. For the Spinozism of the young Hegel's conception of ethical life, see K. Ilting, Hegels Auseinandersetzung mit der aristotelischen Politik, in Philosophisches Jahrbuch 38–58 (1963–64); Riedel, Hegels Kritik des Naturrechts, in Studien zu Hegels Rechtsphilosophie 42–74 (M. Riedel ed. 1970).

14. On the origin of Hegel's "spirit of the people" from Montesquieu's *Esprit des lois*, see H. Trescher, Montesquieus Einfluß auf die philosophischen Grundlage der Staatslehre Hegels 77 ff (1917).

15. See J. Habermas, Technik und Wissenschaft als "Ideologie" 9–47 (1968).

16. On Hegel's Jenenser decision to base ethical life on spirit understood as self-consciousness, see the developmental historical Hegel studies from Rolf Peter Horstmann, especially Über die Rolle der bürgerlichen Gesellschaft in Hegels politischer Philosophie, in 2 Materialien zu Hegels Rechtsphilosophie 276–73, 290 ff (M. Riedel ed. 1975).

17. For the allocation given here for the construction of the philosophy of right to that of the logic see Schöpf, Subjektivität und Sozietät: Studien zum Ansatz der Sozialphilosophie bei Fichte, Hegel and Husserl (1973) (unpublished postdoctoral

thesis Munich). Schöpf attempts to "distill the basic features of a dialectic logic of intersubjectivity from the philosophy of right" by structuring the development of thought to Hegel's inferences. He keeps to the Heidelberger Encyclopedia that refers abstract right to the immediate concept, morality to reflection as judgment and ethical life to inference (see HE § 401). I should like to thank Schöpf here for access to the part of his manuscript on Hegel.

18. Hegel mentions this individuality only in connection with his justification for the universality of the will: the will is "universal, because in it all limitations and particular individuality is sublated . . ." (§ 24). At the same time the introduction presupposes the "particular individuality" from the start.

19. What this means in more detail must remain unexplained here. With respect to the dialectic of negativity, Hegel also says that the particular "is balanced with the universal through reflection in itself" (§ 7 F). See Baum, Gemeinwohl und allgemeiner Wille in Hegels Rechtsphilosophie, in 60 Archiv fur Geschichte der Philosophie 175–98 (1978).

20. Landau, Hegels Begründung des Vertragsrechts, in 2 Materialien zu Hegels Rechtsphilosophie 176–97 (M. Riedel ed. 1975).

21. See K. Ilting, Rechtsphilosophie als Phänomenologie des Bewußtseins der Freiheit, in Hegels Philosophie des Rechts, Die Theorie der Rechtsformen und ihre Logik 243 ff (D. Henrich & R. Horstmann ed. 1982).

22. Translator's footnote: When the author wants to contrast other people with other objects, he often uses the masculine definite article ("der") with the noun ("Andere") to refer to the former and the neuter definite article ("das") with the noun to refer to the latter. This is indicated, insofar as it is possible, by capitalizing the "O" in "other" for other persons and leaving it as is for normal objects. At yet other passages, where no such contrast between persons and things is intended, either "otherness" or "other" is used.

23. In footnote 18 of his article, cited supra in note 19, Baum's main thesis is that Hegel's concept of the freedom of the will as "being-with-oneself in otherness" in fact covers every realization of ends and is, accordingly, underdetermined. Baum thus appears to go further in his criticism and examines critically the concept of freedom that I use to measure my criticism. It is to be noted, however, that his argumentation presupposes an understanding of "otherness," according to which this is only the other (as an object), whereas I, certainly extending beyond Hegel, intend the Other as well when I speak of being-with-oneself in otherness.

24. Compare: "The freedom of thought has only *pure thoughts* as its truth, which is without the fulfillment of life; and is also thus only the concept of freedom and not 'living' freedom itself" (PhS § 153). I view this "living" freedom and the "living" good in objective connection.

25. Hegel remarks so the sentence according to which "the will has itself as an object" (§ 10) in handwriting: "that is, has it as content and end." A *replacement* of the concept of object with the concept of end lies in this remark. That Hegel nevertheless says in § 21, that the free will, in and for itself, has itself "as its content, object and aim," must perhaps be traced back to this tendency. He appears to have disregarded his concerns about the expression "object" in the face of the sublation of instrumental action in the thought that makes itself its object.

26. See Horstmann, Subjektiver Geist und Moralität: Zur systematisches Stellung der

Philosopiedes subjectiren Geistes, in 19 Hegels philosophische Psychologie 191–99 (D. Henrich ed. 1979) (supplementary volume).

27. See Guinle, Le sens de l'abstraction dans la philosophie du droit de Hegel, 8 Man and World 383–93 (1975).

28. See Horstmann, supra note 26.

29. See J. Ritter, Hegel und die französische Revolution 69 ff (1965). For a critical response to this, see Horstmann, supra note 16, at 227 ff. Baum, supra note 19, at 190, even says that the Hegelian state is "indiscernable" from civil society.

30. For this see Emil Angehrn's exposition, supra note 3, at 184 ff, on the "objectivity" ("Sachlichkeit") of relations, also self-relations, in abstract right. For the basic problematic, see also Flickinger, "Das abstrakte Recht" Hegels Kritik des bürgerlichen Rechtsbegriffs, 62 Archiv fur Rechts—und Sozialphilosophie 527–48 (1976). Hegel also takes his "starting point at the Roman empire as the basis for civil right" according to Joachim Ritter. Ritter interprets the portrayal of abstract right, however, not as critical, but rather conversely as a portrayal that reveals "the truth of abstract civil right:" the liberation of human beings from the natural state and from merely naturally grounded government. See J. Ritter, Metaphysik und Politik: Studien zu Aristoteles und Hegel 34–81 (1977).

31. The "abstract idea of the good" is itself already a self-contradiction, namely insofar as the idea, as unity of concept and reality, is defined by its concreteness. In this manner, Hegel portrayed the good, which shows into morality, as contradictory already in the transition to the last section, in § 128, as the contradiction that consists of the fact that the good, on the one hand, is supposed to be the "fulfilled" universal that contains particularity in itself, and, on the other hand, is derivative from the "conscience" in which the subject spreads out in its particularity and, thus, becomes evil in the end.

32. See H. Schmitz, Hegel als Denker der Individualität 105 (1957).

33. In his contribution to *Hegel's Philosophie des Rechts, Die Theorie der Rechtsformen und ihre Logik*, Henning Ottmann shows the nullity of right and morality, which I supported with the example of abstract right by pointing out the assignment of judgment forms, extending Alfred Schöpf's thesis (see note 18) by providing an explication of the corresponding inference forms that goes beyond the actual text. Ottmann's contribution was originally conceived as a co-talk to mine at Fontenay-aux-Roses. Considering the extensive reworking of the paper to which Ottmann refers, I have asked him to omit the designation of 'co-talk' for his subsequently submitted contribution.

34. One should keep in mind that the idea of life guided Hegel's early criticism of private property as well.

35. See Ilting, supra note 21, at 225 ff. I perceive it as pleasant that Ilting gives the vexing book a perspective from which it can be productively worked out. Several points of Ludwig Siep's alternative interpretation also seem worth mentioning. See Siep, Intersubjektivität, Recht und Staat in Hegels "Grundlinien der Philosophie des Rechts," in Hegels Philosophie des Rechts, supra, at 255 ff. I shall be supporting and extending it too in the following. I do not think it sufficient in principle to refer to "system coherent plausibility." That the *Philosophy of Right* fits into the systematic unity of subjective, objective and absolute spirit well—

who would want to deny that? That problem is that it fits into the system too well.

36. See footnote 20 of his contribution, cited supra in note 21.

37. Although Hegel does not have the political crime in mind in the *Philosophy of Right*, which would completely upset the framework of abstract right, his earlier, also politically oriented conception of the criminal, according to which the criminal's action becomes "universal" itself due to the universality of the law broken by him, may be at work secretly in this theory (JS § 278).

38. "Property," which is dealt with by the first section of the first part of Hegel's philosophy of right, is initially and as such *private* property. It is so much so private property that Hegel cannot see in common property, which is to be more than the figment of imagination of guild's ideologies, more than a summation of private parts in themselves into which it can also be dissolved (see § 46) so that the maintenance of the community would be due to mere "arbitrariness" (§ 46 N). This conception of common property corresponds to the pejorative concept of commonality about which I will soon talk. The identification of property with private property coheres with the logic of the philosophy of right. It results from the subject of property, as with abstract right in general, being an "*immediate* individuality," see text accompanying note 19, that is, individuality in the determinacy of "formal universality." See infra text accompanying note 59. For in this determinacy the subject is a reflection only in itself, in which it does encounter all others, but with them as excluded and, from their side, as excluding (see § 34). With regard to "the important theory of the necessity of *private property*" (§ 46A), one should distinguish between its legitimacy and the demonstration of its primitive position, which it occupies in the presupposed, thus civil, society. In 1821, in contrast to his early period, Hegel is concerned with its legitimacy as well. However, it is contradictory. Thus Hegel affirms personal property on earth with the legitimacy of private property (that functions as a paradigm) of soil and land, ignoring the peculiar, ultimately theological problematic of precisely this kind of acquisition of property, although he knows that the elementary is opposed to "being particularized into a private possession." The demonstration of the primitive position of private property is, I think, successful not only within his system, but also substantially. It is also to be accepted, according to my judgment, including his premise that private property is not itself based on a normative, intersubjectively recognized, legal order. The subjectivistic justification of formal rightfulness of private property from the necessity, "that I as a free will am in objective possession of myself and thus also for the first time a real will" (§ 45), especially pictures reality insofar as it derives private property from force.

39. See T. Hobbes: Leviathan 192 ff (C. Macpherson ed. 1968). Just as one can ask whether what Hegel calls a "contract" really is one, one can ask the same of the contract theories. With respect to Hobbes, there is much in favor of saying that the covenant, in the sense of a "Covenant of every man with every man," id. at 227, that is needed in the theory of the initiation of the state, is no contract in the true sense and is also, thus, no "contract of benefit," but rather a silently executed legal act whose validity is connected to the condition of equal treatment of all. See Kulenkampff, Die Schöpfung des Leviathan, 37 Zeitschrift für philosophische Forschung 218–27 (1983).

40. See Siep, supra note 35, at 266.

41. See Ilting supra note 21, at 234 ff; Siep, supra note 36, at 266 ff; see also L. Siep, Anerkennung als Prinzip der praktischen Philosophie: Untersuchungen zu Hegels Jenaer Philosophie des Geistes 285 ff (1979) (on the *Philosophy of Right*). A. Wildt's book, supra note 5, is also important for the problematic of recognition.

42. That Hegel is portraying "the civil natural right tradition" here, see H. Schnädel-bach, Zum Verhältnis von Logik und Gesellschaftstheorie bei Hegel: Aktualität und Folgen der Philosophie Hegels 62–84 (V. Negt ed. 1971).

43. The structural similarity of Hegelean conceived knowledge and civil property acquired through labor is studied by H. Schnädelbach, supra note 44, at 63 ff.

44. See Ritter, supra note 30, at 281–309.

45. See M. Riedel, Bügerliche Gesellschaft und Staat bei Hegel 44 ff (1970).

46. In the division of the work (§ 33), Hegel's handwritten insertion, "i.e. other subjects" behind an "external world," refers to morality, not only ethical life. Support for this are the important notes to § 113.

47. Josef Derbolav, in contrast, sees in the section on intention and welfare "the conceptual place of the world-historical individual." See Derbolav, Hegels Theorie der Handlung, in Materialien zu Hegels Rechtsphilosophie 210–16 (M. Riedel ed. 1975).

48. On this point see Baum, supra note 19. Baum maintains in his well-thought-out study the position that Hegel wants to undercut the alternative in which the tradition of political theory remains caught, namely either to entrust the state with welfare or to admit to the state the government of the universal will over the citizens. He also maintains that the opposite goals of the state diverge in his concept, however. The second section of the paper, supra at 183 ff, contributes a substantial amount to understanding universality in civil society, which is to be analyzed at the end of the present study.

49. The thing with which "*jus ad rem*" is concerned (§ 40 F) is also not a purely natural thing. See J. Ritter, Person und Eigentum, 268 (1974).

50. See A. Reinach, Die apriorischen Grundlagen des bürgerlichen Rechtes (1913).

51. I should like to add to this from my own point of view, which cannot claim to rest on Hegel's self-understanding: the second moment is also the last moment. The conflict between negative and positive dialectic is infertile because the truth lies neither on the one nor on the other side, but rather in the self-reflection of the "negative," the second moment. The further step that Hegel takes in his theory of dialectic away from the second moment towards "the *third* moment" (L II 497) leads to all of the difficulties that make an immediate Hegelianism appear suspicious to me. This conviction underlies even the present study and especially the analysis of the result of the genesis to be portrayed here.

52. For this concept see M. Theunissen, The Other 88 ff, 150 ff (1984); M. Theunis-sen, Sein und Schein, supra note *, at 237 ff.

53. See Ilting, supra note 21, at 234 ff.

54. See Derbolav, supra note 47, at 205 ff.

55. On this dubious concept of action, see E. Lange, Das Prinzip Arbeit: Drei metakrit-ische Kapitel über Grundbegriffe, Struktur und Darstellung der 'Kritik der Poli-tischen Ökonomie' von Karl Marx 24–49 (1980).

56. Hegel's references, left out in the quote, are obviously false. The point *alpha* does not refer to § 109, but rather to § 110, point *beta* not to § 112, but rather to § 111.

57. In his essay on natural rights from 1802 Hegel attempted to mediate both sides, whose cross constitutes the dividedness of civil society, through a "theory of sacrifice," "whose achievement lies in separating the other of absolute ethical life as the realm of necessity and fate from the zone of living ethical life and retaining it, as fate of living ethical life, in a relation to that whose other it is." Horstmann, supra note 16, at 283.

58. Hegel must already search for universality in the family because he construes the sequence of family, civil society and state as that of universality, particularity and individuality. He finds it in the immediate, spiritual-substantial unity that qualifies the family for the beginning of ethical life (see § 255).

59. See S. Avineri, Hegels Theorie des modernen Staates 170 ff (1976). On Hegel's "system of universality reciprocal dependency" from his essay on natural rights from 1802, see Horstmann, supra note 16, at 281.

60. See Ahrweiler, supra note 8, at 105 ff.

61. One of the basic experiences that Hegel takes on his path of philosophizing is the unity of particularity and universality, realized in the I, which means that every time I say I I means myself as this one and, at the same time, one who is identical with all others.

62. See H. Fulda, "Kapital" von Marx 204–10 (1974).

63. See H. Kittsteiner, Naturabsicht und Unsichtbare Hand: Zur Kritik des geschichtphilosophischen Denkens (1980).

64. See Riedel, Natur und Freiheit in Hegels Rechtsphilosophie, in Materialien zu Hegels Rechtsphilosophie 109–127, esp. 121 ff (M. Riedel ed. 1975).

65. Thus in 4 Lectures on the Philosophy of Religion § 4: The Absolute Religion. See Puder, Hegels Gottesbeweise, 16 Neue Deutsche Hefte 4, 17–36 (1969). I also owe the reference to "magical power" quoted below to this paper.

66. See Ottmann, Hegelsche Logik und Rechtsphilosophie, in Hegels Philosophie des Rechts, Die Theorie der Rechtsformen und ihre Logik 388 ff (D. Henrich & R. Horstmann eds. 1982) (points 10 and 11).

2

Hegel's Ambiguous Legacy for Modern Liberalism

Charles Taylor

I am going to try to put together a rather long argument of connected issues concerning Hegel's contribution to modern liberalism, but more particularly to a set of issues concerning the relation between law and politics that is central to modern liberalism. I think the interest partly lies in their connection. Hegel's contribution to modern liberalism is complicated, ambivalent, and double-sided. There is something very important in it, and also something potentially disastrous.

I want to start from a very common distinction that is often made in political theory about the priority of the right over the good or the good over the right. A word of explanation of this hermetic language, which may be familiar to some but not entirely clear to others, is in order. We can pick it up first of all as a discussion of the nature of moral theory. There has been a powerful movement in modern times, from about the seventeenth century, to replace ethics which are grounded on the good, with ethics that are grounded on a concept of right. Let us take Aristotle as our starting point for ethics grounded on the good. In Aristotelian ethics, the key concept is a notion of the good life towards which we ought to aspire: the kind of life that is good for human beings. The issue of what is the right thing to do at any given time is determined for ourselves in terms of this prior, more fundamental, and more important concept of the good life. The right thing to do is that which will contribute, to put it simply, to the good life in any given situation. For a variety of reasons, in the modern period we have a widespread, and widely ramifying movement against not only Aristotle as such, but against this whole structure of thought. Let me just mention some of these arguments quickly, because they keep surfacing. One argument derives from a set of reasons involving epistemology, or with a sense of moral skepticism. We are not as certain as

Aristotle was about what a good life is. This is a contentious or uncertain matter, and we cannot base anything solid on it. That is an epistemological argument.

Also, there is a set of moral/political arguments centering on human freedom, or a new, modern definition of freedom defined as giving oneself one's own purposes or one's own law. And there are corresponding conceptions of equality, that everyone ought to be equally entitled to the freedom to determine their own ends and purposes. Now this sense of freedom and equality has also generated a certain suspicion towards Aristotelian notions of the good life, for these notions seem to assume that there is, after all, one clearly set standard. Perhaps not everyone realized it, but the wise certainly saw it as the right standard and it applied to everyone whether they recognized it or not.

So for a very complex set of reasons which have to do both with epistemology and with morals—the kind of overdetermined set of reasons which actually underlie most philosophical changes at any time, even though the motives are not always recognized by philosophers who make the changes—there has been a move to supplant Aristotle. This type of ethical structure and ethical thinking was to be replaced with one that puts first what I call the right, that is, one which purports to be able to determine what we ought to do, the right, without grounding this on a prior concept of the good. The way in which it is purported that one can do this is to develop some kind of procedure, grounded supposedly in reason, which will allow one to generate through a rational procedure what is the right thing to do in given circumstances without having to use as part of one's premises a particular concept of the good. Now right away you will see that I shall be using the distinction between the right and the good in a different way than it is usually invoked. The way I have set it up here, it actually encompasses more thinkers and movements among those who put the right primary than it is usually taken to include. I am borrowing the terms, of course. Originally, I think it was the intuitionists, David Ross and Harold Pritchard, who used this language of the right and the good. They used it to oppose a Kantian-derived theory to a utilitarian theory. "Deontological" and "teleological" are another set of buzz words that has been used for this purpose. I have rewritten this distinction with the important aim of including the utilitarians among the primacy-of-the-right theories. The utilitarians have a notion of the good, in the sense of a goal we aim for, but it is not the good in the sense in which Aristotle used it. The good as it figures in the utilitarian argument is simply the de facto desire. It is not the good in the Aristotelian sense of what is shown by nature to be a higher goal that we bound to follow by its very nature; what I call a strongly valued good. And in the sense that it rejects a concept of a strongly valued good as a cornerstone of ethics, utilitarianism is a precursor of Kantianism.

Utilitarianism also has a procedure; the procedure is maximization, the summing of desired ends. Now of course, Kant rebels against this variant of utilitarianism and sees all sorts of problems in it which I do not need to rehearse. He provides another kind of procedure; and also since then we have had a number of other proposals, most notably from Rawls, and more recently another variant of proceduralist ethics from Habermas. This incorporates important changes in relation to Kant, but still has this basic structure.

We also have at the beginning of the modern era independent application of this turn of thinking to politics—independent, that is, of its application to morals. Proceduralism can be something that you take on board as your whole theory of morality or it can be taken on board in a narrower compass as your theory of a political right independent of considering what a good life is for an individual. We have at the beginning of the modern era this analogous move restricted to the political sphere. I want to look at the rise of contract theories in the seventeenth century in this light. The crucial question about judging society is not what is a good society, that is, a good form of life that it embodies. The crucial issue is that of origin or procedure, did it come about through consent? This is a shift from a good-oriented theory to a right-based theory which makes some procedure central.

Now I want to bring this all together to look at an influential theory at this time in the United States. I am particularly thinking of Ronald Dworkin's definition of liberalism. Dworkin says, in his definition of liberalism, that a liberal society is

> one where political decisions must be as far as possible independent of any particular conception of the good life, or of what gives value to life. Since the citizens of a society differ in their conception, the government does not treat them as equals if it prefers one conception to another.[1]

Treating people as equals is fundamental to Dworkin's definition of liberalism. He has defined it in such a way that the political structure must be grounded again on the right. We must not take a concept of what the good life is as the basis for a given political structure, or even in some variants of the theory, for particular legislation in that structure. On the contrary, we need to have normative standards for both structure and legislation come from a normative theory which puts the right as fundamental and therefore eschews the issue of the good or leaves it open to individuals. The case of Dworkin is interesting because his view is different from the mainstream position, in that he separates himself from any arguments of moral scepticism. Dworkin has stated consistently that he has no quarrel with the concept of the good life, the fundamental seriousness of which is cognitively understood. But the other motivation I mentioned, the historic motivation of freedom and equality, is of course central to his political view.

Now over and against this picture of modern liberalism, is what we call the civic humanist position. Civic humanism profoundly influenced Hegel, and it has a view of politics that portrays this kind of liberalism as impossible. It offer a critique of liberalism on two levels, branding it as undesirable in one way, while arguing that in some important sense, it is impossible in another. I will return to this later, but first I would like to explore the inner logic of this position in order to confront it with the liberal one that I have been describing.

Let us go right back to the models of Greece and Rome, which were so important throughout our modern history. Again and again, there are writers who reach back and take them as models. Here we have societies of citizen self-rule. A key concept among them is that which I call citizenship dignity.[2] Freedom in one of its meanings carries this notion of citizen dignity, and the underlying intuition here is that as a citizen, I am an agent—I act in the world, I do significant things—as against a metic, or a slave, or a noncitizen who lives in a purely private sphere prior to any public life. Now this depends on an all-important set of distinctions which turn on the difference between private and public. Already the concept of significance which figures in this formulation, in the idea that action for the polis is significant in a way that action in private life is not, depends on one concept of the public. What makes the action significant is that it is action for the polis; it is action which preserves or enhances or allows the polis or the republic to continue. So that significance is tied in with concern for the community, in contrast to that which concerns my situation in life or my particular interests.

Significant action, in turn, was linked very closely with fame and glory and linked in a much closer way then we tend to allow for in our modern concept. Our modern understanding of human life has generated such a powerful conception of the private person and of inwardness that we tend to loosen the connection which was much closer for the Greeks. Thus, that fame which attached to greatness or significance of action in public life was not thought of as simply the consequence of this action, if we mean by this the purely contingent kind. It was thought of as the obverse to greatness, as belonging normally to greatness. Of course, there could be some special and reprehensible set of interventions, whereby citizens out of jealousy or ill-will would try to frustrate this connection by dishonoring an important person. But the idea was that greatness and fame intrinsically belong together. Now fame presupposes a very strong concept of the public. I think this is one of the key differences between the first kind of liberalism and civic humanism. The strong concept of the public here is the concept of what I want to call shared significance. Perhaps "shared" does not quite capture the important distinction, because there are two kinds of sharing: there is a strong and a weak kind. I want to call the weak kind convergence; that would be the case where I privately think something is important and you privately think something is important and it turns out that most of us or all of us feel the same. That is significantly different from sharing in the strong sense where we share public space, the difference being that in this case the good we share in part effectively turns on our sharing; the sharing in itself is valued. In the first case, this does not apply. As you look at a good like fame which was terribly important to people of that age, you can see that it presupposes a strong sense of shared significance. It is not fame in the sense of a lot of people privately admiring someone. Fame is recognition in public space. This distinction between the strong and weak publicity, or sharing/convergence is a distinction not just between two kinds of beings to whom something is important, but actually is a distinction which is significant in itself. It is something that can be desired or can be important too.

Now there is a particular notion of a public institution which turns on this strong concept of shared space, the concept of what bonds citizens to the polis or republic. The set of public institutions and practices—the "laws"—were based on the understanding that they were the common repository of the citizens' dignity. Citizens love the laws because they are the common repository of their freedom (if you use this word in its ancient sense). Why is this form of life a repository for our freedom? Because without this law we would slide into despotism, which is the rule of one person alone. And in case of the rule of one person alone, that person would be the only one who would be honored and have fame. In despotism, there is in some sense no public space at all, or, if you want to use the term in another sense, there is a quite different kind of public space, one which is nourished simply by the despot, in which there is no other free and unconstrained people. Of course, despots commonly have themselves praised, like Stalin who had people write poems about him in Pravda. But, as is well known, this is something which is fundamentally different from fame in the sense of praise and glory in the mouths and judgment of the people. It is different not because the same good is distributed unequally to one person in the despotic case compared with its distribution to many in the other, but rather it is a different kind of good. So here again this notion of the significant is tied to a certain type of public space, which in turn is tied to a certain kind of equality. These are all linked together noncontingently, and that is why the citizens love the republic as a repository of their common citizen dignity.

This common allegiance militated against what otherwise would have been tremendously disruptive forces in the republic—disruptive because this kind of polity allowed full scope for rival ambition. Rivalry and ambition were almost the name of the game. Life was striving for fame. Not everybody could be the most famous leader, and there was an agonistic feature to this society. What could nevertheless hold it together is the obverse of this good that everyone seeks for themselves. The obverse side is that his good itself presupposes solidarity in maintaining the laws, a condition of there being genuine fame. Of course, great, ambitious people can aspire to overturn this and seek something else which they then enjoy as despots. But in principle, the love of the fame is linked to the preservation of the laws, and hence contains its own safeguard. This common love of the laws was a shared good in a strong sense.

Now the great alternative to this view about what holds free society together is the one propounded by some modern theorists, conceptions of society ordered by what we can call invisible hand mechanisms.[3] The prime example is the market. But not only the market. There is a very interesting mixture among the thinkers who put together the Constitution of the United States 200 years ago. In some parts of their minds, they were responding to the rhetoric and the thought of republicans. In other parts of their minds, they were responding to new developments in modern theory which concerned how to put together a Constitution, so that regardless of the motivation of the particular citizens, their action in public life would tend to sustain freedom. The Constitution would be so designed that the energies would be channeled towards the maintenance of stability and freedom. There is a kind of thinking that says: let the motivation of the players be what it may be—be it the most self-regarding or private that one may conceive—nevertheless the structure of the society will ensure that their actions will redound to the good. This is of course the radical alternative to the civic humanist view which, on the contrary, looks on the privatization of peoples' motivation as corruption and as preparing the way for despotism.

So we have these two conceptions of what can make a free society possible; one which makes common meanings and shared good absolutely central to the preservation of the society and the other which says that the motivation issue is unimportant. The latter says we need structure which, in invisible-hand fashion, behind the backs of the subjects and independent of the forms of motivation, will lead their actions towards certain patterns that preserve freedom.

Now there is no question where Hegel stands on this issue. He did indeed note the operation of an invisible-hand mechanism at a certain level of civil society, but this could never be the adequate form for the state. In this sense, Hegel is to be placed in the civic humanist tradition. And that is why we can derive important arguments from Hegel about why the liberal society as described by Dworkin is in a sense impossible.

Let us explore the characteristics of the humanist society to see which of these are conceivable in a modern free society. The humanist society is founded on a common understanding about the good life. In its original version everyone believed that significant public action was something admirable and worthy of fame and honor. And the argument was that if that common understanding ever failed, then there would be danger for the freedom of the society. Secondly, there is this common recognition that the laws by which we organize our life are something admirable. That again is part of the shared understanding of the good. But thirdly, what we have here is not just a general conviction that the public and laws follow this model. This model also incorporates the common recognition of this. But now once we take that under consideration, we see that something else has entered the picture, because this model of society incorporates the sense that citizens with a particular history, a particular condition, and particular institutional forms, are bound together in one such enterprise. In other words, this ethos does not just incorporate a general belief that free societies are a good thing, a belief that anybody could hold—and which may be now held by many in northern Moscow, or southern Santiago. To have a viable society requires not just that I and others think it is a good thing, but that we come to a common recognized understanding that we have launched a particular common enterprise of this sort, and this creates a particular bond around this society, this tradition, this history.

This raises two issues. There are two ways in which this kind of society seems to run against the Dworkin-type liberalism or any type of liberalism that makes the right preeminent alone over the good. There seems first to be some common sense of what the good life is, and secondly, it seems to require that citizens have not just a strong sense of the appropriate universal ethical principles like freedom, equality, and fairness, but also that they have a strong moral allegiance to this particular bonding which has come about in their society, whether it be their institutions, their history, or their tradition. Now this second feature calls for a common allegiance to the particular, and this centrality of the particular is one of the most important issues raised by Hegel in his concept of *Sittlichkeit*.[4] This is one of the things that distinguishes ethical life from morality. Hegel talks in paradoxical formulations about the obligations of ethical life, where we are obliged to bring about what already is. This is the kind of obligation we have under *Sittlichkeit* or ethical life, by virtue of being members of one of the ongoing bonded communities of common life and common freedom. As pure individuals outside of any such going entity, that is in southern Santiago or northern Moscow, and so on, we are bound by *Moralität* and we can have *Moralisch* obligations there. In some cases, these may even drive us to dream about a totally different society. But that is not the kind of obligation we have under *Sittlichkeit*, which presupposes this common existing entity.

So we have here, as it were, a cross between two kinds of distinction: one between those goods that are purely sought by individuals as against goods that are sought by the community together, and the other between a morality of purely universal principals and a morality which is tied up with obligations to a particular community. These are two ways in which a viable free society in civic humanist terms must differ from a society purely based on the right according to the liberal outlook today. Now what I think is interesting in Hegel, beyond his being another member of this long tradition of civic humanism, is his way of formulating the mainline humanist argument that a free society cannot remain a free society without these elements of bonding. I think there are two things that are extremely interesting and insightful. One is this way of making a distinction between *Sittlichkeit* and *Moralität*,[5] between ethical right and morality, which shows the importance of bonding to a particular, and the other is that Hegel has not just drawn this point about the impossibility of maintaining the free society without common bonding out of a reasoned observation of history and society, as for instance de Tocqueville does very brilliantly. But Hegel has connected it with some of the most fundamental features of human right and of what the new, modern subject is. I think it is fascinating to see how this works out in Hegel.

For instance, you can see that this worked out in one way in a very famous dialectic of the master and the slave,[6] where Hegel makes the point of some inner link between self-consciousness and recognition. I think you can reconstitute the argument behind that fundamental link by combining two philosophical points which together produce this connection. One is that counting as a person is intrinsic to being a person. Recognizing persons is inseparable from being obliged to treat them in a certain way: according them respect, giving them rights to speak in modern terms. But even looking at our lives monologically, we seek a sense of worth. We cannot construe our lives narratively in a way which makes sense of them without incorporating this issue of their worth. Thus we may conclude from either of these ways that one can say that persons exist only in a certain space of evaluation. That is one point.

The second point that comes together with this Hegelian insight that personhood involves recognition, is that the space of evaluation of the person's existence is intrinsically and inseparably a public space. We come back to this very important strong sense of the public. Hegel's underlying argument should perhaps be constructed in the following way. The link between the space of evaluation for which persons exist and public space is that this kind of evaluation requires language. That is, the issue of the evaluation of persons could not arise for us unless we could in some way articulate the evaluation or give expression to it. The issue only arises for language animals. But language does not arise monologically. It arises in conversation or between people. Each of us is inducted into language by conversation with others so that the language I speak is not at first my language but our language. We learn the words that can express evaluation by applying them, and we learn to apply them in conversation. So we learn them out of common application and that is why, to use Wittgenstein's expression, we have to agree to some degree in judgments. I become a person by entering the space of value, and this space of value is one elaborated in a common language; so I cannot flourish as a person if this space of value is so laid out as to negate or denigrate me.

In fact, this is the point which underlies the Hegelian dialectic of the master and the slave. To be persons, we crave recognition and we are ready to fight for it, but the fighting over it is in itself a contradictory action because both the acknowledgement that we need recognition and the media or language which sustains the common space of evaluation that allows recognition has to be constituted by conversation between us. What powers the master-slave dialectic, and drives it on, is that the very struggle to gain recognition is fated to self-frustration because it can never be properly achieved until we achieve the kind of community described in the passage which ends this section of the

Phenomenology: a society where the I is a we and we is an I.[7] Thus Hegel has anchored the civic humanist reflection of the importance of common valuation for a free society in a philosophical anthropology linking personhood to the very nature of language.

Coming back now to the issue of how this applies to our modern liberal society, let me go back to the practice of contemporary societies. How do we see the contemporary American republic in the light of both of Dworkin's liberalism on the one hand, and the humanist-derived sense of the importance of ethical life on the other? Interestingly, in the contemporary American polity there is a partial recognition of, or embodying of, this civic humanist requirement and a partial distancing of self. Let us go back to the two points which emerged from the civic humanist tradition as critical of the Dworkin-type liberal position. First, there has to be a common sense of the good life, which directly contradicts Dworkin's provisions. And secondly, that the requirements of a free society according to humanists differs from the liberal one, in that it requires not just the wide acceptance of universal ethical principles but the strong sense of bonding to a particular set of institutions. Now it seems to me that whether or not the contemporary American public involves an embodiment of point number one, that is, a strong common sense of the good life, it certainly embodies point number two, that is, a very strong attachment to particular institutions; and I would argue that the civic humanists' case for the essential nature of this is wonderfully illustrated by recent American history. The public reactions to Watergate and the Iran-Contra affair were excellent illustrations. The reactions displayed a deep sense of respect for and allegiance to a particular political community—not just to the general principles but to the principles as embodied in a particular set of institutions and traditions. These were terribly important to the identity of a lot of people and therefore made them react in anger when they saw how their President had acted. Their reaction had an extremely important political effect and goes on having an important political effect, in preserving whatever these institutions preserve, the kind of freedoms and immunities they embody. Now it is also clear that that kind of reaction, powered as it is by a particular bonding of patriotism rather than simply by widespread acceptance of totally unconnected universal principles, also poses a danger, and opponents of Hegel have made this point again and again. This criticism is not without merit; this kind of patriotism can lead to blind actions that override the ethic of the public life. The paradox of one Oliver North is especially striking: he possesses a tremendous love of country that could take the form of subverting all the principles of that country. This is not a surprising or unusual phenomenon; it is something that exists everywhere and can be a very dangerous force. I do not deny its danger, but the fact that it also takes the form of a bulwark of freedom seems to me to be undeniable. But there is one feature of this allegiance which does not entirely fit with the civic humanist tradition. That is, that the reaction of the American public in defense of the laws seemed directed more as a repository of right, of the rule of law and equal treatment, than as a repository of citizen self-rule. By citizen self-rule, I mean something rather strong and special. I do not just mean the existence of parties and elections, whereby the forms of democracy are built in as part of the rule of law. I mean something more subtle but very important. I am talking of a political culture, where political participation in the process of making a majority, of forming a government, of ruling, would be rather devalued and seen as an activity of secondary importance. But what the serious people who want to act as guardians of the law or adjuncts to guardians of the law would consider important would be judicial action, retrieving rights. Indeed, some consider appointing the Supreme Court justices to be the most important function of the American President.

This is a kind of participation which is very adversarial and looks on political power as "them" against "us," and looks on political action as the retrieving of rights or the retrieving of certain important, very circumscribed goals. So one would have a pattern of political action which is either punctually aimed at a particular goal and/or generally oppositional. That is, its stance would be that the citizens should defend themselves against government as something beyond them, almost an enemy. The objective is to make sure that, among the other bad things, government does not affect this particular interest or that particular group.

There is a pattern of political action here which would turn on the legal process of defending rights rather than the representative institutions as a medium of collective self-rule. Citizen dignity, therefore, would be defined more and more as the capacity to retrieve one's rights, either through the courts, through oppositional campaigns or through the single-issue type of political organization. And correspondingly, the sense of participation in the political process, that is, being elected and sharing in power tends to be devalued. This is different, in an important sense, from the classical civic humanist position in that it would have dropped what I call point one, the general understanding that participation, ruling, and being ruled in turn, was something valuable as a form of life. That would disappear. One would still have something important from the civic humanist tradition, namely, some sense of commonly valued institutions and the laws—that is, those centered around the treatment of right, but not the classical notion of participation.

This gives rise to several questions. Is that what is happening here? If it is, is that a good thing? If it is, is it a viable form of defending freedom in the long run? I mean viable for the defense of freedom. Now, on the other side, there is a sense that there is such a thing as participating in rule, not necessarily just as a politician or in government, but as a member of a large membership mass party trying to elect a government, or as a member of some citizens' group linked in some way to government, or as a worker in a party trying to elect a form of government. There is a sense that this is a valid thing to do, an admirable mode of life. In other words, a sense that citizen dignity partly connects with being connected to rule.

Here are two ways of perceiving the role of law in politics. They both lie within this basically Hegelian civic humanist framework. What they both exclude is a picture of a society run purely by invisible-hand mechanisms. This is a formula which is seen as quite unviable in this framework. There needs to be some strong sense of common values and this has to be particularized and bonded to a particular people in history. But, in my perhaps overdrawn distinction, we have a rather different picture of that around which the bonding occurs, and the difficulty is that it is hard to combine the two. That is, the more that place of one grows, the more it can constrain or take the place of the other. And questions arise, not only as to which of these is the better but, more fundamentally, whether the one organized around judicial review is viable in the long term. I have questions about whether a society, organized around common values and a common sense of the rights, and a rather adversarial attitude toward the legal process, is viable in the long term.

Now, Hegel would have had no difficulty deciding this question. In the *Philosophy of Right*, Hegel writes: "The Many . . . are of course something connected, but they are connected only as an aggregate, a formless mass whose commotion and activity could therefore only be elementary, irrational, barbarous, and frightful."[8] That was his view. It is the point where one can see how the whole Hegelian model is flawed. A Hegelian model, as a model of critical society, is flawed by its Fichtean roots. I think this goes for everything good Hegel did in the way of overturning epistemology and atomism. His argument was powered by a fundamental concept of subject/object identity, which he gets from Fichte, and which has some roots in Rousseau. It is a model for a kind of unity of society which, in the end, gives no place to the agon, to competition, to unresolvable differences. That is why Hegel can make these kinds of remarks, not about the wild West in the 1870s, but about even well-ordered societies that have elections from territorial constituencies. That is why he can make these kind of remarks about institutions that work through checks and balances, which work in adversarial form, and not simply in a form that brings them together. Hegel had this completely unrealistic view about how representative institutions could work simply in a one-way direction to bring people in and create a consensus, rather than to be the arena in which deep dissensions can be worked out in a way that nevertheless helps to bond to a common allegiance. I think that is one way of framing one of the great realizations of liberal democracies when they work—that they manage to achieve this. That, of course, means that in order to reconstruct the whole Hegelian synthesis, you have to do what he did; one has to go down as deep as he did, to the roots of all of this, in a conception of human being rooted in the language and in the way that we relate to language. I think it can be done, but Hegel offers us this very difficult legacy. Hegel gives us an unparalleled depth of understanding and philosophic underpinnings for posing these questions about the nature of a free society, and I think he lays to rest the false view that one could have a society that is organized entirely around invisible-hand mechanisms. Moreover, by posing these issues and showing, I think, the tremendous importance of the bonding around a particular history and tradition, Hegel allows us to pose the more finely grained issues which arise in comparing a society which defines citizen dignity in terms of retrieving one's rights with a society which identifies citizen dignity with participating in rule. In all of that I think Hegel is tremendously revealing and helpful. But, at the same time, his view suffers from a great inadequacy, in that the ultimate metaphysical idea that in Hegel's magnificently consistent way runs through and informs his whole work is a conception of subject/object identity, which is both metaphysical and incredible, and I think in the end a very bad model for a political society. So, in a sense, we have very good reason to use Hegel, but we have to use him with great care.

NOTES

This Essay is adapted from the Keynote Address delivered at the Hegel and Legal Theory Symposium, March 27–29, 1988, at Benjamin N. Cardozo School of Law, Yeshiva University.

1. Dworkin, Liberalism, in Public and Private Morality 127 (S. Hampshire ed. 1978).

2. If you want to go to the Greek this is what "ελευθερια" is in one of its meanings.

3. The first and most prominent of these theorists is Adam Smith. See A. Smith, The Wealth of Nations (E. Canaan ed. 1937). Hegel reinterprets Smith's invisible hand as the cunning of reason. G. Hegel, Philosophy of Right § 199 (T. Knox trans. 1952) (1821) [hereinafter Philosophy of Right].

4. " 'Sittlichkeit' refers to the moral obligations I have to an ongoing community of which I am a part." C. Taylor, Hegel 376 (1975).

5. For a more detailed explanation of the difference between *Sittlichkeit* and *Moralität*, see C. Taylor, supra note 4, at 376–78.

6. See C. Taylor, supra note 4, at 153–57.

7. See G. Hegel, The Phenomenology of Mind 241–67 (J. Baillie trans. 1967).

8. Philosophy of Right, supra note 3, para. 303.

3

Persons and Masks: The *Phenomenology of Spirit* and its Laws

Robert Bernasconi

The *Phenomenology of Spirit*[1] has many laws. Most prominent are the law of force in chapter three; the laws of thought, the laws of the heart, and law as commandment in chapter five; the human and divine laws in the first part of chapter six; and the moral law and the natural law in the final part of chapter six. But is there a law to these laws? Is it possible to detect a law which governs them all? The question is not to be understood as an attempt to find an abstract concept of law, which embraces the laws just mentioned, so that the many laws would collapse into one law—a law of laws. That would be to repeat the dialectic of the one and the many, introduced by Hegel in chapter two of the *Phenomenology* and against which he is on guard throughout (115/§ 150). Rather, the questions would concern the necessity governing these laws. Was Hegel's appeal to precisely these laws essential? How are they related?

The questions would ask about the necessity governing the presentation of the *Phenomenology* itself. It would ask about the law—the order—that saves the *Phenomenology of Spirit* from the chaos which, according to Hegel himself, threatens to overtake every first reading of *Phenomenology*. As he wrote in an advertisement which, as editor, he inserted in the *Bamberger Zeitung* in June 1807: "The wealth of the appearances of the spirit, which at first glance (*dem ersten Blicke*) seems chaotic, is brought into a scientific order which presents them according to their necessity in which the imperfect ones dissolve and pass over into higher ones which constitute their next truth."[2] The necessity which determines the order of the *Phenomenology* shows itself only for a *second* glance, a rereading. At least that is what Hegel implies in this work and others. Unfortunately, we still await a commentary on the *Phenomenology* which would meticulously mark and clarify the character of such a rereading. In the absence of the perspective that such a commentary would provide, discussion of the *Phenomenology* is liable to distortion. Because this paper is largely confined to one particular moment of Hegel's discussion of law, I too shall be guilty of displaying Hegel only through a distorting mirror. I hope to mitigate the charge by focusing on the very partiality of my account.

The shape of consciousness I shall be examining will be the very one in which the language of law as I have considered it thus far is itself apparently put in question. For although I have catalogued a number of senses of law in the *Phenomenology*, that list was far from exhaustive. This is because I confined myself to only one of Hegel's words for law, albeit the most common word, the word *Gesetz*. There is also law as *Recht*. *Recht* has its moment in the *Phenomenology* and it is that moment which I want to consider. The distinction between *Gesetz* and *Recht* is not easily rendered in English. Knox's translation of the *Philosophie des Rechts* as the *Philosophy of Right* has helped establish what now seems the most obvious option and the one which I will follow: law for *Gesetz*, right for *Recht*.[3] But what do these words mean for Hegel? This is not easy to determine. It should be emphasized that the distinction is deep-rooted and reflected in other languages apart from German, such as Latin (*lex/ius*) and French (*loi/droit*). It is in the *Philosophy of Right* that Hegel is most careful to clarify the difference between *Gesetz* and *Recht*. Indeed, he marks a passage from *Recht* to *Gesetz* in the center of the section on *Sittlichkeit*, which follows the discussion of *Das abstrakte Recht* and *Die Moralität*. *Recht* becomes *positives Recht*. *Recht* becomes *Gesetz* when it is posited (*gesetzt*) in objective existence—when it attains the form proper to its universality, its true determinacy.[4]

It is a commonplace that the order of the *Phenomenology* is not that of the *Philosophy of Right*. Unfortunately, I shall not here be able to reopen the question of the relation between the *Phenomenology* and the *Philosophy of Right* in terms of which the different direction of the two works must be approached. This could only have been done if the *Philosophy of Right* had been restored to its place in the System of Science from which it is so often abstracted and if we possessed a better understanding of the ambiguous place of the *Phenomenology* in relation to the System of Science which it introduces and of which it is simultaneously the first part. I can note, however, that the reversal does not arise only because *Sittlichkeit* in the *Phenomenology* precedes *Moralität* and not the other way round as in the *Philosophy of Right*. It also goes further than the fact that the brief discussion of *Rechtszu-*

stand, which follows *Sittlichkeit* in the *Phenomenology* and seems merely to be appended to it there, is made the starting point of the *Philosophy of Right* as *Das abstrakte Recht*. In the *Phenomenology* there is a transition not from *Recht* to *Gesetz* as in the later *Philosophy of Right*, but the other way around. It is not as clearly marked as in the latter work, because Hegel seems less strict in maintaining the separate meaning of the two words. Nevertheless, it seems that *Gesetz* is most prominent in the first five chapters; that at the beginning of chapter six (the chapter on spirit) Hegel uses both *Gesetz* and *Recht* to describe the Greek world, with the emphasis perhaps on the former term, and that at the end of the first part of the sixth chapter, Hegel's attention shifts exclusively to *Recht*. It is that shift which will serve as my starting point. Certainly, this is not the end of the discussion of law—later in the chapter, for example, the French Revolution is discussed in terms of the concept of law rather than of right—but here Hegel clearly marks a transition between conceptions of the law.

Hegel is perhaps most explicit about this transition in a sentence which follows his account of the conflict between Antigone and Creon. He writes: "Only in the downfall of both sides alike is absolute right [*das absolute Recht*] accomplished, and the ethical substance as the negative power which engulfs both sides, that is, omnipotent and righteous Destiny [*das allmächtige und gerechte Schicksal*], steps on the scene (337/§ 472)."[5] Hegel is saying that absolute right, which had been sought in human law, cannot be found there. The downfall is experienced by both Antigone and Creon in the guilt they feel. Antigone, following the divine law, is guilty before the human law. Creon, following the human law, is guilty in the face of the divine law. The two laws are not simply opposed to each other. In the first part of the chapter, Hegel had shown how the two laws were interdependent by examining the interrelation of the substances—the polis or the family—in *one* of which each individual finds its element. Only then does he introduce the situation in which they come into conflict. The suffering brought on by the experience of guilt frees the participants from their respective characters—in the sense of their allegiance to the separate laws which differentiated them—and the belief arises that nothing counts except *das Rechte* (336/§ 470). Absolute right is therefore found not in human law or human right where it had been sought, and the tie between the individual and its substance is broken.

This discussion marks the transition from the familiar and relatively long discussion of *Sittlichkeit* to the brief and largely neglected section on *Rechtszustand* or "legal status." The section has been neglected—like much else in the *Phenomenology*—through commentators reducing it to a story or narrative. This is a widespread practice, not least because Hegel himself has appeared to authorize this approach by describing the *Phenomenology* as "the history of the *education* of consciousness" (67/§ 78 emphasis in original). The description seems to fit the chapter on spirit because it follows the course of history from ancient Greece to Hegel's own times. On these terms, the section on legal status is transitional, albeit only in the rather disarming sense of trying to fill a gap of well over a thousand years. It is impossible to say precisely how long the gap is, because of the lack of explicit historical reference points both in the discussion of *Rechtszustand* and the discussion which immediately follows. It is perhaps not accidental that the narrative details which would allow Hegel's reader better to identify the historical moment are withheld. Perhaps it is more surprising that Hegel is sometimes as specific as he is. It is far from clear that the necessity governing the *Phenomenology* is clarified by every additional historical reference that assiduous commentators succeed in identifying. Such references do more to sustain a first reading of the *Phenomenology* than they illuminate the book's order, the law of the book. For example, it can be shown that the discussion of *Rechtszustand* in the *Phenomenology* corresponds to Hegel's discussion of the Roman Empire in the *Lectures on the Philosophy of World History*.[6] This does not mean that the discussion in the *Phenomenology* is *about* right in the Roman Empire. Most of the section's five pages are concerned with establishing parallels to the earlier account of Stoicism and Scepticism in chapter four. Only when we are better able to explain why Hegel's own focus lies in drawing these parallels will we have learned to read— or rather reread—the *Phenomenology*.

The first time reader, however, will not be impressed by these structural parallels between various sections of the book. Indeed, the first time reader is more likely to be struck by Hegel's curt condemnation of the concept of person. It comes at the end of a crucial but difficult sentence: "Consciousness of right, therefore, in the very fact of being recognized as having validity, experiences rather the loss of its reality and its complete inessentiality; and to describe an individual as a 'person' is an expression of contempt (345/§ 480)." The observation is not an isolated one. Hegel repeats it many years later in the *Philosophy of Right* where he writes: "Man's summit is to be a person, and yet in spite of that bare abstraction, 'person' is a somewhat contemptuous bare expression."[7] In the *Phenomenology*, Hegel seems to be saying that insofar as the law construes the individual as a "person" it holds the individual in contempt, an observation which would amount to a devastating contempt of court (*Mißchtung des Gerichts*) on Hegel's part. Or perhaps one should say there is a more fundamental form of "contempt of court" than the one that is usually recognized—the court's own contempt of the individual.

What is the context of Hegel's suspicion of the concept of person? Hegel explained the collapse of the Greek ethical life in terms of the contradiction between the human law and the divine law. The community which replaces it is sustained not by ethical substance, but by law as right. It survives only by suppressing the spirit of individualism (341/§ 475) and so becomes a soulless community (342/§ 477): it is no more than a multiplicity of individuals all of whom count the same. Before the law, all individuals are equal. But they have been equalized only on the basis of an impoverished conception of the individual as a "person." In the *Lectures on the Philosophy of World History*, Hegel captures in a graphic image the dissolution undergone by the living body of the state when political organization is reduced to the atomism of a plurality of private persons: he says that it reminds him of when a physical body rots and each of its parts acquires a life of its own, the wretched life of a worm.[8] This suspicion of the concept of person extends to the concept of right insofar as the two terms are closely correlated.[9] Hegel is ill-disposed to the language of rights, and particularly the notion of equality which belongs to it. In a famous passage of the *Philosophy of Right*, he says that the demand for equality belongs to "empty understanding which takes this abstraction and its 'ought' as real and rational."[10] Such abstractions seem to be endemic to the law, but the point is particularly appropriate to a discussion of Roman law. In his 1802 essay *Natural Law*[11] (*Naturrecht*) Hegel quoted Edward Gibbon's *The Decline and Fall of the Roman Empire*: "'The minds of men were gradually reduced to the same level, the fire of genius was extinguished, and even the military spirit evaporated.'"[12] The question is whether this is Hegel's main concern in this section of the *Phenomenology*. Why does Hegel come to focus on the word "person" and subject it to his invective? To what is the language of personhood opposed?

The word "person" is very telling for Hegel's purpose. Thomas Hobbes provides the best introduction to Hegel's discussion. Hobbes writes in *Leviathan*:

> The word person is Latin: instead whereof the Greeks have [prosō-pon], which signifies the *face*, as *persona* in Latin signifies the *disguise*, or *outward appearance* of a man, counterfeited on the stage; and sometimes more particularly that part of it, which disguiseth the face,

as a mask or vizard: and from the stage hath been translated to any
representer of speech and action, as well in tribunals, as theaters.[13]

Hobbes here observes a difference between the Greek and the Latin
languages. In terms of this difference, the passage from Greek civilization to Roman civilization amounts to a passage from the face to the
mask. This would correspond quite closely to the transition Hegel
makes from the fullness of ethical life, which he calls "the living immediate unity of individuality and substance (342/§ 477)," to the abstract
impoverishment of the Roman world. Is the transition from *Gesetz* to
Recht therefore to be understood as a passage from face to mask?

Before calling Hobbes to Hegel's aid, it should be noted that Hobbes,
whose linguistic sensitivity is normally so reliable, missed the mark on
this occasion. Does not *prosopan* also mean mask? This appears to have
dawned on Hobbes also. The Latin edition of *Leviathan* (published in
1668, seventeen years after the original English edition) tried to salvage
the text by saying that in Latin *person* "more frequently" (*frequentis-
sime*) meant "mask."[14] The point was made more precise in Hobbes's
response to Dr. Bramhall's *Catching of the Leviathan.*[15] Hobbes said
that it may be possible to render the Latin word *persona* in English
with accuracy, but there is no Greek equivalent—a point readily illustrated by the history of Church doctrine.[16] The underlying claim, which
survives the recognition that both *prosopan* and *persona* can mean
mask, is that with the Romans the word is given political significance.
Or, to put it another way, even if there never was a pure face free of
all masking, it is the Romans who made it a virtue of entering the
political arena in disguise.

The word "person" played an important role in Roman law. Roman
law distinguished between the law which pertains to persons (*jus ad
personas*) and the law which pertains to things (*jus ad rem*). Nevertheless, Roman law did not regard all human beings as persons. Slaves
were things according to the law. That is to say, "persons" possessed
legal rights, but slaves did not.[17] Hegel, however, seems to neglect this
usage in his characterization of law within the Roman Empire and not
only in the *Phenomenology*. In the *Lectures on the Philosophy of World
History*, in the course of a discussion of the position of individuals as
persons in ancient Rome, Hegel said not only that individuals were
"perfectly equal . . . and without political right," but also that in
respect of equality "slaves made only a trifling distinction" (*einen
geringen Unterschied*).[18] Hegel seems to have overlooked the important
role played by the question of the *status* of the person (*condicio perso-*

nae) in Roman law. He ignores, for example, the distinction between the *honestiores* and *humiliores*.[19] One wonders how Hegel can attack the conception of person for proposing an abstract equality without raising what seems to us the obvious point: that this equality, such as it was, was itself only sustained by inequality. Is that not precisely the kind of point one would expect Hegel, of all people, to be making? And not without good reason. In the *Philosophy of Right*, Hegel shows that he is fully aware of the confusions which arise from the classification of the law into *jus ad personas* and *jus ad rem*[20] as well as the deficiency of the definition of "man" in Roman law for excluding the slave: "The very status of slave indeed is an outrage on the conception of man."[21] Why then are such considerations absent from the discussion of legal status in the *Phenomenology*? Indeed, why does Hegel not do more to amplify his understanding of the law and the person in the *Phenomenology*?

My answer, as I have already intimated, is that he is more concerned to establish a parallel between legal status on the one hand and Stoicism and Scepticism on the other. Hegel sets out the parallel in the following way. Stoicism is the abstract form of legal status. It is the *thought* of independence (*Selbständigkeit*) which posits its essence in the unity of pure thought. What in Stoicism was only implicit in an abstract way becomes in legal status an actual world (343/§ 477). But in both cases there is a detachment from what might sustain it. Just as Stoicism is detached from actual existence, the law of the person is "not attached to a richer or more powerful existence of the individual as such" (344/ § 479). That is to say, the law of the person is superficial. The abstract form of legalism amounts to a formalism.[22] The alleged parallel with Stoicism's passage to Scepticism is the context for Hegel's observation that legal status similarly passes into confusion and dissolution.

This is not the only parallel in play. Hegel also says that "[t]he free power of the content determines itself in such a way that its dispersion into an absolute *multiplicity* of personal atoms is, by the nature of this determinateness, at the same time gathered into *One*, a spiritless point alien to them . . . (345/§ 481) (emphasis added)" Thus, at the very point where Hegel establishes the parallel with Stoicism and Scepticism, he also introduces an echo of the dialectic of the one and the many, first introduced in the chapter on perception and often returned to (particularly in the context of discussions of law). A further parallel is established when the *one* of the one and the many is identified. The one, the gathering point of the multiplicity of persons, is identified by Hegel as the "master of the world," a solitary single individual that "thinks of itself as being an actual living god (345§ 481)." Because Hegel couches the discussion in terms of the "master of the world," it is possible to see here a reference to the master-slave dialectic. The necessity of the *Phenomenology* lies in the repetition of structures and so emerges only retrospectively as these come to be multiplied. Hegel thus requires that his reader should constantly relate the section at hand with previous sections. The importance of the early sections of the book, which are often given the most attention, is not recognized until they are seen not only as forms of consciousness, but also for their role as moments of subsequent forms.

The reference to the master-slave dialectic provides an initial explanation of why Hegel is content to ignore the difference between slaves and freemen within the Roman Empire and turn his back on the Roman usage of the word "person" at the very time he appears to be exploring it. His justification has a structural basis in the law of *Phenomenology*. The subjects over whom this master exercises his power relate to one another through him. He is, in Hegel's phrase, "the continuity of their personality" or, as he also says, the "whole content" and the "real essence" (345/§ 481). But the master also destroys his subjects' personality.[23] Hegel wants to suggest that from this perspective, slaves and persons alike are all deprived by the master and that only the collapse of this whole "world" will resolve the problem. If Hegel is not more explicit on this question, it is perhaps in part because he is aware of how readily it might be misunderstood, how insensitive it might appear to be to the condition of slavery. But it is also because the issue at this point is essentially not the historical one, but in keeping with the very project of the *Phenomenology of Spirit*, the structure of the shape of consciousness under examination. This structure is defined in terms of its relation to other shapes of consciousness now conceived at its moments.

Hegel summarizes the whole movement as follows: "Legal personality thus experiences that it is without substance, in that the content which is valid for it is alien to it" (346/§ 482). The same idea is explicated more concretely in the *Lectures on the Philosophy of World History*. Private right, which was initially proposed as the correlate of personality, turns out to be a "not recognizing of personality" to the point of being its disappearance.[24] The contradiction which Hegel calls the "misery of the Roman world" and also its "discipline" is that "[e]ach person is, according to the principle of personality, entitled only to possession, while the person or persons lays claim to the possession of all such persons, so that the single right is at once sublated and deprived of right."[25] If the problem of ethical life is that every right has to be treated as a true right, (336/§ 470) the problem of legal status is that absolute right proves to be a loss of right.

This reference to the *Lectures on the Philosophy of World History* is, I think, like references to the *Philosophy of Right*, helpful in clarifying the discussion of legal status in the *Phenomenology*. But the different purposes of these works means that cross-referencing cannot be our main recourse and it must be done only with extreme caution. Above all, we must guard against pillaging Hegel for arguments to be applied elsewhere. Following Hegel's own frequent cross-references to different parts of the book is more important for understanding the *Phenomenology*. These are the means by which he sought to establish the book's structure and rigor. Some of the references to the section on *Rechtszustand* are to be found later in chapter six where it emerges that Hegel sees *Rechtszustand* as part of a movement of increasing abstraction.[26] But the discussion of legal status in the chapter on religion is even more important.

The chapter on religion has a special status in the *Phenomenology*. The debate over whether or not it is in direct continuity with the preceding chapter on spirit raises important issues, but seems to have drawn attention away from the more important fact that the two chapters should be seen as complementary in relation to absolute knowing: religion provides the content, but lacks the form already attained at the end of chapter six. This is already made clear by Hegel at the beginning of the chapter on religion. He marks the division between chapters six and seven by distinguishing the standpoint of consciousness as consciousness of absolute essence from absolute essence in and for itself, or the self-consciousness of spirit (473/§ 673).[27] Chapters one to six provide an account of spirit in its mundane existence, whereas chapter seven tells of spirit that knows itself as spirit. The distinction will be dissolved in absolute knowing as represented by the final chapter (479/§ 682).

There are, of course, grounds for asserting continuity. The moments which have already presented themselves as separate shapes of consciousness continue to structure the account of religion. The three forms of natural religion correspond to the first three chapters of the book. Religion in the form of art, which culminates in a discussion of tragedy and comedy, is said to correspond to the account of ethical spirit. It is followed, at the beginning of the section on revealed religion, by a three-page discussion of the speculative proposition, "The self is absolute essence" (521/§ 749). Here, Hegel not only returns to a discussion of legal status, but indeed emphasizes the importance of understanding this proposition with the reference to the shape of spirit that expresses it. Hence the proposition, "The self is absolute essence" comes to be understood to mean, "The self as such, the abstract person, is absolute essence" (522/§ 750). In this way, Hegel returns in chapter seven to the themes already dealt with in the first parts of chapter six and offers a rereading of them. This rereading of legal status is an anticipation—albeit a far from simple one—of the rereading of the whole book to which I referred earlier.

I shall not try to take up all the questions raised by Hegel's return to the topic of legal status in the course of his discussion of religion, but I would like to remark upon certain surprising aspects of that discussion. Indeed, it would be possible to claim that they confirm the *first* impression that Hegel's *Phenomenology* is a chaos. Perhaps most puzzling of all is that legal status as discussed in chapter six is said in chapter seven to correspond to the discussion of comic consciousness: "In the condition of right, then, the ethical world and the religion of that world are submerged and lost in the comic consciousness and the unhappy consciousness is the knowledge of this *total* loss" (523/§ 753 emphasis in original). the discussion of comedy, though, does not appear to be about Roman comedy—far from it. The most explicit references are to Aristophanes.[28] How can Greek comedy correspond to *Recht* in the Roman Empire?

Although it is true that Hegel finds personhood to be dominant in both of them, this is not what sustains the parallel even though it might be thought to contribute to its persuasiveness. In chapter seven, Hegel introduces the concept of the person in the context of the tragic hero. The tragic hero is split into the actual self of the actor and the mask of the person or, as one might say in this context, the mask of the *persona*. In comedy, by contrast, the mask that the tragic actor used to be "the person represented" (*un seine Person zu sein*) is "dropped" or, Hegel will even say, "played with." Why? Because the self wants to be something genuine, something right ("*es . . . läßt die Maske fallen, eben indem es etwas Rechtes sein will*") (518/§ 744). Hegel understands the loss of the distinction between actor and *persona* which takes place once the mask is taken off as meaning that the actual self of the actor—and the self of the spectator, too—coincides with his or her *persona* (520/§ 747). So long as the mask is in place, the self has not yet *become* a person. Nevertheless, it is not in terms of personhood that Hegel establishes the parallel between legal status and comic consciousness, but in terms of the proposition, "The self is absolute essence." If Hegel seems to disregard chronology by analogizing legal status within the Roman Empire to Greek comedy, then this appears as a problem in large measure due to the assumption that the later sections of the *Phenomenology* get their persuasive character from the historical references they contain. Were that indeed the case, any fudging of these references would diminish the alleged necessity of the work. There is, to be sure, a rather different reading whereby commentators have sought to establish that Hegel's discussion is governed not by its historical references but by its relevance to his own day.[29] But that reading also is ultimately in historical terms and disregards an instruction which Hegel himself introduces at the beginning of the chapter on religion. Hegel began the chapter by indicating that in relation to religion, Spirit is not be represented as occurring *in* time (476/§ 679). Indeed, in the final chapter Hegel clarifies that it is not just for religion but also for science that a historical presentation is not appropriate. (557–58/§§ 800–02). The historical reading falls away, or more precisely, the historical and scientific approaches must coexist in the form of what Hegel calls "comprehended history" (*begriffne Geschichte*) (564/§ 808). The *Phenomenology* calls first for a historical reading according to which it is an introduction to science. Such a reading places *Phenomenology* within history in the course of justifying the claim that Hegel's time is the time for a introduction to science. Alongside that reading, or rather following it as its corollary, is another, according to which the *Phenomenology* is already science. These two readings need each other.

Hegel marks the second reading all the more intensively as the first reading comes to its close. This is exemplified in the way that what might be called structural considerations dominate narrative ones. More familiarly, the *Phenomenology* as science becomes more prominent than the *Phenomenology* as history. Not that the one ever displaces the other altogether. The double play of the passage from narrative to structure can most readily be exhibited by turning to Hegel's presentation of the proposition, "The self is absolute essence" at the beginning of the section on revealed religion. This is a speculative proposition, showing in a particularly acute way that "inhibition of thought" which provokes the common complaint that philosophical works must be read again and again before they can be understood. As Hegel puts it in the Preface to the *Phenomenology*, the reader experiences that something is meant other than what the author thought he meant: "this correction of our meaning compels our knowing to go back to the proposition and understand it some other way" (52/§ 63). Not that this second reading of a speculative proposition corresponds exactly to what I have called a rereading. It would be better simply to say that such a proposition upsets any attempt to contain it within "one-track" reading. Following Hegel's own account of speculative propositions in the Preface, the proposition "the self is absolute essence" passes into the proposition that "the absolute essence is the essence of the self" (521–22/§§ 749–50). The speculative proposition is read in such a way that it combines two converse propositions without setting one against the other.

The historical reading depends on maintaining order, let us say the order in which the shapes of consciousness appear. The law of such a reading, which is not the law of the *Phenomenology*, depends on sequentiality. That is why an historical reading of the *Phenomenology* finds itself obliged to play down the movement of the moments that can be seen retrospectively. In alleging a connection between legal status and comic consciousness, Hegel is offering a particularly complicated form of this discussion. The connection is established because both legal status and comic consciousness are expressed by the proposition, "The self is absolute essence." It is with reference to it, rather than in terms of any alleged historical coincidence, that the parallel between them is to be understood.

I noted above that "The self is absolute essence" can be interpreted to mean that, "The self as such, the abstract person, is absolute essence." Because substance has here sunk to the level of a predicate of the self, the sentence records the loss of substance suffered by the individual in the transition to legal status from the Greek ethical world where the self was an accident of the substance. But at the same time, absolute essence is the essence of the self. That is to say, the inessentiality of the person is sustained by the self which is lord of the world. Hegel expresses this in the section on legal status with the phrase "self-consciousness, as absolute essence, is *actual*" (346/§ 483 emphasis in original).

The saying, "The self is absolute essence," also records the dissolution of divine substance through comic consciousness. The expulsion of the gods from their heaven, which began with tragedy, is completed in comedy. The self takes the place of the gods as absolute essence. With the advent of comic consciousness there is a loss of essentiality on the part of the alien. Consequently, the individual self takes the character of self-certainty and enjoys well-being (520/§ 748).At the same time, however, consciousness finds that the divine substance—until now embodied in a form opposed to consciousness, such as a statue or some other work of art—is not something separate from it. Having externalized itself as a thing, self-consciousness makes itself a universal self. The connection with unhappy consciousness, which had already been drawn for legal status in chapter six, is extended in chapter seven to comic consciousness. Unhappy consciousness is said to complete comic consciousness in spite of the well-being that comic consciousness was said to enjoy. This is because comic consciousness is the complete alienation of substance such that substance becomes self-consciousness (523/§ 749).

For both legal status and comic consciousness, therefore, the speculative proposition, "The self is absolute essence," can be read in two ways. The proposition does not carry the same meaning in both cases, and the difference corresponds, in part, to the different interest of the two chapters: whereas the analysis of legal status refers to consciousness, the analysis of comic consciousness refers to the self-consciousness of spirit. However, on rereading the *Phenomenology* from the point of view of the system of science, one recognizes that comedy and legal status are both to be understood in terms of the proposition, rather than the other way around.

Hegel speaks here, as elsewhere, with a number of voices. He records the path of consciousness, but also offers the dialectical observations of the "we"—"we" who recognize the contradiction into which consciousness falls and so see how the new true object arises out of the old through its experience. "We" see this only from the standpoint of absolute knowledge. Through rereading the book, "we" have access to the structures which emerge in the parallels drawn between the difference forms of consciousness. There are also the asides, the extrinsic comments like those in the *Science of Logic*, which sustain a polemic against Kant independently of the systematic work of the *Logic* itself.[30] Hegel's rejection of the term "person," his contempt of court, seems to have a similar status to these asides, because it neglects the systematic role of personhood in the discussion, where the *necessity* of its appearance is the primary issue. The first reading, which operates at the level of critique, is sustained by asides like the condemnation of the concept of person. The interest in such asides falls away in the second reading.

At first glance, Hegel's account of legal status is simply negative. To call someone a person, as right tends to do, is, according to Hegel, an expression in contempt.[31] Further, Hegel evokes chaos in the course of his discussion. Having observed how persons find themselves in their solitary master who in turn depends on them, he considers the character of a solitary self cut off from the universal multiplicity of individuals. "Cut off from this multiplicity, the solitary self is, in fact, an unreal, impotent self. . . . Liberated from the negative power controlling it, is the chaos of spiritual powers which, in their unfettered freedom, become elemental beings raging madly against one another in a frenzy of destructive activity" (345/§ 481). Indeed, some commentators have understood the passage from the Greek ethical world to the condition of right only as a collapse into chaos and disruption.[32] The very meaning of the *Phenomenology* is lost if right is identified as a form of chaos. Hegel has attempted to bring to chaos an order which was not simply that of a teleology. This order emerges in rereading the *Phenomenology*. The character of such a rereading has been prepared by Hegel's own commentary on the speculative proposition, "The self is absolute essence." But it has only been prepared for, and I cannot here satisfy the demand to reread the sections from the standpoint of absolute knowing. As a result, this paper has only a provisional status as regards its presentation of Hegel's text, not to mention the tentativeness which is called for simply on account of the sheer difficulty of Hegel's text at every point.

The discussion of legal status, like so much else in the *Phenomenology*, is therefore to be divorced from the underlying purpose of the book only with great caution. One law of the *Phenomenology* which the section on legal status illustrates very well is that one can pluck from Hegel's work arguments of broader significance at one's peril. But then, might not the same also be true of the *Philosophy of Right* which, like the *Phenomenology*, is too often seen in isolation from the system of which it is only a part and by no means the culmination? This has serious implications for whatever we might attempt to do under the title "Hegel and Legal Theory." I noted above that if the problem of ethical life is that every right has to be treated as a true right, the problem of the juridical condition is that absolute right proves to be a loss of right. Even to say that absolute right is not simply loss, but is also gain, is still to fall short of speculative truth. A first reading of the *Phenomenology* will look to what arises out of the discussion of legal status for its truth. It will find its truth in the course of history, its linear succession. We know enough to know that a rereading of the *Phenomenology* would find its truth in the systematic presentation of the whole. A piecemeal treatment of Hegel, such as the present one, will always fall short of such a presentation. That is one law of the *Phenomenology* which should not be evaded.

NOTES

1. G. Hegel, Phänomenologie des Geistes (F. Meiner ed. 1948) [hereinafter Phäno-
    menologie]; G. Hegel, Phenomenology of Spirit (A. Miller trans. 1977) (the author
    has made occasional revisions to Miller's translations)[hereinafter Phenomenol-
    ogy of Spirit]. [Editor's note: Unless otherwise indicated, citations will refer first
    to the page number of the German text and then the section number of the English
    translation of the *Phenomenology*.]

2. "Selbstanzeige der Phänomenologie," Phänomenologie des Geistes, in 9 Gesammelte Werke 446 (F. Meiner ed. 1980).

3. It should be noted that prior to Knox, the book had already been translated twice as the *Philosophy of Rights* and once as the *Philosophy of Law*. See G. Hegel, Philosophy of Rights (T.C. Sanders trans. 1855); G. Hegel, Philosophy of Rights (S.W. Dyde trans. 1896); G. Hegel, Philosophy of Law (J. Loewenberg trans.), in 7 German Classics of the 19th and 20th Centuries (1914).

4. G. Hegel, Philosophy of Right, § 211 (T. Knox trans. 1952)(1821); see Kaufman, Hegel's Concept of Personality in the *Philosophy of Right*, 6 Graduate Fac. Phil. J. 75, 101–02 (1977).

5. This sentence must be read in conjunction with an earlier one which reads: "Its absolute right is, therefore, that when it acts in accordance with ethical law, it shall find in this actualization nothing else but the fulfillment of this law itself, and the deed shall manifest only ethical action." (333/§ 467).

6. G. Hegel, Vorlesungen über die Philosophie der Geschichte, in 12 Werke (Suhrkamp 1970) [hereinafter Philosophie der Geschichte]; G. Hegel, The Philosophy of History (J. Sibree trans. 1956) [hereinafter Philosophy of History].

7. "Das Höchste des Menschen ist, Person zu sein, aber trotzdem ist die bloße Abstraktion Person schon im Ausdruck etwas Ver*chtliches." Philosophy of Right, supra note 4, § 35, Zusatz.

8. Philosophie der Geschichte, supra note 6, at 384; Philosophy of History, supra note 6, at 317.

9. Hegel says elsewhere that the proposition of right is that "each should be treated by the other as a person." G. Hegel, Texte zur Philosophischen Prop*deutik, in 4 Werke 233 (Suhrkamp 1970); G. Hegel, The Philosophical Propaedeutic 23 (A. Miller trans 1986).

10. Philosophy of Right, supra note 4, § 200, Zusatz.

11. G. Hegel, Jenaer Kritische Schriften, in 4 Gesammelte Werke (F. Meiner ed. 1968) [hereinafter Jenaer Kritische Schriften]; G. Hegel, Natural Law (T. Knox trans. 1975) [hereinafter Natural Law]

12. G. Hegel, Jenaer Kritische Schriften, supra note 11, at 492 (quoting E. Gibbon, 1 The Decline and Fall of the Roman Empire 56 (J. Bury ed. 1925)); G. Hegel, Natural Law, supra note 11, at 101–02 (same).

13. T. Hobbes, Leviathan 125 (M. Oakeshott ed. 1962). For more general explorations of the concept of person, see The Category of the Person (M. Carrithers, S. Collins & S. Lukes eds. 1985) and Problèmes de la Personne (I. Meyerson ed. 1973).

14. T. Hobbes, Leviathan, in 3 Thomae Hobbes Opera Philosophica Que Latine Scripsit Omnia 123 (G. Molesworth ed. 1841).

15. T. Hobbes, An answer to a Book Published by Dr. Bramhall, Late Bishop of Derry; called the "Catching of the Leviathan," in 4 The English Works of Thomas Hobbes (W. Molesworth ed. 1840).

16. Id. at 311 (noting that in their discussion of the Trinity, the Greek Fathers employed the word *hypostasis* (substance) instead of the word *persona*); see also An Historical narration concerning Heresy, and the Punishment Thereof, in 4 The English Works of Thomas Hobbes, supra note 16, at 387, 400 (same).

17. J.B. Moyle, Introduction to Book One, in Imperatoris Iustiniani Instituitionum 85 (5th ed. 1912).

18. Philosophie der Geschichte, supra note 6, at 383 (authors translation); The Philosophy of History, supra note 6, at 316.

19. On these and other indications of inequality in Roman law, see M. Finley, Ancient Slavery and Modern Ideology 144 (1980); P. Garnsey, Social Status and Legal Privilege in the Roman Empire 200–03 (1970).

20. Philosophy of Right, supra note 4, § 40, Zusatz.

21. Id. § 2, Zusatz.

22. Hegel elaborates this parallel in his lectures on the philosophy of history. He observes that Stoicism, Epicureanism, and Scepticism share an indifference to everything that actuality has to offer. Hegel believes the same is true of abstract law. Philosophie der Geschichte, supra note 6, at 385; The Philosophy of History, supra note 6, at 318.

23. To contribute to the task of multiplying references, Hegel's account may again have been suggested by Edward Gibbon. In his 1802 essay, *Natural Law*, Hegel continued the quotation to include these lines: "They received laws and governors from the will of their sovereign . . . . The posterity of their boldest leaders was contented with the rank of citizens and subjects. The most aspiring spirits resorted to . . . the standard of the emperors; and the deserted provinces, deprived of political strength or union, insensibly sunk into the languid indifference of private life." Jenaer Kritische Schriften, supra note 11, at 492; Natural Law, supra note 11, at 102.

24. Philosophie der Geschichte, supra note 6, at 387; Philosophy of History, supra note 6, at 320.

25. Philosophie der Geschichte, supra note 6, at 387–88; Philosophy of History, supra note 6, at 320.

26. "The movement of the world of culture and faith sublates this abstraction of the person, and, through the completed alienation, through the ultimate abstraction, substance becomes for spirit at first the universal will, and finally spirit's own possession." (423/§ 596).

27. For a survey of—and contribution to—the continuity debate, see Flay, Religion and the Absolute Standpoint, 56 Thought 316–27 (1981).

28. See the editorial notes to *Phänomenologie des Geistes*, in 9 Gesammelte Werke 519, 520 (1980).

29. For example, citing Rousseau's importance for the French Revolution, Hyppolite understands the presence of the discussion of legal status in the text of the *Phenomenology* in terms of the high regard in which the ancient city was held in Hegel's time. This observation might be valid, but it remains extrinsic to the *Phenomenology's* self-presentation. See Hyppolite, L'etat du Droit (la condition juridique)), Hegel-Tage Toyaumont 1954, 3 Hegel-Studien Beiheft 181–185 (1966).

30. See G. Hegel, Science of Logic (A. Miller trans. 1969) (1812).

31. See supra note 7 and accompanying text.

32. See, e.g., Shklar, Hegel's 'Phenomenology': An Elegy for Hellas, in Hegel's Political Philosophy 73–89 (Z. Pelczynski ed. 1971).

Part Two

Abstract Right and Private Law

4

Hegel's Legal Plenum

Arthur J. Jacobson

BREAKING THE CORRELATION OF RIGHTS WITH DUTIES

The jurisprudence in Hegel's *Philosophy of Right* is one of three sorts of jurisprudence taking a position against an assumption we now attribute to Hohfeld.[1] Hohfeld's assumption is that legal rights must always be correlated with legal duties and vice versa. Hegel's is a jurisprudence of right. The other sorts of jurisprudence attacking the correlation of rights with duties are the jurisprudence of duty and, surprisingly, Common Law. Hegel's jurisprudence, as a pure and perfect jurisprudence of right, breaks or alters Hohfeld's correlation of rights with duties in one of the three ways it can possibly be broken.

The jurisprudence of right alters the correlation of rights with duties by suppressing, if not eliminating, duty. Duty is sometimes present in this jurisprudence as auxiliary to right, sometimes only as a way of talking about rights. Theorists of right give it the least possible role in the jurisprudence. A jurisprudence of duty breaks the correlation outright by eliminating right. Unlike the jurisprudence of right, the jurisprudence of duty does not preserve right as a way of talking about duty.

Two sorts of jurisprudence depend on maintaining the correlation. These, which in some combination underlie most contemporary jurisprudential discussions, are positivism and naturalism.

Common Law also alters the correlation of rights with duties, but suppresses or eliminates neither right nor duty. Both right and duty play crucial roles in Common Law. Consequently, Common Law is commonly mistaken for a Hohfeldian system, one combination or another of positivism and naturalism. Yet it is not.[2]

Ronald Dworkin's *Taking Rights Seriously*[3] is a recent example of a jurisprudence of right. Indeed, Dworkin is one of the few writers I know of in our tradition who understands that jurisprudence may be right-based or duty-based.[4] He even understands that jurisprudences which are either right-or duty-based put the individual at the center. He does not, however, do much with the distinction, especially in the historical analysis of actual jurisprudence.

As we shall see, the jurisprudence of right starts from the twin impulses of legal persons to gain recognition of their rights from other persons, and to love or take care of other persons. Dworkin has versions of both impulses.[5] Theorists of right prior to Hegel, such as Hobbes in his *Leviathan*[6] and Adam Smith in his *Lectures on Jurisprudence*,[7] had versions of the jurisprudence of right which were defective because they lacked understanding of the role of love in the legal system of right. After Hegel, such misunderstanding is impossible.

Examples of the jurisprudence of duty are sacred legal systems, such as Jewish law, and Kant's *Metaphysical Elements of Justice*.[8] Socialist law and legal theory provide practical examples.[9] Recent proponents of Common Law jurisprudence include Edward Levi and Guido Calabresi. Karl Llewellyn is the most notable of the last generation.

Common law has been theorized, but never philosophized. The reasons for the absence of Common Law philosophizing provide fascinating speculation. An adequate philosophy of Common Law does require reference, however one arrives at it, to the discoveries of Hegel. Certainly the hard-headed, anti-intellectual practitioners of Common Law in England were not prepared to put the two together. The Continent-trained Llewellyn found more fertile ground in the United States, whose Common Law, being chosen, is an idealized version of the English system.

DIFFERENCES BETWEEN BREAKING AND MAINTAINING THE CORRELATION

The jurisprudences maintaining the correlation differ from those breaking or altering it in at least four respects: (1) whether the source of law is inside or outside the legal system; (2) whether enforcement of law is separate from legislation; (3) whether the legal system constitutes what I call a "plenum"; and (4) whether the legal system is dynamic.

The five types of jurisprudence are ideal in the sense that no one type exactly captures any real legal system or even any single legal theory. They are not ideal in the sense of Weber. Weber's ideal types serve only the interest of understanding on the part of observers, not the interests of action on the part of participants in a society and culture. The ideal types of jurisprudence, by contrast, are meant for participants, as well as observers. They suggest themes for lawyers to weave into their theories and systems.

While Weber's ideal types are approximate because they must speak to common situations across societies and cultures, the ideal types of jurisprudence are approximate because no person holding one of them can permanently sustain it. No sooner has a system or theorist adopted one type, then the others immediately appear as challenges. The system or theorist then integrates a response to the challenges into the adopted type. The type thus transformed occasions further challenges, further responses and further integrations. The practical and theoretical possibilities are endless, even though we start with only five root types.

Unlike Weber's ideal types, which serve only the observer, these types also serve the observed. Ultimately no one in jurisprudence is just an observer. Hence the types are as much visions as models of jurisprudence. They are the legal possibilities of the universe, which people then use as they will in making their worlds.

Source of Law

The source of law in the correlation-altering jurisprudences is inside the legal system.[10] Typically it is the legal subject, or person. The source of law in the correlation-maintaining jurisprudences is outside the legal system. Though the exact source of law in such jurisprudences is often open to question, it is certainly never the person. The role of the person in the correlating jurisprudences is thus to be legal subject only. The role of the person in jurisprudences altering the correlation, by contrast, is to be source of law as well as subject.

Enforcement and Legislation

The correlation-altering jurisprudences do not distinguish enforcement of law from legislation. When jurisprudence does distinguish them, then persons cannot be the source of either. Pure legislation devoid of enforcement always comes from outside the legal system, from heros or assemblies of heros. Legislation is possible only in a jurisprudence where the source of law is outside the system, in a correlating jurisprudence. By the same token, pure enforcement is also possible only in a correlating jurisprudence. Enforcement is the sole authentic legal action in systems whose source of law is outside the system.

Persons can be the source of law, as they must in a correlation-altering jurisprudence, only in ordinary interactions with other persons. Legislation is the only action in legal systems which must always be prior to or in preparation for other action. Legislation is extraordinary; it can never be ordinary interaction. Likewise, enforcement is the only legal action persons can accomplish after the action the enforcement seeks to regulate. Therefore, enforcement, like legislation, stands in opposition to ordinary interaction. Jurisprudences altering the correlation recognize neither legislation nor enforcement as extraordinary actions regulating ordinary interactions.

Furthermore, distinctively legal institutions in these systems, such as legislatures and courts, are subordinate to ordinary interactions. Correlation-altering jurisprudences either discard distinctively legal institutions or weave them into the system of action. The legal system of such jurisprudences, being ordinary, is an ordinary incident of interaction. Indeed, it is *the* ordinary incident. The law of the correlation-altering jurisprudences defines or creates interactions. Apart from law, interactions in these systems cannot even be imagined. Every interaction, no matter how intimate, requires the issuance and realization of norms. Law is the most ordinary component of action. In the correlating systems, by contrast, law always smacks of the extraordinary.

The Legal Plenum

The persons of the correlation-altering jurisprudences attempt as one of the ordinary burdens of legality to fill the universe with as much law as possible.[11] To be a subject of law is also to be a source of law. Persons cannot fulfill the ordinary burdens of legality without creating fresh legal materials. The universe in such jurisprudences is not full. Instead, its occupants are perpetually filling it with legal materials. It is not full, only fillable. Were the universe ever full in fact, its occupants could not continue to do the ordinary work of filling it, hence could not "fulfill" the burdens of legality. Or, if you prefer, the universe *is* full, but only in the sense that it is always being filled, much like the electron in quantum mechanics, whose probable presence at a point occupies it as completely as possible. Rather than call the universe of the correlation-altering jurisprudences a "full legal universe" (which does not do justice to the strangeness of the conception), I use the term "legal plenum" to indicate a legal universe constantly filling with legal materials. Hegel's jurisprudence possesses, we shall see, one sort of plenum, a legal universe which persons throughout the *Philosophy of Right* are passionately filling with rights.[12]

The correlating jurisprudences do not have occupants constantly filling the universe with legal materials. The source of legal materials in such jurisprudences is not driven, as persons are, to fill portions of the universe with materials which otherwise occupy the universe only in principle. The legal universe of correlating jurisprudences is actually full, or so it seems, but it is, in any case, not in a state of perpetual fulfillment.

Hohfeld defines the legal universe to be full in the following manner. Suppose I sue you for not showing up at my house for dinner, when you accepted the invitation and I purchased the food, cooked it, and did not invite someone else. The court will say I have "no right" to a remedy against you on the basis of the causes of action which I have stated in my complaint. The judgment will read: "Not guilty."

Hohfeld believes that "not guilty" contains two correlative declarations: (1) plaintiff has "no right" to compel defendant to come to dinner, and (2) defendant has a "privilege" not to come. Since each statement is correlative with the other, the court need not make both statements for a legally complete description of the relations between you and me over the dinner. Just because courts choose not to talk about defendant's privilege not to come to dinner does not mean defendant does not have one by virtue of the judgment. By leaving the defendant's decision not to come to dinner unregulated, Hohfeld would argue, courts are nonetheless making a legal statement about the decision. The defendant's legal status is to have a privilege. The arguing point is that through the conception of "privilege," law regulates even those actions which it seems not to regulate. Hohfeld's legal universe has no legally empty corners. Corners we might in fact regard as legally empty Hohfeld fills with privilege.

Hohfeld's completion of the legal universe in this manner has a basic flaw. Judgments (at least in Common Law) never state that defendant has a privilege, only that plaintiff has not suggested a right for the violation of which the court imposes a liability. Judgments never say, in other words, that plaintiff has "no right," only that plaintiff has not successfully suggested a right.

It so happens that our doctrine of res judicata usually forbids a losing plaintiff from suing defendant again for the same incident on the basis of different rights. Sometimes res judicata does not forbid the second suit, however, and even when it does, the doctrine is not rationally deducible from fundamental conceptions. One could easily imagine a legal system with a more limited or even nonexistent doctrine of res judicata. The most we can say is that judgment for defendant grants him privileges with respect to the specific rights actually suggested by plaintiff. We cannot say that defendant has a privilege over all possible rights. But defendant does not effectively have a privilege if the privilege extends over only certain rights, and if we cannot assure him that it extends over all possible rights. Plaintiff may not have successfully suggested a right on the basis of which a court is prepared to render judgment against defendant, but defendant does not yet have what he needs in order to embark on the action, which is assurance that under all possible circumstances he may perform the action without liability. "Privilege" means little to one planning action if we confine it to rights a possible plaintiff happens to articulate. "Privilege" in the sense Hohfeld must mean it is trivial: it contributes nothing to a jurisprudence-governed system of action.

Plaintiff's "no-right" thus does not reflexively lead to defendant's "privilege." The two states are not correlative, since defendant's inquiry supposes a perfect plaintiff articulating all possible rights, whereas plaintiff's inquiry supposes only that he articulate a single right leading to liability. Thus the universe is legally full—states of unregulation constitute legally privileged states—only if we imagine a universe of perfect plaintiffs. The legal universe of positivism and naturalism often supposes the perfection of plaintiffs, but there is nothing in either theory to require it. Hence the legal universe of positivism and naturalism may or may not be legally full. Some portions of the universe, legally unregulated, may be empty of legal materials.[13]

DYNAMISM

Jurisprudences breaking or altering the correlation are dynamic, in the sense that persons occupying the legal system formed according to such jurisprudences must alter the universe of legal norms in order to follow a single one of them. The law-abiding occupants of systems whose source of law is within the system find that they can obey a legal norm only in the process of creating it.[14] Obedience to law in such systems is personal legislation. (In Common Law the equation of obedience with personal legislation is quite explicitly captured in the doctrine of precedent.) Jurisprudences maintaining the correlation, by contrast, are nondynamic, since change never comes from within the system in its ordinary operation. Though change may (or even must) occur in such systems, the impetus for it need not and often will not be internal. Whether it be politics, religion, or other considerations, no agent or occupant from within the system is driven by passion (as in the jurisprudence of right) or self-perfection (as in the jurisprudence of duty) or uncertainty (as in Common Law) to transform the system in its ordinary operation.

HOHFELDIAN JURISPRUDENCE:
POSITIVISM AND NATURALISM

The two varieties of Hohfeldian jurisprudence are positivism and naturalism.

Positivism is the jurisprudence which asserts that the only rules governing social life are those which are positively enacted according to a correct procedure. The validity of rules in positivism stems not from their content but from their correct legislation according to the procedure. The only issue positivism recognizes is the correct application of the rules to those whom the rules are supposed to apply.

Naturalism is the jurisprudence which asserts that the rules governing social life are those which may be rationally perceived by an observer. The legislative issue in naturalism is determining the qualifications of the observer, just as the issue in positivism is following the correct procedure. The enforcement issue in naturalism is that rules which the observer rationally perceives must in fact be the rules for ordinary participants in the system.

Since most discussions of jurisprudence today assume Hohfeld's correlation of rights with duties, common opinion holds that all jurisprudence must be one variety or another of these two. Furthermore, virtually all academic descriptions of real legal systems reproduce reality out of positivism and naturalism alone, suppressing and concealing the very live correlation-breaking or -altering materials infusing real legal systems. Our system, for example, has mixed elements of Common Law and the jurisprudence of right, alongside positive and natural elements. Other legal systems share different mixtures, and some, especially socialist systems and the new theocracies, include a jurisprudence of duty.

Both positivism and naturalism are Hohfeldian, because they require rights and duties always to be in correlation. The idea of a right not correlated with a duty or a duty not correlated with a right simply has no meaning in either system. The reason a right cannot be without a duty or a duty without a right is different in each, because positivism and naturalism have very different accounts of right and duty.

Positivism regards right as the ability to compel legal subjects (one would hardly call them persons) to do or refrain from doing specific actions. Similarly, duty is subjection to this ability. The source of the power is invariably said to be a superpersonal agency, called "sovereign," a hypostatization of the procedure. The superpersonal agency always speaks in correlations. The correlation in positivism is established by the uniformly reflexive behavior of the superpersonal agency toward both the beneficiary and the subject of the power. The correlating talk of the superpersonal agency we call "legislation." Naturalism regards right as the shared goal of both participants in an interaction. Duty is the means of attaining the shared goal. Unfortunately for those who would like natural systems to be simple, an agreed-upon goal does not necessarily specify a single means of attaining it. Hence, duty is often problematic in natural systems, requiring intervention by qualified observers, or enforcers.

Positivism and naturalism differ by focusing, respectively, on legislation and enforcement as the extraordinary, the distinctively legal, actions in the legal system. The focus in positivism is on legislation. Positivism reduces enforcement to an automatic consequence of legislation, so that all legal determinations have been made and can be known prior to ordinary interaction.

> Some versions of positivism do not insist that law-making focus exclusively on legislation. These modified positivist visions, such as Kelsen's and Hart's, are responding to the challenges of the other jurisprudences.

Naturalism focuses on enforcement. It requires ordinary interaction to have taken place before legal determinations can be made or known, since action itself determines the content of the determinations. Action in naturalism is not just an occasion for the application of predetermined norms, as in positivism, but the very moment of legislation.

> Naturalism is easily the most complex and variegated of the major categories of jurisprudence. Some versions of naturalism suppose that an eternal, unchanging body of laws governs every possible sort of society. These versions would seem to contradict the notion that action determines the background laws that regulate human association. These versions of naturalism, however, invariably invoke an eternal, unchanging core of actions which justify and nourish the body of laws. Action determines law as cogently as in natural systems which tolerate changes in action and law. The only difference is that action in the stable systems is as eternal and unchanging as the body of laws.

Natural systems resemble correlation-altering systems in that legislation in them folds or disappears into action. Unlike correlation-altering jurisprudences, however, naturalism insists that enforcement be separate from and subsequent to action. Hence naturalism preserves the extraordinary character of legal action.

Positivism and naturalism also differ in the manner each derives law from outside the system. Each jurisprudence employs a distinctive attack on legal personality. Positivism attacks the idea of personality itself. Naturalism attacks its presence in real legal persons. The nature of these attacks needs to be explored a bit, starting with the positivist attack.

The source of law in positivism is a superpersonal agency, a "sovereign." The positivist agency characteristically finds law in the results of procedures rather than in the actions of persons. A positivist system can, of course, locate the law-making procedure in a single person's expression of will. The essence of law-making in such systems, nonetheless, is the procedure, not the will of the person. More commonly, positivist systems adopt a procedure for combining two or more wills through election, which is clearly distinct from the will of one person. The result of election is impersonal even if the process leading to it calls for expressions of will through voting. There is some question whether positivism can ever totally dispense with expressions of will, whether it must always even indirectly refer to personalities. The source of law can, for example, be an omen. Though omens are impersonal, they must always be interpreted by persons claiming expertise in omens. Even so, a person interpreting omens supports the interpretations with statements about the character of omens, not by reference to his or her will. Certainly the virtue positivism claims for itself is striving to eliminate personality from law-making and law-applying. Thus persons are nothing in positivism because personality is nothing, or ought to be nothing, when positivism is working.

The attack by naturalism on personality differs from the positivist attack. The source of law in naturalism is the idea of personality itself, which some versions identify with a world-system. Unlike positivism, naturalism preserves personality as the source of law. It does not, however, preserve a role for particular persons, except insofar as they conform to the idea of personality or play a role in the world-system. Persons make law only because they themselves are thoughts of the world-system. "Persons" in the sense of historic, living human beings count for nothing. Personality thus plays a role in natural systems only because the persons possessing it consent to deal with each other impersonally.

WHY COMMON LAW IS NOT HOHFELDIAN

The practice or principle defining Common Law as a jurisprudence is the doctrine of precedent. Common Law as a jurisprudence with universal significance, not a family of systems sharing a common ancestor, includes any system whose fundamental practice or principle is the doctrine of precedent.

The doctrine of precedent holds that legal norms cannot exist apart from specific applications. By "application" I mean any action that refers to law as a means to, or an end of, the action. "Application" thus includes ordinary actions having reference to law as well as official enforcement. The idea that law exists only as application has three components. First, persons start knowing law only by studying prior applications. Second, persons know law completely only once they have completed their own application. Third, law must always be the product of both.[15]

The first component—persons start knowing law only by studying prior applications—means that reports of cases, not black-letter rules, are the first place to look for rights and obligations. Though cases often state rules (often they do not), the rules per se are never the law, only a way of talking about its formulation. Only rules-anchored-in-cases are law.[16]

> So purveyors of black-letter compilations and lawyers who confine their practice to those compilations without studying cases are traitors to Common Law. Handbook practice is a species of positivism, where legislation is the compiling of handbooks. Likewise, handbook lawyers are not common lawyers, but a species of Continental notary.

If rules per se were the law, as they are in positivism, then the judges' refusal to state rules before applying them would make no sense at all. Nor would their willingness to change rules make sense. The most that can be said of a rule applied in a prior case is that it was the rule for that case,[17] and must be considered in the formulation of law in subsequent cases. The rule does not suddenly leap out of cases into positivism because it has once been formulated in a case. Rules, like parties in Common Law, have only claims in applications.

> Whether a Common Law jurisprudence asserts that rules which have not yet been applied are nonetheless "there" is a church quarrel, since the rules cannot be stated or form "the law" until they are

applied. It is difficult to say how rules which have not been applied are "there" in a system which depends strictly on application.

Hence the second component: Persons know law completely only once they have completed their own application. Law in Common Law systems is the procedure for its own application. The legal norm is procedurally thick, thus substantively indeterminate. It is a book of cases rather than a general statement about the cases. It exists on many levels at once and through many different phases of a relationship.[18] The abstract statement of a rule may contain everything persons can know or need to know about the legal norm at the beginning. But concrete circumstances and detailed determinations—the cases in their fullness—will be of greater interest in the middle and at the end.

The third component—law must be the product of both—has two consequences. First, law must change with every fresh application, since the latest application must be added to the book of cases constituting the legal norm. Even a case which is "on all fours" with cases already in the book must also be added. Unless everything about the case *and the world* is identical to a case already in the book (which is impossible), then application of the legal norm to the new case, apart from asserting the continuing life of cases in the book, must also be asserting that the changed circumstances do not prevent the fresh application. The legal norm is new, even though it seems old hat. Old statements about new worlds are new statements. Second, law may change only in certain directions in the fresh application.[19] The constraint is dictated by reciprocity amongst persons applying the norm proceeding from uncertainty about its application.[20]

The uncertainty which is at the heart of Common Law has two sources. First, judges are always in principle free to reverse the rule component of the legal norm, changing abstract winners under the rule into abstract losers and losers into winners.[21] The second source of uncertainty in common law systems is that even if judges do not reverse the rule component of the norm, they may always disappoint the expectations of a concrete person that he or she ought to be classified as a winner under the rule.

Common law judges disappoint expectations by using two techniques well known to common lawyers.[22] First, they may decide to use a different rule altogether, whilst maintaining the other components of the norm. Second, they may refuse to classify the person in the winning category, even though the person seems to fit either judge-made or common sense indicia of the category. Such decisions are effectively shielded from appellate scrutiny as "findings of fact," even if the finding is by a judge rather than a jury.

The uncertainty described above yields reciprocity for two reasons. The first is that persons who expect to be classified as winners under the rule-component of the norm must always behave as if either they could be classified as losers under the rule, or all winners under a reversed rule could become losers. Uncertainty is *part of the norm.* To behave as if the result of law application were certain—as if the legal norm were certain—is to violate the norm. The exercise of rights must be tempered by the consciousness of uncertainty. Winners must always behave as if they could be losers, and losers may behave as if it would be possible for them to become winners. The legal norm always includes a requirement of reciprocal behavior. Not to act reciprocally is to violate the norm. Winners can always turn themselves into losers by behaving unreciprocally.

> As we shall see, in the jurisprudence of right, temperance in the exercise of rights proceeds from both love and the drive for recognition of rights, which is the legal corollary of love. Continental legal systems bridle the intemperate exercise of rights through the doctrine of abuse of rights. In Common Law abuse of rights does not form a separate doctrine, but is pervasive, often in notions of equity.

The second reason uncertainty yields reciprocity is that persons must always impress the judge and the jury that they have the character of acting reciprocally in their dealings with other persons. The judge has the power always to switch to a different rule-component of the norm under which the winner may become a loser. The jury (the fact finder) always has the power to refuse to classify the person under the winning category. Both judge and jury can and will disappoint a winner who behaves as if he is exercising the norm without consideration for the right always latent in the loser's position.[23] Respect for the latent rights of losers is an essential component of the character of persons in Common Law systems.

> Persons freshly applying a norm (and if necessary courts) must also put themselves in the mind of persons (or courts) who have already applied the norm, for whom the application is over and done with. This would include losers under the norm, as well as winners. Fresh applications must not betray the persons who have already suffered or enjoyed past applications. Losers might still object to the norm, and might even win in the fresh application. Winners, after all, would

now feel free to join them. Or they might not. Or the losers might join the winners. Persons, then, who are applying norms must approach one another as if they once had a selfish interest in the content of the norms, but no longer have the interest.

Any legal system depending on the doctrine of precedent is not Hohfeldian for the following reasons. First, it is dynamic. It does not, as Hohfeldian systems, assume correlations as given. It *wrestles* rights and duties into correlations through the operations of the system. The character of Common Law is a perpetual wrestling of rights and duties into correlations. And the correlations themselves are dynamic. Every correlation dispenses with prior correlations through the doctrine of precedent.

The second reason Common Law is not Hohfeldian is that it fills the legal universe, or is constantly in the process of filling it. The Common Law system can always at any moment resolve any dispute, even those which the system has so far refused to resolve. By the same token, Common Law may at any moment drop disputes it has traditionally resolved. Hence, persons must always deal with each other as if the legal system might at any moment resolve their disputes. The shadows of rights and duties fill every corner of life in a Common Law system. Persons simply cannot interact without formulating the consequences of the interaction in terms of rights and duties. At the same time, they cannot know their rights and duties without interacting. Shadows of rights and duties fill the universe, but *only* shadows. Persons cannot count on an enforcer to work out their relationship for them, since the enforcer may always choose not to. Since they cannot look to the state, they must look to each other (and their attorneys) as minor legal notables. Authority is everywhere, because authoritative pronouncements are nowhere. Common Law persons are in the exact position of the philosopher in Plato's cave: they constantly look for rights and duties because they never can find them, but know they are there. The rights and duties, it turns out, are just the search for them by ordinary persons.

The third reason that Common Law is not Hohfeldian is that the source of Common Law is internal. Ordinary persons are the ones who in the ordinary operations of the system are driven to wrestle rights and duties into perpetual successions of correlations. Enforcers (such as judges) appear in Common Law, separate from persons, only when persons call on them to help achieve a correlation. In these moments Common Law resembles naturalism, which also separates enforcement from action, suppressing legislation. The resemblance is superficial. Enforcers in Common Law, unlike enforcers in naturalism, cannot act on their own, only at the instance of persons. When enforcers do act in Common Law, they respond to the character of the persons at whose instance they are acting as part of the norm they are enforcing. Enforcement is the drama of these persons.

For these reasons, Common Law is not a correlating jurisprudence. Yet it is not simply a jurisprudence of right or a jurisprudence of duty. It is distinguished from either of them by including both of them. Unlike these other two correlation-breaking or -altering jurisprudences, Common Law does not achieve dynamism by suppressing right or duty. By joining the jurisprudences of right and duty, Common Law also transforms them. We will explore some salient characteristics of the one jurisprudence that breaks or alters the Hohfeldian correlation symmetrically only after examining the simpler (and stranger) jurisprudences that break or alter the correlation asymmetrically.

HEGEL'S DISCOVERY OF THE JURISPRUDENCE OF RIGHT

Hegel discovered the jurisprudence of right through his criticism and rejection of Kant's *Metaphysical Elements of Justice.*[24]

Kant's jurisprudence is an attempt to found a jurisprudence of duty on rational premises. Kant's position is twofold. First, the legal person of Kant's jurisprudence asks the same question as the moral person of his practical philosophy: What are my duties?[25] Second, the person can deduce the answer using a parsimonious criterion of rationality.[26] The duties of persons *inter se* are those which a rational being would legislate as a universal rule for rational beings. The laws of the jurisprudence are determined as surely by this criterion as the laws of logic by the principle of noncontradiction. Should the person ask, Why should I perform my duties?, the only answer jurisprudence can give is, You must if you wish to be rational.[27]

As the next two sections will show, Hegel's criticism of Kant is also twofold. First, a jurisprudence of duty cannot be founded on rational premises. Only a jurisprudence of right can, and only according to a different criterion of rationality than universal legislation.[28] Second, Hegel's answer to the question, Why should I perform my duties?, is that you love the person to whom you owe the duty, not that you wish to be rational.[29] Both elements of the criticism are fundamental to any jurisprudence of right, not just Hegel's. Let us analyze them in order.

HEGEL'S CRITISISM OF KANT

First, a jurisprudence of duty cannot be founded on rational premises. For universal legislation cannot recommend specific duties. It creates morality, the bare idea of duty, but not a jurisprudence of specific duties. It is able to produce specific duties, or laws, only by the addition of elements extrinsic to the rational foundation of the jurisprudence. These elements typically take the form of empirical assumptions about either the personality or the world. Persons never obey laws for the reason that it is their duty. Morality respects reasons; jurisprudence does not. Persons obey laws because they fear not obeying them, or because obeying laws pleases them for some other reason. They can disobey laws and still consider themselves rational. Hegel understood this fundamental character of states and persons, while Kant did not.

Second, persons fulfill duties out of love, not because they wish to be rational. The question Kant cannot answer is why persons choose to have duties in the first place. Kant's philosophy cannot commend persons to undertake duties rather than live as a hermit.[30] Living the life of a hermit is perfectly consistent with Kant's jurisprudence. Once we choose a sociable life, Kant's jurisprudence makes some sense.[31] Hegel's jurisprudence includes the route through which we require the jurisprudence. It commends sociability to persons.

THE JURISPRUDENCE OF DUTY

The true foundation of the jurisprudence of duty is similar to Kant's universal legislation. The answer to the question, What are my duties?, is that they are what God has commanded. The answer to the question, Why should I perform my duties?, is that if I do not, I shall be a stranger to God. Every jurisprudence of duty, one way or another, gives these answers.

The questions themselves simply cannot be conceived by one who does not believe God to be issuing the commands defining his duties and never concerns himself whether he is a stranger to God. Such a person is interested in duty, if at all, only as a correlative of right. This is the position persons take in positivism or naturalism or the combinations of positivism and naturalism we commonly take for jurisprudence. Alternatively, the idea of duty yields altogether to the passion of love. This is the position persons take in the jurisprudence of right.

The source of law in the jurisprudence of duty in the first instance is God, the issuer of commands. Were this the end of the matter, the jurisprudence of duty could hardly be distinguished from early versions of positivism, which define law as the command of the sovereign. Then the only issue, as in positivism, would be agreeing upon a procedure for divining the will of the commander. Early positivism and the jurisprudence of duty differ sharply, however, in two respects.

First, the commander in the jurisprudence of duty is a person, whereas the commander in early positivism is not. Commands in early positivism, as in all positivism, stem from a procedure by which the governors of the system discover the will of the commander; they do not stem from the will itself. Commands in the jurisprudence of duty do stem from the will of the commander. God "reveals" law to his subjects. By so doing God necessarily reveals a personality. God has an empirical substance in the jurisprudence of duty. Sovereigns in early positivism do not.

Second, the subject of the commands, the ordinary legal person, is God's partner in law-making. The relationship between God and ordinary persons is not the relationship between sovereign and ordinary persons. In early positivism, ordinary persons do not obey law because they wish to emulate the sovereign—how could they?—but because they seek pleasure and fear pain. Ordinary persons in the jurisprudence of duty do obey law to emulate the commander, the sacred person. Legality in the jurisprudence of duty is thus an *imitatio dei*. Persons do not obey law so much as they reenact revelation. By obeying law they walk with God.

The relationship of command to obedience is thus quite different in the jurisprudence of duty from that in early positivism. Obedience in the jurisprudence of duty is the self-perfection of the legal person. In early positivism obedience is the rational response of the person to eudaemonic calculation.

Persons in the jurisprudence of duty are God's partners under three conditions. Either God has specified and revealed a complete list of duties, or only a partial list, or God has specified and revealed no duties at all.

In the last case the person presses on with discovering or creating duties no matter how many duties he or she has already discovered or created. Since God has not specified and revealed a list of duties, the person can never know whether he is fulfilling a sufficient number of duties in order to walk with God. Obedience is a ceaseless striving for duty after duty.

In the second case, where God has specified and revealed a partial list, the person is virtually in the same position as in the last case. The only difference is that duties which God has specified and revealed provide a model for persons to emulate as they strive to complete the list (which may or may not be capable of completion).

The first case, where God has specified and revealed a complete list, is closest to early positivism. The person's role in the creation of duties is clearly at a minimum. Nevertheless, the person still must strive to obey the specified duties as an *imitatio dei*, not in order to seek pleasure and avoid pain. The person in this form of the jurisprudence of duty must obey the duties even if breaching them would bring pleasure. The person must also resolve all doubts about the duty in favor of obligation. No statement of duty—even from God—can completely specify or foresee every situation in which the duty might be applicable. The duty in the jurisprudence of duty is different from the rule in positivism. The statement of duty is merely the premise from which the self-perfecting person starts his or her investigation of divinely inspired behavior. Even if a statement of duty would seem to allow the self-perfecting person to "get away with" self-interested behavior, the jurisprudence of duty brooks no loopholes. Rather, it requires the person to give up the self-interested behavior in favor of a broadened version of the specified duty.[32] The legal accountant of positivism would never engage in supererogatory behavior, unless supererogatory behavior happened to tickle its fancy.

The jurisprudence of duty is dynamic—the persons of it fill the legal universe with duties—because persons themselves are responsible for fulfilling—for recognizing and obeying—their duties. God's commands give no one the right to enforce them. You must perform your duties whether the beneficiaries of your duties want you to or not. The beneficiary of a duty must bring violations of it to the attention of a human tribunal, because the beneficiary has a duty to alert the tribunal to infractions of God's commands, not because he has a right which he may, if he chooses, ask the tribunal to enforce. Furthermore, the duty to enforce applies to certain of the commands, never all of them. Persons impose duties on themselves by obeying God. Fulfilling duties is the one work of God that God alone cannot accomplish. God enforces commands only through the collaboration of persons obeying or disobeying the commands.

HEGEL'S JURISPRUDENCE OF RIGHT

As in the jurisprudence of duty, the starting-point of the jurisprudence of right is the person. Hegel thus begins the *Philosophy of Right* with a portrait of the creature whose first thought in its dealings with creatures of its kind is that it is a person.[33]

Hegel's creature, though, is a person in a sense we have seldom seen since Hobbes. Let Hobbes' account of the person stand for the complex traditions of correlating jurisprudence, mixing positivism and naturalism, against which Hegel's account is so striking.

Hobbes' creature submits to legal relations out of expediency. It regards personality as an instrument of its desires. The desires themselves come from within the creature. Legal personality is assigned to the creature from outside. The creature does not desire legal relations for their own sake. The creature does not need personality in the sense that it needs shelter, sex, or food. Like other instruments of desire, personality is an artifice, an arrangement we make with each other to avoid inconveniences in the state of nature, where by definition we pursue desires without the aid of personality.

Unlike Hobbes' creature, Hegel's does not submit to legal relations out of expediency. Nor does it regard them as instruments of desire. Hegel's creature passionately seeks out legal relations. This is not to say, however, that it desires them. Expediency and desire are not the only triggers of action for Hegel. Hegel agrees with Hobbes that the creatures of their systems do not regard themselves as desiring legal relations for their own sake. But he disagrees that they must therefore regard them as merely expedient. Quite the contrary. Hegel's creature desires only because it is *driven* to enter legal relations. Legal relations are not merely expedient. They are the condition of desire.

Desires present choices. Desires are components of the will, favoring some desires over others, saying no to yet others. Drives, on the other hand, present no choices. They stake the claim of *eros*, the claim of the species on its members, often against the members' wills. Hegel's proposition, then, is that the erotic claim on these creatures is to fill the universe with every legal relation imaginable. The only matter which their wills may not scrutinize is their drive to enter legal relations. They may choose, if they will, to die or to be celibate, but they cannot choose to live without legal relations. The creatures at the beginning of the *Philosophy of Right* thus hunger for legal relations more powerfully than they hunger for food, shelter, or sex.

The specific hunger legal relations satisfy is the hunger of the creature at the beginning of the *Philosophy of Right* for recognition of its personality by other persons.[34] The *Philosophy of Right* describes the cultivation of this creature to a consciousness of the institutions in which the quest for recognition leads it to participate. The *Philosophy of Right* is the *Bildungsroman* of the legal person.

The rationality serving the creature at the beginning of the *Philosophy of Right* is not Kant's universal legislation. Hegel's person achieves the recognition it must have through the rationality of exchange, not universal legislation. The rationality of exchange allows two persons to earn recognition of each other by working to establish an equivalence in exchange. The recognition exchange establishes is a recognition of persons as individuals. It is personal recognition, actual respect. Kant's universal legislation abstractly demands that persons treat each other with respect, not supposing they have to earn it through deals. As a consequence, the respect Kant's persons get is a respect having nothing to do with their achievements as individuals. Kant's condition of respect is that persons give up individuality. Persons thus establish individuality only by departures from universal legislation. Kant's jurisprudence suggests to persons that actual recognition of personality can only be achieved through hypocrisy or criminal behavior. Pursuing universal legislation is weak tea for the passionately right-seeking creature, driven to seek recognition as an individual by the erotic demands of the species. The rationality of exchange is strong medicine for such a creature, but the erotic rewards of participating in legal institutions far outweigh the side-effects of the medicine.

The passionately right-seeking creature respects the rights of others, not because it wishes to be rational or seeks self-perfection, but because only by respecting the rights of others can it achieve recognition. The right-seeking creatures at the beginning of the *Philosophy of Right* are simply not interested in court enforcement of rights for its own sake. Holmes' "bad man" is not the person these creatures would deal with in the first place. The passionately right-seeking creatures want recognition from their fellow creatures, and the goods of a deal are the occasion for recognition. Enforcement interests these creatures only as it supplies or corrects the failures of recognition.

Rights for these creatures are never merely facilities for mobilizing duties. Enforceable promises are not interesting to these creatures. *All law for them is the law of contractual conditions.* What the passionately right-seeking creature wants and never stops wanting, even in enforcement, is recognition. Suppose this creature has met a condition, triggering a duty of another. Breach of the duty is merely the condition of a judgment, a further recognition. The judgment sets a further condition, requiring further recognition. Finally the right-seeking creature creates the entire system of the modern world, all to make good the original condition. But this system is open. Ultimately the creature is remitted to war. He or she must fight for recognition. All legal systems can do is sustain the quest for rights to a limit. Legal systems cannot give the creature rights, at least not rights in the Hohfeldian sense of defined facilities for mobilizing duties. Nor would the right-seeking creature want rights of this sort. The rights the passionately right-seeking creature wants begin in personality and end in war. Both are boundless.

Persons have a hunger for recognition, because they love other persons. Without loving others, the person would have no noninstrumental need for them. We need regard only from persons we love. At the same time, loving other persons causes us to want to care for them. The recognition we get from them gives us a stake in their welfare. We feel responsible for them, not because we have duties towards them, but because we love them, having given us recognition. Love even tempers the demands we make on them in treating for exchange. Persons have specific reasons for engaging other persons individually, not general reasons for engaging them en masse. The jurisprudence of right is rooted in sociability.

> Abstract Right describes the legal program of the passionately right-seeking creature where the love and caring implicit in striving for recognition is still "unconscious." The process of the *Philosophy of Right* is the discovery by this creature of love and caring as conditions of its program.
>
> Abstract Right is what the creature dreams it wants from creatures of its kind who are also passionately seeking rights. It is the legally erotic fantasy, which objectively results in the genesis of freedom in the community these passionately right-seeking creatures establish. All the person is driven to get is recognition of its claims of right from the very creatures whose sole quest is likewise to get their claims of right recognized. Recognition from a creature who is not likewise strictly seeking claims of right would not satisfy the lust for recognition. It is the difference between servants and competitors praising one's accomplishments and skills. The passionately right-seeking creatures need from each other exactly what none of them is prepared to give, and the unavailability of the object is exactly why they need it.
>
> It is the logical and practical impossibility of the parallel quests for recognition that makes recognition so critically valuable, and allows the quest for recognition to energize the successive interactions of these creatures. Persons are not impelled by logic to enter into the successive legal transactions and institutions of the *Philosophy of Right*, but find that only by entering into these transactions and

institutions can they satisfy the initial need that led them to seek recognition in the first place.

The law the passionately right-seeking creature dreams on its own is thus unstable, for the reason that what the creature seeks to get by it is by definition unavailable. The game, though, is not over.

The creatures who need from each other what none of them is prepared to give can accomplish a substitute recognition. Each can establish its claim by giving up, by transferring, precisely what it is claiming to the other. By accepting transfer of what the first is claiming—no less and no more— the second recognizes the claim, but only in the context of the first giving up the claim. Once the transfer is complete, the property of the first has become the property of the second; the second recognizes the property of the first, because the first's property is now the second's, which the first recognizes in turn because only as property in the hands of the second can the first get recognition of its claims.

Similarly, the first recognizes the property of the second by accepting transfer of precisely what the second is claiming. The two right-seeking creatures get mutual recognition of their claims to right by accepting recognition of only such claims as each resigns to the other. Persons hold only that property which satisfies the need of others for recognition. "Your own" property is always in the hands of another, and becomes "your own" in fact (to another) only once it ceases to be your property.

Hence, the condition of recognition by these right-seeking creatures who claim in parallel what by definition they cannot get is that they give up the notion of direct ownership of property by a single person. They are driven to make contracts with each other in order to get the recognition they had originally sought in property. From the perspective of the erotic career of the species, then, contract is substituted recognition, a sublimation of the drive for property.

Persons are forced to care for each other on the limited terms contract offers, because only by caring for each other in contracts can they get recognition of their property. Contract breeds love for other persons. It makes property social, and property reflects personality only when it is social.

Every successive move in the *Philosophy of Right* reveals further connections and further dependencies whereby the passionately right-seeking creature realizes the connection of the program of Abstract Right with caring for other right-seeking creatures. "Purpose and Responsibility" and "Intention and Welfare" are the next steps. There are more.

The passionately right-seeking creatures are led, finally, to recognize each other as individuals ("*Individuen*")[35] in an array of ethical laws and institutions ("*Gesetze und Einrichtungen*").[36] The person of Abstract Right can "be a person and respect others as persons"[37] only once ethical laws govern every legal person. The subject of Morality can at once protect its welfare and realize the good only once it has cultivated its ends to be the ends of a participant in ethical institutions.[38] Hegel gives the name "freedom" to the reciprocal recognition of individuals in ethical institutions governed by ethical laws.[39]

DUTY IN THE PHILOSOPHY OF RIGHT

The jurisprudence of right assigns one of three roles to duty.

A jurisprudence of right can treat duty as a necessary evil. Duty in this vision never contributes to the success of the jurisprudence. It is a hedge against the failure of the jurisprudence. This version of the jurisprudence of right tends to regard duty as positivists regard it, as a compulsion to recognize right rather than recognition freely given out of love. This first version of duty resembles the notion of duty held by participants in voluntary organizations or in collegial institutions with strong commitments to shared values.

A jurisprudence of right can also treat duty as a prudent public way of talking about the love persons bear one another. "Christian duty," for example, falls in this second category.

A jurisprudence of right, finally, can assign duty a role in the success of the jurisprudence—one, however, which is subordinate to right and whose purpose is to cultivate right as the jurisprudence defines it. This last choice is Hegel's.

The positive role of duty in the *Philosophy of Right* is to propel the individual along the path of mutual recognition. Duty is the way legal persons, moral subjects, particular wills, or single things have of talking about the sacrifice of personality, subjectivity, willfulness and singularity in order to achieve recognition as individuals. Passion alone will not transform the right-seeking creatures into individuals living in ethical institutions. The right-seeking creatures must possess the Kantian virtue of setting aside natural desires and impulses in favor of the cultivated ends of free individuals. Duty is the lament of these creatures for the uncultivated state in which they dream they may assert rights without connection to the welfare of other creatures. "In duty the individual liberates itself for substantial freedom."[40]

Rights and duties appear to be separate and distinct only in the preethical stages of Morality and Abstract Right. Only there do duties and rights need correlation. In the full ethical life of free individuals rights and duties "collapse" together:

> In this identity of the universal and particular wills duty and right then collapse, and through ethics Man has rights insofar has he has duties and duties insofar as he has rights. In Abstract Right I have the right and another has the duty against that same right; in Morality the right of my own knowing and willing, just as my welfare, only *ought* to be united with duty and objective.[41]

However, Hegel's doctrine, as he makes clear in § 148, is not a "doctrine of duties:"

> The difference of this presentation from the form of a doctrine of duties lies alone in that in the following the ethical determinations show themselves as necessary relationships, stopping here and the postscript to each of these not being added, "This determination is also a duty for Men."[42]

Nor does the collapse of rights and duties in ethics destroy the fundamental character of Hegel's work as a philosophy of right. The creatures of Hegel's work are driven to become individuals living an ethical life by their hunger for recognition. The end state of their quest, as one would expect in a theorist of Hegel's honesty and thoroughness, involves these creatures in a transformation appropriate to the jurisprudence of duty, as well as positivist and naturalist moments. The root of the quest, the home of Hegel's jurisprudence, is the project of right. Hegel's, no less than any mature jurisprudence, reconstructs the other possibilities of jurisprudence from its own unique position.

COMMON LAW AND THE RATIONALITY OF RECIPROCITY

Correlations are always possible in Common Law, but definitely never permanent. Common Law thus always has two moods: one where it shows off correlations persons have achieved and another where it smashes those correlations.[43]

"Open terms" perfectly illustrate Common Law in its correlating mood. Sometimes judges treat open terms naturally. When, for example, the reasonableness standard in negligence refers to a common sense of fitness, then it is naturalism. In this moment, Common Law bids the inquiry to leave the confines of the Common Law and to refer to the external world of spiritual facts. When, instead, reasonableness refers to clear and distinct rules articulated by judges in advance of behavior, then it is a chapter heading of positivist legislation. The perpetual debate in commercial law, whether rules or standards best promote certainty, is another example.[44] We have only just begun to understand when and why Common Law chooses between positivism and naturalism.[45] Surely the considerations are not wholly instrumental. Yet neither set of ideas—those expressed in rules and those in standards— exceeds the grasp of ordinary jurisprudence. Common Law does.

Take, for example, the strange idea that there should be no naked rights or duties. One expression of this idea is the doctrine of consideration. Another is the allergy of Common Law to good samaritans and officious intermeddlers. Another is the reluctance of judges to change the rule of contributory to comparative negligence. Ordinary jurisprudence looks at these doctrines and inhibitions as odd remainders. They *are* odd. But Common Law always will come up with such mad doctrines and inhibitions. It is, after all, not a correlating jurisprudence. It is not rational in the sense that the correlating jurisprudences are rational. From the correlating perspective, each of these doctrines and inhibitions is perfectly arbitrary. The only rationality that correlating jurisprudences impose on a right is that some person, not the holder of the right, possess the correlative duty.

Consider the sudden reluctance of Common Law judges to legislate the rule of comparative negligence. A positivist would be no less surprised by this than by Jack the Ripper getting squeamish about swatting a fly. By what possible criterion can the judges decide when they may legislate and when they may not? A naturalist would question whether the judges really consider comparative negligence rational (in the sense a naturalist means rational).

Yet Common Law judges could answer both positivist and naturalist. Application of a novel rule may or may not require legislation. It depends on whether the novelty promotes reciprocal behavior. Comparative negligence does not. Look closely at an accident in which both persons who were injured were negligent. We can set up one of three rules. Either both persons recover for the injuries caused by the other's negligence, or neither recovers (the rule of contributory negligence), or each recovers in proportion to the quantum of negligence the other contributed to the accident (the rule of comparative negligence). The first choice is inconsistent with the requirement that the negligent act cause the victim's injury. It is impossible to say which person's negligence caused one persons's injury where both were negligent. To choose the first leads to punishing persons for "negligence in the air," that is, negligence that does not cause injury (since we cannot possibly know whose negligence "caused" which injuries). The third choice also offends causation, but softens the offense by instituting a version of compromise verdict.

Common Law forbids compromise verdicts, because persons who face such verdicts cannot use them to deal with each other after the verdicts.[46] In the case of the two negligent parties to an accident, a compromise verdict gives the following message: you must be careful only to persons who are also careful. If you are lucky enough to have an accident with a person who is also not being careful, then you are released of a portion of your obligation to be careful. Since you cannot tell in advance with whom you will have an accident, you may adjust your behavior to a standard of care which is appropriate to facing persons who have an average level of carelessness, not to persons who are always careful. This lesser level of care in turn communicates a lesser obligation to be careful on the part of those other persons, and so on. Comparative negligence eliminates the spirit of reciprocal care which Common Law strives to inculcate.

Other examples would illuminate Common Law's rationality of reciprocity in different ways. Each, I believe, would confirm that the rationality of reciprocity is a rationality of exchange (the jurisprudence of right) that includes duties as well as rights in the exchanges. Persons swap duties, just as they swap rights. So besides pursuing recognition through swaps of rights, they pursue self-perfection through swaps of duties.

> The key question in Common Law is whether a field is dominated by swaps of rights or swaps of duties. Our Constitutional Law, for example, tends to be dominated by swaps of rights, a lesson the Hohfeldian Judge Bork learned to his sorrow.[47]
> Fields other than Constitutional Law are governed by swaps of duties. The vast law of fiduciaries is the broadest (perhaps not the only) example. Most fields—contracts, property, negligence, etc.— are replete with both swaps of rights and swaps of duties.

The key to reciprocity is that right, if anything, is correlated with right, and duty, with duty. We smell reciprocity in Common Law where the impulses driving it are the self-perfection or liberation of persons. Self-perfection always appears in the guise of duties without correlative rights, or unenforceable duties. These we find, for example, in the law of trusts, and in certain constitutional doctrines. The person fulfills the duty, not because another person has a right, but because the person fulfilling the duty seeks self-perfection. Often self-perfection will enhance the rights of the person fulfilling the duty. But it need not. By the same token, liberation always appears in the guise of rights without correlative duties, rights whose exercise generates rights in other persons, not correlative duties. We find liberation in other constitutional doctrines and in the law of contracts.

> The legal Left in the United States has traditionally regarded the legal system as an inert instrument of those with power. The politics is to get power over the instrument. Legal institutions are not an authentic source of politics. The notion that the legal system itself has a politics has traditionally been the province of the legal Right. Recently, however, the legal Left has become interested in the dynamic potential of the legal system.[48] Thus the Left is contesting the Right on a new front.

ANTI-HOHFELD

The goal of the correlating jurisprudences—both positivism and naturalism and the mixtures of the two that we find in ordinary jurisprudence—is order. The goal of the jurisprudence of right is liberation of the person. The goal of the jurisprudence of duty is salvation of the person. The goal of Common Law is each of these—order, liberation, and salvation—transformed through the reciprocal alliances which Common Law generates.

Common Law can achieve order—more precisely, orders[49]—where positivism and naturalism cannot. Unlike positivism and naturalism, Common Law does not attempt to achieve a single order at one moment (positivism) or forever (naturalism). The effort to achieve a single order produces disorder instead.

In positivism the disorder is an explosive and irreconcilable struggle over content. Persons will always engage in this struggle, since law determines more than order. Positivism cannot hide from the fact that law tells people how to live and what to live for. Positivism works, Kelsen and Hart recognize, only if *every* law is a procedure, only if no law has a content. Sooner or later, however, law must have a content.

In naturalism disorder stems from disagreement over the credentials of the rational observer. Rules that the observer perceives must in fact be the rules for participants in the system.

Common Law suffers from neither disorder—the disorder of substance or the disorder of procedure—since the jurisprudence of Common Law allows, but does not determine, a substance of orders. Nor does Common Law insist on a single procedure, or even any procedure. It foments orders, not order.

The legal systems of positivism and naturalism serve only the production of order. Common Law, like the other correlation-breaking jurisprudences, serves personal goals as well as the production of order. Law is the instrument of reciprocity, of salvation and liberation in the context of orders. Persons use Common Law to achieve reciprocity.

The tragedy of Hegel's jurisprudence is his failure to recognize the virtues of Common Law. His hatred of Common Law was in part motivated by ignorance, in part by his fanatical rejection of Kant. Hegel opposed salvation, but he did not oppose liberation, as the highest virtue of persons. Common Law haters, such as Bentham, typically denigrate all the virtues. Hegel was not a typical Common Law hater. Common lawyers can learn from him.

NOTES

1. See W. Hohfeld, Fundamental Legal Conceptions as Applied in Judicial Reasoning and Other Legal Essays (1923).

2. The indented sections are asides, or thoughts about the argument. They are not quotations.

3. R. Dworkin, Taking Rights Seriously (1978).

4. See id. at 172 (1977). I do not count as in "our" tradition Moshe Silberg's masterly exposition of Jewish Law (*Mishpat Ivri*) as a jurisprudence of duty. See Silberg, Law and Morals in Jewish Jurisprudence, 75 Harv. L. Rev. 307 (1961). This paper is but a generalization of Silberg's contribution. Robert Cover's last piece, Obligation: A Jewish Jurisprudence of the Social Order, 5 J. of Law and Religion 65 (1987), shows that he too understood.

5. "[A] natural right of all men and women to equality of concern and respect." Dworkin, supra note 3, at 182.

6. T. Hobbes, Leviathan (C. MacPherson ed. 1982).

7. A. Smith, Lectures on Jurisprudence (R. Meek, D. Raphael & P. Stein eds. 1978).

8. I. Kant, The Metaphysical Elements of Justice (J. Ladd trans. 1965) [hereinafter Kant's Elements].

9. See the jurisprudence of Comtean sociability, especially the works of Duguit: L'État, le droit objectif et la loi positive (1901–1903); Manuel de droit constitutionnel, Intro. & ch. 1 (3d ed. 1918); Traité de droit constitutionnel, Intro. & ch. 1 (2d ed. 1921); Le Droit social, le droit individuel et la transformation de l'état (3d ed. 1922) (all cited in Allen, Legal Duties, 40 Yale L.J. 331, 332 n.4 (1931)). For an account of Duguit's doctrine, see Allen, supra, at 332–40.

10. People usually use "legal system" to refer to legal institutions only, or perhaps to

legal institutions together with the body of rules, but not to the system of social action which the jurisprudence governs. I prefer to include the actions governed by the jurisprudence in my definition, since legal systems do not necessarily include legal institutions. In other words, the legal institutions may be diffused throughout the entire system of action. Even if they are not, the decision to differentiate legal institutions should be regarded in the first instance as a characteristic of the social system.

11. Robert Cover broached the idea of a legal universe in his reference to *nomos* in Cover, The Supreme Court 1982 Term, Foreword: *Nomos* and Narrative, 97 Harv. L. Rev. 4 (1983).

12. Michael Moore has noticed a sort of plenum in Dworkin's *Taking Rights Seriously*: "Prima facie, Dworkin's right answer thesis correspondingly is . . . a thesis about legal *concepts*, namely that they and their apparent contradictories do exhaust the logical space . . . ." Moore, Metaphysics, Epistemology and Legal Theory, 60 S. Cal. L. Rev. 453, 478 (1987).

13. The two discussions of empty corners are: Kennedy and Michelman, Are Property and Contract Efficient?, 8 Hofstra L. Rev. 711, 767–68 (1980); Singer, The Legal Rights Debate in Analytical Jurisprudence from Bentham to Hohfeld, 1982 Wisc. L. Rev. 975, 1025–1056 (1982).

14. Robert Cover, shortly before his death, was involved in exploring the dynamism and world-creating attributes of legal systems. See Cover, supra note 11.

15. In a paper subsequent to the publication of this paper in the Cardozo Law Review, I included fresh applications of a norm fully developed in an actual case as part of the norm itself. In other words, the norm includes prior applications (precedents), the application in the case at hand, and future applications using the case at hand as precedent. See Jacobson, The Idolatry of Rules: Writing Law According to Moses, With Reference to Other Jurisprudences, 11 Cardozo L. Rev. 1079 (1990). I have decided not to incorporate this change into the republication of the original paper.

16. See E. Levi, An Introduction to Legal Reasoning, at 1–8 (1948) (Common Law as "reasoning by example"); K. Llewellyn, The Common Law Tradition: Deciding Appeals, at 183–84 (1960) ("The Law of the Singing Reason").

17. Even this cannot be said. See Yablon, Law and Metaphysics, 96 Yale L.J. 613 (1987).

18. I. Macneil, The New Social Contract (1980).

19. Cf. D'Amato, The Limits of Legal Realism, 87 Yale L.J. 478 (1978) (suggesting that realist judges are constrained to follow predictions of what they will do).

20. See Rosenfeld, Affirmative Action, Justice, and Equalities: A Philosophical and Constitutional Appraisal, 46 Ohio State L.J. 845 (1985) (uses the concept of reciprocity to parse affirmative actions cases); Cornell, Beyond Tragedy and Complacency, 81 Northwestern L. Rev. 693 (1987) (philosophizes reciprocity in Common Law). For a discussion of legal uncertainty, see D'Amato, Legal Uncertainty, 71 Cal. L.Rev. 1 (1983).

21. I am, of course, talking about judges in general, since the canon of authority to overrule is complicated, depending on such factors as the state of the rule and the role of the judge in the judicial hierarchy.

22. See Kennedy, Freedom and Constraint in Adjudication: A Critical Phenomenology, 36 J. Legal Educ. 518 (1986).

23. See D'Amato, Judicial Legislation, 1 Cardozo L. Rev. 63 (1979).

24. Kant's Elements, supra note 8.

25. Id. at 18 ("Of the Subdivision of a Metaphysics of Morals").

26. Id. at 21 ("Rudimentary Concepts of the Metaphysics of Morals").

27. Id. at 14 ("Of the Idea and the Necessity of a Metaphysics of Morals").

28. Compare G.W.F. Hegel, Grundlinien der Philosophie des Rechts §§ 135, 148 (1955) (Hegel's discussion of Kant's theory of duty) [hereinafter Philosophie] with id. § 258 (discussion of the rationality embodied in the state).

29. The same content which retains the form of duties and then virtues is also the content that has the form of impulses (see Remark to Paragraph 19). Also the impulses have the same content as their foundation, but in impulses this content still listens to the unmediated will and to natural feeling, and has not been cultivated toward a determination of ethics.

    Id. § 150R. I use my own translations of the text, since Knox's translation is inadequate for exact work. My translation is awkward, but tries to preserve Hegel's almost algebraic linguistic precision.

30. Id. § 135R: "That no property occurs, contains for itself just as little contradiction as that this or that single people, family, and so forth, does not exist, or that no men live."

31. Id.: "If it is otherwise fixed and presumed that property and human life are supposed to be and to become respected, then it is a contradiction to commit theft or murder . . ."

32. The doctrine lifnim mi-shurat ha-din (staying within the line of the law) in Jewish Law is an example.

33. Philosophie, supra note 28, § 35.

34. Id. § 71.

35. The "Individuum" first appears in Philosophie, supra note 28, in § 145, at the beginning of the third part on "Ethics". The word "Individuum" appears only four times before, to my knowledge, in Paragraph 124, and in the Remarks to §§ 132, 137 and 140. The first appearence of "Individuum" in § 124 is in the second section ("Intention and Welfare") of the second part ("Morality"). The second section of the second part is at the center of the work. This center section has ten paragraphs (119–128). Paragraph 124 is the first paragraph of the second half of the center section. It is thus, in one sense, the first paragraph of the second half of the Philosophy of Right. The "Individuum" opens the second half. "Person," "Wille," "Einzelne" (single thing), and "Subjekt" dominate the first half. The "Individuum" is the participant in ethical life. The reference to the "Individuum" in § 124 involves the satisfaction of its ends ("Zwecke"), hence necessarily a reference to ethical life.

36. Philosophie, supra note 28, § 144.

37. Id. § 36.

38. Id. § 141.

39. Id. § 142.

40. Id. § 149; see id. § 134:

> Because action demands for itself a particular content and determined end, and the abstraction of duty contains nothing of the sort, so the question arises: What is duty? For this determination nothing is available so far [i.e., in the stage of Morality], but this: Do the right and care for the welfare, your own welfare and welfare in common determinations, the welfare of others.

41. Id. § 155. I am grateful to Agnes Heller for the suggestion that Hegel treats the correlation of rights with duties at the level of Abstract Right differently than at the level of Ethics.

42. Id. § 148.

43. Guido Calabresi's recent book, A Common Law for the Age of Statutes (1982), is an extended meditation on these two moods.

44. Standards can promote certainty more effectively than rules when, for example, the content of the standards is filled by an evolving code of commercial practice or a course of dealing between persons.

45. See, e.g., Kennedy, Form and Substance in Private Law Adjudication, 89 Harv. L. Rev. 1685 (1976).

46. See Coons, Approaches to Court Imposed Compromise—The Uses of Doubt and Reason, 58 Northwestern L. Rev. 750 (1964).

47. See Greenhouse, The Bork Battle: Visions of the Constitution, N.Y. Times, Oct. 4, 1987, § 4, at 1, cols. 1–3. Greenhouse, Court Nominee Clarifies How He Differs from Bork, N.Y. Times, Jan. 14, 1988, at A27, cols. 1–3. See also The Bork Nomination: Essays and Reports, 9 Cardozo L. Rev. 1 (1987).

48. See, e.g., Cover, supra note 11.

49. For the notion of "orders," see 1 F. Hayek, Law, Legislation and Liberty: Rules and Order (1973).

5

Hegel and the Crisis of
Private Law

Alan Brudner

INTRODUCTION

The modern evolution of legal thought and practice consists in the manifold expression of a single theme. In the sphere of thought, this theme takes shape in the two dominant revisionist movements of the last decade: in the movement toward comprehending private law in terms of nonlegal "perspectives" that reduce to surface rhetoric the discourse by which private law articulates and understands itself; and in the movement toward interpreting the common law in terms of intractable tensions between visions of the good—tensions that allegedly destroy the power of law theoretically to constrain the subjectivity of judges.[1] In the sphere of practice, the manifestations of the theme are even more varied and numerous. They range from the statutory embodiments of the welfare state to more recent developments in the common law of property, contracts, and torts. Among the latter we may include: the movement from fault to strict liability as a means of socializing risks and encouraging optimal investment in safety; the broadening into a general unconscionability doctrine of the ground upon which courts will void coercive contracts; the further limitation of the sanctity of contract by an expanding doctrine of mistake; and the regular judicial appeals to policy and the public welfare in the determination of entitlements to property.

What unites these diverse phenomena into an articulated whole is the denial of the autonomy of private law. If we understand by private law an ordering of human interactions that is independent of an ordering by the common good, then the dominant theme of modern legal culture can be expressed as a crisis in the legitimacy of such an ordering. No doubt it is impossible to conceive of order except in terms of something common. Yet in each of the domains of law traditionally called private, there is a discourse that honours the distinctiveness of this law by appealing exclusively to a commonality between persons who recognize no good or end as uniformly theirs, and whose interactions are therefore those of self-interested monads. Such a discourse has been called "individualistic" or "rights-based" in order to distinguish it from an understanding of order based on the primacy of the human good and of the duty to promote it. More important than any label, however, is the fact that the recent history of the common law is largely a tale of the displacement of this discourse—or at least of its decline—in favour of one that would shape common-law adjudication into a functionally rational instrument of the public good.

Against this movement toward the hegemony of public law some isolated voices have been raised in protest. In particular, Richard Epstein, George Fletcher, and Ernest Weinrib have sought to render tort law perspicuous by means of theories that make no reference to public goals.[2] However, these protests are inherently incapable of stemming the tide, for they have been mounted from a standpoint conceptually more primitive than (and so historically prior to) that of modern public law, and are thus bound to appear one-sided and reactionary. The defense of private law as a necessary and distinctive form of order has hitherto been based on the very atomistic ontology that stands (in part) repudiated by the contemporary dominance of public law. Specifically, it has been based on the premise of the priority of the right over the good. When analyzed, this premise yields a constellation of principles comprising the outlook of a certain form of liberalism traditionally identified with Locke and Kant. It implies, first of all, that human individuals, as self-conscious agents, have ultimate reality and worth in their immediate isolation from and indifference toward one another; that justice, understood as the mutual respect for this worth, is thus conceivable independently of a conception of the common good and so without any reliance on the possibility of a natural virtue; that private law, or the law ordering the interactions of otherwise dissociated individuals, exhausts the content of natural right and is therefore law in its focal or archetypal form; that, by contrast, public law is the outcome of political choices among contingent goods, a sphere of positive and instrumental law normatively constrained by prepolitical natural rights; that corrective justice, as the formal structure of private law, is therefore the only form of justice that judges acting independently of legislatures can nontyrannically apply. All of these claims are simply antithetical to those on which the contemporary primacy of public law rests and so can only be pitted dogmatically against an equally one-sided adversary. In this conflict, moreover, the defenders of private law are bound to come off badly, because the identification of natural with private law leads ineluctably to the dissolution of the former. Inasmuch as this identity postulates a right to the natural liberty of acquisition, it is silently permissive of social hierarchies originating in contingent differences of premoral nature, and which, lacking moral justification, collapse natural right into the interests of the stronger. Indeed, it is precisely this crisis in the libertarian conception of natural right that engendered the latter's reconceptualization as the conditions of authentic community, a revision that underlies the modern ascendancy of public over private law. Accordingly, if the latter is to be justified in terms that are morally cogent, it must be justified on foundations that have absorbed the critique of classical liberalism and that are now invulnerable to it.

In this essay I shall interpret the legal philosophy of Hegel as providing such a justification. As we shall see, it is the unique achievement of this philosophy to have offered a vindication of private law from the standpoint of a principle of justice more comprehensive than that of modern public law, one that therefore *subsumes* the latter's critique of private law as a self-sufficient elaboration of right. Indeed, not only does Hegel's philosophy incorporate this critique; it also purports to disclose the conceptual necessity for the modern subordination of private to public law even as it then reinstates the former to its full integrity and vigour. One may expect, therefore, that the weapons with which communitarian thought subdued classical liberalism will be broken on a vindication of private law that incorporates the partial truth of the modern paradigm.

I can restate the latter point more precisely by explaining that Hegel offers a vindication of private law from the standpoint of the priority of the good. Now of course there is no dearth of such purported vindications. One might, for example, find good utilitarian reasons for maintaining a regime of private property and contract, and, in a world of fallible judgment, for insulating this regime from direct appeals to the utilitarian standard.[3] One might also view private law in perfectionist terms as part of the totality of communal arrangements tending to promote the realization of distinctively human capacities.[4] However diverse in other respects, both kinds of theory share the view that private law is instrumental to an end outside itself and that its true nature is thus something other than the one presented to the lawyer. Plato's *Laws* gives us the form of all such externalist accounts. In Book Nine, for example, the Athenian stranger turns his reformist attention to the law of delicts. The latter is seen as having a conventional origin in moral indignation, a basis that explains its preoccupation with the distinction between voluntary and involuntary conduct.[5] For the Athenian, however, the true end of criminal law is the cure of souls ignorant of their good and to whom the distinction between the voluntary and the involuntary does not apply. Thus the inherent nature of criminal law is something other than the significance it has for opinion (for the slave doctors of slaves),[6] and the problem for the legislator is to fashion laws that, while ordered to their natural purpose, make the necessary concessions to prejudice.

In his early writings on the philosophy of spirit, Hegel himself conceived private law in a manner consciously modelled on the Platonic.[7] Though ostensibly an autonomous system based on the right of private property, private law is in reality (he argues) an obscure or lower-order manifestation of the primacy of community. Its natural function, therefore, is to be an infrastructural support for the maintenance of a "class of courage," in which the primacy of the good is reflected as in a perfect medium. For the young Hegel as for Plato, then, the truth of private law is contrasted with the way in which private law appears. It appears to be independent of the priority of the good; its essential nature, however, is not this appearance, but rather its subordination to the good. Moreover, this subordination is revealed decisively in war, wherein "there is the free possibility that not only certain individual things but the whole of them, as life, will be annihilated and destroyed for the Absolute itself or for the people . . . " (NL 93).

Now the problem with Hegel's early account of private law is the same as that which besets all contemporary externalist accounts. The problem is that, by asserting the truth of private law over against the way in which private law appears, the theory reveals itself as an artificial construction of private law rather than as a true account of it. Private law is understood to be instrumental to a good that is not private; hence it is justified not as private law but as an instantiation of public law. Qua private, private law is the superficial play of appearances in which something else (community, efficiency) pulsates. And because its true nature lies outside itself, its own self-understanding as an autonomous order intelligible from within is error and illusion. Insofar, however, as the philosophy of private law contradicts the law's own self-understanding, it too becomes mere opinion and its claim of truth an arbitrary dogmatism. This is why serious private law theorists have insisted that a faithful account of private law must rest on the priority of the right, or on the ontological primacy of the state of nature. The idea is that such an account must be internalist, and that an internalist account of private law must rest on the empty principle of agency rather than on any substantive conception of the good. Accordingly, the fundamental opposition is one between internalist accounts of private law whose internalism is based on an exclusion of the good as an explanatory principle, and teleological accounts that are externalist. In this opposition, of course, both sides have a right against the other. For if the nemesis of external approaches is a functionalism that destroys the notion of private law, that of rights-based theory is a formalism that, while preserving private law in its account, never explains why we should be committed to it.

Now Hegel is significant for this controversy because he is the only philosopher to offer an internalist account of private law from the standpoint of the priority of the good. This means that he is the only philosopher to attempt a genuine mediation between teleological and rights-based accounts of justice, or between public good and private right. The fundamental insight—and the one we shall have to elucidate—is that the common good necessitates a regime of private right from which the good is hidden as that without which it would not be objectively the common good. For the mature Hegel, in other words, the good is constituted by its positing within itself a sphere wherein its priority is suspended, so that while the independence of private law is still an appearance, its essence now consists precisely in this appearing and not in direct subordination to the good. The implications of this position for adjudicative theory are, I think, far-reaching and profound. In the first place, a theory that grounds private law noninstrumentally in the common good will provide a better fit with the common law process than either rights-based or instrumentalist accounts of law. Whereas the former might reasonably have claimed to underlie the common law of the nineteenth and early twentieth centuries, it now finds itself embarrassed by a growing number of "mistakes" involving the recognition of a duty of concern for others as intentional agents.[8] On the other hand, instrumentalist theories can easily integrate legal doctrines imposing a duty of altruistic concern, but find cramping and irrational the binary adjudicative structures in which that duty comes to be enforced;[9] or else regard as incoherent the contractual allocation of power which these doctrines must, so long as their principle is not generalized, endlessly correct with ad hoc adjustments.[10] Since neither rights-based nor instrumentalist theory can demonstrate itself as the immanent or thematic principle of private law, neither can make a convincing claim to be the ultimate premise of doctrinal elaboration. By contrast, a theory of justice that offers a dialectical synthesis of private right and public good will reveal the inner unity of classical and modern phases of the common law and will thus advance the most persuasive claim to be the latter's indwelling and original principle.

The latter observation suggests a further implication of Hegel's legal thought for adjudicative theory. To the extent that Hegel succeeds in mediating the antagonism between public good and private right, he provides the only possible response to those who assert a fundamental indeterminacy at the heart of legal reasoning.[11] At its strongest, this thesis flows from the supposed bifurcation in the right created by the irreconcilable opposition between the social and individualistic poles of human nature. Since the standard of right is internally sundered, legal cognition itself breaks up into opposing rhetorical modes, neither more cogent than the other, leaving a judge with no oracle but his passions. Now insofar as Hegel succeeds in restoring unity to the right, he also restores the possibility of a rational and coherent adjudication. Here again, however, his solution will be one that eschews dogmatism and one-sidedness. For rather than asserting unity over against dichotomy, Hegel (we shall see) offers a principle of unity that incorporates dichotomy as an essential phase of its self-realization, one which therefore acknowledges the historical truth of the claim of indeterminacy.

My thesis, then, consists of a number of claims concerning the contemporary relevance of Hegel's legal philosophy. I argue, first of all, that Hegel supports the autonomy of private law on foundations conceptually more advanced than those upon which the modern ascendancy of public law rests; and that his vindication of private law is thus invulnerable to arguments that "deconstruct" the dichotomy between the private and the public. I argue, secondly, that Hegel provides an internalist account of private law from the standpoint of the priority of the good, and so is able to capture the phenomenon of positive common law duties without rendering incoherent the transactional basis of private law. Finally, I argue that by virtue of both these achievements, Hegel vindicates the possibility of the rule of law against its contemporary detractors.

The division of the essay reflects these themes. The first section sets out Hegel's critique of private law insofar as the latter purports to embody justice abstracted from any ordering by a common good. The import of this critique is to disclose the inherent necessity for the transition to a moral understanding of right and for the consequent subsumption of private under public law. The second section elucidates this necessity and deals with a contemporary argument that claims it can be resisted. The third section then outlines Hegel's critique of the moral standpoint and brings into focus the ground upon which private law is restored to honour. Finally, I present Hegel's view of the place of private law in a full theory of justice, and sketch some implications of this view for current problems in the theory of adjudication.

PRIVATE LAW AS SELF-ESTRANGEMENT

Hegel's most elaborate account of private law appears in the section of the *Philosophy of Right* entitled "Abstract Right" (§§ 34–104)[12] An understanding of this section requires a preliminary grasp of the structure of the *Philosophy of Right.* as a whole. The subtitle of Hegel's book about justice (*Recht*) is: *Outline of Natural Law and Political Science.* It would appear that for Hegel as for Plato the true theory of right is coextensive with the true theory about the inner nature or idea of the state. This identity is confirmed by the text. Thus the state is called "the actuality of the Ethical Idea" (§ 257), which in turn is identified with the Idea of freedom (§ 142), whose actuality is said to be "the system of right" (§ 4). The *Philosophy of Right.*, however, does not begin with anything remotely resembling a naturalist theory of the state. It begins instead by considering a theory of right that presupposes the solid reality of persons in a prepolitical state of nature. So far, in other words, from assuming the naturalness of the state, Hegel begins with persons who define themselves independently of any association with others, and for whom there can thus be no such thing as an inner "nature" of the state in the sense of an order given independently of human will. Accordingly, Hegel's book on natural law does not commence with what for Hegel is the true theory of right. It does not do so, for this would be to present the latter as "shot out of a pistol"[13]—that is, dogmatically, and so in a manner contradicting its claim of truth. The book, therefore, is divided into three parts. Each part treats of an understanding of natural law based on a particular conception of nature (the Concept) or of the inner essence or cause of reality. The nature or concept of a thing tells us what the thing objectively is as distinct from the way it appears, and so tells us what a thing must become if it is to exist intelligibly, necessarily, and immutably. The nature of a thing thus prescribes a law for the thing, the content of which will vary depending on the particular conceptualization of nature. Now abstract right is the content of natural law unfolded from a perspective that identifies the essence of reality with the ego of the singular individual exclusive of all other egos (§ 34). It is natural law from the perspective of the Stoics and of the Roman jurists. It is also natural law from the most conceptually primitive standpoint consistent with the notion of law. That is, we begin at a point where self-consciousness or the universal claims causality *vis-à-vis* the sensible world, but at which it has least penetrated or reconstituted the atomism definitive of that world. The self that claims to be the end of existence is the self of the atomistic individual external and indifferent to all other individuals.

The section entitled "Morality" embodies a conceptual advance. Here Hegel treats natural law conceived from the standpoint which identifies nature not with *this* particular ego but with the universal or inclusive ego immanent in a plurality of individual subjects. It is natural law from the standpoint of Kant and of the postKantian intuitionists. This formulation is an advance over the previous one, because the universal, in comprehending and expressing itself in diverse individuals, has been grasped in a way more adequate to its presumed causality and hence also to its universality. Finally, the section entitled "Ethical Life" is the theory of natural law elaborated from the standpoint which defines nature as Spirit, or as the dialectical unity of the universal and particular ego whose perfect embodiment is the rational state. Accordingly, it is only when we reach "Ethical Life" that we arrive at the standpoint at which Hegel's distinctive philosophic principle is self-consciously thematized. The first two parts are intended to justify Ethical Life as the foundation of natural law by revealing the phenomenality of standpoints rival to Hegel's, that is, by revealing them as the semblance rather than the reality of natural law. The import of the first two sections is thus primarily critical or aporetic. The truth of abstract right turns out to be crime, that of the moral standpoint nihilism. The outcome of these sections is not, however, solely aporetic. It is the characteristic feature of Hegel's principle of natural law—a feature required by its claim of universality—that it embraces all rival principles as imperfect instantiations of itself, and is nothing but the rationally connected and hierarchically ordered totality of these principles (§ 1, Phen. 68, 89–90). Thus, while abstract right and morality are negated as foundations of natural law, they are negated only insofar as they claim to be the whole truth about right, or only insofar as they claim validity outside the architectonic structure of ethical life. They are, however, preserved as elements or partial manifestations of that life, and the content of right unfolded from them is absorbed into ethical life as part of the total content of natural law. Accordingly, Hegel's treatment of abstract right will be partly negative and partly positive. It will consist partly in surrendering to the self-existence of the standpoint of abstract right in order to demonstrate the inner necessity of its downfall and transition to a higher principle. But it will consist also in revealing what is unknown at that standpoint, namely, that abstract right is a prefiguration of the perfect community and a necessary phase of its self-realization.

Let us begin by focusing on the negative movement of abstract right. In Hegel's lexicon, the qualifier "abstract" denotes privation: it refers to an entity or concept torn loose from the fusion of form and matter through which its being is first mediately validated, and that claims reality in this isolation, one-sidedness, and immediacy (Phen. 114– 15).[14] Right is initially abstract in at least two senses. First, it is the objective realization of an abstract, thin, or formal conception of personality. At this stage personality signifies a freedom conceived as a reflex from all dependence on another into a transcendental point of agency emptied of all material content (§§ 5, 35; Phen. 501 ff). Freedom, in other words, is here defined as a pure capacity or possibility of spontaneity, a capacity isolated from the material interests, talents, and instruments through which it comes to be actualized. A freedom of this sort is abstract, not because its home is thought, but because it claims self-sufficiency in detachment from the conceptually necessary medium for its objective realization. It is abstract because divorced from the means of its reality. Secondly, right is initially abstract because it postulates human beings who are abstract. That is, it posits individuals who lay claim to a final worth outside the social and political orders through which alone that worth is actualized, who thus claim natural rights without acknowledging the natural duties they presuppose. At the stage of abstract right, duties are either self-regarding (be a person) or correlative to rights of formal liberty (respect others as persons) (§ 36). There are no positive duties of citizenship, for the individual here deems himself to be self-sufficient, owing his worth or reality to no one but himself. There is, moreover, a connection between these two modes of abstraction. Once the individual is accorded a stable reality in his natural immediacy and isolation, he can claim the status of a being only by virtue of an abstraction from all particularity of aim and character, for particularity now has the significance of the fortuitous and nonessential, of what is brutely given in nature. Correspondingly, once the atomistic individual is posited as a constant, the sole basis for a public world is the bare capacity for choice abstracted from determinate aims now identified with the idiosyncratic and the subjective.

The abstraction from determinate purposes into purposiveness itself Hegel calls the person. The latter thus implies an antithesis between (on the one hand) the specific or concrete individual who is dependent on external objects for the satisfaction of want and who is himself a contingent object in the sphere of nature, and (on the other) the abstractly universal ego exclusive of all determinate characteristics (§ 35). Abstract right, then, is the legal order unfolded as the objectification of the person's claim to be the sole essential reality. The critique of this claim consists in a demonstration that its outward reality in fact contradicts it. The self-supposed essential reality will suffer the negation of its reality; and since the ego's claim to be the essence of reality is also its claim to freedom, to independence of an "other," the negation of its being will simultaneously be the negation of its freedom. Furthermore, these negations will occur precisely in the process through which individual self-consciousness objectifies its claim to ontological priority, so that the negations will be immanent to the standpoint rather than asserted from without. Abstract right as a whole will thus turn out to be the estranged or self-contradictory realization of individual self-consciousness as the foundation of freedom and of right. And in understanding it in this manner, we understand the inner necessity for the collapse of private law as a self-contained content of justice.

The consequences of the isolated ego's claim to essential reality are revealed, to begin with, in the structural features of private law (§§ 37–38). It is a phenomenon of the nonpolitical legal order that a certain dimension of the parties to any dispute is considered irrelevant to a just determination of their rights. In adjudicating between litigants, the judge is bound to ignore their individual characteristics—their wealth, moral virtue, motives etc.—and to have regard instead only to their equal status as right-bearing persons. So, for example, the remedy in law for a violation of that equality is not specific relief responsive to the particular projects or circumstances of the plaintiff but an award of money damages in which the particularity of the parties' situations is submerged. Furthermore, duties in private law are (as we saw) characteristically negative duties not to interfere unreasonably with the liberty of others; positive duties of assistance do not arise here unless the failure to confer a benefit is properly construable in the circumstances as the violation of liberty. Both of these features of private law Hegel deduces from the latter's origin in a narrow conception of personality. At the standpoint of abstract right, the individual is considered worthy of respect only in his formal capacity as an agent. As a determinate individual with specific aims and needs, he is a "thing" devoid of essential reality and so also of rights (Phen. 503) ("The empty unit of the person is . . . as regards its reality, an accidental existence, a contingent insubstantial process and activity that comes to no durable subsistence"). Because that which pertains to the concrete individual has the significance of the contingent and the relative, the universality of law can come forward only as a relation of compatibility between abstract wills. To admit the circumstances and characteristics of the parties as relevant to the outcome would here subvert the right, because the judge has no criterion other than his preferences for assessing the importance of these factors. Similarly, since no rights attach to the individual's specificity, there is no right to intentional action, that is, to action that realizes the agent's concrete projects. Rather, the only right of personality is that which protects the formal capacity for choice that personality (at this stage) is. As a right *of* liberty rather than *to* inner-directed action, such a right generates nothing but prohibitions. Since there is no right to see in one's deeds the embodiment of one's purposes, there is no right to the concern of others for one's freedom in this larger sense, hence no duty on others to manifest it (§ 49).

Now if the foregoing is a deduction of the formalism of private law, of its exclusion of a family of considerations pertaining to the concrete welfare of individuals, then clearly it is a deduction of an ambiguous sort. For while it in one sense reveals the necessity of this formalism, it also shows that necessity to be relative to a particular conception of personality and of what is essential to personality. Moreover, far from absolutizing that conception, Hegel's analysis reveals the structure of private law as already in part a negation thereof, so that the structure is also negated as a necessary feature of the right as such. The negation consists in this: the objectification of the person's claim of final worth is a legal order in which the concrete individual is of no account. An individualistic foundation of being and of freedom has generated an order indifferent to individuals. In the *Phenomenology of Spirit*, Hegel describes the subject of this order as an "unhappy consciousness," wavering between a certainty of his substantiality as a person to one of his nothingness as a determinate individual (249–51, 506).

However, while the structure of private law mirrors the disdain for individuals implicit in the hypostatization of personhood, it does not yet negate abstract personality as such as the foundation of being and of right. This occurs in the course of the person's self-objectification in property. By virtue of its abstraction from particularity, the person now stands over against a sensible world apparently alien and indifferent to it. This show of independence poses a problem for personality, for the latter's certainty of being the foundation of reality is now infected with subjectivity (§ 39). The latter is experienced as a privation, moreover, because the subject pole of self-consciousness is inherently inconceivable except in relation to an object from which it primordially distinguishes itself (Phen. 139).Just as an object exists only *for* the self, so does the self exist only as subordinating the object to its causality.

Because self and object are thus mutually constitutive, the disparity between belief and objectivity is experienced as an inner contradiction in self-consciousness itself, and hence too as a desire, wholly noumenal in origin, to remove it (Phen. 219–20). Accordingly, personality is the urge to objectify its certainty of being the foundation of reality, and to do so by reducing sensible things to something notionally "of" the self—that is, to property.

However, instead of confirming the person as the natural end of things, property will actually negate it as such. The necessity for this outcome is already latent in the one-sided definition of reality as abstract personality. The being and freedom of the individual have been conceived in such a way as to repel from their notions dependence on an object, for objectivity here (that is, to the atomistic individual) has the significance of a sensible world fortuitously given to the self, of something external and alien. This means, however, that the objectivity of personality as the foundation of being will take place in a sphere "determined as what is immediately different and separable from it" (§ 41). That is, objectification will take the form of the self-*alienation* of personality, of its submission to an object external to and independent of it. The actualization of the person will be "reality estranged from it" (Phen. 506), an external and autonomous object in relation to which individual personality will appear nonessential and unfree. Let us now examine this process in some detail.

The person's conquest of external things occurs in three phases representing progressively more adequate validations of the person's claim to be the *telos* of existence. Possession is the most primitive phase because it leaves the thing with a positive existence over against the person, so that the instability of the thing in its independence of the self is not yet demonstrated (§ 55–58). In use, by contrast, the thing's independence is objectively cancelled; it becomes explicitly a means to the satisfaction of need and its physical character is altered to that end (§ 59–62). However, use too is inadequate, for it establishes the person's mastery of the thing in the self-contradictory mode of being dependent on it. Because use is driven by desire or need, every act of consumption reinstates the independence of nature, thereby stimulating a renewed desire *ad infinitum* (Phen. 225, F 229). Furthermore, when I appropriate a thing by grasping and using it, my ownership remains *soi-disant* or subjective. Since I have unilaterally excluded other persons whose self-validation likewise requires the thing, my claim to the object is a particularistic one, an expression of power rather than of right. Hence the thing is not objectively mine, nor conversely is my final worth a reality for me. What is needed, therefore, is a mode of acquisition in which I simultaneously release the thing (thereby both demonstrating my independence of it and making it available to others) and establish it as mine.

The dimensions of this problem will perhaps be appreciated if we compare Hegel's formulation of it with that of Locke or Nozick.[15] In general terms, the problem is to determine the conditions that will legitimate exclusive possession under conditions of scarcity. For Nozick, individual appropriation is justified if no one is rendered worse off as a consequence.[16] Since he regards this proviso as satisfied if appropriation leaves at least as much for others to use even if they no longer have liberty to appropriate, it is clear that by "worse off" Nozick means a comparison with the initial situation in terms of welfare. Yet a welfare constraint on appropriation seems inconsistent with the framework of natural rights, for such a constraint implies that rights are a function of welfare, whereas Nozick must surely say that the level of welfare to which one is entitled is limited by respect for liberty. The advantage, however, of a welfare proviso is that it can be very weak.[17] A's appropriation is justified as long as B enjoys no less than the meager amount he consumed in the initial situation of unowned objects. The strongest proviso capable of being generated by a welfarist interpretation of "worse off" is that of Locke, who seems to allow A's appropriation only up to the point where B's *prospects* for enjoyment are not adversely affected.[18] In either case, however, A's property right can be established by unilateral acquisition in a presocial setting—that is to say, without the cooperation of B's will.

Suppose, however, that instead of formulating a proviso in terms of welfare, we formulated one in terms of agency. Thus A has a right to manifest his causality *vis-à-vis* X provided he does not preclude B from doing likewise. Here we have a proviso consistent with the framework of natural rights, but the problem now is that the constraint seems impossibly stringent. A and B each require everything, so that *any* appropriation by one leaves the other worse off in terms of agency. Under this proviso, clearly, no unilateral acquisition of property is possible. And since every single object is an object of competition, consensual property seems equally beyond reach.

Now Hegel's account of property is immensely interesting because it faces up to the stringent constraint required by the framework of natural rights and shows, not how it ought to be met, but how it already is met in private law. The desideratum, once again, is a kind of acquisition that is simultaneously an appropriation of an object and a surrendering of it to another. Such a mode of acquisition is contract, which is therefore the completion of the inchoate property embodied in possession and use. In contract each person relinquishes his possession to another and receives back an equivalent value in recognition of his property right in the thing relinquished. Thus each person's objective mastery of the thing is mediated through the recognition of another person. In this way, contract resolves the two contradictions that seemed to make property impossible. On the one hand, it establishes the person's mastery of the thing in the very act of his abandoning it; on the other, it permits consensual property between persons with mutually exclusive desires for infinite accumulation. Each person can recognize the exclusive ownership of the other without foreclosing his opportunities for unlimited acquisition, because property is constituted only through a system of exchange and free alienability in which everything is in principle available to others.

Now the foregoing analysis of property has revealed the latter not simply as a private relation between a person and a thing but primarily as a social bond between formally equal agents. This bond, moreover, has a dialectical structure, in that the free personality of each constitutes and is constituted by the free personality of the other. By renouncing its possession in favour of another, the self cancels its isolation and makes itself a means to the property of the other. Yet this self-renunciation constitutes the *property* of the other only because it is not that of a slave who surrenders from a contingent fear of death to a master (Phen. 234 ff, F 230 ff), but that of a free self who also claims to be the end of sensible things. It is the surrender of a free self, however, only by virtue of the fact that the other likewise renounces his possession in favour of the property of the first. Accordingly, property embodies a common will, in that each self receives confirmation of his causality from the other, and does so only because each reciprocally recognizes the other as an end (§ 71, F 237 ff).

However, if property is a social bond between equals, the conception of freedom of which property is (at this stage) the embodiment is fundamentally individualistic or asocial. An individualistic freedom is possible, however, only as a flight from the only world capable of validating it, and in contract this divorce between the form and reality of freedom has become explicit. Substantial in thought, the person is in fact dependent for the confirmation of his being on material things now under the rightful control of the free will of others (§§ 73, 195; Phen. 504). In Hegelian terms, the realization (*Verwirklichung*) of the person has taken the self-contradictory form of an alienation (*Entausserung*) thereof, with the result that the object now stands estranged (*entfremdet*) from the self.

Now we can distinguish two ways in which contract represents (at this stage) the self-estrangement of personality. It does so, first of all, by empowering a common will abstracted from, and so indifferent to, the concrete subjectivity of persons. Since contractual rights are fully constituted by the mutual recognition of formal wills, they are enforceable provided only there is formally voluntary agreement on both sides. The fact that economic necessity led one party to submit to the terms of the other, or that one party was, to the knowledge of the other, mistaken about the quality or value of the thing exchanged, is at this point irrelevant to the contract's validity, because there is here no right to intentional action, or to the outward embodiment of one's self-chosen projects (§ 37, 112A). Thus contract, while purporting to perfect the person's dominion over things, in fact sanctions his subjection to every stronger will.

There is another side to the common will's indifference to determinate individuality. That indifference is manifested not only in the enforceability of contracts divorced from inner intention, but also in the lack of protection for individual projects outside the bounds of the formal identity of wills. Thus, since property is established only through exchange, there is no room for the enforcement of unpurchased promises even where the promisee has relied to his detriment, or where consideration has been given by someone other than the beneficiary seeking enforcement. Moreover, because property is realized only in alienating the thing to others, it is consistent with a loss of control over the thing subversive of one's efforts to acquire it in the first place. In the case of public goods like information and spectacles, for example, competitors may appropriate and so render worthless the efforts of the producer without violating abstract right.

Nevertheless, a critique of contract in these terms is not a fully immanent critique, for it compares the institution of contract to a more robust conception of personality than that which contract initially embodies. Specifically, it compares contract to a conception of personality as embracing concrete projects rather than to a personality conceived as the pure capacity to author projects. A truly immanent critique, therefore, is one which shows how contract negates as foundational the very concept of personality it is originally meant to realize.

It does so with the genesis of a species of contract that reflects the freedom of personality in the way most adequate to it. This, according to Hegel, is the executory contract, and because the latter is the best embodiment of personality as the ground of being, it is also contract in its ideal or paradigmatic form. In simple exchange, the person's lordship over things was realized only from one transaction to another.

Consequently, its freedom was still self-contradictorily immersed in sensuous existence, both in the sense that it was involved in the succession of finite points comprising temporality, and in the sense that the noumenal desire for property was still enmeshed with the sensuous appetite for things. An executory contract, however, is an "ideal exchange" (F 238). While standing for a temporal exchange of things, it is in reality an exchange of words whereby a separation is achieved between covenant and temporal performance. Here, therefore, personality rises to its most crystalline abstractness and hence to the limit of its power to master existence. Through an exchange of promises, each will transcends the momentary appetite for this or that thing, renouncing the latter as its principle. Further, each renounces appetite for the sake of the personality of the other, thereby making possible the reciprocal subjugation of time. By virtue of the obligatoriness of mutual promises, the futurity of performance is on the one hand cancelled, and on the other absorbed into an ideal or conceptual present, so that not only appetite is conquered by the person but temporality itself (§ 79, F 239). We have here an account of what many modern contract theorists regard as deeply perplexing.[19] In particular, Hegel has explained why certain promises are enforceable even without reliance by the promisee or benefit having passed to the promisor; why the consideration of another promise selects the promises that are enforceable in this way; and why the promisee has a right to the value of his expectancy. Promises of a certain kind are enforceable without more because they implicitly objectify personality's claim of causality over the sensible world and so conceptually demand enforcement for their completion. Contractual obligation is not simply a species of promissory obligation, distinguished from the genus by the external addition for policy reasons of legal enforcement. Rather, it is an obligation which, in contrast to promissory obligation, objectifies a prior claim of right in the promisee to subdue chance, and which thus implies enforcement by its very nature. Hence no reasons extrinsic to a promise intended to serve another's will are required to trigger legal consequences. On the other hand, such promises are immanently enforceable only for consideration (of which another promise is the paradigm instance) because only if each makes possible the mastery of the other is the self-abnegation of one consistent with the equal causality, hence *right* to performance, of each. Finally, contractual promises are enforceable for the value of the promise, because only then is the future assimilated to the conceptual present and the person's domination of nature thus complete.

In that it signifies a conquest of spatio-temporal existence, the executory contract exhausts the potentiality for freedom of the isolated person. Yet instead of confirming freedom, this institution actually contradicts it. By effecting a separation between word and deed, the executory contract removes the last fetter to the arbitrary freedom of the particular will, thereby placing in constant jeopardy the objective freedom embodied in contract (§ 81, F 238). The insecurity of contract, moreover, is not simply the result of the potential waywardness of appetite. Were this the case, it would have no implications at all for the person's claim of freedom nor for the stability of a private law that embodies it. Rather the contingency of performance is just the inner consequence of that claim, and is therefore its very refutation. Contracts are necessarily insecure at this stage, because they bind not the individual's *will* but only his *appetite* for specific things. "The compulsion," writes Hegel, "applies not to the person, but only to its determinateness, to its existence" (F 240). This is so because the common will embodied in contract is so far something merely conventionally posited by the parties for the sake of the freedom of the particular ego (§ 75, 82). No doubt the freedom of the person is objectified only in consensual transactions; but it is objectified therein *qua* arbitrary or particular, and it is the latter side which the wrongdoer isolates in the form of a claim of right. Accordingly, since the particular will is at this stage logically prior to the common will, respect for property is a matter of choice, and the person is thus dependent for the reality of his freedom on the arbitrary will of others (§ 81).

Now it might be objected at this point that, while anarchy is doubtless the immanent negation of the isolated ego's claim to ontological priority, this hardly counts as a demonstration of the incompleteness of private law as the content of natural right. For the insecurity of objective in the face of formal freedom merely shows that the true basis of freedom (and so of right) is the common will hitherto treated as conventional, a will wherein each person make himself a means to the other in order that each might gain objective reality as an end. The content of the common will, however, is just private property, exchange, and contract, which, so far from being undermined by the negation of the particular will's primacy, are solidified thereby.

A full answer to this objection will be attempted in the following section. We can here hint at its weakness, however, by pointing to a distinction between Hegel's theory of abstract right and Kant's ostensibly parallel treatment of private law in his *Rechtslehre*.[20] For Kant, the content of private law originates in a state of nature wherein the common will is *already* ontologically dominant. The problem with the state of nature for Kant is not that wrong masquerades as right, but

that right is self-contradictorily dependent for its enforcement on partial agents none of whom has any reason to trust each other's respect
for rights.[21] Since the common will is implicitly regnant from the
beginning in the state of nature, the transition to a juridical order does
not alter the conception of right nor, therefore, the content of right
unfolded in the prelegal order. Rather, it merely actualizes that content
in the impersonal mode which the content requires. For Hegel, by
contrast, the supremacy of the common will is not a starting-point but
an achievement. Since the common will is a unity of distinct elements,
it represents a logical advance on a conception of the will as lacking
internal difference, that is, as identifying the particular with the universal will. Furthermore, the content of private law, Hegel has shown,
originates from this more primitive conception. It develops from a
Hobbesian rather than a Kantian conception of natural right. Now it
may be true that this content will be confirmed by the transition to an
order implicitly governed by the common will. The question, however,
is whether it will be confirmed just as it is, or as part of something
richer in which it is altered.

MORALITY AND THE CRISIS OF PRIVATE LAW

The transition from the supremacy of the particular to that of the
common will marks the transition from abstract right to morality. It
is important to bear in mind that this is not a movement from a self-
contained doctrine of right to a self-contained doctrine of the good.
We do not leap, in other words, from a theory of law to a theory of
virtue as we do in Kant's *Metaphysics of Morals.* Rather, we move
from an abstract to a more comprehensive foundation of right, which
must therefore reconstitute and reshape the former.

Now the subsumption of abstract right under a morality of the
common will does not threaten the autonomy of private law if the
moral standpoint merely solidifies the negative rights posited but left
unactualized at the previous standpoint. This would be the case if the
moral standpoint generated no new rights of personality or if a new
generation of rights were simply harmonious with the abstract right to
property and to freedom of contract. As we shall now see, however,
neither of these conditions obtains.

Let us first attempt to understand the new conception of nature that
has emerged here. At the level of abstract right, the supposed essential
reality was *this* personality, exclusive of others, a personality conceived
as a bare capacity for choice abstracted from a material content taken

as foreign to the self. At the moral standpoint, by contrast, the essential reality is personhood explicitly grasped as a universal immanent in a multitude of individual subjects (§§ 105–06). Now once the universal ego is grasped as the foundation of right, there is disclosed a content for the individual will whose origin is not nature but the will itself. That is to say, the will now potentially has for its content the law under which the liberty of each may coexist with the equal objective freedom of all (§§ 103–04). This means that the person is potentially free in a richer sense than before. He is free not simply in the sense that he can choose between contents given *ab extra*, but in the sense that he can choose contents conformable to the will's freedom because rationally determined by the concept of freedom itself. Accordingly, the grasp of the common will as the foundation of right yields the insight that the essence of personality is not simply choice but self-determination, the requisites of which constrain choice (§§ 21, 107).

There is a further implication of the primacy of the common will. Whereas previously the essential reality was a bare point of agency repelling all particularity of content, it is now differentiated internally as a universal or pure agency expressed in the actions of an intentional subject. This means that the willing of some determinate content is now contained within the concept of essential reality as the medium through which pure agency proves its constitutive power over things (§§ 109–11). We have, therefore, a new and more expansive conception of the self. Earlier, the interiority of personality was incapable of embracing the specific projects of the individual, for these had the significance of something brutely given in nature. Now, however, the self has interiorized particular interests and projects as expressions of the pure capacity for purposive action necessary for the latter's self-realization. Because, moreover, concrete purposes are now seen as belonging to the self rather than to what is other-than-self, the concept of action really emerges here for the first time (§ 113). At the stage of abstract right, conduct was voluntary but not intentional—that is, not the outward realization of an inner purpose or conception of the good. Hence it was not action in the fullest sense. At the moral standpoint, by contrast, the essence of personality is grasped precisely as this capacity to unfold or to externalize what is inward, to transform existence in light of a project self-consciously grasped.

Now what are the implications of this richer understanding of selfhood for the institutions generated at the previous standpoint? It is clear, first of all, that the new concept confirms and solidifies the rights to physical security and property left inchoate at the level of abstract right. The common will, after all, emerged as the universalization of the particular person's claim to freedom of acquisition, and so establishes at a minimum the person's rights against involuntary transactions as well as against breaches of mutual promises. For the libertarian rights-theorist, these negative rights are the only ones entailed by the supremacy of the common will, and on this restricted content of natural right he bases his claim concerning the autonomy of private law. No distributive considerations need enter the determination of private right, for the latter is independently intelligible as the embodiment of negative freedom. Indeed, at first sight it seems impossible to refute him. Ostensibly the common will adds nothing to the negative rights claimed at the previous standpoint except the form of consistency. How can the universalization of claims to negative rights yield anything more than negative rights?

Let us attempt to construct a dialogue on this point between Hegel and the libertarian rights-theorist. The latter will agree that the foundation of rights is the common will understood as the universalization of the individual's claim to the liberty to do as he chooses. If he is serious about rights, however, he must also make a claim about the ontological status of the common will. Specifically, he must claim that this will (which is reason) is not naturally subservient or instrumental to the satisfaction of appetite, for were this the case, one would never emerge from the sphere of contingent obligation into that of strict law and rights. He must claim, rather, that the common will has deontic force, or that it is itself a potential end or principle of action, one whose choice entails the renunciation of the principle of isolated self-interest. However, once the common will is thus accorded ontological primacy, the individual agent is now seen to be free in a more inclusive sense than before. For by virtue of that primacy, the law is potentially related to the agent not solely as an external and coercive restriction of selfish liberty, but also as an end immanent in his own will, as that in virtue of which his personal rights are first guaranteed. Thus, solely by virtue of the objective status of the common will (a status required for the intelligibility of rights), the individual agent is potentially self-determining, or capable of acting from contents generated by the will. And since the libertarian rights-theorist must acknowledge that status or cease to be a rights-theorist, he must admit that agents are potentially free in a sense broader than that which originally inspired the exclusive claim to negative rights.

The libertarian might object that, while the hypostasis of the common will might disclose a human capacity broader than that which generated an order confined to negative rights, this new potentiality does not logically require the expansion of rights beyond the negative ones. All that it requires is that the libertarian acknowledge the existence of a sphere of private virtue alongside the sphere of law. That is, it merely shows that a theory of rights cannot pretend to be an exhaustive account of moral duty. In addition to the duties correlative to rights, there are also purely moral duties to become the autonomous subject one inherently is. There is no necessity, however, to regard self-determination as something to which agents have an enforceable positive right, since the content of right-claims that were initially universalized were negative ones. Indeed, this seems to be the position of Kant.[22]

There are at least two responses one can make to this argument. In the first place, the libertarian's claim of right to negative liberty was originally based on a conception of personality that identified it with the abstract freedom from external determination or with the pure capacity for action. That capacity supported a claim of right only because it was thought to be the sole unconditioned and essential reality. But if the reason for claiming a right of negative liberty was a certain conception of personality, and of what is essential thereto, then the libertarian cannot coherently insist on that restricted claim in the face of a revision to the idea of personality that he is required to make. If the nature of personality determines what rights persons have, then an expanded conception of the person must entail an expanded inventory of rights.

Secondly, negative rights against coercive transactions are themselves explicable only on the basis of a right to self-determination in the concrete sense. No unconsented to taking of property, after all, can touch the liberty of the formal will, for the latter is capable of transcending, and so of ceasing to identify itself with, any attachment to a particular thing. Since the will is able to renounce any specific desire, it is coercible only to the extent that it chooses not to do so, which is to say, it is not coercible at all in determinate objects (§ 91). Hence no taking of property or threat thereof can infringe a right to the formal liberty of choice. If such takings or threats are wrongful, therefore, it can only be because they interfere with freedom objictified in intentional action. That is, they implicitly deny the right to the expression of freedom in property, or else they force the victim to choose between options neither of which he would have chosen for himself. But if the libertarian thus postulates a right to intentional action, can he coherently limit that right to its negative embodiments? Must he not also acknowledge a positive right to the conditions that make intentional action possible?

Once again the libertarian will appeal to the logical origins of the right to self-determination. That right originated, he will argue, in the universalization of right-claims to negative freedom, and in this process only negative rights were generated. Consequently, there is no necessity to regard the right to self-determination as having an independent or transcendent life so as to require the unfolding of its entire implicit content. On the contrary, that right has a specific logical derivation, and its content cannot be greater than that which was present in its germ.

It is at this point that the form of the transition from abstract right to morality provides the decisive answer. The common will, it is true, is merely the universalization of the claim of right of the particular will. However, this means that if we logically excavate the order constituted by the common will, we find a more primitive order based on the supposed primacy of the particular ego, an order in which the common will is derivative or posited. Moreover, the demonstration that the common will is the basis of right is just the process whereby the particular will (a) objectifies its right-claim in social property, (b) claims a right (in crime) to negate its objective reality, a claim that is self-contradictory, (c) acknowledges the priority of what it has hitherto regarded as its creature. Accordingly, if the common will is now grasped as an ontological *prius* (as it must be if there are any rights), this can only have occurred through its *emancipation* from its origins in the particular will and through its hypostasis over against the latter (§§ 82, 104–05). Indeed, the universalization of the claims of formal liberty is nothing but this process of emancipation. But once we see that the right to self-determination is born not *from* the particular will but precisely in the common will's emancipation from the latter, we also see that the content of that right cannot coherently be tethered to the negative claims of the particular ego. Rather, its entire implicit content must now be unfolded as a content of right. The universalization of claims to negative freedom yields rights not only to negative but also to positive freedom. The libertarian can resist this conclusion only by resisting the hypostasis of the common will. But then he must cease to be a rights-theorist.

The right of the individual to self-determination must be developed to the full extent of its implications. Now some second-generation rights of autonomy will be easily accommodated by the structure of private law as developed under the previous paradigm. For example, the agent's right of self-determination implies the right to have imputed to him only those deeds that are either explicitly or implicitly contained in his intention (§§ 107, 117–118). Such a right against strict liability is obviously consistent with the framework of private law, since it actually enlarges the scope of negative liberty. On the other hand, the right to self-determination also implies the right to treat one's welfare or the satisfaction of one's determinate aims, as a legitimate object of concern (§§ 114, 121, 123–24). When universalized as an independent moral end, moreover, this principle yields a duty of concern for the welfare of others, and ultimately for welfare in the abstract (§ 125). Such a duty is much less obviously consistent with the principle of private right; indeed, the possibility of conflict is ever-present. Since the content of welfare is at this point drawn from the immediate preferences of agents, while the right consists in respect for agency itself, any harmony of the good and the right is purely a coincidence (§ 125).

Nevertheless, the moral duty to promote the general welfare does not at this point threaten the autonomy of private law. Where welfare is understood as the satisfaction of contingent preferences, it is true to say that the right is prior to the good and so a constraint on its pursuit. The right is prior because, as Hegel says, "my particularity . . . is only a right at all insofar as I am a free entity" (§ 126). The satisfaction of agent-relative projects is an object worthy of moral concern only because it expresses and realizes a pure capacity for self-activity. That capacity is prior to its instantiations in concrete action for specific goals and is the basis for the latter's ontological status. Accordingly, the greater good of others can never justify invading the very ground upon which welfare first rises to moral significance.

On the other hand, the potential conflict between the positive duty to promote the general welfare and the negative right of respect for agency reveals the inadequacy of each as an embodiment of the right to self-determination. By itself, the right to respect for abstract agency entails no positive right to the material conditions of intentional action, or even to the means for the legal vindication of one's negative rights. For its part, the moral criterion of welfare submerges the right of personality not to be used for ends external to its own. Pursued one-sidedly, each pole leads to consequences destructive of the right to self-determination. Accordingly, that right is intelligible only as a synthesis of welfare and abstract right (§ 128). The right to self-determination implies a right to the goods needed by everyone in order to ensure that action realizes self-chosen projects. Conversely, welfare becomes the object of moral concern not as the satisfaction of contingent preferences but as the realization in each individual of the human capacity for intentional action. This synthesis of welfare and abstract right Hegel calls the good (§ 129).

It is at this point that the moral standpoint threatens to submerge the sphere of private law. To see why this is so, consider the relationship of the good both to welfare and to abstract right. Here we should attend to Hegel's own words:

> In this idea [of the good], welfare has no independent validity as the embodiment of a single particular will but only as universal welfare and essentially as universal in principle, i.e. as according with freedom. Welfare without right is not a good. Similarly, right without welfare is not the good; *fiat justitia* should not be followed by *pereat mundus*. Consequently, since the good must of necessity be actualized through the particular will and is at the same time its substance, it has absolute right in contrast with the abstract right of property and the particular aims of welfare. If either of these moments becomes distinguished from the good, it has validity only in so far as it accords with the good and is subordinated to it (§ 130).

In the good defined as the individual actualization of concrete freedom, abstract right and welfare have been in one sense cancelled and in another sense preserved. Abstract right is cancelled insofar as it signified a right to property and to freedom of contract enforceable without regard to their consequences for the welfare of others. *Fiat justitia* should not be followed by *pereat mundus*. Those rights are now inwardly limited by consequentialist considerations of a particular sort—specifically, by the equal right of all agents to the necessary conditions of self-determined action. On the other hand, property and contract are preserved as essential embodiments of individual autonomy and so as part (but only part) of the totality of objective goods to which agents have a right. Likewise cancelled is the moral criterion of welfare insofar as it enjoined the satisfaction of contingent or agent-relative values. It is preserved, however, insofar as it is reconceived as the individual actualization of the pure capacity for autonomy, and so as demanding the satisfaction of objective or agent-neutral needs related to that end. When rights of property and of contract are limited for the sake of welfare so conceived, they are limited not by the particular good of others but by the common good of freedom, and hence for the sake of the right itself.

If we now look back over the course we have travelled, we discover what is perhaps a surprising development. Beginning with a claim of unconditional reality on the part of the particularistic and formal will, we were driven by a logic internal to the notion of the unconditioned to a universal will establishing equal rights of objective freedom. Moreover, because this will attained the status of the unconditioned by freeing itself from the particular will and negating its primacy, the right to objective freedom had to be specified as an autonomous principle. Thus, negative rights against misfeasances had to be subsumed under a broader principle of right that included positive rights of self-determination and their correlative duties of concern. Accordingly, the standpoint of the priority of the right has, by a necessity immanent to its own principle, driven us to a common good inwardly constitutive of private rights.

It is this necessity which constitutes the logical ground for the contemporary crisis of private law. Under the new paradigm of right, proprietary and contractual rights are internally limited by distributive considerations. Hence consequentialist arguments are now relevant to the determination of individual entitlements, while duties of assistance, because correlative to prior rights, become suitable for legal enforcement. At this stage, moreover, the alienation of autonomy in abstract right—the necessity by which deeds estranged from intentions are empowered against individuals[23]—now appears as a contradiction of right and so as something to be removed. This means, at a minimum, that legislatures may, without violating rights, enact positive legislation limiting property rights and contractual freedom for the sake of the autonomy of all. However, does it not also mean that judges must, in determining rights in private disputes, apply the criterion of the common good so as to enforce positive duties of concern for others as intentional agents? Must they not (in general) seek to cancel the self's estrangement in abstract right by annulling the power of deeds divorced from concrete intentions? Must they not (in particular) invalidate a contract of adhesion formally consented to or void a contract mistakenly agreed to (or agreed to under circumstances unexpectedly altered) if doing so will upset no morally justified expectations in the promisee? Must they not, on the same ground, restrict the consent defence in tort by requiring not simply a formal consent to risk but a concrete acceptance of the consequences of formal consent? Must they not protect as "quasi-property" public goods already alienated for value as well as reasonable reliance on promises? And finally, must they not seek to shift losses due to personal injury and property damage to the party best able to distribute them so as to avoid the ruin of a single individual? The point is that, once private rights are seen to be constituted by distributive justice, it is difficult to see how a judge of a private dispute can avoid reference to that standard without perverting the court into a tool of privilege. The primacy of the good thus threatens to collapse the distinction not only between private law and public law but also between adjudication and progressive taxation.

Before considering what Hegel teaches us about the resolution of this crisis, we should first examine an argument purporting to vindicate the autonomy of private law adjudication from the standpoint of the requirements of distributive justice itself. Ever since the appearance of Lon Fuller's *Forms and Limits of Adjudication*,[24] it has become commonplace to argue that private law adjudication is structurally unsuited to the implementation of distributive goals. For one thing, these goals make relevant the claims of persons disenfranchised by the binary model of adjudication, so that judgments informed by distributive considerations will likely skew the distribution in favour of someone randomly selected by the occurrence of a cause of action, while imposing on the loser a disproportionate share of the compensation burden. Such an imbalance can be avoided only if judges take into account the distributive ramifications of a rule of decision and expertly make the necessary adjustments. However, this requires a managerial perspective capable of surveying the distributive system as a whole, as well as access to information typically beyond the competence of a judge to gather and process. Furthermore, the criterion of the good is indeterminate with respect to the manifold ways of realizing it, and so requires a discretion for which political accountability is appropriate. Finally, it is irrational, one might argue, to pursue a patterned distributive goal in the *ad hoc* fashion demanded by the nature of adjudication. For in doing so, we tie the achievement of this goal to chance transactions between individuals, even though transactions are quite incidental to the distributive purpose. Again, therefore, we are self-contradictorily selective in the application of our principle of distributive justice, granting a windfall to someone whose incapacity was caused by another human being.

Now clearly, the first two of these arguments do not tell against the use of adjudication *per se* for the realization of public law goals. They merely indicate the need for a transformation of common law adjudication from a binary to a more participatory model in order to render it a more efficient instrument of the public good. The inadequacy of an existing institution to the dominant conception of right can hardly be said to demonstrate its independence of the conception; rather, it attests to the historicity of the institution. The third argument no doubt points to the shortcomings for distributive purposes of any transaction-based apparatus, however extensive the participation or managerial the decisionmaker. Yet this argument too has its limitations. In the first place, it is in no sense a vindication of private law as such; it has nothing to say, for example, against the total submersion of tort law in a legislative scheme of social insurance, or against the displacement of contract by central planning. Secondly, it is an argument only against using common law adjudication as a substitute for a comprehensive and rational scheme of social welfare. Once such a scheme is in place, however, the argument has no force against the interstitial application of distributive criteria to private disputes in the lacunae left by the welfare system or in circumstances where the system breaks down.[25]

Furthermore, there are modes of actualizing the good that are not inconsistent with the randomness of the occasions for doing so. This is the place to draw a distinction that will later prove important in reconciling the independence of private law with the priority of the good. The distinction is between an autonomy jurisdiction of courts that, while having a redistributive effect, aims at no distributive goal or pattern and one that does have such a goal in view. An autonomy jurisdiction with a redistributive purpose might impose strict liability on enterprises capable of distributing losses, or might impose liability on the party better able to bear the loss; and it would block any attempt by these parties contractually to exclude their responsibility. In adopting such redistributive strategies, the court undoubtedly creates a tension between the aim of adjudication and the transactional framework within which the aim is pursued. For example, the accident victim may have a right to insurance against severe misfortune, but why should the defendant be singled out from the community to be the insurer? The plaintiff has a right to welfare only because the idea of a common will is unintelligible otherwise; his right is thus the correlate of the state's duty to conform to the notion of a state. This means, however, that his right counts only against the collectivity, not against any specific individual. Imposing liability on the defendant, therefore, amounts to coerced beneficence, a violation of right.

There is, however, another way in which courts might actualize the agent's right to autonomy. They might do so by cancelling the power of abstract right insofar as the latter would, if strictly enforced, negate the right to intentional action. So, for example, they might prevent someone from asserting his property right in circumstances where doing so would amount to oppression; or they might guard persons against legal detriment for deeds bearing no connection to their interests where doing so would frustrate no morally reasonable expectations in the party standing to benefit. Because it aims at no global distributive pattern, an autonomy jurisdiction of this limited sort encounters no anomaly in a transaction-based medium, involves no random tax on losers, and makes relevant no interests unrepresented in the litigation. To be sure, the court imposes on the party seeking enforcement of an unconscionable contract a duty to forgo an advantage for the benefit of another. Yet this is not coerced beneficence, because here the right of the defendant does indeed single out the plaintiff as the bearer of the correlative duty. The plaintiff has no coercive duty to confer a benefit on the defendant independently of any transaction. He does, however, have such a duty once a transactional nexus is established, for the right to self-determination is concretized in transactions as a right to be held accountable only for deeds that embody some reasonable definition of one's interests. Since this instantiation of the right is a right with respect to transactions, it demands a bilateral form of dispute resolution just as tightly as does the correlativity of right and duty in abstract right.

In that it remains coherently tied to transactions, the limited autonomy jurisdiction just outlined does not fundamentally undermine the independence of private law. At this point, however, such a limitation is arbitrary, for the inner constitution of the right by the good is pregnant with more farreaching implications. Specifically, the transition from the paradigm of abstract right to that of morality fundamentally historicizes—and so destabilizes—the model of corrective justice and the binary form of adjudication it presupposes. It creates an impetus toward the submersion of corrective in distributive justice, toward corollary reforms in causation and liability rules, and toward the remodelling of the adjudicative process itself so as to make it a fit instrument for distributive purposes. It creates pressures, too, for the displacement of tort law by a scheme of social insurance, for the subordination of contract to a regulatory regime that would allow advantage-taking only when it serves the common good,[26] or for the negation of contract itself as the primary engine of the social distribution of advantages. Against the momentum toward the abolition of tort law, Professor Weinrib's claim that the latter is coherent only as an embodiment of corrective justice self-confessedly has no power.[27] But neither does that argument tell against the movement to restructure tort law from within (through strict liability and relaxed causation requirements) in conformity with its newly conceived purpose. For if the argument states that the *idea* of private law is unthinkable except as corrective justice, then it is true but tautological, establishing no essential connection between the model of corrective justice and the historical existence of tort law. Hence the model exerts no normative force *vis-à-vis* the common-law process. If, on the other hand, the argument is that corrective justice is the essential nature of tort law in history, then (absent an account of corrective justice from the standpoint of the good) it does no more than arbitrarily elevate certain historical features of tort law (causation, fault) into the essence of tort law as well as eternalize a particular historical form of common-law adjudication.

THE CRITIQUE OF THE MORAL STANDPOINT

Once the basis of right is conceived as the self-determination of the will, there is no vindication of private law from the standpoint of the priority of the right. For that standpoint has been shown to be radically unstable and finite. If private law is to be restored to independence, therefore, it must be restored on new foundations. Specifically, it must be rehabilitated on the basis of an immanent critique of the moral standpoint itself, one that will bring into view an even more comprehensive foundation of freedom and of right.

What, according to Hegel, is the defect of the moral standpoint? In the *Philosophy of Right.* he writes:

> The subjective will, directly aware of itself, and distinguished from the principle of the will . . . , is therefore abstract, restricted, and formal. But not merely is subjectivity itself formal; in addition, as the infinite self-determination of the will, it constitutes the form of all willing. In this, its first appearance in the single will, this form has not yet been established as identical with the concept of the will, and therefore the moral point of view is that of relation, of ought-to-be, or demand. And since the self-difference of subjectivity involves at the same time the character of being opposed to objectivity as external fact, it follows that the point of view of consciousness comes on the scene here too . . . The general point of view here is that of the will's self-difference, finitude, and appearance (§ 108).

The moral standpoint was attained by universalizing the claim of final worth implicit in the agency of the atomistic person. Hence that standpoint continues to posit as its initial and underived premise the isolated individual in the state of nature, investing that individual with a fixed and stable reality. What is merely given and nonrational is thus arbitrarily accorded the status of an absolute reality. The individual is posited "outside reason" (NL 72). It is true that the natural self is conceived differently than before; his aims are now understood as determinations of a self rather than as brute impulses of nature and so as inherently worthy of regard. Nevertheless, because determinate aims are identified with those of the isolated individual, they have the significance of the relative as *opposed* to the absolute, of the subjective as *opposed* to the objective. A disparity thus emerges between the concept or potential of the will as self-determining and its existence as dependent for expression on a content particular to the individual (§ 131). The will must therefore overcome this contradiction and become the autonomous will that it inherently is. However, because determinateness signifies the one-sidedly subjective and particular, the universal good of self-determination must again be conceived by abstraction from determinateness *per se* and so as the abstract autonomy of wills that will nothing but the equal freedom of persons for duty's sake (§ 133). This good now stands opposed to the pursuit of particularistic conceptions of welfare as to a sphere of arbitrary liberty and heteronomy outside it. Hence the good assumes the significance of an "ought" forever opposed to a foreign and intractable "is". This fixed opposition (between the impersonal and the personal) the moral standpoint takes to be an objective or metaethical reality, one which it merely discovers. Yet it is the moral standpoint itself which, by virtue of its atomistic presuppositions, generates the opposites with which it is constantly preoccupied.

The opposition of the good to existence is, however, only one side of the picture presented to the moral outlook. The good, after all, is only truly the good if it is the inner essence and truth of what is, so that the moral standpoint is the contradiction between the claim that the good is the inner essence of reality and that it stands opposed to an alien reality (§ 109). Correspondingly, it is the contradiction between the claim that the self-seeking self has no solid and independent reality and the claim that it is precisely the fundamental reality. This dualistic concept of nature implies two equally eligible possibilities of human motivation. The individual agent may either make his particularistic welfare the end of his activity, or he may will the universal good for its own sake. Because each of these contrary possibilities has the sanction of nature, each must be taken as separately grounding a necessary form of the good's realization (NL 84).[28] In this way, the dualistic self of the moral standpoint causes a fissure in the moral life between two mutually exclusive spheres of endeavour, each of which will, by virtue of its exclusion of the other, effect a dissolution of natural right.

If we initially presuppose the agent in pursuit of particularistic values, then the vindication of the common good as his essential nature takes the form of a legal order constraining his outward actions by means of external compulsion (NL 85). Thus a contingent possibility of human motivation generates a legal order whose inherent nature is to be indifferent to inward character and coercive. The law is no doubt coercive only for the bad man; but it is the perspective of the bad man that here defines the essential nature of law. The natural coerciveness and externality of the legal order, moreover, has the effect of transforming each of its poles into its respective opposite. Given the natural egoism of the subject, the sole basis for the purely legal obligation to obey the law is that of compulsion. Within the legal order, therefore, the common good has no *moral* force and is thus indistinguishable from arbitrary human violence; the right becomes the wrong. Conversely, since legal obligation rests on coercion alone, it follows that it must repose on the agent's amenability to coercion. Accordingly, if circumstances are such that the law cannot possibly deter him, his obligation ceases and therewith the authority of a court to punish him: the wrong becomes the right.[29] Again, were the common good ever completely victorious in the legal sphere, the result would be an order in which the property, talents, and energies of the agent belong to the common will rather than to himself. But since the common good is precisely the universalization of *freedom*, its complete vindication would be simultaneously its negation. Hence the life of the legal order must consist in a restless tension between the poles of universal and individual freedom, wherein the good must seek at once to realize itself and restrain itself from self-realization. This tension, however, effects a bifurcation in the notion of the right. On the one hand, a natural right of personality could find no repose outside a common good inwardly constitutive of individual rights; yet the realization of the good is just the alienation of personality, the very foundation of the good. Thus, each pole of the legal order (the good and liberty) seeks the other for its own reality and yet, since they are also antithetical, each must shun the other to preserve its reality. This means that, from each side, the other is both something positive and essential and something negative and contingent. Therefore, each side is to itself at once positive and negative, which is to say that each has an acknowledged right against the other. At the level of adjudication, this means that the forms of distributive and corrective justice may now with equal justification (and so with equal barrenness) claim to be the paradigmatic form of right. The bifurcation in the right is, however, the negation of right, for the determination of rights is now subject to an unconstrained ideological choice as between the primacy of the individual and the primacy of the good.

If in the legal order, the moral law is an external force, and if in this externality it is self-contradictory as a moral law, still, it *should* be self-legislated, the individual will should be united with the universal, and in this union both the moral law and the individual should be realized.[30] Accordingly, if we now take as primary the common good and its inner constitution of reality, then its vindication as the essential nature takes the form of a private morality wherein the agent endeavours to purify his will of particularistic ends and to will only the universal good for its own sake. The morality here is private: just as the legal order was reflexively determined as coercive in opposition to morality, so the moral life is reflexively determined as private in opposition to the public and objective order of legal rights. Because, in other words, the public order is essentially coercive, genuine autonomy is possible only outside it—in the solitary communion of the will with itself. Furthermore, because all material content of law has been laid at the door of the isolated subject, the willing of what is universal must be a willing of the abstract form of law rather than of any determinate laws. Moral action, however, of necessity entails the willing of some specific duty, and the question now is whether the moral agent can act and still remain moral.

The answer to this question depends on whether the form of law can determine a content conformable to its universality and necessity, either by way of inward specification or by way of external application to a given material. Now since the universal good was conceived precisely by abstraction from material content, there is no possibility here of an immanent specification from the good of a content adequate to its universal form. A will whose essence is to be devoid of content cannot spontaneously determine itself without self-negation (§ 135, Phen. 440–45, NL 75–76). If, however, the good cannot generate duties in the manner of a legislator, can it test contents given *ab extra* in the manner of a constitutional court? Kant's first formulation of the categorical imperative suggests noncontradiction as a possible criterion. A given maxim of the will must be capable of universalization as law without self-destruction. Yet as Hegel points out, one must presuppose as necessary the principle negated by a given maxim of the will before the destruction of that principle constitutes a contradiction (§ 135, Phen. 447 ff, NL 77). For example, the universalization of theft destroys the notion of property. But the absence of property is a contradiction of something only if one initially posits the institution of property without the aid of the Kantian test. And if one initially posits the institution of property, then of course the categorical imperative is quite superfluous as a formula for deriving duties. At best, therefore, the categorical imperative works only if one assumes the very content to be demonstrated as necessary; at worst, it is indiscriminately permissive, since it offers no guide as to which of two contrary principles (e.g. property or no property) should be established as necessary, leaving this choice to the caprice of the agent. But to make one's inclinations the principle of one's actions is precisely the essence of immorality (Phen. 450, NL 78).

Whether as a legal or as a moral order, therefore, the objectification of the good as the essential nature of the agent is in reality the collapse of natural law into a radical indeterminacy of moral choice. In the one case, its self-validation required it to suppress the very self whose good it claimed to be, and thus to reveal itself, from the individualist's point of view, as the bad. In the other case, its self-verification required the moral action of the individual agent and so implicated the very particularity it had deemed incompatible with its nature. Now a critical consciousness views the indeterminacy so generated as itself an immutable feature of reality, and sees the task of legal cognition as one of continually reproducing it out of the fixed dichotomies of legal discourse.[31] As the reflective self-awareness of the entire preceding episode of thought, this criticism consists in the confounding of notions which a naive formalism holds far apart, in the debunking of law as a mask for passion and in the praise of passion as that which alone has essential reality. By means of this enterprise, the agent finds in moral rebellion the objective worth that eluded him in moral action. For by expressing the vanity of impersonal and disinterested structures, criticism simultaneously affirms the reality of the isolated ego.

Yet this reality is itself vain. Aware of it only through the unreality of impersonal orders, the critic must depend for his being on a regime which he continually shows to be unstable. Moreover, in positing indeterminacy as an objective fact, the critical consciousness reveals itself as sharing the same assumptions as its dogmatic opponent regarding the fixed reality of the atomistic self and the unalterable tension between "individualist" and "communitarian" natures to which the former prejudice inevitably leads. What this consciousness fails to see is that radical indeterminacy was the *result* of a particular way of conceptualizing the good. Specifically, it was the result of conceiving the good in such a way as to exclude from its essence the very action and knowledge of the individual agent upon which it depended for self-confirmation. It was the outcome, moreover, of the refusal of the poles of consciousness to remain in the fixed opposition assumed by both the moral and the critical standpoints. The good obtained objective realization as the good only through the moral action and insight of the agent; while conversely the agent attained his essential reality not in his immediate and isolated existence, but only in self-transcending action for the sake of the good. Grasped in thought, this unity of the good with the action and knowledge of the agent is Ethical Life, and we now have to understand both its structure and its relation to the institutions developed under the previous paradigms of right.

PRIVATE LAW IN ETHICAL LIFE

At the stages of both abstract right and morality, the concept of freedom was rendered abstract and one-sided by its having been reflexively conditioned by the empirical agent. Because the isolation of the agent from other agents was assumed to be a necessity of nature, all particularity of inclination and willing signified the exclusive and hence purely accidental particularity of the atomistic individual. Consequently, the universal structure of freedom had to be grasped by abstraction from the required medium of its self-expression, so that the latter process entailed the will's surrender to something foreign. Now at the stage of Ethical Life, we no longer assume the constancy of the isolated agent, that assumption having been refuted by the very *praxis* of morality. Hence, too, we no longer allow the finitude of the atomistic self to define or to obscure the nature of the unconditioned. The latter is now conceived not as a subjective causality forever limited by a reality bereft of immanent purpose, but rather as the indwelling and objective end of reality itself.

Regarded as a concept, then, Ethical Life is the idea of freedom emancipated from the limitations of the empirical agent and thus allowed to develop unperturbed the elements intrinsic to its nature. So conceived, freedom implies, first, the differentiation of a capacity for spontaneity from the external necessity that, despite all its inward organization, characterizes the physical world. This capacity is the will or self-consciousness. By virtue of its spontaneity, moreover, the will necessarily affirms itself as the end or cause of that from which it originally distinguished itself. Because, in other words, spontaneity originates in an irruption from nature rather than by appearing ready-made alongside it, it primordially produces nature as an object in the very act by which it affirms itself. Inherently, therefore, the being of nature is not its immediate, atomistic existence but its existence as mediated by or attorned to the will. Furthermore, because an unactualized end is not objectively an end, freedom implies, secondly, the outward transformation of nature into a medium for the realization of the will's causality, this transformation taking place through the mediation of some specific project as well as through the instrumentality of the body. The objectification of the will's causality would, however, remain forever incomplete as an external and one-sided domination of the object if the outward movement of the will were not met by the spontaneous self-transcendence of the object toward its own immanent reality. Freedom, therefore, is the dialectical unity formed by the interpenetration of distinct elements, each of which is itself the whole (§ 142–43). The substantive or universal will presupposes the free recognition of its causality by the particular desiring agent, just as (therefore) the particular agent presupposes the universal will as the foundation of its essential reality. Accordingly, the bond between the universal and the particular will such that each sees in the other, not an indifferent or hostile object, but its own confirmation and support, is the concept of action or of freedom. The standard of right is the actualization of the causality of this concept, that is, its existence as a political life wherein public and private spheres, though distinct, are mutually confirming.[32]

When it first appears in the *Philosophy of Right*, the concept of Ethical Life (the Ethical Idea) is one-sided and incomplete. The historical reality to which it corresponds is the *polis*, which Hegel in his maturity regarded as an imperfect and ultimately self-contradictory embodiment of Ethical Life. The limitations of the Idea will become apparent when we consider the dilemma that a philosophy of law based on this principle must encounter. Were philosophy to interpret private law in terms of the causality of the objective will, the former would be revealed as, in its real existence, a dim prefiguration of man's communal essence, naturally subordinate to the clearer reflections visible in explicit acts of citizenship. Private law may assert itself to be an autonomous system; however, its independence, one could argue, is nothing serious, as Athena shows when, in Aeschylus' play, she vanquishes the Eumenides and placates them with a subordinate role in the city (NL 105). Because it is oriented to a human good conceived objectively, an interpretation of this sort would doubtless account for the normativity of private law, but it would do so at the cost of the immanence of the explanation. The object of cognition will have been transformed in the account into something other than its existence for itself, and the latter will have been asserted to be a nullity. Such a disjunction between the object as cognized and the object as it exists in itself would, however, embarrass cognition, for the latter could no longer claim to be cognition *of* the object (Phen. 141–42). On the other hand, to avoid this *cul-de-sac*, philosophy might surrender to the self-existence of private law, interpreting it in terms of the presumed causality of the person. Since, however, the principle of free personality is not contained in the Ethical Idea, such an interpretation would lose contact with the good and so, while achieving immanence, would have done so by sacrificing normativity. That is, an account of private law in terms of the priority of the right would lead to the normative impasse already described.

Now it is Hegel's position that this tension between immanence and normativity is surmountable, or that there can be an internalist account of private law from the standpoint of the priority of the good. The possibility of such an account is given precisely by the limitations of the *polis* as an ethical community. The original form of Ethical Life is imperfect, because it has not yet made conceptual room for the concrete individual agent who asserts *himself* as an end and who seeks objective confirmation for that certainty (§§ 185, 260A, Phen. 434, 501). Hence the substantive will lacks proof of its causality in the extreme of individual self-seeking, or in the extreme of individual choice, intention, and insight. At this point, the standard of right is the objective ethical *order* standing over against the individual, an order towards which the agent is directed unreflectively and which thus has the significance of immemorial custom (§ 144–45, Phen. 478 ff., 498). The appropriation or internalization of that order by the existing subject is at this point deemed inessential to the right, even though the Ethical Idea, as the dialectical unity of thought and action, implicitly contains this moment. Thus the ethical order is called "a circle of necessity" to which individuals are related as "accidents to substance" (§ 145). "Whether the individual exists or not," writes Hegel, "is all one to the objective ethical order" (§ 145A). Liberal critics have fastened on such statements as evidence of their view that Hegel exalts the state at the expense of the individual. They are not mistaken in concluding that the Ethical Idea submerges the concrete individual subject, but only in assuming that the Ethical Idea is Hegel's last word about right. "The concept of this Idea," he writes, "has being only as Spirit" (§ 157). Precisely because the ethical order is one-sided in relation to the independent individual, it must realize its causality by *subduing* the very individual upon whom it depends for confirmation, thereby negating itself as the good in the very process of its self-realization (Phen. 484–99). Moreover, this outcome manifests the tension latent in the Ethical Idea from the start. In concept, the Ethical Idea is a dialectical unity of the conceptual and the practical, of the universal will and its realization in the patriotic action of citizens. *Qua* concept, however, it incorporates the agent's activity only as something ideal or universal, only as the thought of activity, and is thus again one-sided in relation to existence. As such it is self-contradictory: its undifferentiated existence contradicts its implicitly dialectical nature. But the self-discordance of the Ethical Idea *qua* Idea reveals the necessity in reason of that which is radically distinct from the Idea. It reveals the necessity, namely, of the concrete individual who asserts himself as an end and who, in doing so, repudiates the causality of the objective will (Phen. 501–02).

This repudiation is a mistake, but a necessary mistake. It is necessary because the individual's self-assertion is inconsistent with, and so ultimately destructive of, the ethical order whose unity was based precisely on the exclusion from being of the concrete particularity of the individual. In the ethical order, the individual acquired substantial reality only as an instance of the universal, only as a citizen and warrior devoted to public causes; as an independent individual existing for himself, he was an "insubstantial shadow" (Phen. 470). Accordingly, the individual's self-affirmation must take the form of a rejection of the naturalness of community and hence of a claim of reality for the *isolated* self. On the other hand, the repudiation of community is mistaken, because this very self-assertion is necessitated by the Idea's self-discordance, and so is inherently embedded within the causality of a whole (Spirit) of which the Idea is one moment and the ethical action of the individual the other. Stated otherwise, it is the Ethical Idea which organically distinguishes subjective freedom from itself, and which therefore suspends or conceals its own priority, abandoning itself to the assumed primacy of the isolated agent. In doing so, moreover, it sunders itself internally into the antithesis between the universal and the particular will to which the assumed priority of the individual necessarily leads. It therefore posits within itself the appearance of the individual's independence as well as the appearance of dichotomy in order that, through the dissolution of dichotomy, through the return of the individual to his ground, and through the consequent reinstatement of the whole, it might be vindicated as the foundation of the real. However, this restored totality is not the one-sided ethical order that constituted the starting-point of the process. Rather it is this order inwardly differentiated so as to include the process of its objectification, which process necessitates individual freedom and is thus the ultimate basis of its rights (Phen. 80–81).

It now becomes apparent how Hegel can claim to offer an immanentist account of private law from the standpoint of the priority of the good. That claim rests on the premise that the objective ethical order, by virtue of distinguishing the self-centered agent from itself, dwells within the state of nature *as viewed from the amoral perspective of the agent.* Because the Ethical Idea organically differentiates free personality as an isolated person, a contradiction arises between the latter's subjective claim of final worth and the objective reality of this claim in the whole. Consequently, the person's activity will consist in confirming his certainty of final worth by receiving it back from another self whose finality and hence validating power he reciprocally constitutes. This activity will belie the presumed naturalness of the atomistic individual as well as the connected claim to self-sufficiency of abstract personality. The latter will be revealed as requiring confirmation of its finality through the mutual self-renunciation of empirical individuals in contract. In this way, private law will instantiate the structure of interlocking wholes that characterizes the Ethical Idea, but it will do so precisely as an objectification of the presumed natural right of the agent, to whose perspective the philosopher can thus surrender without losing hold of the Idea. Accordingly, instead of dissolving private law in a monochrome and static idea of community, philosophy will reveal community in the determinate (i.e. legal and abstract) shape peculiar to persons who spurn community, thereby simultaneously reclaiming the state of nature for the Idea and expounding private law from its own point of view. The philosophy of private law will thus be as much an account from the standpoint of the priority of the right as it is an account from the standpoint of the priority of the good, and it will be the one *because* it is the other. The immanence (and hence reality) of the good will be confirmed by the philosopher's revealing it in the self-oriented activity of the agent; while the normativity of right will be guaranteed by the necessary link between this activity and the reality of the good.

Hegel's solution can be further clarified by contrasting his mature position with that of his youth. Recall that in his early writings, the priority of the right was an appearance that obscured the true subordination of private law to the good. The appearance, though necessary for the self-objectification of the good, was essential only in the sense of providing a foil against which the good could manifest its supremacy by conquering its other. It was not a constituent element of the good itself and so had no positive significance: its truth was realized in negation (NL 93 ff, 98 ff, 103 ff). In the *Philosophy of Right.*, the priority of the right is still an appearance, since it is posited within the priority of the good. Now, however, the appearance is a necessary, constitutive element of the good itself, that in virtue of which alone the good is confirmed as the good *of* the agent. This is so in a double sense, corresponding to the two sides of the whole. On the one hand, it is only through the cultivation of, and protection for, a self-affirming and intentional agent that the good can ultimately be validated in the individual's free and intelligent devotion to the whole as to the objective support for his particularity (§ 187). Hence ethical life will incorporate and rationally establish the first generation rights of property and contract, whereby the individual affirms himself and is recognized by others as an end. It will also absorb and solidify the second-generation rights of self-determination, for the realization of the Ethical Idea as the good requires the cultivation not only of a choosing agent but also of one capable of choosing something as *his* good. It requires, in other words, an intentional self capable of organizing his commitments so as to give expression to a coherent and self-chosen conception of value. From the side of the Idea, therefore, private law will be significant as a realm of *Bildung* or education, wherein is developed an agent capable of self-consciously validating the priority of the Idea. Yet the agent will be capable of doing so precisely because the Idea makes room for the presumption of the priority of the agent and the rights entailed thereby in order to manifest itself as the essential nature of the individual. It is only through the suspension of the priority of the good so as to leave scope for the causality of the agent that the good is immanentized in the concrete individual, or that the individual can will the good as his *own*, as the rational foundation of his strictly private rights. The ethical order has surrendered its primacy to that of the individual agent; *therefore*, the individual can devote himself to the ethical order as to the basis of his distinctive reality. For the mature Hegel, then, the truth of private law is not something other than its appearance of independence; rather, it is just this appearance. Private law *is* the appearance of the priority of the right, because it is the Ethical Idea in its essential phase of self-concealment. The appearance itself, therefore, has ontological stability (Phen. 105) ("Appearance is the process of arising into being and passing away again, a process that itself does not arise and does not pass away, but is *per se*, and constitutes reality and the life-movement of truth.")

That the abandonment of the priority of the good is itself a necessary phase in the vindication of the good is the formula that secures at the heart of being the autonomy of private law. So conceived, this autonomy is no longer vulnerable to deconstruction, because it is no longer based on the presumed reality of a natural will unmediated by self-consciousness; rather it is now rooted in the inward and rational articulation of self-consciousness itself, in the conceptual requirements of freedom. Still, this solution raises more questions. First, how does the autonomy of private law survive the reinstatement of the whole in a fully realized Ethical Life? Second, if the priority of the right is an essential appearance posited *within* the priority of the good, the connection or inherent subordination of the right to the good must also be reflected in some way. How then does the autonomy of private law hold out against the bond that links this autonomy to the priority of the good?

Hegel's response to the first question can be formulated in the manner of his critique of Schelling in the preface to the *Phenomenology of Spirit* (77–84). The totality that is reinstated is not one that has left behind the pathway by which it came to be; rather, it is this pathway itself—the entire process of the Idea's self-objectification, a process revealed by philosophy as the integrated series of the Idea's manifestations. Each of the stages on the road to the philosophical grasp of the whole is itself an essential instantiation thereof, for the whole is truly such only as interiorizing its own process of validation in what is ostensibly other. This means that the realized whole—the whole explicitly posited as such—must be embodied institutionally in a way that does not swamp the phases in which the whole merely glimmers (§ 263–67). Specifically, it must be embodied not throughout the whole length and breadth of law but only in constitutional law, that is, in the law by which the legislative and executive organs of the state are integrated with the organic associations of society (§ 272–311).

The second question raises more difficulties. It cannot be doubted that, since each phase of the Idea's objectification is a progressively more adequate instantiation of its unity, the phases are ordered hierarchically within the totality. Thus the first generation rights of property and contract are subordinate to the rights of self-determination, which are in turn subordinate to the supreme right of the whole as manifested, for example, in national emergencies (§§ 230, 236, 258, 323–24). The problem, then, is to reconcile the subordination of abstract right to morality with the necessary concealment of the priority of the good in abstract right. At the moral standpoint itself, of course, this problem did not arise. Since the good opposed the sphere of private choice, the subordination of the right to the good took the form of the thoroughgoing submersion of the right in the good. In institutional terms, this meant the loss of support for the distinction between adjudication on the one hand and the political functions of legislation and administration on the other. In Ethical Life, on the other hand, this is precisely the form subordination must not take; the appearance of the priority of the right must be preserved no less than the reality of the priority of the good. And the way in which this reconciliation is embodied is through an institutional division between adjudication and administration, or between an institution whose specific intelligibility rests on the priority of the agent and one whose specific intelligibility rests on the priority of the good (§§ 229–30). Thus the full-blown differentiation between adjudication and administration, so problematic both from the libertarian standpoint of abstract right and from the communitarian standpoint of morality, becomes coherent for the first time within Ethical Life. Moreover, this difference is reflected in the structural features peculiar to each. Since adjudication determines the rights of isolated agents *vis-à-vis* one another, its focus is transactional and its aim corrective justice, from which supratransactional considerations of the good are excluded. Since administration implements the good, its work is purposefully redistributive and independent of transactions. The upshot is that Hegel provides a vindication of the structure of corrective justice more powerful than was available from the standpoint of the priority of the right. This is so because corrective justice is here vindicated not simply as an idea of reason bound in a heavenly embrace with the idea of a private law.[33] Rather, it is vindicated as the essential form of the historical law of transactions, just as binary adjudication is confirmed as the paradigmatic form of adjudication. It is not simply the case, in other words, that corrective justice is the formal structure of a law of transactions *if* there is a law of transactions. *That* there is a law of transactions is itself necessary, according to Hegel, for such a law embodies the concealment of the priority of the good that is required by the objective realization of the good itself.

TOWARD A UNIFIED THEORY OF PRIVATE LAW

To the strict institutional division of matters pertaining to the right and those pertaining to the good one qualification must be made. I shall introduce this qualification in the form of another question. Does the preservation of a sphere of activity ordered to the causality of the agent demand so rigid an exclusion of considerations of the good as to require the restoration in all its pristine independence of abstract right? Does it, in other words, demand a private law so narrowly ordered to the formal will of the person as to be utterly deaf to the claims of the intentional subject?

Here again Hegel's position takes the form of a bridge between abstract extremes. Because its rights are negative ones, rights-based theory has difficulty accommodating modern common law doctrines imposing what amounts to a positive duty of concern for the fruition of the projects of others. For example, the nascent duty of a promisee to inform the promisor of significant background facts of which he knows the latter to be ignorant cannot without strain be accounted for by a rights-based theory of contract law. No doubt a promisor's mistake as to the *terms* of the agreement will afford a defense under abstract right, provided the promisee knew or ought to have known of the error. For in that case the promisor has not actually assented to the agreement to which he manifested assent; the agreement as concluded no more proceeds from his will than it would have done had the promisor uttered the words in his sleep. Where, however, the promisor subjectively assents to the very terms to which he manifests assent, but is excused because, known to the promisee, the contract fails fundamentally to execute his purposes in concluding it, he is being accorded rights to disclosure not recognized under abstract right. Specifically, he is being accorded a right to the externalization of his concrete projects, something from which abstract right precisely abstracts. The same principle underlies the move to a general doctrine of inequality of bargaining power as a ground for rescinding an agreement. Fraudulent misrepresentation aside, the only coercive contracts that are voidable under abstract right are those extracted by duress of the person. Since the formal will (the only subject of rights here) can transcend and so renounce everything but itself, it is coerced only when threatened with the loss of the necessary conditions of its existence. Only in that case can it be said that external pressure has negated the voluntariness of assent. When, therefore, a court invalidates an agreement simply because one party has exploited its market power to dictate one-sided terms to another, it is once again enforcing rights that are invisible under abstract right. Here there is no question of involuntariness, since the weaker party can always renounce the preference that places him in the power of the stronger. Nor is there a lack of equivalence in the value of the things exchanged, for (as rights theory must acknowledge) there is no standard of equivalence between things independent of the equality of assenting wills. The agreement that is unconscionable under the modern doctrine is, accordingly, neither unjust in a purely procedural sense divorced from substance (the contract is voluntary) nor unjust in a purely substantive sense divorced from procedure (the values are equivalent). Rather it is unjust by a standard that demands a connection between the substantive terms of the contract and the subjective interests of both parties. If the weaker party is excused from performance of a one-sided bargain, it is because he has a positive right to the externalization of values he can recognize as his own; while the other party has a corresponding duty to forego any advantage which, if pressed, would sever the connection between the deed and any reasonable conception of the defendant's good.

Given the plethora of private law doctrines that embody a right to positive freedom, it is perhaps now timely to speak of the exhaustion of the theory of abstract right as an internalist account of private law.

On the other hand, instrumentalist theories of law, while entirely comfortable with legal doctrines imposing positive duties of social responsibility, have no principled means of stopping them from bursting the transactional framework of private law. Those, for example, who integrate such doctrines under a communitarian "countervision" to the model of abstract right have no reason to treat the existence of a contract between litigants as anything more than one factor among many (including fault, reliance, relative ability to pay) to be weighed in a "fair" allocation of losses.[34] From this standpoint, indeed, any attempt to contain the theoretical momentum of the counterprinciples within the individualistic framework of classical contract law gives rise to a fundamentally blind series of *ad hoc* compromises and adjustments that shatters the coherence of doctrine. The same marginalization of transactions on the part of instrumentalists is evident in contemporary theories of tort law. Thus wealth maximizers concerned with optimal deterrence must allocate losses due to accidents to the *category* of actors most likely to minimize costs rather than to the particular individual involved in the accident;[35] while those concerned with the distribution of losses have no reason intrinsic to their principle either for treating causation as a prerequisite of liability or for limiting the matter of redistribution to losses caused by human agents. Moreover, in circumstances where risk is generated from more than one source and injury results to a plurality of victims, neither loss distribution nor deterrence provides any reason for linking liability to a causal nexus between defendant's activity and plaintiff's injury. In such cases, the traditional form of litigation becomes a facade for the administration of a compensation scheme funded by a proportional tax.[36]

Now Hegel's philosophy of private law seems to account for the evolution of common law rights of welfare in a way that coherently preserves the transactional basis of private law. In doing so, moreover, it manifests stronger internalist credentials than formal rights theory, for it reveals the inward continuity of classical and modern phases of the common law, and thereby saves more of the phenomena without having to torture them into a classical mold. If private law is the appearance of the priority of the right necessarily posited within the good then judges must honour not only the distinctiveness of private law but also the architectonic structure within which this difference is first securely established. This means that they must respect the subsumption of first generation rights of liberty under second generation rights of intentionality to the extent compatible with the individualistic basis of private law and with the centrality of the transaction. It would seem that this reconciliation is accomplished to the extent that courts disempower abstract right whenever the latter conflicts with the right to self-determination of the agent. They disempower abstract right when, for example, they prevent the assertion of property rights to frustrate reasonable expectations known to the party wishing to assert them; when they excuse from contractual performance a party labouring under a mistaken assumption that could have been dispelled by the party seeking enforcement; and when they refuse legal effect to an agreement concluded under circumstances where one party has exploited vastly superior power to extract grossly one-sided terms.

In elaborating such doctrines, the courts are not, as Kant might have thought, incoherently enforcing with legal sanctions duties of subjective virtue. Rather, they are enforcing prior rights of self-determination—rights that were implied in the conceptual transition from a Hobbesian to a Kantian state of nature. Nor are the courts enforcing "counterprinciples" whose inner, communitarian logic explodes the individualistic foundations of contract. From the perspective of Hegel's thought, these principles represent, not a break with contract, but rather the bringing closer to its own notion of an institution whose initial shape contradicted the project it was intended to realize. That is to say, the enforcement of these principles actualizes the self-determination of the agent by revoking on various fronts the alienation of self that was sanctioned under the regime of abstract right. Such an enterprise in no way entails the subordination of contract to amorphous considerations of communal solidarity, for rights of intentionality, no less than the formal rights they subsume, actualize the causality of the individual agent. Hence the enterprise consists precisely and intelligibly in *ad hoc* corrections to an institution that remains the paradigmatic embodiment of individual autonomy. While the corrections are *ad hoc*, however, the confinement of the court's autonomy jurisdiction within bounds consistent with the integrity of transactions is not. No doubt it appears as such from the standpoint of morality, where the right of autonomy appeared as an undifferentiated principle of distributive justice whose operation transcended the narrow confines of bilateral transactions. From Hegel's standpoint, however, the limitation is conceptually demanded. For although it is true that private rights presuppose the good as their ultimate foundation and support, this is so only because the good also presupposes a sphere of private right as that which confirms it as the good. Accordingly, by enforcing a positive right to self-determination in a manner consistent with the coherence of transactions, common law courts pay instinctive regard to the dialectical structure of natural law.

Finally, the unity-in-difference of the right and the good restores the distinction between law and politics in a way that concedes as little to formalists as it does to critical theorists. It rejects formalism because it rejects a distinction between law and politics based on the crude dichotomy between a private sphere of natural right emptied of the good on the one hand, and a public sphere of contingent choices among competing values on the other. It affirms instead a distinction between law and politics based on the internal articulation of a unified concept of natural law. The distinction now is one between the enforcement of a right to self-determination in a way that preserves the necessary appearance of the priority of the agent and the enforcement of such a right in a way that affirms the hierarchical superiority of the good within the architectonic of ethical life. Furthermore, by healing the rift between private right and public good, Hegel's principle cancels the indeterminacy of moral choice that seemed to collapse the liberal conception of law into the liberal conception of politics. A court is not free to choose between abstractly individualistic values and abstractly communitarian values; for in choosing the former, it ignores the substance that first sanctifies the individual, and in choosing the latter, it ignores the element that alone renders the community the individual's good. The court is, therefore, *bound* to do precisely what is implied by the historical fusion of law and equity and what, for the most part, it actually does: affirm a private right inwardly informed by the good to the extent compatible with the idea of a good inwardly constituted by private right.

NOTES

1. See, for example, The Politics of Law (Kairys, ed. 1982).

2. See R. Epstein, A Theory of Strict Liability: Toward a Reformulation of Tort Law (1980); Fletcher, Fairness and Utility in Tort Theory, 85 Harv. L. Rev. 537 (1972); Weinrib, Legal Formalism: On the Immanent Rationality of Law, 97 Yale L.J. 949 (1988).

3. See Sumner, The Moral Foundation of Rights 175–98 (1987).

4. J. Finnis, Natural Law and Natural Rights 298–308 (1980).

5. The Laws of Plato, § 866e–867b (T. Prangle trans. 1980).

6. Id. § 857c.

7. G. Hegel, Fruehe politische Systeme 97 ff, 327 ff (Goehler ed. 1974); G. Hegel, Natural Law 93 ff (Knox trans. 1975). [Editor's note: *Fruehe politische Systeme* will be abbreviated as *F*, and *Natural Law* will be abbreviated as *NL*; page references will be placed in the text.]

8. For example: the doctrines of mistaken assumptions, promissory estoppel, and

unconscionability in contracts; the protection of "quasi-property" in intangibles through the tort of unfair competition; and the duty of a surgeon or a researcher to disclose all pertinent information to a patient or a subject.

9. See Fiss, Forward: The Forms of Justice, 93 Harv. L. Rev. 1 (1979); Chayes, The Role of the Judge in Public Law Adjudication, 89 Harv. L. Rev. 1281 (1976).

10. Unger, The Critical Legal Studies Movement, 96 Harv. L. Rev. 561 (1983).

11. See Unger, Law in Modern Society (1976).

12. Editor's note: Unless otherwise indicated, all section numbers in the text refer to the *Philosophy of Right* (Knox trans. 1967).

13. Hegel, The Phenomenology of Mind 89 (Baillie trans. 1967). [Editor's note: The *Phenomenology* will be abbreviated as "Phen.," and page references to the Baillie translation will be placed in the text.]

14. See also The Logic of Hegel, § 80 (Wallace trans. 1892).

15. See Locke, The Second Treatise of Government § 25–51 (1952); Nozick, Anarchy, State, and Utopia 174–82 (1974).

16. Nozick, supra note 15, at 178.

17. See Cohen, Self-Ownership, World-Ownership, and Equality, in Justice and Equality Here and Now 125 ff (Lucash ed. 1986).

18. Locke, supra note 15, § 33.

19. See Fuller & Perdue, The Reliance Interest in Contract Damage, 46 Yale L.J. 52 (1936).

20. Kant, The Metaphysical Elements of Justice (Ladd trans. 1965).

21. Id. at 71–72.

22. Id. at 13–14, 18–21.

23. For example, in strict liability, in formal consent or assumption of risk as a tort defence, and in narrow contractual doctrines of mistake and coercion.

24. 92 Harv. L. Rev. 353 (1978).

25. See London Borough of Southwark v. Williams, 2 All E.R. 175 (1971).

26. Kronman, Contract Law and Distributive Justice, 89 Yale L.J. 472 (1980).

27. Weinrib, supra note 2.

28. c.f. Hegel, The Difference Between Fichte's and Schelling's System of Philosophy 142 ff (Harris & Cerf trans. 1977).

29. I refer here to Kant's account of the law of necessity; see Kant, supra note 20, at 41–42.

30. Hegel, The Difference Between Fichte's and Schelling's System of Philosophy, supra note 28, at 149.

31. See Kennedy, Form and Substance in Private Law Adjudication, 89 Harv. L. Rev. 1685 (1976).

32. For an understanding of what follows, it is essential to grasp the shift in the meaning of "universal will" that occurs at the stage of Ethical Life. There the universal will is no longer the universalization of subjective right-claims to liberty; it is no longer a common or general will built on individualistic foundations. Rather, it is a supra-individual will that constitutes a natural ethical order or

"substance", one given independently of individual thought and volition (see § 144–46; Phen. 451–61). Hegel marks this change by referring to the universal will of the ethical order as the "substantive" or "objective" will (§ 257–58).

33. See Weinrib, Law as a Kantian Idea of Reason, 87 Colum. L. Rev. 472, 487–500 (1987).

34. Unger, supra note 10, at 638 ff.

35. One of several reasons for this is that the particular plaintiff or defendant might externalize the burden. See G. Calabresi, The Costs of Accidents: A Legal and Economic Analysis 244–50 (1970).

36. Sindell v. Abbott Laboratories, 26 Cal. 3d 588, 607 P.2d 924, 163 Cal. Rptr. 132, cert. denied, 449 U.S. 912 (1980).

6

The Priority of Abstract Right and Constructivism in Hegel's Legal Philosophy

Peter Benson

A first task of a philosophy of law and morals is to try to make explicit and authenticate a standpoint that allows for the evaluation of things in normative terms. It cannot begin straightway with conceptions of the right, the good or the moral worth of persons. For these are notions whose adequate elucidation presupposes that we are already occupying a standpoint which, taken by itself, is unqualifiedly normative and complete. The account of what I shall refer to as "the standpoint of the normative" is thus prior to the explication of the criteria and contents of our normative conceptions.

How is this standpoint to be characterized? If the "ought" is to constitute a genuine and categorially distinct reality, the standpoint of the normative must, I think, fulfil at least the following three conditions. First, it must be self-sufficient, in the sense that it must not be derived, even in part, from the representation of things as merely causally determined happenings: the normative is grounded in and framed in terms of itself. Second, it must entail a conception of objective validity that is proper to the distinctive, self-sufficient character of the normative: the normative must articulate a standard that identifies and excludes the morally arbitrary. Third, it must be postulated with respect to a self that is conceived in terms of a capacity for self-conscious and responsible choice and that, as such a self, is necessarily subject to this standpoint: the standpoint of the normative must in itself express a conception of validity that does not merely apply to choice but is the unique standpoint from which a choosing subject must always judge itself in its capacity as a responsible agent. There must be no *locus standi* within the elucidation of responsible agency that entitles the subject to choose independently of or to limit that conception of validity.

Now this third condition, namely, postulation with respect to a choosing self, may be approached in two fundamentally different ways, yielding two different conceptions of the standpoint of the normative. The standpoint of the normative may be conceived either as a moral order that is given, even in part, prior to and independent of the free activity of the choosing self, or, alternatively, as one that is wholly immanent in and expressive of its agency. Let us call the second conception "constructivist." In a constructivist conception, the content of the normative is worked out or "constructed" from a standpoint that is immanent in and constitutive of responsible agency: normative conceptions, such as the right or the good, are not viewed as objects that are fixed prior and given to the choosing self independent of its activity; rather, they are conceived as entailments of that activity, posited by and wholly expressive of the choosing self as the basic unit of responsible agency.[1]

In this essay, I wish to consider this second, namely, the constructivist, conception of the normative. My intention is not to compare these two conceptions, much less to uncover and argue for the presuppositions of the constructivist approach. Instead, I want to explore the following question: What must the normative *first* consist in when it is conceived as unqualifiedly immanent in responsible agency? By framing the question in these terms, I suppose for now, first, that a constructivist account of our normative conceptions may have a complex structure, in the sense that it may comprise a sequence of mutually distinct but interconnected parts that must be elucidated each in its turn, and, second, that these parts are ordered in accordance with a conception of lexical priority.[2]

To explore this question, I believe it will be most useful to consider Hegel's account of the normative in the *Philosophy of Right*. Like Kant's conception of practical philosophy, Hegel's may, I will suggest, be viewed as constructivist. However, Hegel is perhaps even more explicitly attentive to the question of the proper order of such an account. Briefly stated, a central thesis of the *Philosophy of Right* is that what Hegel calls "abstract right" is the lexically first part of the normative. In this essay, I hope to set forth the essential steps of his argument for that claim.

By way of introduction and in order to help fix ideas, let me for now simply assert some fundamental features of Hegel's constructivism. What is merely stipulated here will hopefully be explained and justified, at least to a certain extent, later on.

A first premise in Hegel's account is that the standpoint of the normative is identical with what I shall call the "*general* concept of the free will." Now Hegel analyses this general concept under the two aspects of form and content.[3] For present purposes, we may take the aspect of form as representing an understanding of individuals as free and equal responsible agents or, more exactly, as possessing the moral powers that are necessary for them to be such agents. This conception of the person is not something that must itself be constructed. Rather, it is something that can be elicited from our moral experience of responsible agency and it serves as the basis of construction, as that from which construction begins. The aspect of content, on the other hand, refers to any mode of existence in which this conception of the person is realized. This content, which Hegel calls "right," includes *every* kind of normative reality. Thus, it is not restricted to the right, as distinguished from the good, but incorporates both and more. And right is not a content that is given prior to and independent of the activity of free will. On the contrary, it is a generated world that is entirely constructed by free will and that is wholly expressive of its powers, namely, the moral powers of free and equal personhood.

Moreover, in Hegel's constructivism, the general concept of free will is made *specific* in the following way. The aspect of form becomes specific through an ordered sequence of different forms or structures of free will.[4] The conception of the person with its defining moral powers (in other words, the form of free will) is something complex. Thus the conception of the person as free and equal that serves as the basis of construction is not complete *ab initio* but is elucidated (though not itself constructed) through its own sequence. This sequence exhibits, step by step, the progressively adequate and complete determination as well as integration of the different moral powers that characterize free and equal persons. Similarly, the aspect of content is made specific through an ordered sequence of distinct yet interconnected modes of right (ranging from the right as embodied in bare interaction between two individuals to the right as realized in complex social and political institutions). And each different mode of right rests on and expresses a different structure of free will, a different moment, as it were, in the sequence of the forms of free will. So, for example, we shall see that abstract right is based on the specific form of free will (with its distinctive and relatively incomplete articulation of the moral powers of free and equal personhood) which Hegel refers to as "personality."[5]

The essay has three parts. I begin, in the first, by indicating briefly in what way Hegel's conception of the normative is constructivist. More exactly, I try to identify the central features of the general concept of free will and try to show how they imply a constructivist conception of the normative. In the second and third parts, I try to explain why

Hegel's constructivist conception must begin with the specific form, personality, and why the mode of right that rests on and expresses personality must be abstract right. My main object is to identify which moral power or powers constitute personality and which features characterize abstract right as, respectively, the lexically first specific form and the lexically first specific content of free will in this constructivist conception of the normative. Hence the title of this essay.

I

In a constructivist conception, the standpoint of the normative is conceived as wholly immanent in the activity of the choosing self. Constructivism postulates a certain conception of responsible agency and elucidates the normative in terms of that conception. What, then, is the conception of responsible agency that informs Hegel's constructivism and how does his understanding of the standpoint of the normative in terms of the general concept of free will satisfy the constructivist requirement of immanence? I can address these important questions here only in the briefest way.

At the basis of Hegel's constructivism lies a conception of responsible agency that is, in its fundamental terms and import, very much like that of Kant.[6] The general concept of the free will, as explicated by Hegel, views responsible agency as self-conscious purposive activity which is unqualifiedly self-determining in character. Hegel refers to the free will as a "thinking" will.[7] Being purposive, such activity begins with, and is directed toward, the realization of a *conception* formed by the subject; it is rooted therefore in thinking rather than in instinct or in some other merely natural necessity. More exactly, free will postulates a self-conscious subject that views itself as wholly independent of everything given to it prior to its activity and that therefore has itself *qua* free for its object. And it is in virtue of this thought of itself as free that the subject is self-determining.

Now the fact that the subject is free just insofar as it views itself as such is itself something which the subject knows and which it seeks to make explicit. It does this by making the realization of this conception of itself its essential aim and purpose. The free will is thus thinking that gives its conception of itself existence in the element of self-conscious purposive activity. Or, conversely, it establishes self-conscious purposive activity as an exhibition of its conception of itself as free. Thinking in its *theoretical* function, or as cognition, has an object that, in relation to itself, must at least in part be taken as prior and independent. In contrast, thinking in its *practical* function, or as free will, gives itself an object that is wholly constituted through its own activity—an object that, far from being different from or independent of it, is the subject's very same conception of itself as free, only in the form of *realized* existence.[8]

As I said in the introductory remarks, the general concept of free will is analysed under the two aspects of form and content. I also suggested that we may view the aspects of form and content as referring respectively to the moral powers of free and equal persons and the ensemble of conditions (both internal and external to the self) in which that conception of the person is realized. Let us now take a closer look at what these two aspects entail. The general concept of free will, viewed under the aspect of form, has a structure that may be analysed in the following three steps. I shall briefly present these steps each in turn as distinct presuppositions in the understanding of responsible agency, without attempting, as Hegel does, to explain the way in which they may be conceptually interconnected.[9]

First, if the will is to be conceived as a faculty of *unconditioned* free agency, that is, as endowed with a self-originating power to set ends for itself, we must postulate a subject which views itself as having a capacity to posit ends that are not in any way given to it independently of and prior to its activity of choosing. This power implies, at the least, an ability to choose that is not inevitably tied to or framed in terms of any particular object(s) as such. Accordingly, the subject regards itself as having a capacity to abstract from, that is, to distinguish itself from and to stand above, every determinate feature of experience, whether it be something that is internal to the subject, such as its inclinations, needs, or aims, or something that is external, such as its circumstances or relations with others. One who is accountable must, as such, be able to view every determinate content as a restriction which it can dissipate and transcend. It follows that what is *not* given to the subject is whatever remains when it views the determinate as something from which to abstract. And this can only be the consciousness of oneself as wholly unqualified by anything particular. Being without particular content, such self-consciousness entails a standpoint that is formal and universal. Now this standpoint constitutes the will's *negative freedom*: in virtue of it, the will is independent of everything that is extrinsic to its activity of choosing and it is thus fitted to be self-determining.10 If, however, the free will were defined *only* as independent of any content, it would not be represented as having a determinate content of its own—it would be simply undetermined. In this case, it would not be a will, for agency entails the willing of *something*: choice is directed toward the realization of *this* rather than *that*. Thus the first aspect, taken by itself, articulates only a necessary but not a sufficient condition of free agency. We must also postulate the subject's capacity to give itself a specific content. This is the second step in the analysis of the free will, in virtue of which the will is conceived as determinate activity, as incorporating reference to particularity, and therefore as something actual rather than merely potential.[10]

But, further, if the free will is to be represented as *self*-determining, it must, in willing something particular, will itself alone. The free will *is* the activity of realizing its conception of itself as free: In willing something determinate, the subject must express its capacity to set ends for itself independent of the given. Therefore, in willing something particular, the subject must know the restriction as something which is its own, in which it is confined only because it has put itself there, and which it wills in order that its freedom may have determinacy and reality. The standpoint of formal universality entailed in the first step must be carried over and fulfilled in the second: this constitutes the will's *positive freedom*. And the integration of the two in the manner just indicated articulates, according to Hegel, the essential nature of the free will.

In sum, by the first step, the will is intelligible as potentially self-determining; by the second, as actually determined; and by their unity, as actually self-determining. This, then, is the form or structure of the general concept of free will. It represents the intelligibility of unqualified self-determining agency.[11]

Viewed under the aspect of content, the general concept of free will is the right. As previously discussed, right is to be understood as the ensemble of conditions that express and realize the conception of the person as free and equal or, more exactly, as possessing the moral powers proper to this conception of the person. We have just seen that the form of free will entails the unity of the universal and particular in self-determination. Right may be viewed as the actualization of this unity in the shape of a constructed world or, in Hegel's words, like a second nature.[12] In contrast to nature proper, right is not a world that is given prior to and independent of free activity, but rather one that is actual through and expressive of such activity.

Now insofar as right is nothing other than a mode of existence that realizes and expresses the concept of free will, it must always be respected as an end in itself. The reason is this. Because, as free will, the subject has the conception of itself as independent of the given for its sole object and goal, it necessarily views itself as unqualifiedly self-relating, as self-determining. Accordingly, this is what it is from the standpoint of the normative. Consequently, the free will cannot, consistent with this standpoint, be treated merely as a means to and as conditioned by something else. The free will and all that it entails must be respected as an end in itself.

We are now in a position to see how the general concept of free will seems to satisfy the requisite conditions for conceiving the standpoint of the normative in constructivist terms. A constructivist account, I said, invokes a conception of the person, with its defining moral powers, that may be elicited from our moral experience of responsible agency. More precisely, we have seen that Hegel's constructivism is informed by an idea of responsible agency in which the subject is characterized by two essential features, namely a capacity to conceive of itself as independent from anything given, and a capacity to choose ends in accordance with the entailments of this self-conception. These two features completely and exhaustively articulate the most fundamental structure that is presupposed in the understanding of responsible agency: the first identifies the standpoint that must orient agency if there is to be accountability; the second explicitly relates this standpoint to the aspect of the choice of ends (which aspect is essential to the intelligibility of agency as such).

The form and content of the general concept of free will integrate these features in a manner that satisfies the three conditions of a constructivist account of the normative. Take the matter of self-sufficiency: in virtue of the subject's conception of itself as independent of everything given, that is, on account of its negative freedom, the free will and its entailments are represented as categorially independent of natural causal determination. In this way, the free will is conceived as self-grounded and as explicable only in terms of itself. Moreover, the required conception of validity is provided through the form of universality that is necessarily entailed by negative freedom. As a result, everything having to do with the mere particularity of the subject, such as inclination and subjective preference, is disqualified *ab initio* as a determining ground of choice: a conception of the normatively arbitrary is identified and excluded. In turn, the subject's positive freedom signifies that the justificatory basis of the choice of ends must be framed in terms of this form of universality: the categorially independent conception of normative validity is the unique perspective from which a responsible agent is to judge the propriety of its choice of ends. The standpoint of the normative is conceived here, not as an order that is given independent of and prior to the activity of choice, but as a form or structure that is wholly immanent in it. Finally, right, as the content that embodies this structure, is already implied by and is the completion of the very meaning of free will: for free will is nothing but the self-grounded and self-relating activity of practical thinking, that is, of thinking that is oriented toward its realization in the element of self-conscious purposive activity, and right is a world that is wholly constituted by and expressive of this activity. In brief, right is a freely constructed world, understood from a practical point of view.

II

With this understanding of the standpoint of the normative in mind, let us now turn to the central question of this essay: What is the first part of an account of the normative when the normative is conceived as wholly immanent in responsible agency? As I have already indicated, "first" is to be understood here not temporally but rather conceptually, as entailing lexical priority. To prevent misunderstanding, it seems desirable to emphasize at this point that, in Hegel's view, the lexical priority of a normative conception does not imply that it is the sole or even the most adequate expression of normativity; on the contrary, as merely the first, it is the most limited fulfilment of free will and it gives way to (while being preserved by) other, more adequate conceptions.

To answer this question, it is necessary to elucidate not merely the general concept of free will but a *specific* form and content of free will that embody the general concept. In doing so, I hope to substantiate, at least in part, the claim that the conception of the person is complex and that it must be analysed in terms of specific forms of that conception, forms that belong to an ordered sequence in which the moral powers of free and equal persons are, step by step, determined and integrated in a fully adequate way. I believe we may also see more clearly how a content—a mode of right—can be said to rest on and to express this conception of the person.

Accordingly, we can restate the central question as follows: What is the lexically first way of conceiving free and equal persons and their essential moral powers, and what is the lexically first conception of right that rests on and expresses this understanding of the person? In the light of previous discussion, let us say for now that the answer must at least be: whatever is *minimally* entailed by the subject's negative freedom and *minimally* required to realize its positive freedom. If we can establish what these involve, we may then be able to see why they constitute an irreducibly distinct stage in the account of right and why their relation to other categories of right may properly be framed in terms of lexical priority.[13]

The subject's negative freedom minimally entails the mere possible consciousness of itself as undetermined by everything determinate. It therefore consists *just* in the subject's power to distinguish itself from whatever object it may happen to want or from whatever condition in which it may happen to find itself: it is this feature that exhibits the subject's capacity to break the power of the given as such and to establish itself as not inevitably tied to any particular determination.

The elucidation of the subject's negative freedom begins, then, with relation to the given, but the postulated relation is wholly negative, because the subject has established every restriction as completely negated and transcended, and has denied all validity to it: the determinate is represented as something that has been categorially excluded as a possible justificatory ground of responsible choice. This negative relation to the given has, in turn, the following positive significance: *qua* distinguished from and independent of the given, the subject now has itself alone for its proper object; in knowing itself as a subject that has transcended every particular content and in having itself, conceived exclusively in this way, for its sole object, the subject is a self and necessarily views itself as an end in itself. In short, the subject's negative freedom minimally entails, not a general consciousness of itself as an ego concretely determined in this or that way, but rather a consciousness of itself as "a completely abstract ego in which every concrete restriction and value is negated and without validity."[14] Insofar as the subject conceives of itself in this way, it is, to use Hegel's term, personality. Personality is thus the specific form of free will that is minimally postulated in Hegel's account of the normative.[15]

It is true that the elucidation of personality presupposes that individuals possess the requisite natural endowments and the acquired aptitudes to engage in self-conscious purposive activity as well as to recognize and honor the normative entailments of participation in it. However, the only *moral* power expressive of free will that is specifically attributed to a subject in virtue of its being personality is the faculty of knowing itself as undetermined by everything given and of having itself, conceived as independent, for its object and goal. It should be stated at the outset that although persons are represented as having this moral power, it does not follow that, from the standpoint of personality, individuals need have this conception of themselves explicitly before their minds. Personality, we shall see, implies merely that they can, on reflection, recognize this view of themselves as implicit in and presupposed by their understanding of responsible agency. According to Hegel, it is only when individuals have the status of "moral subjects" (in contrast to being mere persons) that they can be represented from the standpoint of the normative as explicitly adopting this conception of themselves as their own.[16] With these remarks in mind, let me try to identify more exactly what personality entails.

Personality is a form of self-consciousness in which the subject has for its object itself, unqualified by anything particular or determinate and utterly without internal differentiation or complexity. The self that the subject has for its object is both formally and substantively *simple*: it is a formally simple "I" that is not yet explicitly defined as a unity of many "I's"—its identity is not yet the more complex "we" that signifies a many-in-one; and it is a substantively simple "I" that does not yet contain in itself, but on the contrary abstracts from, the multiplicity of concrete factors that constitute the particular aspect of purposive activity. These factors may be internal (such as natural endowments and features, determinate needs or purposes) or external (for example, ties of relationship with others, contingent natural or social circumstances in which an agent is placed). The standpoint of personality is thus that of a simple unit inwardly aware of its sheer independence from everything given. And inasmuch as personality postulates the subject's unconditioned relation with itself, personality—and all that it implies—must be respected as an end in itself and never treated merely as a means to something else.

To prevent misunderstanding, it should be emphasized here that the attribution of independence does not imply that individuals can somehow strip themselves of their particular features and can exist, disembodied and unindividuated, without them. What is at stake in this attribution of independence is not the *existence* as such of these particular features (which the elucidation of personality simply assumes) but rather their *normative significance* when we view ourselves as capable of free choice.

Now insofar as the standpoint of personality is unqualified by any particular content, subjects are necessarily *identical* in their capacity as persons: each is necessarily and identically a self-originating locus of negative freedom.That all individuals, *qua* persons, are indistinguishable and in this sense equal is necessarily contained in each subject's awareness of its being independent from determination by the given and thus of its being an end in itself: the "I" that each knows as independent is necessarily the same as every other "I." Let us call this entailment the "postulate of formal (abstract) equality."[17]

Being an entailment of negative freedom, the postulate of formal equality constitutes an unconditional normative criterion that must be respected in all our choices. It does not add to or alter in any way the utterly simple and contentless self-consciousness that characterizes personality but merely represents the universality that is inherent in this first formulation of negative freedom. Note that this form of universality is just the bare identity that subjects share as persons. Like personality itself, universality here is simple and contentless—it is formal or abstract universality. And, as we shall see, it is this abstract universality that must be preserved in the articulation of the subject's positive freedom.

This, then, is, briefly stated, the minimally presupposed specific form of the subject's negative freedom. But free will, we saw, entails the determination of the subject's negative freedom as positive freedom. How are we to construe its positive freedom consistently with the standpoint of its negative freedom? Positive freedom, it will be recalled, consists in the subject willing a *determinate* object in a way that embodies the very same conception of self contained in its negative freedom. Here, therefore, a determinate content would have to be postulated that reflects nothing save the formal self-relatedness and independence of personality as well as its entailment, the idea of formal equality. The question is then: Given that the subject, as choosing agent, must choose *something*, how are we to conceive its determinate choosing such that it exhibits nothing other than the subject's capacity to have itself, *qua* independent, for its object and end? If we can answer this question, we will have found the minimally presupposed content of free will, the "embodiment of personality," to use Hegel's phrase. And this content, we shall see, constitutes abstract right. To begin, let us consider what the subject's negative freedom *excludes* as a possible conception of its positive freedom.

First, with respect to form, the standpoint of personality entails that the determinate aspect cannot figure as an end which expresses the subject's freedom: positive freedom cannot be framed in terms of an end that is to be attained. To see why, we must keep in mind that the freedom of personality (and therefore its constitutive moral power) consists *solely* in the subject's capacity to distinguish itself from, and to know itself as independent of, every particular determination: the exclusive aim, as it were, of the subject *qua* personality is to maintain its independence from every determinate aspect of purposive activity rather than to form and pursue determinate ends of action through which it can express its freedom. Notwithstanding the rich concreteness and apparent value of the content represented by these particulars, they are wholly without validity from the standpoint of personality, being given to the choosing self prior to and independent of its activity. That they lack validity is just what must minimally be established by the subject if it is to be vindicated as self-determining, and this is established through the subject being a person. Thus while the subject, as a choosing agent, always chooses something (*this* rather than *that*) and therefore, we assume, has determinate ends, the *normative* significance of its choice, considered solely from the standpoint of abstract personality, lies neither in its determinate content nor in its being directed toward an end as such but only in its compatibility with the subject's independence from every determination and with whatever such independence implies. In order to reflect this standpoint, the determinacy postulated in positive freedom must not, then, be framed in terms of ends, the pursuit of which is deemed to be constitutive of the subject's freedom.

We may put the fundamental point this way: unless the subject just *is* personality, that is, is realized *as distinct from* the determinate aspect of its agency, it cannot have the realization of the freedom of personality (and whatever this entails) in that determinate element for its end and object; and conversely, unless the determinate aspect is first posited by the subject as something that is *not* given to it prior to and independent of its activity, the determinate element cannot provide the subject with an object which is directly suitable to express its free purposive capacity. When the form of free will is still personality, directedness toward ends is not as such part of self-determination.[18]

Second, in terms of content, the determinate aspect in positive freedom cannot lie in personality itself, since, we have seen, it is wholly and inherently indeterminate. Nor can that determinacy be found in the relation of personality to personality: taken by itself, the personality of the second is just as indeterminate as that of the first; and the relation between them, which at this point can be framed only in terms of the postulate of formal equality, states nothing more than their identity as wholly without determinacy. In contrast to personality, the concrete features of purposive activity *are* particular and determinate. As such, they constitute the only material that can possibly function as a determinate aspect expressive of the subject's freedom. However, as just discussed, they cannot do so in the form of ends or purposes of action through which the subject is to realize its freedom. Under what condition, then, can these concrete features function as determinate aspects of choice in such a way that they are constructed by practical thinking and thus reflect the standpoint of personality alone? The required condition, as I will now try to explain, is that they be treated as *things that persons can have as their exclusive individual property*. We shall see that the minimally presupposed articulation of positive freedom is that subjects be respected as persons having a juridical capacity to possess things as their individual property.

Since the freedom of personality consists in the subject's distinguishing and detaching itself from everything particular, the subject establishes the latter as something that is immediately different from personality and therefore as something that is *not* self-related or free. Notwithstanding the rich concreteness of content represented by these particulars, they share, at the start, the same form of being given to and not by practical thinking. In relation to free will, their only significance is that they do *not* have intrinsic validity: this is what they *are*, that is, this is their essence, from the standpoint of the normative. Being without the form of self-relatedness, they can therefore, consistent with this standpoint, be used merely as means to something else. The normative significance of the particular aspects of purposive activity, insofar as they count as merely distinct from personality, is only that they are something *usable*. In normative terms, they are things.

"Thing," like "personality," denotes a mode of existence rather than an entity as such, and more specifically a mode of existence that contrasts with the self-relatedness of personality: a thing is anything determinate—whether a capacity, an action or an object in the external world—that, being established as immediately different from personality, is, normatively, something which can be treated merely as a means. The concrete features of purposive activity are considered solely in relation to the standpoint of personality; they are represented, not in terms of their different particular contents, but formally, as abstractly identical things. The characterization of their essence in these terms constitutes the first step in the conceptualization of a determinate aspect of willing that is given by and not to practical thinking.[19]

Thus far, we have reached the conclusion that the normative intelligibility of the particular aspects of purposive activity necessarily consists in their being things that can be used as means to external ends. In the light of what has been said, it follows that it must be normatively possible, that is, permissible, for a free agent to subordinate things to its purposive capacity. Stated in terms of its opposite, there can be no prohibition that would place usable things beyond the purposes of persons.

For there to be such a prohibition, it would have to be required either by the nature of a thing or by the nature of personality. But insofar as something falls under the category of thing, it contains nothing that can exclude its being subordinated to extrinsic purposes or that can determine the normatively possible purposes to which it may be put. And, similarly, there is nothing in personality that precludes such an object being used as a means. As already discussed, *qua* personality, the subject's relation to particular determinations is negative: it knows itself as independent of and undetermined by everything given. This negative relation has the following two implications: that the particular, being distinguished from the subject, *can*, in normative terms, be used merely as a means, and that the subject, being under no positive requirement to realize its personality in the element of the particular, is *not obliged* to subordinate things to its purposes. The conclusion that it must be *permissible* for a subject to use things is consistent with these implications. The contrary conclusion would signify that there can be no determinacy expressive of the subject's negative freedom at this first stage of its freedom and, consequently, that its positive freedom is inconceivable. This would entail, in short, the impossibility of elucidating responsible agency as an expression of unconditioned freedom. This consequence cannot be required by or explicated through negative freedom, for the latter would then have to be postulated as a capacity for self-determination that precludes the possibility of its own actualization—which is absurd.[20]

Now, if the capacity to use of things merely as means to one's purposes is to constitute the most elementary articulation of positive freedom, it remains to be shown more exactly how this capacity can be construed to reflect exclusively the conception of self entailed by negative freedom. We must be able to construct a conception of permissible (but not obligatory) use that enshrines nothing save the postulate of formal equality. In this way alone can there be determinate willing that is wholly given by practical thinking and that thus embodies only the standpoint of personality. More specifically, the conception of permissible use must reflect the specific character of freedom entailed by personality which, I have said, consists in this: that the sole aim of the subject is to maintain its formal independence from particularity in whatever it happens to choose. Let me try to explain how such a conception of permissible use is to be construed.

First, the relation of subject, *qua* personality, to thing is one of ownership. The connection between the two must be conceived such that it preserves the categorial difference between person and thing. Therefore, the relation between subject and thing must not be construed as one of identity: in relation to me, a thing cannot count as another "I" but only as a determinate "mine."

Second, the subject that relates to a thing as its own is the utterly simple and contentless self postulated in negative freedom: as we saw, one views oneself as "I," as a bare self-relating locus of responsible agency. Accordingly, subjects count merely as identically separate persons. The capacity to relate to things as one's own is—and at this point can only be—attributed to and exercised by subjects conceived in this way. Ownership is thus individual or private in character.[21]

Third, the conception of ownership that is at stake here is *merely* the *capacity* to have things as one's own. This is what constitutes the subject's positive freedom and what must be accorded respect. I have referred to this capacity for ownership as juridical in nature. That it is to be so characterized follows, I hope to show, from the specific nature of the freedom entailed by personality.

To begin, let us recall the conclusion that, given personality's essential indifference to and transcendence of everything particular, we can only hold that it must be normatively *possible* (but not necessary) for individuals to use things as means. Consistent with this premise, neither ownership itself, nor any constituent element in the account of ownership, nor even the requirement to respect the capacity for ownership, is to be construed in terms that presuppose that the subject's freedom is constituted through its adopting anything whatever—whether it be a substantive content of some sort or the requirement of respect itself— as its end: the relevant standpoint here is not that of virtue.[22] Those aspects of purposive activity that may be significant in judging conduct or character from the standpoint of the adoption of required ends are therefore irrelevant. Moreover, the justificatory basis of the capacity for ownership cannot be that it satisfies any interest or need, or that it is necessary for individual moral development, if such interests or development go beyond the bare (highest-order) interest of the subject in affirming its contentless and simple conception of itself as independent from everything given, whether from within or from without. Otherwise, ownership could not signify merely the preservation of the standpoint of personality in whatever one happens to choose. Of course, individuals choose to make things their own in order to serve their particular interests, purposes, and needs; however, this alone does not make such factors normatively relevant. It is only in relation to the standpoint of the normative that such relevance can be determined. And where we are considering the most elementary mode in which that standpoint is expressed, it is personality—and it alone—that can provide the criterion of relevance.

More specifically, conceived in the light of the freedom of personality and its entailment, namely, the requirement to respect formal equality, the juridical capacity for ownership has the following three characteristics: it is negative, interactional, and external. I will discuss each of these in turn.

(A) The requirement to respect a person's capacity for ownership is *negative* in character: it stipulates merely that individuals are to do nothing that is inconsistent with the independence of personality.[23] Or, to frame the requirement positively in terms of what can be enjoined: action is not obligatory for the reason, even in part, that through it an end can be realized. Reference to ends cannot figure in any way as a premise in the justification. This follows from the previously discussed point that the freedom of subjects *qua* persons does not consist in the pursuit of anything as an end; on the contrary, freedom here lies solely in their capacity to detach themselves from every particular end as such. Accordingly, the requirement to respect a person's capacity for ownership qualifies the choice of ends as permissible or impermissible, not as obligatory. Its commands are, in the final analysis, always prohibitions, not positive duties: it does not impose a positive obligation upon individuals to appropriate and to make use of things or to assist others to do so. The meaning of this requirement of respect is merely that things must always be treated as susceptible of being owned (by someone) and persons must always be treated as capable of ownership (but never as objects of ownership). Thus, the requirement to respect formal equality is not infringed *just* by the absence of ownership: respect for the possibility of ownership does not entail that any individual must in fact have something as his or her own.[24] From this it follows that it is only when acts affect what *already* belongs to a person that this requirement can be violated.[25]

Moreover, since, with respect to their personality, all individuals are identical, it makes no difference whatsoever *which* individual has acquired ownership. The appropriation of everything by one has the same normative significance as the appropriation of something by everyone: great inequality in holdings and even sheer propertylessness can, as such, be perfectly consistent with respect for each person's equal *capacity* for ownership. The existence or absence of holdings has normative significance only insofar as it may infringe the negative requirement of respect for formal equality, which, we have seen, is independent of the whole sphere of particularity, that is, of all considerations relating to wants, needs, or welfare. Thus, respect for the individual capacity for ownership does not entail that a certain level of welfare must be maintained through the allocation of property entitlements. Whether holdings are fair in the light of a criterion of distribution is categorially irrelevant to their justification. Right is, at this stage, purely nondistributive in conception.

(B) The requirement to respect a person's capacity for ownership is structured *interactionally*: the basic unit of analysis is a relation of correlative right and duty between two separate yet formally equal persons. Here again, we try to derive this feature from the fundamental proposition that, as persons, individuals need not appropriate things for their use in order to realize their freedom: personality, and all that it entails, is fully preserved as an end in itself merely if the subject does nothing that is inconsistent with its simple and contentless independence from every particular determination.

We have seen that, because persons are not obliged to appropriate or to help others to do so, the requirement to respect the capacity for ownership pertains only to something that is *already* one's own. To this we now add the following qualification: it must be something that is already *another's* own. To see why, consider first my choosing to do something with *my* own things. Because I am not obliged to acquire anything or, for the same reason, to continue to own something that is already mine, I need not view the subordination of a thing to my purposes as something that, where I alone am concerned, I must respect as an end in itself: it counts merely as a particular determination from which I can abstract at will, consistently with my independence and freedom. Whatever I do in this regard cannot possibly affect my capacity for ownership.

However, the same cannot be said of my actions that may affect *another's* thing, that is, something which another has already subjected to his or her purposes. I cannot rightly view the embodiment of the other's will as nothing more than a particular determination which I may negate at will. On the contrary, it contains the other's will and, if I affect it, my doing so does not, in itself, express the other's independence (since, from the other's standpoint, my choice counts merely as an external factor from which to abstract) but only my own. Thus, I must treat the embodiment of another's will as an end in itself and, by impinging on it, I can affect his or her capacity for ownership.

If we combine the point, that the requirement of respect only applies insofar as one person can affect what already belongs to another, with our prior conclusions, namely, that the capacity for ownership is attributed to formally equal but separate persons and that each person's capacity must be respected as an end in itself, we arrive at the following idea: whether formal equality has been respected is decided in the context of a two-person interaction, where one has affected in some way what already belongs to another. The requirement of respect is stipulated in terms of a two-person relationship, such that the existence of a relationship of this kind, taken by itself, is not only a sufficient but also a necessary condition of the applicability of the normative criterion. Thus, where interaction involves more than two individuals, it must be possible to conceptualize the interaction, for the purposes of normative evaluation, either as entailing in fact only a two-person relationship or as comprising a number of distinct two-person relationships, each of which must satisfy formal equality. The two-person relationship always constitutes, normatively speaking, the relevant standpoint of analysis.

Furthermore, in relation to others, the exercise of one's capacity for ownership is not to be conceived as a mere *liberty* but rather as giving rise to a genuine *right* that others have a *corresponding duty* to respect. Supposing that an individual's choice has been effectively manifested with respect to the use of a thing that can, consistently with formal equality, be appropriated by that individual, that decision must be respected as an end in itself if positive freedom is to be possible.[26] For an individual's manifestation of choice in these circumstances has, taken by itself, universal import: given that individuals are identical as persons, it signifies that the subject, as free will and thus as necessarily and completely representative of everyone, has chosen with respect to a determinate object. But this is nothing less than positive freedom itself which, because it embodies the standpoint of the normative, constitutes an end that must be respected in every act of choice. The failure to respect another's decision regarding the use of his or her thing *eo ipso* denies the possibility of *any* person—and therefore the wrongdoer also—choosing a determinate object in a way that must be respected as an end in itself. Accordingly, the requirement to respect another's capacity for ownership must be framed as a *duty* to respect another's *right*.

To this it might be objected that it would be consistent with positive freedom for a second person to displace the first without his or her consent, because, in doing so, the second merely substitutes his or her identical will (to use the thing) for the first's. The objection holds that, in this circumstance, the second will can properly be viewed as the equivalent of the first. But this is to ignore that the first person's will has already been expressed and that it must therefore be respected as an end in itself, for which there can be no equivalent. This point can be made in another way. The second can count as the equivalent of the first only insofar as it is identical to it. However, the sameness of individuals consists here solely in their being formally equal ends in themselves. By failing to accord the first respect, the second violates their identity as persons and so cannot be represented as equivalent.

We conclude, then, that the fundamental unit of analysis is a relation between two persons having correlative rights and duties: a person's duty is always owed to another, who has a corresponding right. In other words persons do not have duties toward themselves. Where ownership is private and persons have obligations only with respect to another's capacity for ownership, right and duty cannot coalesce in one person with respect to the same object of ownership.[27]

(C) The final characteristic of the capacity for ownership when it is construed in the light of the postulate of formal equality is what I shall call its "*external*" nature.[28] We start, once more, with the fundamental premise that the requirement to respect the capacity for ownership does not imply that anything, including the requirement itself, must be adopted as an end. Accordingly, the requirement does not determine the propriety of choices in the light of an individual's purposes (subjective understandings, intentions, and so on) as such. This feature has three implications that define the requirement's external character.

First, the requirement applies only to acts that can actually affect another's capacity for ownership: purposes which are not manifested in actions that can do so are as such normatively irrelevant. There must be, in other words, an external manifestation of will that can impinge upon what is already another's. Second, the normative validity of an action is decided, not by reference to its author's subjective intentions, purposes and understandings as such, but in terms of conditions of respect that one ought reasonably to subscribe to when one's actions can impinge on another. The standpoint of evaluation is public and relational. Third, the applicability of the requirement does not depend upon an individual assenting to it. Persons are under its jurisdiction simply in virtue of their having manifested a capacity for responsible choice. Just as the requirement does not oblige individuals to pursue anything as an end—including the requirement of respect itself—so its vindication, in the face of an action that is inconsistent with it, does not depend upon the author of the action subjectively regarding the vindication as a desirable or as an obligatory end: the vindication can, consistently with personality, be exercised upon the agent through coercion.[29]

In sum, the requirement to respect the capacity for ownership commands that one's external actions be consistent with the entailments of positive freedom, that is, with the use of things by persons having the status of an end in itself. However, as I have tried to emphasize, it does not command (as virtue arguably requires) that one will this respect as one's end and that one make its standpoint one's own. This minimally presupposed articulation of positive freedom does not postulate the goodness of intention or of purpose as an aspect of the normative; it determines merely the permissibility of ends through a conception of respect for the capacity to own that, being negative, interactional, and external, is juridical rather than ethical in character.[30]

Let me now try to gather together the main points discussed thus far in this part. What I have attempted to outline is a way of conceiving choice with respect to a determinate object that presupposes only—and adds nothing categorially new to—the standpoint of negative freedom, as it must be minimally expressed. The argument can be summarized in the following five propositions. First, a certain notion of the person, namely personality, must be postulated as the minimally presupposed specific form of free will and as expressive of the subject's negative freedom: unless we begin with this notion of the person, we cannot adduce a normatively valid criterion with which to evaluate conduct. Second, the sole criterion that is implied by this conception of the person and that is therefore minimally but necessarily entailed by the standpoint of the normative is the postulate of formal equality: all our choices must be consistent with it and with whatever follows from it. Third, a conception of positive freedom that exhibits personality must be framed in terms of the possibility of ownership, elucidated in the light of this postulate. This idea of ownership constitutes the most elementary specific content of free will. Fourth, the possibility of ownership is represented as a normative, or more exactly, a juridical capacity inhering in separate yet formally equal persons, a capacity that must be respected in our every choice. Fifth, consistently with the postulate of formal equality, the requirement to respect this capacity is articulated as a negative duty to respect what is already another's own; and this duty can be coercively enforced against an agent insofar as it action can actually impinge upon another's right of ownership. In short, the requirement of respect is negative, interactional, and external in character.

These five propositions suggest an understanding of negative and positive freedom which is, I believe, internally coherent and minimally presupposed in a constructivist account of our normative conceptions. The requirement to respect each person's juridical capacity for ownership *is* abstract right. Abstract right thus represents the most elementary mode in which a subject's willing can be determinate in a way that exhibits its conception of itself as free. The relation between subject and object postulated in abstract right enshrines nothing less—but also nothing more—than the categorial distinction between persons, who, necessarily viewing themselves as ends in themselves, should always be accorded respect, and things, which, lacking unqualified self-relatedness, may be used merely as means. Moreover, because this distinction states the essential first condition under which something is to be accorded respect, it marks the necessary first step in understanding how there can be an unconditional entitlement to anything at all. Accordingly, we may formulate the meaning of abstract right as follows: the individual capacity to make use of things consistently with formal equality represents the first way in which a subject can be entitled to anything as such. The subject of abstract right is a person with a bare capacity for rights.[31]

III

Thus far, I have tried to explain why personality and abstract right are *minimally* presupposed in Hegel's constructivist account of the normative. But I have also suggested that Hegel's claim, more exactly stated, is that abstract right is the *lexically first* content of free will and that it rests on personality, the *lexically first* form of free will. By way of conclusion, I should like to make three very brief comments about the basis and significance of this claim of lexical priority.

First, we are now in a position to see more clearly why the relation of personality and abstract right to other modes of free will must be conceived in terms of lexical priority. Because both personality and abstract right are specifications of free will, that is, of unqualifiedly self-determining agency, they cannot be represented as mere means to something else: whatever they essentially entail must be respected as an end in itself. Supposing that there are other things that qualify as specific forms and contents of free will, these must preserve whatever is essential to the intelligibility of personality and abstract right. And since personality and abstract right are minimally presupposed, the condition of the possibility of such other forms and contents of free will is that they first of all be consistent with and satisfy what abstract right requires. Hence its lexical priority.

Second, personality and abstract right constitute a *distinct* normative whole that gives specific expression to the idea of free agency. As personality, the self is endowed merely with the moral power of affirming a conception of itself in which it is represented as independent of every particular determination. Although, as we saw, Hegel's constructivism certainly accepts that the structure of choice must be characterized by determinacy, that is, choice must be directed toward *this* rather than *that* end, it can only vindicate the idea of free agency if it *begins* with a specific normative category that denies inherent normative significance to the particular and that does not yet incorporate action-directed-toward-ends as part of freedom. Accordingly, the *moral* power ascribed to individuals in virtue of their being personality is not framed in terms of a capacity to realize ends. In other words, the capacity to form, to revise, and rationally to pursue a conception of the good (as understood by Rawls) is not yet postulated as a moral power of free and equal persons. Here, the sole end of the self, the only mode in which it realizes itself, is merely the affirmation of its independence from every determination, from every particular end. When the self is still personality, free agency does not consist in the effort to give determinate expression to personality: agents need not make the conception of themselves as independent their principle in the pursuit of particular ends.[32]

Abstract right, which is constructed on the basis of personality, expresses this limited moral power in the element of determinate purposive activity. Stated negatively, the key to understanding the specific character of abstract right is that here, in Hegel's words, "there is no question of particular interests, of my advantage or my welfare, any more than there is of the particular motive behind my volition, of insight and intention."[33] These considerations presuppose something more than the purely formal equality enshrined in abstract right, namely, a form or structure of freedom that consists in the will being directed toward the realization of particular ends and the satisfaction of particular interests. Indeed, given that persons in abstract right have no end except the bare affirmation of themselves as independent from every determination, not even abstract right's requirement of respect is something which they must adopt as an obligatory end (for they have none) or something which they must follow for its own sake. In abstract right, the capacity for an effective sense of justice is realized just in a purely external mode consisting in this: that a responsible agent is rightly subject to coercion by another (with whatever purpose or intention) if that agent has violated the other's entitlement.[34]

We have seen that the relevant standpoint in abstract right is always framed in terms of an external relation between two formally equal persons in which each is represented as having a bare juridical capacity for ownership. This negative, interactional, and external standpoint differs not only from the inwardness of virtue (which postulates obligatory ends) but also from the normatively more complex distributive standpoint that informs the notion of cooperative association on fair and equal terms. For instance, in light of the abstractness of abstract right, a conception of needs which, in contrast to desires, can express normatively valid requirements, is not yet postulated as an aspect of self-determination. There is accordingly no place yet for a doctrine of primary goods or for a conception of the needs of free and equal persons that can provide a basis for legitimate claims to distributive shares.[35] And because abstract right's requirement of respect is categorially nondistributive in character, it cannot serve to ground a principle of reciprocity or mutual advantage that might regulate the production and the division of the benefits of collaborative undertakings.

However, on Hegel's view, the nondistributive character of abstract right should not be taken to imply that, in a subsequent stage of right, individual entitlements may not be determined in accordance with a suitable principle of distribution. What must be respected in order to satisfy abstract right is every individual's capacity, as a person, to subject things to his or her purposes. As long as things are treated as usable and persons as beyond mere use, personality is respected. Now when the relevant normative standpoint is that of the correlative rights and duties of individuals viewed as separate, though formally equal, interacting persons rather than, say, as members of civil society or as citizens of a state, right entitles individuals to obtain whatever and however much they can through the permissible modes of acquisition (which are, according to both Hegel and Kant, first occupancy and contract). With abstract right, there are as yet no moral considerations that might validly qualify or limit this entitlement. Thus, in abstract right, a person rightfully complains if any thing is placed beyond the possibility of individual acquisition. But this need not be so when the normative standpoint incorporates other categories of right which, let us assume, rest on fuller, more complex specifications of free and equal personhood than does abstract right. It is Hegel's view that the institutions of ethical life, namely the family, civil society, and the state, actually satisfy this criterion. Consequently, the sphere that is subject to unqualified individual appropriation may be determined and limited in accordance with the entailments of freedom embodied in these. Such limitation can be consistent with abstract right because abstract right, in virtue of what I have called its "negative" character, is not a right to any thing or any bundle of things as such. In short, abstract right does not definitively determine either the content or the extent of property ownership.[36]

My third and final remark concerns the way in which a sequence of normative categories is generated. In Hegel's account, the elucidation of a lexically second form and content of free will is effected through the systematic exploration of abstract right's inherent *limits* as an expression of free will.[37] The second category of right is established by showing that it is needed and able to resolve certain fundamental tensions that characterize abstract right and that challenge its self-sufficiency on its own terms. The justification of the second category is thus thoroughly immanent to the analysis of abstract right itself. In specific terms, the transition to the second category is shown to be necessary through a consideration of the meaning of wrong and its annulment. I shall conclude by briefly indicating how.

Because, in abstract right, individuals are not obligated toward any end (including right itself), it is normatively a matter of chance whether an agent's particular choices conform with the abstract equality of personality. Hence abstract right is *inherently* and *necessarily* vulnerable to wrong. Wrong constitutes a particular external expression of choice that violates the abstract equality of persons and that is therefore inconsistent with its own essential normative basis. For this reason, it is intrinsically self-contradictory. However, a wrongful act, as an external manifestation of will, also has a positive existence in the following sense. It alters the world and this alteration, being the outcome of an act of will, seems to challenge the validity of right, which, on a constructivist approach, is conceived as immanent to willing. The alteration must therefore be annulled by a second act of will in order to make manifest that it is without validity. Only in this way can right be genuinely vindicated as something explicitly and actually valid.

But this required annulment can be effected only through an individual's particular will and it is here that abstract right generates a basic problem which it cannot solve with its own resources. Precisely because the determinate aspect of willing is not yet part of the will's freedom and consequently can be something merely arbitrary and subjective, individuals cannot annul wrong in a way that *objectively* establishes it as invalid. Being subjective and contingent in *form*, the effort to annul wrong must be inadequate to the universality and necessity of its import and so it can reasonably be regarded by others as itself a transgression. Because the standpoint of judgment in abstract right is public and relational, how something appears to others expresses its essential character as such. Each response to wrong, entailing as it does the positive action of a particular will, becomes in turn a new transgression that is self-contradictory in character and that consequently needs to be annulled, and so on *ad infinitum*. The sphere of abstract right turns out to be a condition of wrong in the highest degree because here action cannot posit the normative validity inherent in free agency as valid with respect to the interactions it is meant to govern unconditionally.[38]

In short, the requirement to respect formal equality can only be actualized at this point through a means, namely, the will in its particularity, which, being essentially unfree, is categorially unsuited to the task. This tension—that abstract right is vulnerable to and challenged by wrong but cannot annul it in accordance with its own criterion of objectivity—can be resolved only if the exclusion of determinacy from freedom is superseded, so that the will, "though particular and subjective, yet wills the universal as such."[39] What is needed is a form of free will in which the moral powers of free and equal persons are now elaborated such that subjects have a highest-order interest to realize the requirement of respect for formal equality as their end and goal. The account of this form and of its realization belongs to a second stage of right, which Hegel calls "morality," the transition to it being required by abstract right itself.

NOTES

1. For both Kant and Hegel, the first conception of the normative (whatever its content) is heteronomous, whereas the second alone is expressive of autonomy. I have adopted the term "constructivism" from the work of John Rawls. See Rawls, Kantian Constructivism in Moral Theory, 77 J. Phil. 515, 554–572 (1980); Rawls, Themes in Kant's Moral Philosophy, in Kant's Transcendental Deductions 81–113 (E. Forster ed. 1989). Drawing on Rawls' account of Kant's moral constructivism, I have tried in this paper to suggest why Hegel's philosophy of law is also constructivist in character and how the significance of the first part of that philosophy, namely, the section on abstract right, may be more fully brought out when it is viewed in this light.

2. Following Rawls, I shall take "lexical" ordering to mean an "order which requires us to satisfy the first principle in the ordering before we can move on to the second, the second before we consider the third, and so on. A principle does not come into play until those previous to it are either fully met or do not apply." J. Rawls, A Theory of Justice 43 (1971). Rawls notes that the priority of right as found in Kant is a case of lexical ordering.

3. Hegel discusses what I call the form and content of the general concept of free will at §§ 4–7 and § 29 respectively of the *Philosophy of Right* (T. Knox trans. 1952). My conceptualization of Hegel's discussion draws on distinctions suggested by Rawls in his *Themes in Kant's Moral Philosophy*, supra note 1, at 95–102.

4. Hegel refers to the "specific forms" that embody freedom. Philosophy of Right, supra note 3, § 30.

5. To prevent confusion, it should be noted here at the outset that, following Hegel, I will use "personality" to denote a *specific* form of free will. "Personality" is thus to be distinguished from "free and equal persons," "moral persons," and "conception of the person," all of which, as I use them, belong to the *general* concept of free will and are accordingly instantiated in the different specific forms, including personality. Finally, again following Hegel, I refer to individuals, viewed exclusively under the aspect of personality, simply as "persons."

6. I have discussed Kant's conception of responsible agency in Benson, External Freedom According to Kant, 87 Colum. L. Rev. 559 (1987).

7. See, for example, Hegel, Logic, § 53 (W. Wallace & A. Miller trans. 1975).

8. Hegel discusses the distinction between theoretical and practical thinking in several works. See, for example, Philosophy of Right, supra note 3, §§ 4, 4R, 4A; Philosophy of Mind, §§ 443, 469 (W. Wallace & A. Miller trans. 1971); The Philosophical Propaeudeutic 1–3, 10 (A. Miller trans. 1986).

9. Philosophy of Right, supra note 3, § 5–7. It should be noted that, although Hegel thinks that there can be a systematic rational account of the conception of the person as free and equal or of what I have called "the form of the general concept of free will" (which he seeks to provide in the *Logic* and *Philosophy of Mind*), he states that for the purposes of the *Philosophy of Right* he shall not attempt any such demonstration but will assume that the reader can, on reflection, discover that its essential features are latent in and presupposed by his or her everyday experience as a thinking, responsible agent. See id. § 4.

10. It should be emphasized that the independence spoken of here (which is a necessary aspect of the general concept of free will and which is therefore presupposed by its various specific forms) is only independence from the given as such. Each stage in the account of right has its specific way of expressing the will's independence from the given. Moreover, such independence does not imply that the self is to be characterized in abstraction from, or as indifferent to, *normatively valid* ethical ties of family or community, for example. Indeed, at the stage of free will that Hegel calls "ethical life," individuals are related to the ethical order (which comprises the family, civil society and the state) as accidents to substance (§ 145). This relation is possible, however, only if the ethical order can be represented, not as something given or extrinsic to free agency, but rather as its immanent realization. If attachment to family and community or to religious and philosophical views is to have *normative* validity and worth, it must not have its determining ground in a purely given or natural necessity.

11. Kant's discussion of these conditions of free agency can be found in the *Critique of Practical Reason*, (L.W. Beck trans. 1956), especially ch. I, § 2–4 and ch. II, bk. I of pt. I. Definitions of negative and positive freedom are presented in summary form in his *Philosophy of Law* 13–14 (W. Hastie trans. 1887). A contemporary account of agency in these terms is M. Oakeshott, On Human Conduct 35–40 (1975).

12. Philosophy of Right, supra note 3, § 4.

13. I discuss these matters briefly in Part Three of this essay.

14. Philosophy of Right, supra note 3, § 35.

15. Philosophy of Right, supra note 3, §§ 35–36. I note in passing that Hegel's use of the term "personality" seems to differ from that of Kant. For Kant, moral personality is "the freedom of a rational being under moral laws." Kant, The Philosophy of Law, supra note 11, pp. 31–32. In Kant's usage then, personality seems to represent the form of the general concept, and not a specific form, of free will.

16. This is the case in the second stage of right, "morality." See Philosophy Right, supra note 3, §§ 105–7. In the present essay, the discussion of why individuals, as *persons*, need not subjectively regulate or view their ends in the light of this conception of themselves begins at text accompanying note 18, infra, and

culminates with the characterization of the relevant normative standpoint as "external," at text accompanying note 28, infra.

17. See Philosophy of Right, supra note 3, § 49.

18. It is important to keep in mind that the self's *merely* negative relation of independence to its determinate features (native endowments, particular purposes, ties of relationship, and so forth) is characteristic of only one specific form of free will, namely personality, and it reflects the fact that at the start those features must be established as not given to the choosing self. With the other forms in which free and equal personhood is expressed, these determinate features can be progressively integrated, insofar as they are no longer merely given. The distinction between being a person and having the realization of personality for one's determinate aim is Hegel's (§ 104) and it underlies the categorial difference between abstract right and what Hegel calls "morality" or what Kant calls "virtue."

19. Philosophy of Right, supra note 3, §§ 42–43. The division into personality and things is normatively exhaustive and regulative. It is sometimes objected that Hegel has not shown why on his own view the determinate expression (or embodiment) of free will cannot be through an aspect of agency that is not a thing and in which a person need not have a proprietary interest. E.g., Piper, Property and the Limits of the Self, 8 Pol. Theory 39 (1980). In reply, Hegel's fundamental point is that *whatever* determinate feature one wishes to select, its *normative* significance can, at this stage, only consist in its being different from personality and therefore in its being a thing that persons are entitled to use. In this regard, it is important to keep in mind that, as we shall see, persons are under no obligation to use things and that the characterization of freedom in terms of persons and things is categorially independent of—and so need not constitute—the conceptions of value or particular interests that individuals may wish to realize.

20. This argument draws on §§ 44 and 45 of the *Philosophy of Right* as well as on Kant's elucidation of the "juridical postulate of practical reason" in his *Philosophy of Law*, supra note 11, at 62–64.

21. Philosophy of Right, supra note 3, § 46. At this point, ownership that is in common must be the result of a contract among individuals, each with a capacity for exclusive ownership, and it is therefore inherently dissoluble in character.

22. Philosophy of Right, §§ 37, 38, 45, 49, 104. See supra text accompanying note 18. Kant makes this point explicitly:

> As Right in general has for its object only what is external in actions, Strict Right, as that with which nothing ethical is intermingled, requires no other motives of action than those that are merely external; for it is then pure Right, and is unmixed with any prescriptions of Virtue . . . Now such Right is founded, no doubt, upon the consciousness of the Obligation of every individual according to the Law; but if it is to be pure as such, it neither may or should refer to this consciousness as a motive by which to determine the free act of the will.

Kant, Philosophy of Law, supra note 11, at 47–48.

23. Philosophy of Right, supra note 3, § 38. Kant characterizes the juridical postulate of practical reason, which grounds his deduction of the right to have an external

object as one's own, as a "permissive law of practical reason." Philosophy of Law, supra note 11, at 62–63.

With this mention of permissibility, it might be thought that the elementary mode of positive freedom (abstract right) articulates a doctrine of permissible, even if not obligatory, ends and that therefore, contrary to what I have suggested, it does after all refer to ends as part of the account of freedom. But this view is mistaken. To avoid misunderstanding, one should keep in mind the main idea: while the relevant criterion of evaluation, namely, respect for formal equality, applies to action, it is wholly indifferent to the standpoint that informs, and to the interests that are realized in, the pursuit of ends, whether permissible or obligatory. At this point, the pursuit of ends counts merely as a contingent factual happening that is, as such, devoid of inherent normative significance. Here positive freedom resides solely in the maintenance of the abstract standpoint of personality (and of its entailment, respect for formal equality), not in the pursuit of ends as such. To be sure, actions that are inconsistent with this requirement of respect are prohibited. This is entailed by the application of the criterion. So, we may say, positive freedom (abstract right) articulates a criterion in the light of which actions are intelligible as permitted or prohibited. However, in doing so, it merely sets the stage for the next step in Hegel's analysis of right, namely morality, where positive freedom now consists in, and is realized through, the pursuit of permissible ends and the satisfaction of the agent's interests contained therein. This gives rise to a qualitatively distinct complex of rights and duties that directly integrates such factors as the agent's particular intentions, purposes, insight, and needs—factors which were hitherto categorially irrelevant. For further discussion, see supra text accompanying note 18.

24. Jeremy Waldron interprets Hegel to be saying the contrary: "If one never actually gains control of any object then one never gets the benefits of the exercise of one's will on objects; one's will, then, never develops in the way that Hegel thinks it is important for it to develop." J. Waldron, The Right to Private Property 383 (1988). In order to reach this conclusion, however, Waldron must introduce (for example, at 371–74 and 385–89) formal and substantive ethical considerations, in connection with the question of the justification of private property, that are not entailed by the moral power(s) of personality (as set forth by Hegel in the crucial opening paragraphs of Abstract Right, §§ 34–39). Consequently, the bare abstractness of personality is not preserved in Waldron's account of the "embodiment of personality." But, as I have tried to make clear, the embodiment of personality is nothing more than the determinate mode in which the freedom specific to abstract personality is expressed. As textual support for his conclusion, Waldron refers (for example, at 350, 382, 384) to *Philosophy of Right* § 49A (based on student notes) where Hegel says: "Of course men are equal, but only *qua* persons . . . [T]he inference from this is that everyone must have property." Interpreted in context, however, this passage does not, I think, support Waldron's contention. Negatively, Hegel is trying to explain here that the equality of individuals, which at this point consists just in their being persons, does not justify equal property holdings. Positively, and in the light of what Hegel has attempted to establish in the preceding paragraphs, the Addition can only mean that, as a person, every individual has equally "the right of putting his will into any and every thing and thereby making it his." (§ 44). But this right, as Hegel emphasizes, is to be conceived only as a permission and as correlative to a negative duty not to injure what is already a person's property. The phrase "everyone must have

202 / *Abstract Right and Private Law*

property" is the equivalent of "personality must be embodied in property" (§ 50A): in both instances, the "must" expresses the kind of normative necessity compatible with the abstractness of personality.

25. The common law principle that there is no liability for mere nonfeasance can be justified on this basis.

26. In this essay, I do not discuss the possible ways in which persons may appropriate things consistently with formal equality. According to Kant and Hegel, these are essentially twofold: original acquisition in accordance with first occupancy and contractual acquisition in accordance with what they call the parties' "common will." In a forthcoming essay, "The Basis of Corrective Justice, its Priority and Autonomy," I try to show how these modes of acquisition reflect, and are required by, the negative, interactional, and external imperative of abstract right. The account of this imperative and of these modes of acquisition can provide a systematic understanding of the normative basis and structure of corrective justice. Or so I argue.

27. Philosophy of Right, supra note 3, § 155 ("In the sphere of abstract right, I have the right and another has the corresponding duty"); see also Philosophy of Mind, supra note 8, § 486.

28. I borrow this term from Kant. See Kant, Philosophy of Law, supra note 11, at 47–48.

29. For both Hegel and Kant, (abstract) right necessarily entails—and is conceived as—a right to coerce. See Philosophy of Right, supra note 3, § 94; Kant, Philosophy of Law, supra note 11, at 47–48. Here I have identified only one necessary condition of the moral possibility of coercion, namely the external character of the requirement of respect. A more complete discussion of this matter would require a systematic treatment of Hegel's account of wrong and its rectification at §§ 90–101.

30. I believe this account of positive freedom as negative, interactional, and external in character accords with Kant's presentation of the concept of right in the Introduction to the Philosophy of Law, supra note 11, at 44–45. In a recent essay, I have tried to discuss systematically the relation between this conception of autonomy and contemporary contract scholarship, in particular, the theories of Charles Fried, Anthony Kronman, and Michael Sandel. See Benson, Abstract Right and the Possibility of a Nondistributive Conception of Contract, 10 Cardozo L. Rev. 1077, 1077–1147 (1989).

31. Philosophy of Right, supra note 3, § 36.

32. In Hegel's doctrine, the capacity to form, to revise and rationally to pursue a conception of the good is first accounted for as a moral power, that is, as a capacity that belongs to individuals as free and equal persons, only in the second stage of right, "morality." See especially Philosophy of Right, supra note 3, §§ 106–111. Although this capacity is not postulated as a moral power in abstract right, it nevertheless presupposes abstract personality in at least the following respect: it is part of this capacity that individuals' preferences are not to be viewed as propensities beyond their control, that simply happen; individuals are regarded as responsible for their ends. See, Rawls, Social Unity and the Primary Goods, in Utilitarianism and Beyond 169 (A. Sen & B. Williams eds. 1982). The negative

independence that characterizes personality and that is embodied in abstract right expresses a necessary condition of this requirement.

33. Philosophy of Right, supra note 3, § 37.

34. See supra note 29.

35. I have in mind Rawls' account of the primary goods. According to Rawls, the primary goods are introduced so that rationally autonomous parties in the original position can make a rational agreement on behalf of the persons they represent: given the restrictions of the veil of ignorance, they are to do the best they can to advance the determinate good of those persons. See, for example, Rawls, The Basic Liberties and their Priority, 3 Tanner Lectures on Human Values 18–22 (1982). The primary goods are necessary, then, on the supposition that an interest in realizing a determinate conception of the good can be attributed to free and equal persons. But this, I have tried to show, is not yet the case in abstract right. Abstract right does not postulate even a thin theory of the good. This seems to confirm, from within a constructivist approach, Rawls' view that "primary goods are not to be used in making comparisons in all situations but only in questions of justice which arise in regard to the basic structure." Rawls, Social Unity and Primary Goods, supra note 32, at 163.

36. In this regard, Hegel's argument for the lexical priority of abstract right should be contrasted with libertarian approaches. Put in Hegel's terms, the latter view abstract right as being the sole category of right and as establishing an essentially final and normatively adequate determination of entitlements. Hegel's account of the distinctive nature and limits of abstract right may be understood as a systematic effort to show why this view is in fact mistaken.

It is beyond the scope of this essay to consider the relation between Hegel's constructivism and what, in my view, is the most systematic and carefully elaborated contemporary example of this approach, namely Rawls' theory of justice. Nevertheless, I wish to mention one point in this regard, although I cannot provide here the needed discussion. From the standpoint of Hegel's constructivist approach, justice as fairness unites in one conception certain normative notions that both presuppose and develop the more elementary meaning of abstract right. On the one hand, abstract right, or, more exactly, bare interaction between persons viewed exclusively in terms of formal equality, is the lexically first subject of right: with respect to the elucidation of the sequence of shapes of right, the priority of right entails the priority of abstract right relative to the other shapes, including therefore the conception of right (justice) appropriate for the basic structure. On the one other hand, the fundamental intuitive ideas in justice as fairness (such as its conception of the person with the two moral powers, the idea of fair social cooperation for mutual advantage, and so on) can be fully and systematically accounted for on a constructivist approach only through their being built up, step by step, over the several stages of right that follow abstract right and that culminate in the standpoint of what Hegel calls "the state:" justice as fairness is elaborated from a standpoint whose fundamental intuitive ideas are normatively complex relative to abstract right. In my view, this does not deny but, on the contrary, is fully consistent with and indeed substantiates the relative autonomy or free-standing character of the distinctive conception of justice for the basic structure. On the priority of abstract right, it should be noted, Hegel and Kant agree. For Kant, "private right" as he calls it (which is essentially the same as abstract right and which, like it, does not seem to depend even implicitly on any account of the primary goods) is the first part of a metaphysics of morals. For further discussion, see Benson, External Freedom According to Kant, supra note 6; Gregor, Kant's Theory of Property, 41 Rev. Metaphysics 757 (1988).

37. That abstract right is both a *distinct* and a *limited* normative whole is necessary if it is to be part of a lexical ordering. See Rawls, A Theory of Justice, supra note 2, at 43.

38. Philosophy of Right, supra note 3, §§ 102–03; Philosophy of Mind, supra note 8, § 502. Here again, Kant agrees. He explains the categorical imperative to leave the state of nature and to enter a juridical state under distributive justice in the light of the (arbitrary) subjectivity of individual judgment that characterizes the state of nature and that makes it a condition of wrong in the highest degree. Kant, Philosophy of Law, supra note 11, at 156–58.

39. Philosophy of Right, supra note 3, § 103.

7

Property, Contract, and Ethical Life in Hegel's *Philosophy of Right*

Peter G. Stillman

Property has signal importance in Hegel's *Philosophy of Right*.[1] Property is the first major institution discussed in the text; it is raised again in each subsequent section; and later interpreters, from Marx to the present, at least touch on property and its implications. In this paper, I explore some political and legal issues that turn on one central striking feature of Hegel's treatment of property: Hegel commences his political philosophy with abstract right, where he presents extensive individual rights to private property and free contract; but, when he considers the polity's major institutions (family, civil society, and state, which Hegel labels Ethical Life or *Sittlichkeit*), he sometimes asserts and at other times limits or transforms property and contract, according the qualities of the institutions and the needs of individuals, so that his polity contains many different varieties of property and of human relations.

Hegel's striking treatment of property is important from many perspectives. In Hegel's thought, the relation of abstract right to *Sittlichkeit* remains much debated. In modern political thought, the relation of individual rights (such as property and contract) to the state surfaces as a central theme. From Hobbes and Locke to the present, many modern thinkers begin with some version of independent persons, in a pre-social condition, asserting the rights to property, life, and liberty, and then conclude that all important human relations be based on or subordinated to private property and free contract.[2] On the other hand, Hegel rejects such monological thinking and uncovers a variety of forms of property, individuality, and social relations.

In contemporary legal theory also, prominent vexed questions revolve around how and to what extent the law and other social institutions should reflect the norms and practices implicit in private property and free contract, questions of alienability or inalienability of property; restraints on alienation; discrete transactions and relational contracts; and economic, utilitarian, and rational choice analyses of the law. Throughout the *Philosophy of Right*, Hegel wrestles to discern the types of property and human relations most conducive to freedom and individual development within the intersubjective interactions that characterize human life.

1. *Property in the Philosophy of Right.* Hegel first discusses property in the opening section of the *Philosophy of Right*, entitled "Abstract Right." Like many modern political philosophers, Hegel commences his exposition by stripping individuals of their political, social, and economic roles and attainments. Hegel's "abstract right" is a logical construct, whose human actors are logical abstractions from full human beings: they are persons, who have *Willkur* or arbitrary free will ("to do or forbear doing"[3] as they wish), particular characteristics (such as age and height, needs and passions), and the normative imperative, "Do not infringe personality and what personality entails" (§§ 35, 36, 38). Persons face a world of things, which are also logical abstractions from the full world of institutions and shaped nature: things are natural objects and animals, defined by their lack of free will, different from persons, and incapable of rights (§ 42).

Confronting this external world, the person sees that he is limited to being only subjective by this world that, as external to him, appears different and strange. To overcome this limitation, the person "has as his substantive end the right of putting his will into any and every thing and thereby making it his" property (§ 44). A property is a thing that contains a person's will.

At the same time that willing is the essence of property, the person must "occupy"—by grasping, forming, or marking (§ 54)—his property in order that others may recognize it as his (§ 51). The person has full use of his property (§ 59) and may alienate it by letting it fall ownerless, by giving it away, or by exchanging it by contract (§ 65). In a contract, property-holding persons who recognize each others' property rights freely exchange "single external things" of equivalent value according to their own arbitrary wills (§ 75, 77). So persons relate to and recognize each other through the media of things.

"Abstract Right," then, is a realm of private property and free contract among persons who are equal in terms of rights. The capacity to hold property and have other rights depends solely on bare, unencumbered, independent personhood; irrelevant are social status or position in political hierarchy. Similarly, things that can be property are sweepingly defined: rejected is, for instance, any special status or treatment for land or for objects with religious significance. Private property is full and complete: the owner has full use (and abuse), and can completely and cleanly alienate it. Contracts are discrete transactions: the exchange of equivalents in the market by parties who are equal (as property-owners). In short, Hegel's portrayal of persons, property, and contract has many points of similarity with visions of society and freedom varyingly labelled modern, liberal, (1980s) neoconservative, formal, commercial, capitalistic, or market.

2. *Property, Freedom, and Personality.* In "Abstract Right," Hegel presents property as essential for freedom for individuals. In the immanent logical development of the free will, a person's will, hitherto internal and merely subjective (Enc. §§ 480–81), becomes in property "an actual will" for the first time because it gains its "first embodiment" in the external world (§ 45). For Hegel, "man is implicitly rational, but he must also become explicitly so by struggling to create himself, not only by going forth from himself but also by building himself up within" (§ 10A). By putting his will into a thing and making it his property (§ 44), the person goes out from himself to work the external world of nature; through his property, the person goes forth from himself to relate to other men and to build social institutions; and, by developing his will in the natural and social worlds as well as by claiming himself, his life and liberty, as his property, man builds himself up from within as an independent and free individual.

In other words, in owning property, men act in the external world; property is freedom because it gives the individual a scope for action and makes possible his extending and expanding his personality. Through their property, human beings domesticate nature, liberating themselves from its toils. They create social institutions. In shaping the natural and the social world according to their intentions and goals, men develop and express their own capabilities; in reflecting on the results of their actions, they educate themselves about the world of actuality and about themselves—and thereby prepare themselves for additional action. Property—the embodiment of the free will in the world—is essential for human beings if they are to attain a developed freedom and individuality.[4]

But the freedom and individuality of property have, Hegel knows, serious deficiencies. In property the person's will is limited to some extent by the external characteristics of the thing owned and the social context in which he owns it. Moreover, the characteristics of the abstract person are not very appealing: "To have no interest except in one's formal right may be pure obstinacy, often a fitting accompaniment of a cold heart and restricted sympathies. It is uncultured people who insist most on their rights, while noble minds look on other aspects of the thing" (§ 37A). The will that is content to find its freedom in property, the individual for whom his property is his highest concern, the isolated individual concerned only with his own desires and interests—each is defective, narrow both as an individual and socially, unable fully to participate in the possibilities offered by ethical life. So the person needs experience in ways of living that are not exclusively tied to abstract right, private property, and free contract.

Founded on private property, Hegel's political philosophy retains it throughout. Property remains a permanent apparatus for the individual to carry out a life-plan, to give reality to a conception of his own good, his further development, and his self-satisfaction. Similarly, for the fully developed world of ethical life, characterized by a variety of institutions and interactions, property remains a permanent dimension of freedom, actualized and guaranteed in the system of needs and the administration of justice. But Hegel's political thought is founded on property only so that it can transcend property. The fully developed individual is more than the property-owning person of abstract rights, the system of needs, and the administration of justice; the individual has (moral and ethical) ideals and human interactions (in, e.g., family and state) that are not based on private property. Similarly, major institutions of ethical life are rooted in community, impose obligations, and so overcome the atomism and individualism of property and contract. In Hegelian terms, then, property must be *aufgehoben*, both preserved and transcended,[5] so that Hegel can get from the property-centered starting point of "Abstract Right" to a *Sittlichkeit* that is institutionally pluralistic and varied; rich in types of human relations, development, and freedom; and logically and practically coherent as a society.

3. *The Status of "Abstract Right."* The preservation and transcending of property occurs throughout the *Philosophy of Right*. But even in the section on "Abstract Right," Hegel prepares for modifications in private property and free contract. This section and the next two explore three aspects of property in "Abstract Right": the logical status of "Abstract Right" itself; the connection between property and personality; and the distinctions about alienation in the opening discussions.

In Hegel's thought, even the possibility that property be transcended or limited draws on the different role abstract right plays in his overall political philosophy from the role of the state of nature (or similar prepolitical construct) in most other major modern political philosophies, a difference that subsists despite the parallels that can readily be drawn between Hegel's abstract right and constructs from Locke's state of nature through Rawls's "veil of ignorance."[6] From their states of nature, historical or hypothetical, Locke, Kant, and Rawls derive the rights of man and certain rules about social relations, rights and rules which they then hold up as a constant paradigm, norm, or criterion of what contemporary social and political life should be. For instance, once Locke has derived in the state of nature the rights to life, liberty, and estates, the use of money, and the unequal distribution of property, then he sees that the role of government in "civil or political society" is to maintain and protect those rights, money use, and property inequalities. So the state of nature is not only primary— in the sense of coming first in order—historically or conceptually; conclusions derived from it are primary—in the sense of coming first in predominance or, as Dworkin would have it,[7] "trumping": actions, institutions, and ideas that come later in order than those derived from the abstract original condition are always to be tested against, subjected to, and vulnerable to being trumped by the principles derived from that abstract original condition.

Hegel's abstract right functions in the exact opposite way. First or primary in the logical order of the major parts of Hegel's political philosophy, abstract right is for that reason the least adequate part of "objective spirit" (§ 75R); and the specific contents of abstract right— the rights, principles, and paradigms of property, contract, and annulment or punishment of crime—are similarly inadequate: primitive, thin, and insufficient. The models of human being and of social interaction that derive from abstract rights alone are one-sided and narrow: for instance, from rights alone it is difficult or impossible logically to deduce human love and love-based institutions (§ 75R). Moreover, abstract rights are neither self-generating nor self-maintaining but rather rely on norms and values that are external to and prior to rights: neither possession nor exchange can itself generate the rights to property and contract; rights require a preexisting relational structure of reciprocally recognizing persons (with free wills), a structure that has developed historically, that represents the crystallization of certain habits and customs, and that (for Hegel) is characterized as *Sittlichkeit*. As the "minimal mode of human freedom" for individual and institution and as dependent on preexisting social relations for their very existence as rights, abstract rights are "in radical need of correction and completion through contextualizing."[8] Consequently, for Hegel, the abstract rights of property and contract are always vulnerable to being modified, limited, and filled out by later developments in the text.

4. *Hegel's Developmental Idea of Personality.* In addition, Hegel has a very different conception of the person from most social contract theorists. By deriving the person's rights to life and liberty from the right to property, Hegel displays a concern for the education and culturation (*Bildung*[9]) of the individual. A comparison with Locke may bring out Hegel's concern sharply. Locke postulates the individual's property in himself as the original: "every Man has a *Property* in his own *Person* . . . The *Labour* of his Body, and the *Work* of his Hands, we may say, are properly his."[10] Locke assumes that the individual owns himself as his own property and derives property in things from property in self. Because Locke begins with the assertion that individuals own their bodies and minds, he regards that property as a given, not as a task for the individual nor as a problem for his political philosophy.[11]

Hegel, on the other hand, sees the right to property in things as the basis for the rights of the person to life and liberty. The person claims himself as he claims a property, through his will to own, occupy, and modify and transform himself: "it is only through the development of his own mind and body, essentially through his self-consciousness's apprehension of itself as free, that he takes possession of himself and becomes his own property and no one else's" (§ 57). So the individual's appropriation of himself as his own property—his self-conscious apprehension of himself as free—is neither automatic nor easy, but a long struggle in claiming one's self and developing one's individuality, an undertaking that requires moral attitudes, practical experience, and constructive intersubjective interactions.

Concurrently, Hegel holds a developmental idea of society. Again, the contrast with Locke may be helpful. For Locke, political society has a constant and changeless goal: the protection of the natural rights of each citizen. But Hegel insists that private property inheres in persons only because of their relations to other persons in a nexus of mutual recognition of personality; property is social from the start. And the social context adequate to persons with property does not, for Hegel, define and determine the ultimate social context for fully developed individuals; the social and political world Hegel envisions must grow progressively richer—more complex, more various—after abstract right, in order to generate the values and relations that can enrich the developing individuality that citizens pursue and that politics encourages.

5. *Alienable and Inalienable Property, and Contractual and Noncontractual Relations.* Hegel's ability to preserve and transcend property also depends on his carefully differentiating between the person's

alienable property in things and his inalienable property in his life and liberty. Hegel makes this differentiation by following consistently and rigorously his definition of property. Most notably, he insists that the object that is to be the property must be a single external thing, "something not free, not personal, without rights" (§ 42); that alienation is an integral element of property (§ 65); and that the object "about which a contract is made is a single external thing, since it is only things of that kind which the parties' purely arbitrary will has it in its power to alienate" (§ 75).

When a person claims a property by putting his will in the thing, the person has the full use and alienation of that property, so long as— here is where Hegel's definition enters—the thing that is property remains "external" and "not personal" (§ 42). So for Hegel, one kind of property—property in one's self, one's body and mind—must be treated somewhat differently from the paradigmatic case of property as simply the will in the thing. For Hegel, the difference in treatment arises because a person's body and mind are special kinds of things and thus special kinds of property.

Unlike other property in the early discussions in "Abstract Right," the person's body and mind—though at first "things" to the person because they do not yet contain his will, purposes, and personality— are directly part of the person and so not external and not alienable from the point of view of others. A person must be recognized by others as owning his body, because it is only through our bodies—by speech, by grasping, forming, and marking—that we are seen to be and act in the world. It is through our bodies that our free wills manifest and actualize themselves in the world through free actions. If my body did not belong to me, I could not manifest my will in the world, because the words and actions emanating from me would not be mine.

Furthermore, for the person, taking possession of his self means appropriating his mind and body, his willing, thinking, and acting, and his moral, religious, and ethical life; so he gains as his property those substantive characteristics of himself that are not "external by nature" (§ 65) but that are internal to himself and "constitute" his "own private personality and the universal essence of [his] self-consciousness" (§ 66). Once gained, they cannot be alienated because they are not single external things (§ 66R). The inalienability and imprescriptibility of a person's mind and body—life and liberty—are indispensable constituents of the centrality of freedom in Hegel's political philosophy.

In other words, starting from a rigorous (and generally modern and market) definition of private property and free contract, Hegel has shown that persons cannot be property; human beings cannot be slaves.

This inalienability of life and liberty is not "paternalistic," either in the specific denotation or the generally negative connotations of that term.[12] Rather, for Hegel the inalienability of life and liberty is built into the very definition of personality. Inalienability is constitutive of personality, not accidental to or separable from it: persons qua persons have free will—and thus must potentially or actually own, permeate, and control their own minds and bodies (§ 35).[13] Conversely, any political theory that admits slavery necessarily views human beings as things, as nonhuman, or as essentially natural beings—and so remove "human beings" as a universal category from participation in entitlements and rights (§ 45R).

Just as Hegel's discussion of what is alienable hinges on property's being "single external things," so too does his discussion of what can be contractual (§ 75). For Hegel, the strict definition of property and contract means most especially that neither marriage nor the state can be contractual relations (§ 75R). In a lament that could have been made today, Hegel complains that "the intrusion of . . . contractual relation, and relationships concerning private property generally" into thinking about the state "has been productive of the greatest confusion in both constitutional law and public life" (§ 75R). Theorists who see the family and the state in contractual terms "have transferred the characteristics of private property into a sphere of a quite different and higher nature" (§ 75R).

In sum, starting even in the section on "Abstract Right," where property seems at first to be defined in unequivocal, unambivalent, and far-reaching terms, Hegel follows precisely the meaning and implications of his definition of property; and that path leads him to limit private property and free contract to their proper practical sphere—of relations about single external things—and to their proper theoretical and ideological spheres—so that the family and the state, for instance, not be seen purely in contract terms, in property terms, or (as at present) in economic terms.

6. *Property in Civil Society: The System of Needs and the Administration of Justice.* Beyond the limits of "Abstract Right,"[14] Hegel's discussions of property in "Ethical Life [*Sittlichkeit*]" continue to involve precise distinctions and careful attention to circumstances—of the thing that is the property, the human beings and their *Bildung* or development, and the institutional context. As those distinctions and circumstances require, the characteristics defining property in abstract right are modified in *Sittlichkeit*. Because both the system of needs and the administration of justice involve substantially a translation into

concrete terms of the paradigmatic property of abstract right, it may be easiest to begin with them.

In the system of needs in civil society, private property and free contract have extensive play, in what might be labelled the "economic" aspect of property. The human being (*Mensch*) of the system of needs, with his multiplicity of differentiated needs (§ 190), finds himself unable to satisfy those needs through unworked nature or unclaimed things, because almost everything is owned by someone as property. So he can satisfy his needs only through "external things, which . . . are . . . the property and product of the needs and wills of others" (§ 189). These properties can be obtained only through his own work and effort in a complex system of "interdependence of each on all" in which each man contracts with others, alienating his own property (e.g., money) for whatever properties—goods and services—he wishes for the satisfaction of his needs. Following Smith, Say, and Ricardo (§ 189R), Hegel sees the system of needs as a locus of the free play of the individual's arbitrary will and self-interest, as he works, earns, and exchanges freely in order to satisfy his needs, interests, and whims, i.e., to gain properties that he can use. When an individual chooses his vocation and activities, "natural capacity, birth, and other circumstances have their influence"; but "the essential and final determining factors are subjective opinion and the individual's arbitrary will, which win in this sphere their right, their merit, and their dignity" (§ 206).

In the administration of justice in civil society likewise, the major aspects of property have extensive scope, in what might be labelled the "legal" aspect of property. "In civil society, property rests on contract and on the formalities which make ownership capable of proof and title in law" (§ 217), and the administration of justice enforces and determines these formalities. It "gives abstract right the determinate existence of being something universally recognized, known, and willed, and having a validity and an objective actuality mediated by this known and willed character" (§ 209). Abstract right is posited as positive law, known by all, and applicable to specific cases. Hegel strongly advocates codified law (as opposed, for instance, to common law) and sees that his conceptualization of abstract rights is congenial to a sound codification.[15]

In other words, for Hegel the central definitional characteristics of property (and its alienation through contract) exist in concrete, institutionalized form in both the system of needs and the administration of justice. Three important connections must be noted. First, for Hegel, the arbitrary free will that characterizes the person of abstract rights is reproduced in the "concrete person" of civil society (§ 182), who is a mixture of caprice and natural need. The person's voluntariness or capricious choosing is an essential dimension of full subjective freedom for Hegel and the crowning achievement of modern civil society, "which has for the first time given all determinations of the Idea their due" (§ 182A; see § 206R). Hegel values free choice because it encourages individual "particularities": it activates individual energy (§ 206R), it leads to variety (§ 182A), and it inclines individuals to think about their own selves, interests, and private ends (§ 181) and to act in pursuit of these private ends. The freedom of the marketplace and the law courts, the actualized freedom of private property and contract, is a minimal but essential moment of freedom.

The second important connection between abstract right and civil society is that private property and free contract serve as the theoretical basis and justification for the free exchange of the system of needs and the jurisprudence of public, codified law in the administration of justice. Whereas social contract theorists like Locke use property and contract as the bases of the state, Hegel's strict concept of property and contract cannot properly serve as a metaphor for the state (§ 75R). But property and contract can properly "fulfill a *double* function of legitimation: they serve as the philosophical foundation of modern positive law, and they justify modern relations of exchange in the market place."[16] What underlies, justifies, and legitimates modern law and modern market exchange is not any utilitarian consideration (like the wealth of the nation, value, economic efficiency, or GNP) but rather the rights of the person.

Thirdly, however, when freedom is characterized as choice and abstract right legitimates the law and the market, then the limits, partiality, and incompleteness of private property and abstract right surface. To consider freedom primarily as the freedom to choose—voluntariness (*Willkur*) or rational choice—is inadequate because the focus on choice alone ignores the constrained alternatives available to be chosen, the ways in which the individual is dependent on forces beyond his control, and the coercion of the institutional setting, the market, in which choice occurs.

For instance, while the person of abstract right and the man of civil society can choose, the contents of their mind—that which is available for them to choose from—may well be severely limited or constrained: in Kant's idiom, they may be heteronomous; in Rousseau's, they may be slaves to their passions.[17] Equally, their freedom is mean if the alternative choices offered to them by external circumstances are all unpalatable. For Hobbes and his successors, "fear and liberty are consistent; as when a man throweth his goods into the sea for *fear* the ship should sink, he doth it nevertheless very willingly, and may refuse to do it he will: it is therefore the action of one that was *free.*"[18] But for Hegel such circumstances produce at best a thin and constrained freedom.

Moreover, the competitive-contractual system of needs imposes on individuals limited and unappealing ways of thinking and acting. Every man "becomes in some measure a merchant,"[19] caught up in getting and spending, in the quest for mere life; equally, every burgher spends much of his time following the habits of the Smiths (§ 192A), keeping up with the Joneses, or buying goods and services to satisfy a need newly created "by those who hope to make a profit from its creation" (§ 191A). Human relations are reified and instrumentalized, mediated by money in calculated and utilitarian contracts (§§ 75, 80). Men are thrown into positions of subservience and dependence on others,[20] and must obey the imperatives of the system of civil society itself (§ 238).

Equally, however, the system of needs and the administration of justice are limited and inadequate on their own. Most obviously in Hegel's presentation, the modern exchange economy has a constant tendency to fall into disequilibrium and disorder; formally equal contracts in civil society produce highly inegalitarian results in an "inner dialectic of civil society" that leads it to generate a class of poverty-stricken rabble whose distress civil society itself cannot heal (§§ 185, 195, 241–48). Similarly, because the goal of the administration of justice is the "protection of property" (§ 208), law cannot be a final point of political integration or represent true universality.[21] Both the system of needs and the administration of justice require institutions outside of themselves to regulate, order, and guide them. Their own insufficiencies show that they (and the freedom they instantiate) cannot be the final and sufficient institutions of *Sittlichkeit* nor the locus of full freedom.

7. *Property in Civil Society: The Police and the Corporation.* The other two major institutions of civil society are the police (or public authority) and the corporations,[22] whose functions are "provision against contingencies still lurking in [the system of needs and the administration of justice], and care for particular interests as a common interest" (§ 188). In some of their functions, the public authorities uphold property, alienation, and contract: like contemporary police, Hegel's enforce the law (§ 233); like contemporary governmental agencies, they also superintend education (§ 239). But other important functions of the public authority impinge upon free alienation and contract: they are charged with keeping economic order in domestic

trade, minimizing dislocations resulting from foreign trade, maintaining welfare for the needy, and assuring that everyone be able effectively to exercise rights and participate in the system of needs.

The public authority intervenes in the domestic economy to adjust, adjudicate, and balance the "differing interests of producers and consumers" by, for instance, fixing prices (§ 236) of necessities such as bread. The police's "public care and direction are most of all necessary in the case of the larger branches of industry, because these are dependent on conditions abroad and on combinations of distant circumstances which cannot be grasped as whole by the individuals tied to these industries for their living" (§ 236).

Finally, the public authority is charged with the double task of maintaining the welfare of impoverished members of civil society and ensuring that they can participate fully in the system of needs. The public authority uses tax money to act as trustee to some poor (§ 240), to provide public charity for others (§ 242), and to "take the place of the family where the poor are concerned in respect not only of their immediate want but also of laziness of disposition, malignity, and the other vices which arise out of their plight and their sense of wrong" (§ 241). The public authority also acts to assure that the poor still engage in the socializing activities of the system of needs, i.e., that they work, develop needs in interaction with others, and exchange goods and services by contract (§§ 243–45).

In the instance of trade, Hegel advocates intervention and active oversight by the public authority because he thinks that the claims of the universal purchaser, the public, are more weighty than the right of free alienation and contract; in the instance of welfare, Hegel advocates public intervention because he thinks that the physical and mental well-being of all should override strict adherence to property rights. In both instances, Hegel is directly at odds with that strong tradition that advocates a single-minded or blunt use of property rights, a position voiced by David Ricardo, who insisted that "distress" from trade dislocations "is an evil to which a rich nation must submit" and that— regardless of level of wages and the incidence of poverty—"like all other contracts, wages should be left to the fair and free competition of the market, and should never be controlled by the interference of the" government.[23]

Hegel's differences with Ricardo and his followers about the role of the public authority have three roots. One is that Hegel held Sir James Steuart's idea that fair and free markets require "double competition," i.e., competition among both buyers and sellers.[24] For Steuart, "single competition," where for instance one seller is negotiating with a plurality of buyers—as happens with "the commonest necessities of life" such as bread—puts the seller in a powerful position and leads to contracts imbalanced consistently in favor of the monopolist, not conducive to overall fairness or orderliness in the economy, and therefore requiring governmental intervention (§ 236).

A second reason exists for Hegel's advocating the intervention of the public authority where Ricardo, for instance, does not: like contemporary economistic thinkers, Ricardo stresses formal freedom to the general exclusion of welfare in economic society, whereas Hegel stresses rights and formal freedom to the exclusion of welfare only in abstract right and sees that in civil society both welfare and right must be recognized and realized. Consequently, the public authority frequently has to intervene, sometimes to remind men in the system of needs to recognize the rights of others (and not take their property by theft rather than contract), at other times to assure the welfare of those affected by trade dislocations or the normal functioning of the economic system.

A third reason Hegel favors public intervention is the ethical welfare of the members of civil society, especially the poor: their rights must be upheld and their participation in the social benefits of civil society assured if they are to remain full members of their own *Sittlichkeit*, active citizens of their state (§§ 244, 257). Since a free economic order on its own generates potentially alienated poor, the public authorities must act to integrate them.

The free use and alienation of property is also limited in corporations. Although not legally required, membership in a corporation is important for businessmen, because owning "moveable" property or engaging in the "business of exchange" tends to make their relations with their fellow citizens abstract or dissociated (§ 204). Through their membership in a corporation they can obtain stable recognition and respect for their contribution to civil society (§ 253), a sense that they are "somebody" working and contributing valuably in the social order. "The so-called 'natural' right of exercising one's skill and thereby earning what there is to be earned is restricted within the Corporation only in so far as it is therein made rational instead of natural" (§ 254), i.e., made a pursuit of recognition rather than sheer accumulation of money. Recognition and cooperation in corporations also includes aiding the less fortunate members. So the corporation member loses the free use and alienation of his property, practices the virtues of liberality and rectitude in the place of (the person's) arbitrary will, and enters into long-term relations, not only discrete and transitory contracts.

8. *Property in the Family.* Hegel follows his definitions of property, alienation, and contract strictly when discussing marriage and children. So Hegel argues that marriage is not in essence a contract deriving from mutual alienation of property because it involves not "single external things" that can be alienated but rather each party's full personality, which no one can rightly alienate once he or she has claimed it, and in which no other person can rightly claim a property right. Hence Hegel's vehement and famous complaint that "to subsume marriage under the concept of contract is thus quite impossible" (§ 75R); to talk of marriage as such a contract is "shameful" (§ 75R). Rather, "though marriage begins in contract," including the free consents (§ 162) and inclinations (§ 162R) of the partners, "it is precisely a contract to transcend the standpoint of contract" (§ 163R), because both parties "consent to make themselves one person, to renounce their natural and individual personality to this unity of one with the the other" and thereby find in this union "their liberation, because in it they attain their substantive self-consciousness" (§ 162) in a full and intimate community of "love, trust, and common sharing of their entire existence as individuals" (§ 163). So marriage and the family must be seen as a small community based on love (§ 158) in which the participating individuals are viewed as family members.[25]

Since marriage does not involve the assertion of personal rights by the two parties but is a small community, the property of the marriage-partners should be viewed not as the private property of each, to be used and alienated by each separately according to the arbitrary will of each, but rather as the resources or "family capital" (*Vermogen*) of the small community. *Vermogen* extends to include everything that can provide for the subsistence and enjoyment of the family, including for instance the skills and labor of the father (§ 171). The family resources are to be treated as "common property so that, while no member of the family has property of his own [*qua* family member], each has his right to the common stock" (§ 171). In other words, all family members contribute to the family's *Vermogen*, and all can draw on it according to their needs.[26] Based on a type of human relation unrelated to (and indeed excluded from) property-based relations, marriage involves a principle of property that is different from—indeed, as common property, contradictory to—the property of "Abstract Right" (§ 46).

Children also cannot be subsumed under the principle of property of "Abstract Right." As potential adults, they "are potentially free and their life directly embodies nothing save potential freedom. Consequently they are not things and cannot be the property either of their parents or others," such as the state (§ 175). Rather, their status as potential adults means that their parents are obligated to educate them into the principles of ethical life, to "raise" them out of their natural instinctive level, to discipline them to correct and reform them (and not to enforce retribution, as is the purpose of the legalistic punishment of abstract right and the administration of justice, which is not appropriate to the nonproperty-based, feeling community of the family), so that they can attain "self-subsistence and freedom of personality" (§§ 174–75).[27] With children as with marriage, Hegel finds that the principles and practices of private property and free contract retain little scope in the community of the family, and must be replaced by other principles.

9. *Property in the State.* A similar conclusion holds with the state. Like marriage, the state cannot be conceptualized as property or contract, because the state does not own its citizens and because individuals do not own or alienate "single external things" when they become members of a state. Rather, and again like the family, the state is a living community of which the citizens are parts, a community whose norms, ideals, and modes of action shape—and are shaped by—the citizens' habits, knowledge and activity, and goals (§ 257), a community whose overall goal is the common interest or general will of all its citizens, what Hegel calls the universal.

Almost nowhere in the state exist the principles of private property and free contract. The state has a legitimate claim to a portion of each citizen's property in taxes (§ 299). The modern state generally exacts taxes in money, not service, so that the individual can choose how to earn the money to pay the tax.[28] But the one remaining nonmonetary exaction is the state's calling on its citizens in case of war—which puts at risk their lives and properties. "War is the state of affairs which deals in earnest with the vanity of temporal goods and concerns—a vanity at other times a common theme of edifying sermonizing" (§ 324R). The individual citizen's duty is to uphold "the independence and sovereignty of the state, at the risk and the sacrifice of property and life, as well as of opinion and everything else naturally comprised in the compass of life" (§ 324).

In his discussion of the major powers of the state—the monarch, executive, and legislative—Hegel does not assimilate any political relation to his abstract right statements of freely usable and alienable property in things. State positions cannot be private property, much less alienable private property. The legislators in the lower house gain their seats by election, not by purchase, and retain them by re-election, not property-right (§ 308). They are elected by vote of members in a corporation; no formal property qualification determines who votes. (Hegel finds any statewide system of property requirements as external to and abstract from the core issue, political competence [§ 310R], although each corporation may well impose its own minimal standards of property and earnings on prospective members [§ 255R].) Legislative debate aims to "vindicate the universal interest, not the particular interest of a society or Corporation in preference to that interest" (§ 309).

In the executive (i.e., the governmental bureaucracy) and the army, Hegel also minimizes the scope for private property. Members of the executive and the army (§ 277A) do not hold their offices as private property. Not to be regarded as a "single external thing" but as requiring a commitment to the core values of the state, public offices cannot become private property, as was the case under feudalism (and, as Hegel carps, in the contemporary English army [277A]), but must be open to those who have the needed "ability, skill, [and] character" (§ 277A). In the face of state requisites, private property must give way.

For the members of the upper house and the monarch himself, alienable private property must also give way: it becomes inalienable wealth. For full and open communication of all important points of view, the state requires one branch whose members' wills are independent (§ 305), especially independent of the results of state activity and of the imperious demands and fluctuations of civil society (§ 306) and of election campaigns (§ 307); Hegel finds such independence in a legislative upper house whose members are large landowners whose wealth is "inalienable, entailed, and burdened by primogeniture" (§ 306). Similarly, Hegel's hereditary constitutional monarch, whose independent "I will" is so essential to the modern state that has actualized subjective freedom (§ 279), has his politically necessary independence and service assured because his family's wealth is not freely alienable (§§ 280–81).

Throughout the state as throughout the family, then, the practices and principles of abstract right are transformed in order to fulfill the requirements of the political community. The state is not about single external things and so not a contract; the relations of state offices and officers to each other and to the citizens are neither contractual nor relations of ownership. Private property is redefined and transformed to meet the demands of proper political order and action.

10. *Property, Personality, and Sittlichkeit in Hegel's Thought.* In opening stages of his discussion of property in "Abstract Right," Hegel presents what seems to be a extensive, comprehensive, and powerful statement of the person's right to property. Property seems as influential for Hegel as for many other modern political philosophers, since

the right to property is bound up with freedom, personal equality, and the domestication of nature. If anything, property takes on especial importance since for Hegel the person's rights to life and liberty derive from (or are modes of the exercise of) his right to property—private property and possessive individualism at their most extreme, it could be said.

But what appears true for the first few paragraphs in Hegel's presentation of property does not hold true at the end of the *Philosophy of Right*. Hegel does start with a broad and powerful definition of property; but he does so because the distinctions and limitations within property and contract will then, he thinks, become clear, made translucent by his logic, his attention to relevant contextual considerations, and his awareness of the theoretical issues that have surrounded past discussions of property and that would surround post-1821 discussions.

Generally, what allows and requires Hegel to limit the scope of paradigmatic private property (the will in the thing, full and complete, with free use, alienation, and contract) and to introduce other forms of owning are three concerns: first, his sense that property, primary in logical order, is therefore primitive and less developed than later attitudes and institutions in contributing to mature human freedom (section 3, above); his idea of the person as dynamic and developmental, acting in and learning from the world (section 4, above); and the careful logical and contextual distinctions Hegel draws in his analysis of property, alienation, and contract in abstract right (section 5, above) and the attention to circumstances—of things, individuals, intersubjectivity, and institutions—throughout all of ethical life (sections 6–9, above), where Hegel focuses on the matters that are the media of human relations for different institutions of *Sittlichkeit*, the social roles that the individuals play in the different institutional settings; the demands and purposes of the institutions themselves, and the relation between individual and institution, between what is required for the full development of individuals and the rational ordering of institutions.

Because of his first concern, the primitiveness of property, contract, and abstract right generally, Hegel does not wish to impose images, metaphors, or models of private property and free contract throughout all social life; nor to follow economistic theorists in asserting, without much argument or context, that free alienating and contracting are always desirable; nor to follow out the implications in Locke, for instance, that because (abstracted) man in the state of nature relates through property, free alienation, and contract, therefore fully developed and social man can or should only or even primarily relate through them. Rather—and because of his second concern, about the dynamic and development character of individuality—at the same time that Hegel sees private property as essential to the development of individual personality and rational institutions, he also sees that abstract right is limited in its contribution to such development and that nonproperty-based and noncontract-based modes of personality development and rational institutions exist and are necessary to a full individuality and to a full political rationality.

Hegel's third concern—his care, in "Abstract Right," in defining property clearly and in discussing the distinctions of use and alienation, as well as his attention to the specific characteristics and goals of different social structures—allows him to differentiate among types of relations between human beings and nonhuman objects, in plain language among types of property. When combined with his first concern—the primitiveness of full and complete private property—the result is that in the major institutions of *Sittlichkeit* only the system of needs and the administration of justice directly actualize private property. Public authority and corporations limit private property, and the crucial institutions of family and state contain very little of private property and free contract: as the person is transformed into a member of a community, property is transformed into community resources and contract is replaced by different forms of intersubjectivity, relation, and obligation.

Hegel's three concerns, taken together, indicate how he can begin his presentation of his political philosophy with a single person in a presocial condition, from that start derive free and complete private property, and then—because of property's relative primitiveness and because of the logical distinctions (in the subsection on "Property" especially) and the contextual distinctions in ethical life—end up with social structures in ethical life some of which concretize and embody abstract property fully and others of which modify it or are based on altogether different foundations from property and contract.

Similarly, Hegel's three concerns, taken together, indicate how he can begin his political philosophy with the right to property, have the individual claim his life and liberty as property, and yet claim things as alienable, and life and liberty as inalienable, property; and how he can link property and personality, show the limits of the linkage, and construct the nonproperty-based institutions which continue the *Bildung* of personality or individuality, begun in property and still requiring private property. The dynamic and developmental character of personality both requires and is limited by property (section 2); and the transcending of property is built on the existence, in *Sittlichkeit*, of social structures some of which concretize abstract right, others of which do so partially, and still others of which are built on completely different principles. For Hegel, individual development and *Bildung* require that the individual be involved in a variety of institutions, that allow more or less scope for the arbitrary will of property and for the universal will of community; the coincidence or concrete unity of individual and *Sittlichkeit* requires that individual *Bildung* develop to the level of universality; and the state, in order to be a logical and experiential unity, requires a variety of social structures that both encourage individual *Bildung* and produce institutional coherence.

Among the many implications of Hegel's discussion for the contemporary world, three seem to stand out. One is that personal rights and freedoms cannot be alienable: free will is constitutive of personality, not merely an inessential attribute, and so cannot be alienated by the person nor appropriated by another. The second is that any free modern political order requires some scope both for actualized abstract rights and for social practices not based on abstract rights. Private property—the first rights of the person—does need to have some definite scope in social life, so that those essential rights can be actualized. Equally does welfare—the satisfaction of needs and participation in civil society—require realization. Moreover, human development—individual *Bildung*—necessarily requires that there be some scope in social life where the norms and practices of abstract right do not predominate. Political life does not exist in order to extend property rights and rules, but to develop and encourage the many different dimensions of human flourishing.

Finally, and unlike many other modern political philosophers and economists who aim to interpret and enclose as many dimensions of human life in the terms of individual private property with free and full use, alienation, and contract, Hegel's treatment serves to open, not to close, the question of the scope of application in society of the practices and principles of abstract right, formal freedom, and arbitrary free choice: in what types of social structures and individual interactions should private property and free contract be given full scope, and in what kinds of social structures and individual interactions should property (that may be fully usable and alienable in the system of needs or the economists' marketplace) be limited or replaced by norms and goals not based on property, contract, or abstract right?

NOTES

1. G. Hegel, The Philosophy of Right (T. Knox trans. 1945). Citations to the *Philosophy of Right* are placed in parentheses in the text and are to section

number; where the material cited is from the main text of the section, the section number alone is given; where it is from the "remarks" Hegel added to the text, the section number is followed by R; where it is from the "additions" that later editors appended to posthumous editions by collating student lecture notes, the section number is followed by A. The material in the *Philosophy of Right* is presented in briefer compass in G. Hegel, The Philosophy of Mind (W. Wallace trans. 1894), which is Part III of Hegel's *Enzyklopadie der philosophischen Wissenschaften* (F. Nicolin & O. Poggeler eds. 1969) (7th ed.), cited in parentheses in the text, with the section number preceded by the abbreviation "Enc." In this article, "property" means "private property" (except where the context makes clear otherwise). I use "man" and "men" as the generic terms for human beings, partly because Hegel's translators do so but primarily because Hegel's political philosophy sees men (i.e., males) as the major actors in civil society and state, regardless of Hegel's terminology, and so the generic term quietly takes on a strongly masculine identity.

2. The emphasis on private property and free contract exists among many contemporary economists, economic analysts of law (and philosophy and politics), rational choice theoreticians, libertarians, and the like—who can be labelled economistic thinkers, i.e., those who reason deductively from such standard neo-classical economic assumptions as atomistic individuals, pursuing their self-interest, voluntarily, in a condition of formal freedom (or "freedom from").

3. J. Locke, An Essay Concerning Human Understanding 240–41 (P. Nidditch ed. 1975); see also T. Hobbes, Leviathan 54 (M. Oakeshott ed. 1962).

4. These assertions are argued in Stillman, Person, Property, and Civil Society in the *Philosophy of Right*, in Hegel's Social and Political Thought 103 (D. Verene ed. 1980); Stillman, Property, Freedom, and Individuality in Hegel's and Marx's Political Thought, in Property 130 (Nomos XXII; J. Pennock and J. Chapman eds. 1980).

5. "*Aufheben*" is for Hegel a technical term (and for translators a particularly recalcitrant one). It "has a twofold meaning . . .: on the one hand it means to preserve, to maintain, and equally it also means to cease, to put an end to. . . . Thus what is sublated [*aufgehoben*] is at the same time preserved; it has only lost its immediacy but is not on that account annihilated" G. Hegel, *Science of Logic* 107 (A. Miller, trans., 1969).

6. J. Locke, Second Treatise of Govenment c. 5 (C. Macpherson ed. 1980); Kant, Metaphysical Elements of Justice 76 (J. Ladd, trans. 1965); and J. Rawls, A Theory of Justice (1971), c. 3.

7. See R. Dworkin, Taking Rights Seriously 240–58 (1977).

8. Westphal, Hegel, Human Rights, and the Hungry, in Hegel on Economics and Freedom 218–28 (W. Maker ed. 1987).

9. "*Bildung*" is a nearly untranslatable term but a central concept for Hegel's political philosophy. It means education in the broadest sense, formation, acculturation, cultivation, formative development, and maturation to a cultured and liberal state of mind. Knox translates *Bildung* as "education"; I frequently leave the term untranslated or use "cultivation" and "development" as limited English equivalents.

10. Locke, supra note 6, c. 5 § 27.

11. Many Anglo-American theorists follow Locke and Hobbes in not regarding the development of intelligent, informed, and psychologically integrated mature adults as a problem for political thinking. Among contemporaries, for instance, Nozick does not explore what constitutes a mature individual able sensibly to choose for him—or herself, i.e., to formulate a viable life plan and to make the choices needed to carry it out; rather, he admits lack of satisfactory answers by merely stating that "I hope to grapple with these and related issues on another occasion." R. Nozick, Anarchy, State, and Utopia 51 (1974) (indicating in that conclusion his lack of satisfactory answers, or even beginnings of answers). Someone from a different field but with similar paucity of analysis and answers is the (libertarian) pyschariatrist Thomas Szasz. See Stillman, Szasz on Contract, Liberty, and Autonomy, 42 Am. J. Econ. & Soc. 93 (1983).

12. Kronman, Paternalism and the Law of Contracts, 92 Yale L. J. 763 (1983). Kronman seems to think that restrictions on contractual freedom must be paternalistic (id. at 765). But I suspect that "paternalism" as applied to contractual freedom is a term in the discourse of those who favor "negative liberty" or "freedom from." As such, the term is not neutral but persuasive (if conscious) or ideological (when not conscious). It carries strong pejorative overtones (as being suited only to minors and to barbarians). See J. S. Mill, On Liberty (1859). It serves as a red flag to mark interference—most likely to be seen as illegitimate—in negative liberty. In that discourse, contractual freedom is to be seen as the rule, "paternalism" as the exception, requiring justification. Kronman, supra, at 765; see also G. Calabresi & D. Melamed, Property Rules, Liability Rules, and Inalienability: One View of the Cathedral, 85 Harv. L. Rev. 1089 (1972). Similarly with the term "restrictions." Kronman, supra, at 765).

13. When economistic theorists assert that individuals may alienate their liberty, R. Nozick, supra note 11, at 331, they ignore the temporal dimension of freedom. They in effect assert that individuals are free, *now*, to do anything (including alienating their freedom); they do not care about maintaining individuals in a *continuing* condition of freedom (a goal that prohibits certain current actions, such as selling oneself into slavery). They also portray the (bizarre) good society or utopia, id., as one in which not all but only some are free, and others are or may be slaves.

14. For a too-brief discussion of property in "morality," see Stillman, Hegel's Analysis of Property, 10 Cardozo L. Rev. 1031, 1047 n. 62 (1989).

15. For comments about codification and extended discussion of the relation of philosophy of law to positive law, see id. at 1050–51 & n. 73.

16. Benhabib, Obligation, Contract, and Exchange: On the Significance of Hegel's Abstract Right, in The State & Civil Society: Studies in Hegel's Political Philosophy 164–67 (Z. Pelczynski ed. 1984).

17. I. Kant, Groundwork of the Metaphysics of Morals 69–71, 87–95 (H. Paton trans. 1964); J. Rousseau, The Social Contract Bk. 1, c. 8 (J. Masters trans. 1978); see also Thorstein Veblen's sardonic portrayal of hedonistic man, "a lightning calculator of pleasures and pains, who oscillates like a homogenous globule of desire of happiness under the impulse of stimuli that shift him about the area, but leave him intact . . . Self-imposed in elemental space, he spins symmetrically about his own spiritual axis until the parallelogram of forces bears down upon him, whereupon he follows the line of the resultant." Veblen, Why Is Economics Not

an Evolutionary Science, in The Place of Science in Modern Civilization and Other Essays 73–74 (1942).

18. Hobbes, supra note 3, c. 21. Jack Benny played humorously on the meanness of a similar choice: the robber's threat, "Your money or your life!" produced in the miser extended and deep contemplation ("The Jack Benny [Television] Show," passim.)

19. 1 A. Smith, The Wealth of Nations c. 4 (1776).

20. G. Hegel, Aesthetics 149 (T. Knox trans. 1975).

21. H. Marcuse, Reason and Revolution 210 (1940).

22. Corporations are not solely or even primarily business corporations. More like Tocquevillian associations, they are voluntarily organized groups that meet for shared purposes: business corporations, churches, interest groups, charitable societies, etc. In his translation, Knox consistently capitalizes "corporation"; except when quoting, I do not.

23. D. Ricardo, Principles of Political Economy and Taxation c. 19–20 (3d ed. 1821).

24. See 2 J. Steuart, An Inquiry into the Principles of Political Oeconomy c. 7 (1767).

25. Contemporary economistic thinking continues to see marriage in terms of contract and—from Hegel's perspective—continues to ignore love and individual development in marriage. For instance, for Posner marriage contracts resemble other contracts, "a voluntary arrangement in which services are exchanged presumably to the mutual benefit of the parties," R. Posner, Economic Analysis of the Law 62 (1972); "marriages not undertaken for mutual advantage create inefficiency." Id. at 63. Whether love can be defined as a "service" and can be commidified and calculated like any other economic good or service—these two points at least distinguish Posner and Hegel. For Hegel, in economic behavior, the person acts to maintain his independence and autonomy; in love, the "first moment" or aspect is "that I do not wish to be a self-subsistent and independent person and that, if I were, then I would feel defective and incomplete. The second moment is that I find myself in another" (§ 158A) and gain completion and self-subsistence. Love is therefore, Hegel thinks, "the most tremendous contradiction" and not susceptible to comprehension through standard modes of deductive logic (§ 158A).

26. Decisions about *Vermogen* should consider the interests and goals of all family members, but are ultimately made by the husband and father (§ 171); Hegel's is a patriarchal family.

27. Hegel's idea of the family allows him clearly to conceptualize the status and treatment of children. Economistic thinking, perhaps because of its lack of concern with individual development or because it takes voluntariness (*Willkur*) as the full definition of freedom or free will, has difficulty treating children. For instance, when R. Posner considers children in cases of divorce, he notes two standard economistic ways of thinking about children—that the parents can be depended upon to represent the children's interests and that children should be regarded as the property of their parents. He rightly rejects both, the first on sound empirical observation, the second on oddly uneconomistic, un-empirical grounds: "the view of children as chattels does not accord with modern sensibilities" Posner, supra note 25, at 64. These "modern sensibilities" justify extensive "interventions in market processes" to protect the welfare of children. Note that Posner does not

have an economistic way of conceptualizing children (and that he does not use "modern sensibilities" elsewhere to justify intervention).

28. Monetary taxes do respect the arbitrary will of the person of abstract right and the system of needs, because an individual's tax-paying is "mediated through his own arbitrary will" and so his "subjective freedom" is respected (§ 299). Nozick is simply wrong to hold that "taxation of earnings from labor is on a par with forced labor," reorganization. Nozick, supra note 11, at 169; he does not see the world of difference between being taxed at 28% on earnings from a job that he has chosen himself (e.g., professor of philosophy) and being required to spend 28% of his working time doing a job—sanitation worker, ditch digger, or hospital orderly, perhaps on the graveyard shift—that the state has ordered him to do, with no regard for his preferences or skills.

8

Hegel and the Dialectics of Contract

Michel Rosenfeld

There is a sharp division of opinion concerning the meaning of contemporary contractual relationships. Some believe that contract is dead;[1] others assert that it thrives and that more relationships are contractual today than ever before.[2] Underlying this division of opinion lurks a fundamental question concerning the proper relationship between individual-regarding and community-regarding values in legitimate contractual relationships. Contract must include both individual and communal aspects.[3] Nevertheless, contemporary theories of contract have not only generally failed to harmonize these two aspects but also they have not provided adequate guidance for determining an acceptable proportion of communal to individual input in contractual undertakings.

I will argue that Hegel's theory of contract, in the context of the broader concerns of his legal and political theory, provides the means to resolve this troubling question without leading to the seemingly inevitable pitfalls of individualist and collectivist theories. I shall refer to this model as the paradigm of *contract as reciprocal recognition.* Under this paradigm, contract is not only compatible with the reconciliation of individual autonomy and communal values, but it is also suited to foster the mutual determination of the individual and—or, perhaps more precisely, against—the communal.

Any plausible interpretation of Hegel's writings on contract must take proper account of his unique dialectical methodology. Therefore, Part I of this Article discusses relevant methodological issues relating to Hegel's conception of contract to the extent necessary to render the subsequent analysis more fully intelligible. Part II proceeds to an interpretation of the meaning of contract for Hegel, focusing principally on the famous passage in the *Phenomenology of Spirit* concerning the struggle for recognition between lord and bondsman,[4] and then on Hegel's views on contract and on the institutions he associates with, or contrasts to, contract in the *Philosophy of Right.*[5]

THE METHODOLOGICAL BACKGROUND

Modern contract refers to a relatively simple and invariant generic relationship involving, to use Ian Macneil's definition, "the projection of exchange into the future."[6] For Hegel what counts as contract is an abstract right of the abstract person who is the subject of exchange transactions in civil society.[7] Initially, it is not apparent what bearing that may have on the scope of legitimate contractual transactions or on the meaning of contract in the context of Hegel's theory; this is largely due to Hegel's distinctive dialectical methodology. Generally, according to this methodology, nothing which is a part of a larger whole can be understood except in terms of that whole, and conversely, the whole cannot be fully grasped except in terms of the full panoply of determinate relationships that exist among its various constituent parts.[8] To the extent that whole and part are bound together in organic unity, the meaning of anything cannot be established except in terms of the meaning of everything. This would seem to lead to the following methodological impasse: nothing can be truly said unless everything that is true is said at the same time. Moreover, since for Hegel the internal links that bind the parts together and subsume them under the whole are forged in the course of a dialectical process that unfolds in the course of history, no definitive meaning can be established before the end of history. As Hegel states, in the celebrated passage of the *Philosophy of Right*, "[a]s the thought of the world, [philosophy] appears only when actuality is already there cut and dried after its process of formation has been completed."[9] Process, therefore, can only be fully understood in terms of its product.

Since for Hegel the relation of part to whole is fully intelligible only in terms of the relation between process and product, the meanings of the concepts, such as contract, which emerge in the course of the dialectical journey towards totality, should in principle be susceptible to full and final determination. For the succession of perspectives that mark the road from point of departure to end result is not arbitrary. It is determined by the "inner necessity" or inner logic of the concept of a free willing subject. Thus, each of the succeeding perspectives generated in the course of the journey from point of departure to end result is formed specifically to overcome the particular contradictions to which its immediate predecessor was inevitably led and which remained insoluble from the standpoint of that predecessor. And each perspective embodies a partial truth, with the chain of succeeding perspectives representing the requisite sequence of partial truths that necessarily inform the full truth of the for-itself that corresponds to what it is in-itself.

The actual dialectic of the subject as presented by Hegel is often not only dense and difficult to follow in its minute details, but it also takes certain turns that appear to be rather arbitrary.[10] On the other hand, the "onto-logical" process[11] underlying the entire historical progression of the subject towards absolute self-knowledge, and which repeats itself within each stage involved in that progression, is fairly clear and relatively easier to grasp. In the most general terms, this process involves three distinct moments. In the first moment the subject establishes an immediate identity with itself. That identity, however, only establishes that the subject is other than the other, but it does nothing to link the subject to its manifold determinations. Being other than the other establishes mere identity but is wholly inadequate to bring about concrete individuality. Accordingly, the perspective of the first moment is dissolved and the subject passes into the second moment. From the perspective of the second moment, the subject can grasp the manifold diversity of its concrete determinations, but it fails to recognize that these are its own determinations. Thus, in the second moment the subject becomes aware of its diversity but can only do so by losing its identity. Finally, from the perspective of the third moment, which is established through the negation of the negation—that is, through the realization by the subject that the diversity which it perceived as being other is none other than itself—the subject regains its identity amidst its diversity.[12] In the last analysis then, because of the very nature of Hegel's dialectical method, the first (immediate) attempt at grasping the meaning of a relation must fall short, and it is only by subsequently assuming the appearance of its opposite that the true meaning of that relation can be ultimately revealed.[13]

Viewed within this methodological framework, Hegel's conception of contract assumes the following broad characteristics. The abstract person, who is the subject of the right to contract, is a partial portrait of the ethical, social, political, and historical person who enters into relations in the sociopolitical arena.[14] Actually, Hegel's abstract person is very much like Hobbes's individual found in the state of nature.[15] There is, however, an important difference between the two conceptions. Hegel calls his counterpart to the Hobbesian individual the "abstract person," indicating that this person is a construct who has been cut off from the diverse concrete determinations of the real historical person. Thus, whereas the free willing subject who is the protagonist of the *Philosophy of Right* may at first view herself as embodying the characteristics of the abstract person, Hegel is well aware that the abstract person provides only a partial representation of the subject of legal and political relations.[16]

In contrast to the Hobbesian contract, which is the paramount legitimate vehicle for intersubjective relations, Hegelian contract plays a more modest role. Initially, both contractual vehicles are put into use by individuals who seek to satisfy the desires produced by their respective free wills.[17] According to Hegel, a contract results from the arbitrary individual wills of the contractors, but it produces a common will of its own.[18] Each contractor seeks to enlist the cooperation of the other in the pursuit of her own self-interest, but cannot obtain that cooperation without in turn making an agreement that helps to promote the other contractor's self-interest. It may be that by coincidence the common will embodied in the contract is but a mere aggregate of the individual wills seeking satisfaction through the contract. This would occur, for example, when each contractor could exchange an object for which she has no use for a coveted object in the possession of the other contractor. In most cases, however, a contractor must give up something which is of value to her to obtain a more coveted object in exchange. Thus, although the individual contractor may obtain a particular object which she seeks through the contract, to the extent that the full satisfaction of arbitrary will would require the acquisition of all objects of desire, and to the extent that obtaining one object of desire through contract forecloses acquiring some other such objects, the common will generated through the contract no longer appears to be a mere aggregate of the individual wills of the contractors. Provided that the bargaining process preceding formation of the contract leads a contractor to agree to pay more for a coveted object than originally intended or to receive less than what was initially sought, the common will embodied in the contract would still, in part, satisfy the arbitrary wills of the contractors, but it would, in part, frustrate them.

The more the individual depends on the voluntary cooperation of others for the fulfillment of self-interest, the greater would seem the need for an ever larger number of self-imposed sacrifices in order to secure the satisfaction of individual desires. Taken to its logical extreme, in the context of a sociopolitical universe in which contract is the only legitimate vehicle for intersubjective relationships, the necessary cost in self-imposed sacrifices for the securing of individual desires is likely to become so prohibitive that individual freedom would risk turning into individual submission. This is the paradoxical fate of the Hobbesian state where freedom must be sacrificed to secure self-preservation.[19]

There is yet another important way in which Hegelian contract leads to the opposite of what it first seems to establish from the limited standpoint of the abstract person. From the latter's perspective, the contractual relationship appears isolated and severed from the complex of legal and social relations from which it emerges.[20] From the more comprehensive perspective that seeks to embrace all contractual relationships, however, the focus of the overwhelming majority of voluntarily concluded contractual exchanges is the free market economy, which is the dominant institution in Hegel's civil society.[21] Following Adam Smith, Hegel believes that, taken as a whole, all contracts that are the product of arbitrary individual wills seeking to satisfy desire are led by the "cunning of reason" to form a network of social relationships governed by a series of common norms.[22] Thus, in contrast to the limited perspective of the abstract individual, from the broader perspective of civil society taken as a whole, contract emerges as a vehicle for collective undertakings governed by a set of commonly shared legal norms.[23] Once again, as the result of a shift in perspective, contract appears to turn into its opposite, from a vehicle that abstracts the individual from her social milieu to one that taps the individual's eager desire to satisfy self-interest and cunningly turns it into a source of collective cooperation.

Unlike Adam Smith, Hegel does not believe that unfettered competition in the economic marketplace is bound to produce the common good. Quite the contrary, Hegel is convinced that the free market necessarily experiences periodic crises of overproduction resulting in the exacerbation of disparities in wealth and in the creation of chronic poverty which poses a serious threat to the social order.[24] Because of this, Hegel cannot be satisfied with allowing contract to reign virtually free of all constraints over the economic sphere.

If pursuit of individual self-interest often does not lead to the common good, and if exclusive reliance on self-imposed obligations tends to turn freedom into submission, a reevaluation of the meaning of "free will" would be necessary. Indeed, if by free will we mean arbitrary will, it is ultimately self-contradictory since the uninhibited expression of the arbitrary will leads to the abdication of freedom. Accordingly, consistency requires that the exercise of free will must mean something other than the uninhibited pursuit of the endless series of things that qualify as objects of desire. In other words, the will cannot be genuinely free if it is forced by a desire that it cannot control to aim ceaselessly from one object to another. To overcome this inconsistency, free will must find self-expression in a way such that it does not lose self-control. Viewed in this light, the concept of free will should be understood as depending on self-control rather than on mere desire or impulse. Moreover, for Hegel, the person demonstrates self-control by freely willing to perform her duty.[25] Although this may seem paradoxical at first, Hegel maintains that the freedom to follow one's impulses is but abstract freedom whereas freely willing one's duty is substantive or positive freedom.[26] From the perspective of this latter freedom, one is only genuinely free through conscious assumption of one's duty, which not only evinces the achievement of self-control, but also provides the means to overcome the deficiencies of a collective order propelled exclusively by the pursuit of self-interest.

Although self-imposed, the duty that corresponds to positive freedom differs sharply from contractual duties in that it is not dependent on a correlative right or assumed in a trade-off for a particular object of desire. Instead, this duty is a universal moral duty, which in its initial appearances is an expression of *Moralität*—that is, a Kantian duty-based morality that prescribes that all actions should conform to universal maxims.[27] According to Hegel, however, Kantian morality is ultimately without content, and must therefore be transcended.[28] Indeed, *Moralität* stands in opposition to the self-interest of the marketplace,[29] but while it prescribes action in accordance with universal principle, it does nothing to specify the *content* of moral action.[30]

To provide a determinate content to the duty that springs from the true essence of free will, Hegel proposes a transition from *Moralität* to *Sittlichkeit*.[31] Inherent in the concept of *Sittlichkeit* is the notion of community as defined through the amalgam of customs and norms which have been internalized by a people and which have given shape to its collective identity.[32] Moreover, while each people has its own *Sittlichkeit*, Hegel specifies that there is a crucial difference between the *Sittlichkeit* of modern peoples and that of the ancients.[33] Greek ethical life lacked concern for subjective freedom.[34] Modern ethical life, in contrast, involves not only the internalization of common norms, but also the conscious and deliberate adoption of these norms as the determinate objectifications of the self-imposed duty through which the moral subject realizes the true essence of its free will.[35] In other words, modern ethical life consists not only in living together with others in accordance with shared communal norms, but also in freely choosing these norms to govern the life of the community. Thus, in one sense these communal norms are *not* chosen: they are the given norms of the community which are transmitted from one generation to the next and which every member of society finds reflected in the collective institutions in which she partakes.[36] In another sense, however, these communal norms *are* chosen: that is, to the extent that the subject freely decides to make it her duty to abide by them and to act only in accordance with their prescriptions.[37]

Sittlichkeit can only be fully realized in the context of the Hegelian state.[38] Logically, in accordance with Hegel's dialectical method, the state is necessary to resolve the contradictions that flow from the operation of civil society.[39] Specifically, as the political organ of the community, the state must intervene in the marketplace to combat the great disparity in wealth and the chronic poverty that Hegel believes are inevitably created as a by-product of civil society.[40] From the standpoint of the subject, on the other hand, the state represents a new perspective, based on community norms, that contrasts with the individual-regarding and self-interested perspective that prevails in civil society.

Given the logical role of the state within Hegel's dialectic vision, it becomes apparent why Hegel rejects the social contract as the source of legitimacy for the state. Indeed, the state appears necessary and fully justified from a perspective which is constituted precisely to transcend the inherent contradictions of contractarianism. But if the Hegelian state is not *contractual* in nature, that does not mean that it is not ultimately *consensual*. The subject is free to choose, as its self-imposed duty, to abide by the dictates of the communal norms that inform the sociomoral and sociopolitical reality of the state. And this is precisely what Hegel believes that the subject would do upon adopting the ethical perspective of the modern state.[41]

Thus we apparently come to the end of the dialectical process that progressively reveals the full meaning which contract has for Hegel, through a series of reversals and qualifications prompted by the inner logic and requires the above-mentioned shifts in perspective. I have only touched on the broad outlines of the Hegelian conception of contract, leaving for later the task of providing a more detailed analysis. Nevertheless, some important points have already emerged: contract is individual-regarding from the standpoint of the contractors. Through the "cunning of reason," however, civil society as the sphere of all contracts is led to adopt a set of collective legal norms necessary to secure the enforcement of contracts. To the extent that contractual exchanges are also bound to lead to substantial social disruption, however, the individual-regarding aims of contract must be checked and opposed by the community-based goals of the noncontractual state.

Hegel's dialectical methodology avoids the pitfalls of individualism, but this arguably may only be at the cost of falling into those of collectivism. Thus, moving from the perspective of the abstract person to that of the state, the validity of contracts depends less on the fact that contractual obligations are self-imposed than on whether such obligations can be justified in terms of substantive community norms.

This characterization is defective, however, as it rests on an interpretation of the Hegelian state that abstracts the product from the process, the whole from its constituent parts. Indeed, Hegel's methodological approach does not merely imply that the whole be interpreted in terms of its relation to its parts. Hegel's "onto-logic" requires that the particular institutions meaningful in the context of a partial perspective do not simply disappear when that perspective is transcended. The passage from one perspective to the next merely recombines them to make them intelligible from the later perspective. The process whereby the elements of one perspective are simultaneously canceled and preserved in the course of the transition to the next perspective is what Hegel refers to as the process of *"Aufhebung."* As Hegel puts it,

> What transcends (*Aufheben*) itself does not thereby become [n]othing
> . . . . It . . . retains the determinateness whence it started. To transcend
> (*Aufheben*) has this double meaning, that it signifies to keep or to
> preserve and also to make to cease, to finish . . . . Thus, what is
> transcended is also preserved; it has only lost its immediacy and is
> not on that account annihilated.[42]

As interpreted in light of the concept of *Aufhebung*, the advent of the Hegelian state need not signify the demise of the contractual relationships prevalent in civil society. Instead, from the state's perspective, the scope of valid contractual relationships needs only to be somewhat narrowed to avert the adverse collective consequences likely to flow from a regime of virtually unchecked contractual relationships.[43] Under this new perspective, contracts are no longer justified merely because they are contracts, but also because they promote the common good. Moreover, while the extent to which contracts promote the common good may be an open question, if contractual relationships contribute to the common good they are arguably preferable to other means equally well suited to lead to the same result, because of the role which they may play in furthering the development of the person's individuality.[44] Accordingly, it is reasonable to insist that in the modern state, freedom of contract within certain well-defined limits should be adopted as one of the community norms contributing to the definition of the ethical substance of the state.

Hegel, then, avoids the inconsistencies of Hobbesian individualistic contractarianism by conceiving contractual relationships as dependent on noncontractual ones. To obtain a better grasp on that process, it is necessary to consider Hegel's conception of contract in greater detail.

THE MEANING OF CONTRACT FOR HEGEL

The *Philosophy of Right* traces the dialectical journey that leads from the perspective of the abstract person to that of the modern state. The abstract person who is the bearer of the abstract rights of property and contract, while (for-itself) severed from the many attributes of full personhood, is nevertheless not cut off from other persons. Indeed, property and contract cannot be meaningful except in the context of intersubjective relationships based on reciprocal recognition.[45] Accordingly, even the initial perspective presented by Hegel in the *Philosophy of Right* posits a sociopolitical universe in which the right to reciprocal recognition is already an accepted given.[46] Because this right plays such a crucial role in the context of contract, it is important to elucidate it by briefly retracing the process of its formation. Thus, we are led back to the struggle for recognition and to the celebrated dialectic between lord and bondsman which Hegel addresses in the *Phenomenology*.[47]

The struggle for recognition is part of the dialectic of self-consciousness. Self-consciousness for Hegel is desire.[48] In the first instance, desire seeks objects to appropriate and consume them.[49] Moreover, such appropriation and consumption are acts of negation through which self-consciousness seeks to establish its own identity.[50] By appropriating and consuming an object, self-consciousness negates the independence of that object, and simultaneously develops a perception of itself as independent of its objects. Similarly, in contrast to its appropriated and consumed object which loses its identity, self-consciousness retains its identity as that which negates its objects.

To the extent that the negation of the appropriated objects is what allows self-consciousness to maintain its identity, the desire for objects becomes insatiable as each consumed object must be replaced by another object of desire. Indeed, once it is understood that the desire aims to preserve self-consciousness, then it seems logical to conclude, as Hegel does, that self-consciousness can only achieve satisfaction in another self-consciousness. If desire seeks to maintain identity, then self-consciouness must seek an object which provides it with recognition. And the only object which can provide sustained recognition to a self-consciousness is another self-consciousness.

Self-consciousness's desire for recognition can only be satisfied by another self-consciousness, through mutual recognition.[51] Moreover, an optimal way to bring about genuine mutual recognition is through love.[52] Indeed, in love each self-consciousness recognizes the other without attempting to reduce it to being a mere reflection of itself. In other words, in love both self-consciousness are united in mutual recognition, but each is able to preserve its individuality and freedom in the course of its union with the other.

If all self-consciousness could be united through love, individuality and community would not only be mutually compatible but also mutually reinforcing, and no room for contractual relationships would remain. Hegel, however, does not believe that in a large society all social relationships can be founded on love.[53] Even at the level of abstraction of the phenomenology of self-consciousness, Hegel invokes the metaphor of the struggle between lord and bondsman rather than that of love in order to introduce his account of the process that leads to mutual recognition.[54]

In the *Phenomenology*, self-consciousness seeks to satisfy its desire for recognition through another self-consciousness devoted to recognizing and acknowledging its (the first self-consciousness's) individuality. That leads to a struggle, however, inasmuch as each self-consciousness would rather be a recognized self-consciousness than a recognizing one.[55] Indeed, being a recognizing self-consciousness is problematical, as it involves becoming a reflection of the self-consciousness it recognizes, and thus, to that extent, losing one's own identity.[56] Under those conditions, the struggle for recognition becomes a struggle for the freedom of the recognized self-consciousness—a freedom which, to the extent that it requires the subordination of another self-consciousness, cannot be obtained without risking one's life.[57] It is precisely at this point that a choice must be made between two possible attitudes: that of the lord and that of the bondsman. The lord is willing to risk his life to secure his freedom. The bondsman, on the other hand, is primarily motivated by the fear of death, and therefore opts for survival, even though that entails the loss of freedom.

The lord, as the recognized self-consciousness who has overcome the fear of death, imposes his will on the bondsman who, as the recognizing self-consciousness, abdicates his freedom to avert death. The subordination of the bondsman to the lord's will finds concrete expression in the work that the bondsman must perform for the lord.[58] This labor, which must conform to the specification of the lord, becomes the tangible embodiment of the unequal relationship between them. Indeed, from the lord's standpoint, the goods produced by the bondsman are not only objects for the lord's pleasures but also reflections of his power to compel the bondsman to devote himself to giving concrete content to the expressions of the lord's free will. Conversely, from the bondsman's standpoint, production of goods for the lord signifies self-estrangement and apparent resignation to the role of a subordinate who exists to further the will of the lord by suppressing the dictates of his own will.[59]

Because of the fundamental inequality between lord and bondsman, and because the lord views the bondsman as a mere instrument who exists to satisfy the lord's desires, the relationship between lord and bondsman cannot be viewed as contractual in nature, nor as a direct prelude to contractual exchange. Thus, at least in its initial appearance, the relationship between lord and bondsman is much farther removed from contract than that between the warring individuals found in the Hobbesian state of nature. On the other hand, the relationship between lord and bondsman is for Hegel the first in a series of "onto-logical" steps that lead to contract. Contrary to Hobbes, however, Hegel roots the process that leads to contract in inequality rather than equality. This is significant for determining which relationships should be viewed as contractual in nature.

Upon further consideration, the initial impression conveyed by the relationship between the lord and the bondsman turns out to be misleading. Whereas the lord initially appears to be free, he in fact depends on the bondsman for the satisfaction of his desire, and to that extent his freedom turns out to be illusory.[60] Similarly, in the course of performing his work, the bondsman realizes that he is in fact the opposite of what he originally thought he was. First, he realizes that his subordination is ultimately self-imposed and that it was precipitated by his fear of death. According to Hegel, work relieves the dread associated with the fear of death and thus opens the bondsman's eyes concerning the true reason for his submission.[61] Second, work and the products of work lead the bondsman to become aware of the extent of his genuine independence from the lord and the latter's actual dependence on him.[62] Thus, besides freeing him from the fear of death, work forces the bondsman to hold his desire in check, enhancing his self-control.[63] Moreover, although the goods produced by the bondsman may conform to the specification of the lord, as products, they nevertheless stand on their own as independent from the lord. And on contemplating the independence of his product, Hegel maintains, the bondsman discovers his own independence from the lord, and the latter's ultimate dependence on him for the satisfaction of the desire.[64] Therefore, the attempt by self-consciousness to obtain recognition from another self-consciousness without having to reciprocate is led by the inexorable movement of Hegel's dialectic to a dramatic failure. The lord seeks to become a master and to make the bondsman a slave, but in the end, to put it in Hyppolite's terms, the slave becomes the master of the master while the master becomes the slave of the slave.[65]

As Hegel elaborates in the *Phenomenology*, the struggle leading to reciprocal recognition is presented as taking place at a high level of abstraction, at which self-consciousness vie for recognition in a rarified universe devoid of particular social or political attributes.[66] The social consequences of this struggle, on the other hand, are supposed to become manifest in the context of the legal universe in which individuals relate to each other as persons endowed with certain rights. That universe, as already mentioned, is the subject of the *Philosophy of Right*, and its initial stage is that of the abstract person endowed with abstract rights, including the right to contract.

As initially stated, the universe of the abstract person and of contract rights presupposes reciprocal recognition, and is thus logically posterior to the struggle for recognition. Contract itself also can be viewed as the culmination of the process set in motion by the struggle for recognition, and as accordingly rooted in inequality. Further, the struggle for recognition can serve as a metaphor for the process of contract formation, once it is understood that the primary purpose of contract in Hegel's system is to give determinate content to the reciprocal recognition rather than merely to facilitate the acquisition of coveted goods.[67]

To better understand the conceptual link between the struggle for recognition and contract formation, and to better appreciate the implications of rooting contract in inequality, it is instructive to contrast the Hegelian approach to the Hobbesian one. The Hobbesian state of nature is an abstract construct that posits an intersubjective universe from which all concrete social and political institutions have been removed.[68] The equality of Hobbes's state of nature, therefore, amounts to little more than an assertion that different individuals are inherently equal. In the last analysis, the Hobbesian justification of contract appears to be circular. Provided that individuals are formally equal, and provided that all contractual obligations are consensual in form, contracts are valid and should be enforced. This justification thus begs the key questions of substantive freedom and substantive equality.

By rooting contract in inequality, Hegel avoids the circularity that afflicts Hobbes's account. Although the struggle between lord and bondsman is purely metaphoric in nature, the initial relationship between the two bears a much closer resemblance to the historical circumstances that gave rise to the era of modern purposive contract than does the Hobbesian state of nature. Nevertheless, contract is possible only if the formal freedom and formal equality that emerge from Hobbes's account are present. The question that Hegel's own analysis raises, however, is whether the concept of reciprocal recognition upon which he relies to justify contractual relationships ultimately provides a more satisfactory foundation for contract than does Hobbes. To be able to answer that question, it is first necessary to take a closer look at the conceptual similarities between the process of contract formation and the struggle for recognition between lord and bondsman.

Under conditions of freedom to contract, the process of contract formation between two individuals can be schematized as follows: each individual seeks to deal with the other because she believes that she cannot obtain the good she seeks (or that she can only obtain it at a much greater cost) without enlisting the cooperation of the other. As each seeks to obtain the greatest possible benefit at the least possible cost, the two individuals are likely to bargain over the terms of their proposed contractual relationship. Since neither individual is likely to confer a benefit on the other without receiving anything in exchange, if their bargaining leads to an agreement it will be on terms which would be less advantageous for each individual than what she had hoped for initially. Assuming each individual is exclusively motivated by self-interest while committed to respect the constraints imposed by formal equality and freedom to contract, bargaining should only lead to an agreement under the following circumstances: a meeting of the minds is reached on contractual terms such that neither party obtains as good a deal as originally hoped for, but each party obtains a better deal than she would have by not contracting.

In the struggle for recognition, each self-consciousness similarly seeks to obtain the greatest possible recognition while granting its counterpart the least possible recognition. Unlike in the process of contract formation, however, in the struggle for recognition the initial position is one of inequality between the two prototypical figures of lord and bondsman. Also, whereas in contract formation the moment of consent is crucial as it transforms the product of precontractual dealings into a mutually binding agreement, in the struggle for recognition consent plays a much less prominent role. Indeed, the bondsman, prompted by fear of death, agrees to assume the role of the recognizing self-consciousness and to devote himself to serving the lord. But because the bondsman's consent to serve the lord provides no more than apparent recognition to the latter in the context of the dialectical struggle towards recognition, consent does not play the same kind of decisive role in the struggle as it does in the contract formation. Further, while contract formation is carried out through the bargaining process, the struggle for recognition unfolds through the dialectical process. Finally, while both contract formation and the struggle for recognition involve a desire for some object and an element of recognition, the relative importance of these factors is reversed as we go from the former to the latter. Thus, in contract formation the goal apparently is to secure a coveted good, and mutual recognition as formally equal persons who enjoy freedom to contract is but a necessary means towards that goal. In the struggle for recognition, by contrast, the objects which the bondsman produces for the lord are but tokens of recognition while recognition itself is the paramount objective sought by the struggling self-consciousness.[69]

Notwithstanding these differences, the struggle for recognition is conceptually similar to contract formation in an essential respect. Both involve a confrontation between seemingly independent beings, each seeking to make the greatest possible use of the other while making the smallest possible contribution in return. Yet the process in which they both become engaged leads them to accept voluntarily a very different outcome than that originally hoped for. Each willingly agrees to assume a greater obligation towards the other than originally contemplated in exchange for a seemingly smaller benefit than had been previously sought. Thus, in both contract formation and in the struggle for recognition, the particular process involved transforms one-sided perspectives into positions of equilibrium. In contract, this equilibrium is embodied in equality in exchange; in the struggle for recognition, it is found in equality in recognition. Thus, the process of reciprocal recognition is very much like the process of contract formation. Within the Hegelian framework, however, contract presupposes reciprocal recognition because in the context of the struggle for recognition, equality in exchange is subordinate to equality in recognition.[70]

The question remains, however, whether Hegel's definition of contract as depending on a socially achieved reciprocal recognition can lead to a satisfactory reconciliation of the individual and the communal *within* contract. To answer this question, it is first necessary to explore the essential common features of those contracts that satisfy the definition of contract in terms of reciprocal recognition. With this in mind, this Article turns to Hegel's account of contract in the *Philosophy of Right*.

In the sociopolitical universe of the *Philosophy of Right*, in contrast to the much more abstract universe of the struggle for recognition in the *Phenomenology*, abstract persons first recognize one another as owners of property. Such recognition is equal for everyone, for it is not the nature or quantity of property held by a person which accounts for the kind of recognition the latter receives, but merely the *fact* that she has property—that is, her abstract identity as a property owner.[71]

Recognition as a property owner, however, is not much of a recognition, for it only involves an act of forbearance whereby the recognizing person refrains from interfering with the recognized person's enjoyment of her possessions. Because the mutual recognition among property owners is equal recognition, a community of property owners who do not exchange possessions would satisfy the minimum conditions which must be met to overcome the struggle for recognition. But if recognition among property owners is minimal, it seems likely to provide its beneficiaries with a low level of satisfaction. To fulfill her yearning for greater recognition, the abstract person must resort to contract. According to Hegel, contract is "the transference of property from one [property owner] to the other in conformity with a common will and without detriment to the rights of either."[72] Thus, by using items of property as tokens of recognition, abstract persons can confer greater recognition on one another. Indeed, a transfer of property to someone involves greater recognition than mere forbearance from interfering with another's property. Moreover, because the circulation of property in contract is bilateral, and because the items of property which are exchanged in a contract are of equivalent value as tokens of recognition, contract provides equal recognition for all the contractors. Finally, Hegel specifies that contract furthers both the arbitrary will of each one of the contractors and the common will of all of them.[73] That is, each contractor recognizes the will of the other insofar as she gives that other an item of property which that other covets in exchange for an item which she desires. And the contract, as the agreement to exchange designated items of property in the future, enshrines the common will of the contractors, which is the product of a temporary convergence of their respective arbitrary wills. If a contract satisfies the arbitrary will of a contractor, it promotes individual-regarding interests. On the other hand, insofar as it promotes the common will of the contractors, contract also serves to advance collective interests— albeit that "collective" in this context may refer to a small group which may have as few as two members.

Further evidence of the primacy of reciprocal recognition in Hegel's conception of contract—as embraced in the paradigm of executory contract[74]—is that the legal obligations of the contractors become binding at the time of the making of the contract rather than on receipt of a benefit pursuant to the terms of the agreement. Thus, Hegel rejects Fichte's claim that the legal obligation to keep a contract only begins when the other party starts performing her obligations under the contract.[75] According to Hegel, it is not the performance of one party which triggers the other's obligation to perform, but instead the mutual recognition expressed through the exchange of contractual stipulations. By agreeing to particular contractual terms, the parties have already established a common will, and under these circumstances, actual performance under the contract merely completes what each party already recognized as being prescribed. In Hegel's words, "[t]he embodiment of the will in formal gestures or in explicit and precise language is already the complete embodiment of the will as an intelligent entity, and the performance of the covenant so embodied is only the mechanical consequence."[76]

While the abstract right of contract promotes equality in recognition and provides some degree of integration between individual-regarding and community-regarding concerns, the kind of equality and harmony which contract in the abstract yields is purely formal. Indeed, all abstract persons are equal. But, as Hegel points out, that merely expresses an "empty tautology"[77] because the very definition of abstract persons as bearers of abstract right imposes equality by completely excluding all particularity that establishes differences among concrete persons and which thus leads to certain inequalities. Nevertheless, the degree of abstraction displayed by the abstract person found in the initial stage of the *Philosophy of Right* is so extreme that it explains virtually nothing concerning the concrete implications of contract. To be more than an empty construct, contract must therefore involve something beyond disembodied persons acting in a nearly total sociopolitical vacuum.

Significantly, Hegel places the sociopolitical sphere of contract neither in the initial nor in the final stage of ethical life, but rather in its intermediate stage—civil society. In its immediate manifestation ethical life is represented by the family, an institution which displays collectivist features, contemplates no role for the individual except as a part of the whole, and therefore leaves no room for contractual relationships.[78] Following the general pattern of Hegel's dialectic, social organization based exclusively on the family is dissolved because it is inadequate to account for the totality of ethical life.[79] After this dissolution, ethical life becomes alienated from the subject, as it becomes embedded in the sociopolitical organization of civil society. The alienation of ethical life in civil society, in turn, finds expression in the radical split between the subjective individualism of its atomistic members and the objective universality of its community-wide norms.[80] Moreover, the principal vehicle of intersubjective relations within civil society is contract. From the subjective standpoint of the individual contractor, contract is the instrument of individualism;[81] from the objective standpoint of civil society as a whole, however, contract operates pursuant to universal legal norms and promotes the interests of the community.[82] In civil society, therefore, contract is both individualist and communitarian, or more precisely, it is individualist to the extent that it is communitarian and it can only remain that way because the perspective of the individual remains split from that of the community.[83] However, since civil society cannot ultimately succeed in bringing about the necessary synthesis between the individual and the whole, its perspective is dissolved and gives way to that of the state.[84] Within the state, through the work of the dialectical process of the negation of the negation, the subject becomes reconciled with itself and reunited with its ethical life.[85] In the state, individual-regarding interests give way to community-regarding ones and contractual relationships are replaced by consensual ones rooted in the acceptance of common norms.[86] However, because the transcendence (*Aufhebung*) of contract implies its preservation (in a different relation to the whole) rather than its elimination, the Hegelian state should not be conceived as providing for the end of contract or of individual-regarding concerns. Rather, from the state's perspective, contract is legitimate, but only to the extent that it does not conflict with the ethical life of the community taken as a whole.[87]

In civil society, contract provides recognition to the individual as being self-subsistent.[88] The self-subsistent being of civil society, however, is not as abstract as the abstract person initially encountered in the *Philosophy of Right*. The self-subsistent individual is embedded in a concrete society, but one that acquires its particular characteristics by first loosening the bonds of family.[89] In other words, civil society becomes the locus of intersubjective relationships between self-subsistent individuals by first eliminating the primacy of family ties which subordinate the individual to her family unit. Moreover, if we take Hegel's conception of the family as a subject of the ethical life as a general metaphor for all social orders based on status relationships and, in particular, for feudal society with its marked hierarchies and clear subordination of the individual to the whole, then civil society should be viewed as a social order devoted largely to the leveling of hierarchical and status-based relationships. Consistent with this, contract not only provides recognition to self-subsistent individuals severed from their family ties, but also it is an instrument for the repudiation of those preexisting ties that stand in the way of the individual becoming self-subsistent. Contract can only provide recognition to individuals as self-subsistent by refusing to grant any further recognition to the status-based norms and relationships that make self-subsistence impossible. In short, recognition of a person as self-subsistent through contract is only possible if contract does away with, and replaces, the status-oriented norms and relationships which have thus far linked that person to a social hierarchy.

For a person to be self-subsistent in civil society means that she should not be regarded primarily as a family member or as belonging to a particular group. But it does not mean that a person is self-subsistent in the sense that she does not need the recognition of others to satisfy her needs.[90] And to the extent that recognition is achieved through contractual exchange, the magnitude of the recognition that an individual could obtain would depend on the number of contracts which she enters and the number of contract partners with whom she associates.[91]

As long as reciprocal recognition is promoted by the proliferation of contracts, there is a need to ascertain what a person may legitimately alienate through a contract. Hegel asserts that the domain of things that can be alienated legitimately through contract includes all *external* things.[92] This includes not only external objects acquired or produced by a would-be contractor, but also her services and labor power, provided that her labor power is not alienated for a time period that would impair her ability to enter into contracts.[93] Consistent with this stipulation, it would seem that a person could both safeguard her capacity to contract and maximize the number of "external" things under her control available for alienation by splitting herself, on the one hand, into an inalienable *ego contractans* and, on the other, into all her alienable attributes and properties which are not required to sustain the *ego contractans*. Accordingly, self-subsistence would seem to mean reciprocal recognition qua *ego contractans* through contractual exchange of all manner of alienable possessions.

The *ego contractans* appears to be the reincarnation of the abstract person with its abstract rights; but this time it is inserted in a concrete sociopolitical milieu in which it emerges as a consequence of the systematic dismantling of status-based relationships. On the other hand, the subject of recognition, to multiply the instances of recognition and to maximize the intensity of the feeling of being recognized, particularizes and individualizes desire so that each contractual exchange may satisfy a particular, separable individual desire. Moreover, the more arbitrary and capricious a particular individual desire is, the more its satisfaction seems likely to intensify its owner's feeling that she is being recognized as the unique individual that she aspires to be. In this way, there is a correspondence between the increasing abstraction of the subject of recognition as *ego contractans* and the increasing particularization of her desire. In fact, these two phenomena are but the two principal manifestations of a single process that simultaneously produces the abstraction of the particular and the particularization of the abstract.

We have thus far concentrated on the subject of recognition, but the simultaneous process of increasing abstraction coupled with increasing particularization affects objects of exchange. To be in the chain of exchange and to become susceptible to being traded for an equivalent object—a necessary prerequisite for achieving equality in recognition through contract—an object must have a separate and distinct exchange value. This means that abstraction must be made from the bundle of manifold concrete determinations of an individual object to ascribe a quantifiable exchange value to it.[94] Nevertheless, although understanding objects of exchange in terms of their exchange value is essential for rational market transactions, perception of such objects exclusively in terms of that value is insufficient to account for contractual relationships. Indeed, if individual contractors seek recognition in the form of satisfaction of particular desires, exclusive focus on exchange value, which makes all objects of exchange essentially fungible, fails to achieve an acceptable level of differentiation. Accordingly, to become desirable to a potential consumer, an object of exchange must display sufficient particularization to appear capable of satisfying that consumer's particular need or desire. In sum, for an object to be suitable for contractual exchange, there must be abstraction of the particular to extract a commensurable exchange value. There must also be particularization from the abstract—that is, a process whereby the object is perceived as unique notwithstanding the characteristics it shares with other objects.

Abstraction of the particular and particularization of the abstract pull in opposite directions and thus threaten to undermine the recognition sought through contract. The *ego contractans*, understood as the inalienable core of the person which becomes separated from the rest through the process of abstraction of the particular, is but a formal shell. Under these circumstances, reciprocal recognition is reducible to equal recognition as an *ego contractans*, amounting to little other than the establishment of formal equality.[95] Therefore, individuality, self-subsistence, and equality are purchased at the cost of vacuity. On the other hand, particularization of the abstract compartmentalizes desire so that it can be given piecemeal satisfaction through contractual exchange. Taken to its logical extreme, however, the fragmentation of desire could so completely separate individual desires from the background from which they emerge that satisfaction of particular desires could no longer be perceived as a form of recognition. In other words, if fragmentation of desire dissolves the unity of the person, then satisfaction of a particular desire may be akin to quenching a particular thirst but could hardly contribute to the maintenance of a sense of recognition. In the last analysis, through the combined work of the abstraction of the particular and the particularization of the abstract, the ego becomes an empty unity while desire is fragmented into an irreducible multiplicity of disparate atoms. Once that happens, contract becomes meaningless.

Because the same process that sustains contact eventually leads to its dissolution, contractual relations must be bounded by noncontractual ones. Before exploring the boundaries of contract as conceived by Hegel, it is necessary to focus on some of the other apparent contradictions that emerge from the preceding account of contractual relationships. First, the self-subsistent person who contracts to satisfy her desires turns out to be completely dependent on others to achieve her aims. Second, there is a marked contrast between use-value, which seems purely subjective, and exchange value, which seems objective. Third, since satisfaction of desire requires reciprocation, and since recognition demands satisfaction of an increasing number of particular desires, the person who desires recognition must devote a greater portion of her time to work—that is, "other" than satisfying desires— to keep up with her obligations to reciprocate. And fourth, contract seems to depend simultaneously on the individual's arbitrary will and on adherence to universal norms that are binding on the whole community.

All four of these apparent contradictions can be understood as diverse manifestations of a single phenomenon—the alienation of ethical life in civil society.[96] This alienation of the ethical life results in the radical split between the subjective and objective points of view. Moreover, what is remarkable about this phenomenon is not the split itself— which is characteristic of all but the last of the various stages of Hegel's dialectic[97]—but rather that in civil society, the split between the subjective and the objective constitutes the very foundation upon which contractual relationships must stand to become suitable vehicles for the expression of reciprocal recognition.[98] Indeed, recognition itself is only intelligible in terms of both identity—that is, a common intersubjective collective denominator—and difference—that is, a particularity or individuality that makes it possible to distinguish one person from another. Contract, in turn, remains viable only to the extent that individual contractors remain unaware that the individuality which they seek to have recognized is ultimately defined in terms of the common intersubjective meanings that make identity possible. In short, contract is the form of reciprocal recognition of those who fail to realize that identity and difference are two sides of the same coin—that is, spirit (*Geist*) or the absolute subject.

The inner dialectics of contract also lead to other contradictions. One of these contradictions reproduces at a different level of abstraction part of the dialectic surrounding the struggle between lord and bondsman. Contract presupposes that the road to reciprocal recognition is through satisfaction of particular desires—that is, through fulfillment of consumer wants. Moreover, through particularization of the abstract, the number of particular desires susceptible of satisfaction greatly proliferates. Indeed, the seemingly infinite fragmentation of desire both makes it impossible to obtain recognition for every particular desire and tends to devalue the relative importance of obtaining recognition for any individual desire. Thus, once a person embarks on a journey in search of recognition through the acquisition of consumer goods, she seems condemned to enter into an unending series of contractual exchanges without ever achieving the full recognition which she seeks.

The process just described is analogous to the process described by Hegel in the *Phenomenology* by which self-consciousness is led to enter into the struggle between the lord and the bondsman. As will be remembered, preceding the struggle, self-consciousness was seeking to establish its identity through the appropriation and consumption of external objects. The achievement of identity through this process fails, however, for much the same reason as does the process underlying the search for full recognition through contractual exchange: they both depend for their success on consumption of an infinite number of objects. Each of these processes, however, unfolds at a different level of abstraction in Hegel's overall dialectical scheme. Thus, the process whereby the member of civil society seeks recognition through contract, unlike the one whereby self-consciousness seeks identity, involves reciprocal recognition between individual contractors.[99] The failure of this process has to be understood, therefore, not as a failure to achieve purely formal equality in recognition, but rather as a failure to obtain recognition as a substantive self-subsistent subject whose identity is self-contained, defined, and fully realized through the exercise of its own free will. Once again contract leads to formal equality of recognition, but this time at the cost of frustrating the desire for substantive recognition.

A further reversal brought about by the dialectic of contract in civil society concerns the relationship between the subject as consumer and as producer. The constant need to acquire consumer goods through contractual exchanges requires the individual to devote substantial effort to the production of "external" goods suitable for alienation in exchange for coveted consumer goods. Presumably, the individual in civil society produces to be able to consume, and consumes, in large measure, to obtain recognition. Consumption alone, however, does not lead to substantive recognition. But through the cunning of reason, production, which is originally viewed as but a necessary means toward consumption, makes a greater contribution to the achievement of substantive recognition than can consumption.[100] Indeed, production requires a curbing of desire and a postponement of arbitrary gratification which enhances self-control and hence contributes to the unification and integration of the person who otherwise becomes fragmented in the proliferation and particularization of desire.[101] Moreover, production is not only likely to enhance the producer's image of herself but also the image which others have of her.[102] Thus, paradoxically, in a world in which persons seek recognition as satisfied consumers, they can actually achieve greater substantive recognition as producers.

The dialectic between consumer and producer is analogous to that between lord and bondsman, particularly as it relates to the realization by the bondsman that in working for the lord he overcomes his fear of death, masters his own environment, and places his own imprint on the products upon which the lord depends for recognition. Unlike the bondsman, however, the producer in civil society works for herself as well as for those who consume her products. Also, unlike the bondsman who has not yet achieved recognition, the producer who contracts to alienate her products enjoys relationships of formal reciprocal recognition with all her contract partners. Nevertheless, the critical point that emerges is that, even in the face of formal reciprocal recognition, the uninhibited pursuit of recognition through consumption fails to yield substantive recognition. In addition, to project an identity worthy of recognition, the individual must curb her rampant desire to consume to channel her energies towards the production of goods reflecting her creative potential and her mastery over herself.

In her capacity as a producer, the member of civil society begins to give concrete life—most likely without being aware of it—to Hegel's conception of substantive freedom as dependent on self-restraint.[103] Substantive freedom, however, requires that the subject voluntarily assume her duty, and this cannot be achieved fully within the perspective of civil society because of its inability to overcome the alienation of the subject from her ethical life. The reconciliation of the subject with her ethical life therefore requires transcending the stage of civil society and entering into the last stage of Objective Spirit, that is, the stage of the state, in which the subject consciously embraces her ethical life and freely chooses to fulfill her universal duty.[104]

With the advent of the stage, we come to the end of contract as the dominant intersubjective relationship. The principal reason for this and for Hegel's rejection of the social contract as a means to legitimate the state is that he envisions the state's perspective as a collective one.[105] Contract requires arbitrary will and its irreducibly individualistic component.[106] On the other hand, the state, representing the perspective of the community as a whole, cannot be the product of a contract, according to Hegel, because the perspective of society as a whole is that of the universal will *as opposed to* the arbitrary will.[107] From the standpoint of the inner logic of the dialectic of ethical life, it is precisely because civil society and its contractual relationships based on the arbitrary will fail to reconcile autonomy and welfare that it becomes necessary to embrace the more comprehensive perspective of the Hegelian state. In other words, because contract and civil society are not self-sustaining, they ultimately depend on the collective noncontractual outlook of the state for their viability.

CONCLUSION

The preceding analysis demonstrates how contract as mutual recognition serves to maintain an equilibrium between individual-regarding and community-regarding interests in Hegel's system. Viewed from the perspective of the Hegelian system, contract promotes both the individual and the communal by pitting them against each other. Moreover, contract, which finds its logical place among abstract rights, and owes its existence to its original sociopolitical insertion in the realm of civil society, can only survive through the mediation of the noncontractual state.

The fact that contract occupies a meaningful place in Hegel's ("ontological") system does not necessarily imply that it must have some coherent meaning in its contemporary use. Indeed, it is not clear whether contract can continue to serve as a legitimate vehicle for the reconciliation of the individual-regarding and collective values once the particular trappings of Hegel's dialectic of the subject have been removed. More specifically, because of the convergence between logic and ontology in Hegel's system, the validity of his methodology seems inextricably intertwined to the validity of his system taken as a whole. Therefore, to the extent that some of Hegel's ontological conclusions appear to be unacceptable to the contemporary mind, the usefulness of his methodology is questionable. As Charles Taylor has observed, this presents a serious question, for Hegel's actual synthesis has dissolved and become obsolete.[108] In particular, Hegel's notion of *Geist* as cosmic spirit in which reason and reality completely overlap seems highly implausible today.[109]

Notwithstanding these difficulties, Hegel's conception of contract may yet prove to be particularly well suited to contribute to a proper understanding of contemporary contractual relationships. Indeed, the rejection of *Geist* does not foreclose the postulation of an initial position and end result that closely approximate those that emerge in the Hegelian conception of contract. Thus, one might postulate as the relevant initial position that of the abstract rights-endowed person who seeks to satisfy her desires. As end result, on the other hand, one might postulate a sociopolitical milieu in which an equilibrium is struck between individual autonomy and communal solidarity, without recourse to any cosmic spirit. Moreover, the adoption of these postulates is justifiable in light of widely shared contemporary norms and beliefs.

The abstract individual who seeks to satisfy desire is a partial construct of the whole person, which has come to occupy a prominent position in contemporary political philosophy.[110] It is thus the abstract person who is most frequently invoked as the subject of civil and political rights and of political equality in liberal political theory. Further, the abstract person is often made the subject of legal and economic relationships in general,[111] and of contractual relationships, in particular. Consequently, by placing the abstract person in the initial position—which is always partial and one-sided—one not only draws upon a ubiquitous figure in contemporary liberal theory, but also posits that figure as an incomplete and unindimensional representation of the fully constituted person who engages in a multitude of concrete intersubjective relationships.

Postulating as end result some kind of synthesis between individual autonomy and community-oriented solidarity also appears to be consonant with plausible contemporary normative aspirations.[112] From a prescriptive standpoint, it seems reasonable for members of contemporary societies to be dissatisfied with the consequences of individualism as well as with those of collectivism. Accordingly, it is plausible for such persons to postulate as desirable a state of affairs that would compromise neither the dignity of the individual nor the integrity of the community. From a descriptive standpoint, on the other hand, while such a synthesis between individual and community may be more difficult to conceive, there seems to be no a priori reason why it should not be feasible. It is beyond the scope of this essay attempt to describe what a society having reached such a synthesis might look like. For present purposes, it should suffice to recall that a certain degree of indeterminacy may allow some measure of purely individual input in the Hegelian state, in which all intersubjective relationships are shaped by communal norms, and to note that there seems to be no intrinsic reason why a similar degree of interdeterminacy might not lead to a similar result in a contemporary society.

NOTES

1. See, e.g., P. Atiyah, The Rise and Fall of Freedom of Contract (1979); G. Gilmore, The Death of Contract (1974). The principal claim of proponents of the death of contract thesis is not that contractual transactions are in danger of becoming extinct in contemporary society, but that contract law is losing its distinct identity and becoming absorbed into the law of torts. G. Gilmore, supra, at 87–90.

2. See, e.g., C. Fried, Contract as Promise (1981); I. Macneil, The New Social Contract 71 (1980) ("contract has swept the world").

3. Cf. I. Macneil, supra note 2, at 11 (even discrete contract—involving a one-time exchange between otherwise complete strangers—can only take place in a social matrix). On the other hand, there could be no genuine contracts in the absence of a certain minimum of individual-regarding input. See Rosenfeld, Contract and Justice: The Relation Between Classical Contract Law and Social Contract Theory, 70 Iowa L. Rev. 769, 804 (1985).

4. G. Hegel, Phenomenology of Spirit §§ 178–96 (A. Miller trans. 1977) (1807) [hereinafter Phenomenology of Spirit].

5. G. Hegel, Philosophy of Right §§ 72–81 (T. Knox trans. 1952) (1821) [hereinafter Philosophy of Right.]

6. Macneil, The Many Futures of Contracts, 47 S. Cal. L. Rev. 691, 712–13 (1974).

7. See Philosophy of Right §§ 33A, 217, 229; see also Westphal, Hegel's Radical Idealism: Family and State as Ethical Communities, in The State and Civil Society: Studies in Hegel's Political Philosophy, 77, 81 (Z. Pelczynski ed. 1984) [hereinafter State and Civil Society] (Hegel "portrays civil society as the institutionalization of contractual relationships.").

8. See Phenomenology of Spirit §§ 20, see also J. Hippolyte, Genèse et Structure de la Phénoménologie de L'Esprit de Hegel 322 (1946) (for Hegel "the Truth is the Whole and . . . each of its moments only acquire meaning in relation to its place in the overall dialectic.") (author's translation).

9. Philosophy of Right, preface, at 12–13.

10. See, J. Hyppolite, supra note 8, at 431, 441.

11. The term "onto-logic", which reminds us that Hegel's logic is not formal but rather a logic that is also an ontology, has been coined by Hyppolite. See Hyppolite, supra note 8, at 554.

12. As Hegel states in the preface to the *Phenomenology:*

    [The] . . . Substance . . . [or] *Subject* . . . is in truth actual only in so far as it is the movement of positing itself, or is the mediation of its self-othering with itself. This substance is, as Subject, pure, *simple negativity,* and is for this very reason the bifurcation of the simple; it is the doubling which sets up opposition, and then again the negation of this indifferent diversity and of its antithesis . . . .Only this self-*restoring* sameness, or this reflection in otherness within itself—not an *original* or *immediate* unity as such—is the True.

    Phenomenology of Spirit § 18 (emphasis in original). In a similar vein, Hegel further states that the Subject is "essence, or . . . *being in itself*; it is that which relates *itself to itself* and is *determinate,* it is *other-being* and *being-for-self,* and in this determinateness, or in its self-externality, abides within itself; in other words, it is *in and for itself.*" Id. § 25 (emphasis in original). See also 2 G. Hegel Science of Logic 230 (W. Johnston & L. Struthers trans. 1966) [hereinafter "2 Logic"].

13. See Phenomenology of Spirit § 17.

14. See Benhabib, supra note 8, at 159 166. The *Philosophy of Right* itself, however, is launched from the standpoint of a community bound together by collective norms deriving from a process of intersubjective recognition. Id. at 168.

15. See id. at 167.

16. See, e.g., Philosophy of Right § 49R ("the person, as something abstract, has not yet been particularized or established as distinct in some specific way").

17. See T. Hobbes. Leviathan 111–12, 146 (M. Oakeshott ed. 1962); Philosophy of Right §§ 45R, 74.

18. Philosophy of Right § 74.

19. See Rosenfeld, supra note 3, at 864–65.

20. From the standpoint of the individual contractor, the contract looms as the product of the confluence of two individual wills, and creates rights in the contractors which are in the first instance enforceable against each other and no one else.

21. See Westphal, supra note 7, at 81–82.

22. See Philosophy of Right §§ 183 and 184TN; S. Avineri, Hegel's Theory of the Modern State 146–47 (1972); C. Taylor, Hegel, 433 (1975) (Hegel takes the "invisible hand" theory and makes it part of the "cunning of reason.").

23. See Benhabib, supra note 8, at 162; Philosophy of Right §§ 213, 217 and 217A.

24. Philosophy of Right §§ 243–45; see R. Plant, Hegel: An Introduction, 169, 213–14 (2d Ed. 1983).

25. Philosophy of Right §§ 149, 149A.

26. Id.

27. See Philosophy of Right §§ 33, 33A, 34TN, 141, 141A.

28. Id. §§ 135, 135A.

29. The proper place of *Moralität* is in the context of civil society. See id. § 207. Moreover, abstract reflection envisions morality as a constant struggle against self-satisfaction. Id. § 124.

30. See id. §§ 135, 135A.

31. Id. §§ 141, 141A.

32. See Taylor, supra note 22, at 376, 444; Philosophy of Right §§ 151–56.

33. See Walton, Hegel: Individual Agency and Social Context, in Hegel's Philosophy of Action 75, 88–89 (L. Stepelevich & D. Lamb eds. 1983).

34. See Pelczynski, Political Community and Individual Freedom, in Hegel's Philosophy of State, in State and Civil Society, supra note 8, at 55, 57; Philosophy of Right § 260A.

35. See Philosophy of Right §§ 260, 260A.

36. Id. §§ 151.

37. Id. §§ 151A, 151TN.

38. See id. § 258R.

39. See id. §§ 261, 261A, 263A.

40. See Plant, supra note 25, at 169–71, 213–16.

41. See Philosophy of Right §§ 260, 260A.

42. 2 Logic, at 119–20.

43. Cf. Plant, supra note 25, at 224 ("Hegel's state transcends the egoism of the market place but at the same time is not to be seen as an alien institution imposed upon the market.").

44. Hegel makes it clear that the modern state is designed to preserve the individuality of its members. See Philosophy of Right §§ 261, 261R, 261A.

45. See Philosophy of Right §§ 51A, 71R.

46. See Benhabib, supra note 8, at 168.

47. Phenomenology of Spirit §§ 178–96.

48. Id. § 167.

49. See id. § 174.

50. Id. § 175.

51. See Hyppolite, supra note 8, at 157.

52. Id. at 158.

53. Id.

54. Id.

55. Phenomenology of Spirit §§ 185–87.

56. See id. § 189.

57. Id. § 187.

58. See id.

59. Id.

60. See id. § 194.
61. Id.
62. Id. § 196.
63. Id. § 195.
64. Id. § 196.
65. Hyppolite, supra note 8, at 166.
66. See id. at 38, 151.
67. Cf. Philosophy of Right § 40 (Initially, "it is only as owners that . . . two persons really exist for each other. Their implicit identity is realized through the transference of property from one to the other in conformity with a common will and without detriment to the rights of either. This is *contract.*") (emphasis in original).
68. See Rosenfeld, supra note 3, at 852.
69. See Phenomenology of Spirit § 190.
70. While exchanges between lord and bondsman are not contractual in nature in the struggle for recognition, see id. §§ 190–94, once equality in recognition has been achieved, the exchange of equivalents through contract can serve as an expression of mutual recognition.
71. See Philosophy of Right § 49A.
72. Id. § 40.
73. Id. § 74.
74. An executory contract is a "contract in which no performance has yet taken place" and this kind of contract is to be contrasted to the "executed or partially executed contract, that is, a contract in which performance or part performance has already occurred." Rosenfeld, supra note 3, at 823.
75. Philosophy of Right § 79R.
76. Id.
77. See id. § 49R.
78. See id. §§ 158–81.
79. Id. § 181.
80. See, e.g., id. §§ 187, 217, 229.
81. This is reflected in the nature of contract since it is an expression of each contractor's abstract will. See Philosophy of Right § 74.
82. See id. § 183.
83. While the individual concentrates on the pursuit of self-interest, the "invisible hand" or more accurately the "cunning of reason" promotes, albeit without complete success, the common interest. See Philosophy of Right §§ 183 and 184A.
84. See id. §§ 255, 255A, 256.
85. Id. §§ 257–61.
86. Id. § 260.
87. See id. § 261R.
88. Id. § 238.

89. "[C]ivil society tears the individual from his family ties, estranges the members of the family from one another, and recognizes them as self-subsistent persons." Id.

90. See id. §§ 198–99.

91. It may be argued that it is not the *quantity* of contracts and the *number* of contract partners that is paramount, but rather the *quality* of the contracts and the *identity* of the contract partners. In a free-market economy marked by an ever-increasing division of labor, however, each individual presumably becomes more dependent on exchanges with others for the satisfaction of her needs. Moreover, as a more specialized producer, each individual in such an economy is capable of satisfying an increasingly narrower range of needs.

92. See Philosophy of Right § 67.

93. Id.

94. See Rosenfeld, supra note 3, at 834.

95. Cf. Philosophy of Right § 49R ("[I]n respect of their personality persons are equal. But this is an empty tautology, for the person, as something abstract, has not yet been particularized or established as distinct in some specific way.").

96. Following the general pattern of Hegel's dialectic, ethical life is divided into three moments. The first moment, which is the stage of the family, is immediate. On the other hand, in the second stage, civil society, immediacy is lost, and the ethical substance that glues together the individual members of civil society becomes alien as they remain unaware that they are united by the ethical substance. Only in the last moment of the ethical life, when the alienation of individuals is removed, is the internal link between individual, society, and ethical substance fully reinstated at a higher and more fully conscious level of integration, and governed by reason. See Philosophy of Right § 157; Taylor, supra note 22, at 431.

97. Viewing the matter from the standpoint of the *logic*, for example, the Hegelian dialectic is a retracing of the journey of the Idea. As Charles Taylor notes, the Idea is "a process of positing its other and then recovering its unity with itself in its other. This process is a dialectical one. It is a struggle. . . . The whole system hangs together by contradiction and struggle." Taylor, supra note 22, at 330. But whereas the *process* of the realization of the idea is marked by stages characterized by the split between the self and its other, at the culmination of the process, in its ultimate realization as the absolute, the Idea reunites self and other, and encompasses everything within itself. See id. at 330–31.

98. See Philosophy of Right §§ 184A, 183–87.

99. This follows from the fact that abstract right itself presupposes the achievement of inter-subjective recognition.

100. See Philosophy of Right § 199.

101. See Phenomenology of Spirit § 195; Plant, supra note 25, at 219.

102. See Philosophy of Right § 199; Plant, supra note 25, at 220.

103. See Philosophy of Right §§ 149, 149A.

104. See Philosophy of Right § 260.

105. See id. §§ 259, 260, 261R.

106. See id. §§ 75, 75A, 258R, 281R.

107. See id. §§ 260–61, 288–89.

108. Taylor, supra note 22, at 537–38.

109. See id. at 547, 551.

110. The abstract person who is the protagonist of contemporary individualistic political philosophy has its origins in the writings of Hobbes and Locke. See Hobbes, supra note 18; J. Locke, The Second Treatise of Government (C.B. MacPherson ed. 1980); see also C.B. MacPherson, The Political Theory of Possessive Individualism (1962). Among its best known contemporary exponents are J. Rawls, A Theory of Justice (1971), and R. Nozick, Anarchy, State, and Utopia (1974).

111. See C. Dyke, Philosophy of Economics 138 (1981) ("For the purposes of the market we are 'buyer,' 'seller,' 'producer,' or 'consumer.' These simply specify the activities of the rational economic man within the market system. Any further understanding of us as people is barred by the theoretical constraints on how the market must be described.").

112. One attempt to articulate a more communitarian vision in the context of contemporary American political philosophy is M. Sandel, Liberalism and the Limits of Justice (1982).

9

Right and Advantage in Private Law

Ernest J. Weinrib

THE CASE OF THE DOOMED AIRPLANE

Suppose that as Smith is travelling to the airport to catch a plane, she is negligently injured by Jones's careless driving. The incident causes Smith to miss her plane. In the course of its flight to Smith's desired destination, however, the plane crashes, killing everyone on board. It is as certain as anything can be that Smith too would have died in the crash, had she not been injured by Jones. Can she recover in tort for the injuries Jones inflicted on her?[1]

The paradox of this situation is that Smith has benefited from Jones's tortious conduct. Although Jones did not so intend it, his negligence has resulted in a net gain to Smith. Had it not been for Jones's negligence Smith would have reached the plane on time with limbs intact, only to die shortly thereafter. It would seem that Smith has no basis for complaint, since she owes her life to Jones's carelessness. Yet Jones has violated her rights.

Most lawyers, I think, would allow Smith to recover in tort. The fate of the doomed plane has nothing to do here with the juridical relationship between Smith and Jones. The cause of action is complete at the time of Smith's injury, and is not affected by subsequent events. Just as Jones would not have been liable for her death had she caught the plane, so he should not escape liability for preventing her from catching it. Negligence law is concerned with the materialization of unreasonable risk, not with whether the defendant has caused the plaintiff to be or not to be at a certain place at a certain time.[2] Here the unreasonable risk posed by Jones's carelessness has materialized in injury. That Smith consequently missed the doomed airplane is a stroke of luck for her, but not a tort defense for Jones.

Moreover, I think most lawyers would say that the quantum of damages should not be reduced because the airplane crashed. Although tort law is supposed to make the plaintiff whole by putting her in the position she would have been in had the wrong not occurred, this does not mean that Smith must disgorge the benefits that accrued to her (for example, by committing suicide), or even that those benefits must be included in the calculation. The assessment of the plaintiff's loss from the wrong is not affected by the fact that without the wrong she would have suffered another, greater loss. Damages are a valuation of the infringement of the plaintiff's right, not the global calculus of the debits and credits occasioned to Smith by Jones's wrongful behavior.

At the heart of this example is the relationship between a right or a wrong, on the one hand, and an advantage or a disadvantage, on the other. An advantage is something that contributes affirmatively to the contingent level of welfare that someone enjoys at a relevant time, and a disadvantage is something that diminishes that level. Because every right crystallizes certain advantages, the infringement of a right is usually remedied by a damage award that quantifies the value of the advantages of which the victim has been deprived. Having an advantage, however, is not the same as having a right, nor is suffering a wrong identical with suffering a disadvantage. I can infringe your rights without thereby disadvantaging you, as where a court would award nominal damages. I can disadvantage you without infringing your rights, for instance, by starting a business that competes with yours. The case of the doomed airplane dramatically illustrates the lack of congruence between right and advantage, because the wrong to Smith is, at the end of the day, a considerable advantage to her.

My treatment of the case of the doomed plane proceeded on the assumption that private law is concerned with rights, not advantages.[3] This assumption is generally accepted, though not always and not without struggle and reminder. Sometimes the choice between a right and an advantage arises in connection with liability. Is it, for instance, a nuisance for a hotel to build up on its own property and thereby cast a shadow on the beach of a neighboring hotel? A trial court, thinking in terms of advantage, held that a tort had been committed because "no one has a right to use his property to the injury of another."[4] The court of appeal, cognizant that disadvantaging is not equivalent to wronging, reversed with the observation that "the maxim *sic utere tuo ut alienum non laedas* . . . means only that one must use his property so as not to injure the lawful *rights* of another."[5] Sometimes the issue surfaces in the determination of the remedy, as when the victim of a nuisance is restricted to the damages that would make up for the disadvantage suffered but is denied the injunction that would protect the right as such.[6] Occasionally a court, by attending to advantages rather than rights, produces a decision of surpassing eccentricity, as where the injunction won by the victim of a tort is made conditional on the victim's compensating the tortfeasor for the damage that would be done by the injunction.[7]

Behind these controversies lie two competing models of private law. One model, illustrated by my treatment of the case of the doomed airplane, makes the determination of rights primary. Although damages are assessed by reference to value of the advantages expected from the infringed right, advantages do not in this model have an independent status. Their role is a consequence of the structure of rights into which the process of valuation fits. In the second model, the advantages and disadvantages are the original elements of analysis. Theorists of the second model differ on how to characterize these advantages (are they preferences? utilities? wealth? basic aspects of the good?) and what is to be done to them (maximize them? equalize them? satisfy the most urgent? allow Pareto superior moves?). They agree, however, that law is ultimately intelligible only in terms of the advantages that accrue to those who are governed by it. Rights, if they play any role at all, are labels attached to the preferred interests at the conclusion of a legal operation on advantages and disadvantages.

Although the model of rights underlies much of private law, the model of advantages dominates most of contemporary legal scholarship. Private law is currently regarded as a system of economic incentives that maximize the value of advantageous occurrences and minimize the cost of disadvantageous ones.[8] The disjunction between the law and the academic effort to understand it suggests one respect in which Hegel's legal philosophy continues to address current concerns. The treatment of abstract right at the beginning of Hegel's *Philosophy of Right*[9] is the purest and most uncompromising account of private law from the perspective of right. In this Essay, I wish to illustrate how contemporary scholars—even those who claim to be rights theorists— mistake the significance of private law because they ignore Hegel's abstract right.

The central insight of abstract right is that private law abstracts from the particularity of advantage. Abstract right strips the advantages crystallized in private law of their concrete character and thereby makes the distribution of these advantages a matter of indifference. In abstract right advantages are valued not for their own sake but only inasmuch as they represent embodiments of an abstractly free will. Instead of being conceived as the particular benefits enjoyed by particular persons, the rights of private law are seen as expressions of the universal nature of the will's freedom.

The second part of this Essay outlines Hegel's notion of abstract right, drawing special attention to its normative basis and to its conception of interaction. For Hegel the possibility of property is integral to the definition of the interacting parties. Accordingly, the third part underlines the extremism of abstract right by examining the difficulties in Robert Nozick's account of appropriation. I argue that these difficulties flow from Nozick's failure to free his supposedly rights-oriented conception of property from the grip of the advantages model. The fourth part describes how abstract right illuminates the dynamics of interaction. Here I concentrate on two points: first, that the legal category of misfeasance cannot be understood as a mere disadvantaging, and second, that strict tort liability is not—as is often assumed—implicit in the rights model.

ABSTRACT RIGHT

Private law is a normative framework for claims arising out of human interaction. Accordingly, a theory of private law must address three questions. First, what is the normative nature of private law? Second, how are the interacting entities to be understood? Third, what is the appropriate conception of interaction? In a coherent theory of private law these three issues are not merely juxtaposed in the common space of private law litigation. They come together as expressions of a single theme.

The theme of abstract right is that "there is no question of particular interests, of my advantage or my welfare."[10] This observation goes to the core of the lack of congruence between private law rights and advantages. Hegel does not mean that the rights holder in abstract right is without particular interests, but rather that rights are intelligible whatever those interests are and however successful or unsuccessful the rights holder is in satisfying them. Abstract right features the abstraction from—not the absence of—particular interests. I wish to consider what this means and how it affects the three issues set out above.

The Normative Character of Abstract Right

I first outline Hegel's position concerning the normative character of abstract right and then elucidate the elements of that position. Right, defined by Hegel as "[a]n existent of any sort embodying the free will,"[11] is inherently normative. Abstract right partakes of this inherent normativeness because its abstraction from particular interests arises out of the initially abstract nature of willing itself. Accordingly, the normative character of abstract right is a function, first, of the nexus of normativeness and free will, and second, of the nature of free will in abstract right.

The first of these points, the nexus of normativeness and free will, reflects the consideration that obligations bite on action, connecting the actor to the required conduct. From the standpoint of right as Hegel understands it, however, obligations are not imposed from without as a coin is impressed with the image on the die. Rather, they are incumbent on actors by implication from the conceptual structure of acting. Normativeness, in other words, is intrinsic to the operation of free will.

Free will denotes that the actor is a choosing being and thus unqualifiedly active. Only such a being is subject to normative requirements. If these requirements arose extrinsically, their application to the actor would involve the actor in a passivity inconsistent with the freedom of true activity. In contrast, when normativeness is conceived as intrinsic to free will, the actor is held to the obligations implicit in being an actor. What binds the actor to certain conduct is a consequence of the actor's status as a freely willing being.

This brings us to the second consideration, the nature of the free will in abstract right. Abstract right is the normative structure that corresponds to the most fundamental condition for the will's freedom: the capacity to abstract from any particular object of choice. Particular acts can rank as the determinations of a freely acting being only inasmuch as they can be seen in the light of the capacity of such a being to rise above every determining circumstance. Although the freely active being makes particular choices, free activity is more than the particularity of these choices. What makes the particularity conceivable as the outgrowth of choice is the presupposition that the chooser's particular decision could have been otherwise.

Abstract right features abstraction from the particularity of willing. From the standpoint of the will in abstract right, particular acts, as well as the material circumstances and the subjective aims and interests that occasion those acts, have no standing of their own. Particular acts are only the contingent manifestations of free activity: they represent what the agent happened to choose from an array of possibilities. Because freedom presupposes the possibility of choosing to do this or that or something else, any of which would instantiate free activity, the particular content of the agent's choice has no specific significance. Or rather, its significance is negative: the particular act is merely that which need not have been. Although a free will must, to be a will, will something, and therefore must determine itself in a particular choice, there is at this stage no choice in particular that is required by its being a free will.

Because of its indifference to the particularity of choice, the will is (in Hegel's terminology) a universal. Although the will's operation is a series of particular acts, the will is not the same as any act in particular. Free will is related to particular acts in a negative way, through the denial that it is identical with any of them. The universality of free will consists in the will's being neither this particular act nor that particular act, but indifferently this act as well as that act.

The status of the free will as a universal is the ground of the actor's obligations in abstract right. Particular acts must conform to the free will's universality. At this stage the obligations do not go to the content of particular acts by requiring that the actor endeavor to achieve certain purposes. Rather, the obligations reflect the abstract nature of willing itself. Of course, it is in the nature of agency to attempt to execute particular purposes, which flow from the particular actor's particular interests. But abstract right requires that, in the execution of these purposes, whatever they are, the actor's particular acts should conform to the character of free will as a universal. Thus, the normative character of abstract right reflects not the desirability of the actor's particular interests or the optimal disposition of the interests of everyone affected by the act, but the abstractly universal nature of action itself.

Hegel terms the actor conceived from the standpoint of this abstract universality a "person," and he sums up the demands of abstract right in the imperative to "[b]e a person and respect others as persons."[12] Abstract right is the structure of relationships that necessarily obtains between persons understood in Hegel's sense as abstractly universal actors. In arising out of what is presupposed in freely willed activity, abstract right constitutes an intrinsically normative sphere, where the obligations incumbent on the actor reflect the nature of action.

The Interacting Parties

Because the person is not identical with any of his or her particular interests, the person is not intelligible in terms of the inner life of needs or desires. In its indifference to the inner, personality is oriented to an external world. The person is an agent and therefore must act, but the person's acts are significant only for their bearings on the personality of others. Being a person involves existence from the point of view of another. The interactions of abstract right are between externally recognizable units of freedom.

Viewed from outside, personality has two manifestations. One is the body that houses the free will and is the organ of its purposes. The body is that in which the will is directly present. Although someone might consider his own body and its vicissitudes to be something external to him, he is always within his body so far as others are concerned. In abstract right an individual's physical constitution is always the embodiment of personality.[13]

The other manifestation of personality is property. The imperative of abstract right that one "[b]e a person"[14] means that "[a] person must translate his freedom into an external sphere."[15] By putting his will into an external thing that in itself has no will and therefore does not instantiate freedom, a person becomes an owner of property. In Hegel's conception of it, property is not intelligible as a repository of particular interests. The point of property is to allow the freedom of the will pertinent to abstract right to express itself in an external sphere and thus to be recognized by others. Property is entailed by personality and reflects its abstractness. Particular interests, therefore, cannot have a significance for property that they lack for personality.

In relating property to the abstractness of personality, Hegel is not denying the obvious fact that the activity of acquiring and preserving one's property is fueled by the particular needs and interests of the property holder. Rather, Hegel's point is that to be conceived as an embodiment of freedom, property must be an expression of the universality characteristic of freedom. Just as personality abstracts from the particular choices to the universal through which all choices are understood as the operations of a free will, so property abstracts from the particular needs that impel the acquisition of particular things to the universal that makes all property rights intelligible under the concept of right. Just as persons are not entities without needs, but are freely willing actors intelligible as such whatever their needs, so property owners can be understood as property owners whatever their needs and whether or not what they own satisfies those needs. At stake in both personality and property is not the absence of particularity but the abstraction from particularity. Personality is characterized by the possibility of choice rather than by particular choices; in abstract right this possibility assumes the form of a capacity for property rights that is indifferent to the particular property holdings. Because personality does not involve the actor's having particular rights that reflect the desirability of satisfying particular interests, "[p]ersonality essentially involves the *capacity* for rights."[16] In abstract right the significance of particular rights consists solely in their being actualizations of this capacity and not in their contribution to the satisfaction of the rights holders' particular interests.

Every person can exercise his or her capacity for rights by appropriating that which does not contain the will of another person. Everything lies open for appropriation except the bodies of other persons, which are the immediate embodiments of their free will, and the external things into which they have put their will by means of a prior appropriation.[17] If the person did not have the right at least to appropriate things that lack free will, such things would be raised to a status equal to that of persons. If, on the other hand, a person had the right to appropriate even entities that contained free will, such entities would be degraded to the level of unfree things. In either case, the distinction between freedom and its absence would be obliterated. Because right originates in free will, this obliteration would entail the impossibility of right itself.

Thus, appropriation is limited only by the bodily and proprietary boundaries of other persons. So long as the rights of others are not violated, abstract right imposes no limits on the accumulation of property by any single person. Neither does abstract right insist that every person have sufficient property for subsistence. The point of property is not to satisfy needs or to promote well-being, but to provide an external sphere for the operation of the free will. Because free will at the stage of abstract right is itself abstract, the property expressive of the free will is not intelligible as a means of satisfying the particular interests of the property owner. "What and how much I possess, therefore, is a matter of indifference so far as rights are concerned."[18]

Interaction

In abstract right, persons are units of freedom whose interaction is governed by the imperative to respect others as persons.[19] Personality denotes indifference to the particularity of an actor's interests. The requirement on every person to respect others as persons does not, therefore, import an obligation to assist in the satisfaction of anyone else's particular interests. Indeed it denies such an obligation. The abstractness of personality means that the needs and desires of one person exert no normative pull on the behavior of another. No obligation exists as a matter of abstract right to confer a benefit on anyone else.

The exclusion from abstract right of duties to act for the benefit of another is categorical. It is an implication of abstract right as it arises out of the conceptual structure of free will. It therefore does not depend on the size of the benefit, the intensity of the beneficiary's desire, the urgency of his need, or the degree to which it will disrupt the life of the benefactor. Even if I can accomplish the salvation of another with no real prejudice to myself—for example, by tossing a rope to a drowning child, by lifting the face of an intoxicated man from a puddle, or by shouting a warning to a person about to walk with a lighted candle into a room strewn with gunpowder[20]—abstract right imposes no duty on me to do so.

For abstract right all that matters is how the free will of any person has actualized itself. If what someone needs or desires is neither part of his body nor an external thing that he owns, the fact that he needs it or desires it is of no normative significance to anyone else. It is true that his body or property may be seriously injured if the need is not satisfied, and that the need thus operates with reference to an embodiment of his personality. The damage his body or property will suffer if I do not help him is irrelevant, however, because abstract right deals with personality as a universal and thus contains no guarantees as to the condition or the value of any particular embodiment of personality. Conversely, my owning the object of someone else's need makes it an embodiment of my personality and therefore within the sphere of my entitlements. Because my bodily organs and my property are the embodiments of my free will, only I have the right to decide what to do with them. Accordingly, the circumstance that some aspect, however trivial, of my embodied personality may be the means of salvation for someone else imposes no obligation on me to make it available to him.

The imperative to respect another as a person signals a duty to avoid infringements of—rather than to confer benefits upon—the physical and proprietary embodiments of another's personality.[21] The limits of one person's embodiment are, in some way,[22] the limits of another person's freedom. Short of infringing these limits, one's freedom to act is unrestricted. Abstract right is thus constituted by permissible actions that are subject to prohibitions against interference with the embodiments of another's personality. There are no positive duties in abstract right to do anything in particular: positive duties would promote some form of well-being, whereas abstract right abstracts from all notions of well-being. The very abstractness of abstract right entails that its commands are negative. "The result is that there are only prohibitions in the sphere of [abstract] right, and the positive form of any command in this sphere is based in the last resort, if we examine its ultimate content, on prohibition."[23]

Thus, Hegel's exposition of abstract right is a philosophical account of the categorical distinction in common law between nonfeasance and misfeasance. Abstract right postulates that the harming of another's rights is significant in a way that failing to confer a benefit is not. It thereby employs a transitive conception of causation, in which action originating in one person reaches out to infringe the physical or proprietary rights of another. Because abstract right is indifferent to the satisfaction of any particular interest, it does not subordinate the difference between acts and omissions[24] to the achievement of desirable consequences.

In abstract right, the doing and the suffering of harm is a normatively significant feature of interaction. The normative bond takes the form not of an obligation to act for the good of another, but of a duty not to infringe the rights that embody the will's freedom. The relationship of doer and sufferer is thus a relationship of free wills, with the doer expressing his freedom through acting subject to the imperative to respect the personality of others, and the sufferer expressing his freedom through the physical and proprietary embodiments of personality. Because advantages and disadvantages have no significance in themselves, the relationship of doer and sufferer is not oriented toward the promotion of well-being for its own sake.

NOZICK'S PROVISO ON APPROPRIATION

Nowhere is the harsh nature of abstract right more evident than in Hegel's account of property. Because property for Hegel is an embodiment of an abstractly free will rather than a means for satisfying needs and desires, both surfeit and destitution are irrelevant. In abstract right there is no distributive justice.

Hegel's abstract right, accordingly, has some resemblance to Robert Nozick's repudiation of patterned principles of distribution.[25] There is, however, this difference: In abstract right, patterned principles of distribution are excluded because they are incompatible with its abstraction from the particularities of advantage and welfare. Nozick, in contrast, does not object to welfare as such but to patterning. In his view advantages count so long as they attach independently of any patterned principle of distribution.

The focal point of this difference is Nozick's proviso on appropriation. Nozick allows a person to acquire a permanent property right to a previously unowned thing provided that "enough and as good" is left for others.[26] Nozick interprets this proviso as requiring that others either continue to have the liberty to use the thing or be compensated for the loss of this liberty. The result is that one can acquire a previously unowned thing provided that others are not put in a worse position than they would have been had the acquisition not taken place. The situation before appropriation represents an unpatterned welfare level that the appropriation cannot then diminish.[27]

For Hegel, appropriation is unconstrained by a proviso protecting the antecedent advantages of anyone else. The only limitation on appropriation in abstract right is that the object in question should not already be the embodiment of someone's will. The legitimacy of the appropriation is not affected by the consequence that the situation of others will be worsened. Whereas Nozick mixes right and advantage by constraining the former through a proviso dealing with the latter, abstract right relates the interacting persons to each other only as rights holders.

Which of these two accounts of appropriation is more coherent? More is at stake here than the curiosity that Hegel's abstract right is more extreme than the most extreme contemporary rights theory. Nozick poses an unspoken—but nonetheless fundamental—challenge to abstract right. If rights and advantages really can be combined in some such way, then private law, to be coherent, does not require the uncompromising abstraction that Hegel postulates. I suggest, however, that Nozick's account is entangled in difficulties that are absent from Hegel's.

Since Nozick is a rights theorist, one might suppose that his proviso can itself be construed as a right in any beneficiary of the proviso (B) to the undiminished use of the thing that the acquirer (A) wishes to appropriate. Nozick's conclusion is that A can capture all the gains flowing from appropriation so long as B's situation is not thereby worsened. If, however, B has a right to the undiminished use of what A might appropriate, B should also be able to use this right to bargain for a share in whatever value A hopes to realize from the acquisition. The point can be put in Nozick's own terms as follows: Nozick supposes that A should give B what he calls "full compensation," that is, the amount barely sufficient to make B indifferent to the infringement of his right to use the acquired thing. Perhaps, however, B should be compensated at the higher level that Nozick calls "market compensation" by being given what he could have secured through prior negotiations for his consent.[28] Under the proviso, *A* can expropriate *B*'s right without sharing the benefits of a market exchange.[29]

One might reply in Nozick's defense that this last point misconstrues *B*'s right: *B* does not have a right to use the object (with compensation due if the right is infringed), but rather a right to a welfare level that includes either the right to use or its equivalent value. On this view the use and the compensation are seen as fungible components of *B*'s antecedent welfare. *A* is obligated merely to replenish *B*'s welfare loss, not to bestow a welfare gain. Because the benefits *A* realizes from appropriation are not part of *B*'s welfare in the thing's unappropriated state, *B* is not entitled to market compensation.

This reply, however, begs the question, for it assumes precisely what is at issue: that *A*'s potential gain from acquisition is not part of the welfare level to which the object's possible use entitles *B*. There is no reason to exclude the discounted future value of a right from the inventory of one's present resources. The conclusion Nozick requires, that prospective advantages from a more profitable future use are not included in the welfare of someone who is or could be using it now, follows only because it has been assumed at the outset.

The difficulty remains even if we connect the proviso not to rights but to the supposition that a person not disadvantaged has no grounds to complain. The proviso itself cannot settle what is to count as the baseline of disadvantage and thus as the ground of complaint. Nozick's unsubstantiated assumption is that *B*'s situation before the appropriation is to be compared with *B*'s situation had there been no appropriation rather than with *B*'s situation had the appropriation worked to *B*'s benefit.[30] The notion of welfare, however, supplies no reason for differentiating losses suffered from gains not realized. As a matter of welfare, *B*'s failure to benefit from *A*'s appropriation of something is not different in kind from *B*'s loss of the use of the thing. Indeed, in Nozick's theory losses suffered cannot be the only ground for complaint, because that would undercut the validity of appropriation itself. For if one could complain only of losses in welfare, *A* would be unable to complain if *B* refused to recognize *A*'s new entitlement to the welfare gain realized through appropriation.

These problems point to the radically different status of the rights in abstract right and the advantages maintained (or the disadvantages avoided) by Nozick's proviso. Because, as we saw above, abstract right is inherently normative, its rights have immediate justificatory significance. That rights actualize abstract right is, therefore, a sufficient reason for respecting them. Such rights sanctify three aspects of a situation: the time, the object, and a specifically appropriate remedial consequence. First, rights sanctify the present, because it makes no sense to recognize that I have a right and yet to treat as normatively decisive a past time when I did not have it or a future time when I might not have it. Second, my having the right means that the object of the right is set apart from everything else in the world and included within a special normative relationship to me that others must respect. Third, violation of the right entitles one to a remedy (tort damages, expectation damages, restitution, and injunctions for example) that in any given case corresponds to the nature of the right and its violation.[31]

The advantages protected by Nozick's proviso lack this immediate justificatory significance. We are always entitled to ask why normative force is to be ascribed to any particular advantage. An advantage, in and of itself, is just a fact about the world. It does not morally link a specific person to a specific time and object. Nor does it imply the measure of compensation operative on its loss. On what basis, for instance, does Nozick sanctify B's advantages as of the moment preceding appropriation? Further, why is the maintenance of B's welfare level required when A appropriates but not when A engages in other disadvantaging operations (such as competitive activity)?[32] Finally, as was noted above, what justification is there for restricting B's entitlement to full rather than market compensation?

Advantages, unlike the rights in Hegel's account, do not include within themselves the grounds of their own normativeness. Whereas rights are morally relevant because of their conceptual connection with free will, advantages have no independent normative significance: it takes further argument to give them moral force. Consequentialists recognize this when they argue that the justification of a particular disposition of advantages lies in its conformity to or promotion of some favored pattern. Nozick, however, expressly abjures the justification of advantages on the basis of their pattern.[33] The advantages protected by his proviso are left to an unspecified normative netherworld that is neither rights-based nor consequentialist.

The difficulty here is that rights and advantages are constituents of different justificatory paradigms. It is impossible for both to be basic elements in a single coherent theory. Asserting the priority of rights is inconsistent with maintaining an initial level of advantages. Conversely, to worsen an individual's situation is not the same as to infringe his or her rights. A theory of rights cannot, therefore, begin with a mechanism devoted to the preservation of advantages.

WRONGFUL INTERACTION

The distinction between right and advantage is as significant for the rights holders' interaction as it is for the conception of their property. Tort law and the law of restitution amply illustrate that not all disadvantaging constitutes a wrong to the victim and that not all advantaging generates a right in the beneficiary. Here I wish to deal with the framework of wrongful interaction in abstract right.

Disadvantage and Misfeasance

As we have seen, Hegel's abstract right fully preserves the categorical distinction in common law between misfeasance and nonfeasance. The abstraction of the free will from the content of choice means that particular interests have no standing in abstract right. The actor is, therefore, under no obligation to act for the benefit of anyone else. Abstract right attaches significance only to the action of one rights holder as that action affects another. In situations of nonfeasance, the absence of such action precludes the imposition of liability.

The salient point about abstract right is that it ties the relevance of misfeasance to the interaction of free wills. Abstract right insists that there is no liability unless the harm trenches upon an embodiment of the will's abstract freedom. Accordingly, the distinction between nonfeasance and misfeasance plays itself out in the context of rights. Misfeasance in abstract right is not merely the creation of a minus quantity rather than the absence of a plus quantity.[34] The minus quantity must be an infringement of a right, not merely the lowering of a level of welfare.

When private law is conceived in terms of variations relative to an existing level of welfare, the common law's categorical distinction between misfeasance and nonfeasance evaporates. The closest analogue is a distinction between decreasing another's welfare and failing to increase it. However, this distinction is empty, for there is no reason to treat a unit of welfare below the existing level differently from a unit of welfare above it. What matters is whether the level is optimal, not whether it varies in either direction from some other level. Accordingly, once rights are discarded so that welfare becomes significant on its own, the failure to realize an advantage is not qualitatively different from the suffering of a disadvantage. Advantage and disadvantage are merely calibrations up and down the same scale from a contingent starting point.

The consequence is that liability cannot depend on whether the impugned behavior of the defendant is construed as depriving the plaintiff of a benefit or as imposing a burden. In either case the plaintiff is less well off than otherwise. The equivalent status of advantage and disadvantage means that there is no difference between them that can be used to mark off an area of immunity for the defendant's action. Because my harming you is not different in kind from my failing to help you, liability for the former cannot in principle be combined with an exemption from liability for the latter.[35] Thus, no categorical line can be drawn between advantage and disadvantage that corresponds to the distinction at common law (and in abstract right) between misfeasance and nonfeasance.

The dissolution of the nonfeasance/misfeasance distinction into the homogeneity of advantage and disadvantage is fundamental to the currently popular economic analysis of law. The basic idea of economic analysis is that resources should be assigned to those who are willing to pay for them and can therefore be said to value them most. Value is ideally the reflex of a bargaining process driven by the intensity of the bargainers' preferences and their willingness to express these preferences through monetary sacrifices.[36] In the paradigm situation, in which transaction costs do not impede bargains, the party to whom the resource is most valuable will buy it if he does not already own it. If he does already own it, no one who values it less will offer enough to induce him to sell it.

The distinction between nonfeasance and misfeasance has no place in this analysis. Because anyone can secure the coveted resource by investing his limited wealth in it, no one can be regarded as the passive victim of someone else's activity. Economic analysis repudiates the significance of the unidirectional transitivity of doing and suffering. Instead, everyone is regarded as a potential purchaser of advantages; disadvantage is merely the failure to secure a benefit. Accordingly, causation of harm is identified with the potential reciprocity of effect among economic actors in their competition for a scarce resource.[37]

This supplanting of misfeasance indicates that economic analysis is incompatible with private law, conceived as the ordering of relationships between rights holders. For the economic approach, the function of law is not to declare rights but to lubricate the mechanisms that will put the goods to their most valued uses. Indeed, under conditions of costless bargaining, the assignment of rights through private law adjudication is without significance: the judgment does not affect the ultimate use of the disputed resource, but merely marks a point of departure for the bargaining that will move the resource to the person to whom it is most valuable.[38] Only when bargaining costs prevent the market from spontaneously allocating a given good to its most valuable use does law become important.

The economic approach proposes that the law should then do what the market would have done had the market been able to do it: assign the resource to the person who would have been willing to pay the most for it. In the dominant strand of economic analysis, those disadvantaged by this assignment need not be compensated.[39] If, for instance, the owner of a factory would be willing to pay more to pollute than the neighbor would to have clean air, the factory owner should be allowed to pollute without paying the neighbor anything. The value of the air, as measured by the parties' willingness to pay, is at its highest when the entitlement to the air is assigned to the factory owner. Monetary compensation, however, cannot be valued more highly by one party than the other because money is itself the unit of value. Assigning the right to the polluter here maximizes value, whereas transferring a monetary sum does not.

This lack of compensation, it has been suggested, is what makes economic analysis problematic from a rights perspective.[40] If the entitlement really is more valuable to him, the factory owner would realize a profit even if he were forced to compensate others for breathing polluted air. Requiring compensation would satisfy both efficiency and rights: the resource would be put to its most valuable use and no one would have grounds for complaint.[41] The absence of compensation means that the interests of one party are sacrificed to those of the other; this sacrifice is what makes economic analysis incompatible with rights.

The distinction of right and advantage shows, however, that the absence of compensation does not go to the heart of the matter. The objection from a rights perspective is not that the advantages are improperly distributed between those who would bargain if they could, but that the juridical problem has been framed in terms of advantage and disadvantage. The consequent repudiation of the misfeasance/nonfeasance distinction is the point at which economic analysis cuts across the structure of private law.

Strict liability for disadvantaging is, accordingly, incompatible with private law understood as the actualization of abstract right. The focus on advantage makes paramount that from which abstract right abstracts. The norms of interaction in abstract right are not violated merely by adversely affecting another. That the plaintiff's harm can be characterized in terms of an invaded right is a necessary condition of liability.

The Liability Rule

Is that characterization also a sufficient condition? The common assumption is that the answer for rights theory is affirmative. Rights are thought to form the boundary of the moral space that circumscribes the individual. This boundary is the limit both of the rights holder's absolute discretion and of the effects of the actions of others. Whatever lies within this space is at the disposal of the rights holder; any unpermitted penetration of it by anyone else is a wrong. In legal terms, one's rights are protected against even accidental injury by a regime of strict liability.[42]

Proponents of strict liability assume—and, indeed, sometimes expressly claim[43]—that strict liability is conceptually implied in the very notion of a right. Now Hegel's account of abstract right is an exploration of the conceptual connections that render private law a coherent expression of right. Although Hegel says little about tortious liability[44] (in comparison to his elaborate treatment of property, contract, and crime), we can reconstruct the liability regime consonant with abstract right. If there were a conceptual connection between strict liability and the notion of a right, the logic of abstract right would bring it into high relief. If, on the other hand, strict liability cannot be sustained under abstract right, it is unlikely to be as indissolubly connected to the rights perspective as is commonly assumed.

Two arguments in favor of strict liability invite particular attention. The first focuses on the damage suffered by the plaintiff. The second construes the defendant's harmful act as a taking. Neither argument, in my view, succeeds when examined from the perspective of abstract right. I first set out their defects and then indicate why abstract right requires tort liability to be based on fault.

Damage Under strict liability any damage done to the physical or proprietary embodiments of free will is, in principle, ground for liability. The suffering of such damage, however, cannot in itself count as a violation of abstract right. Consider first the standpoint of the victim. When damaged, a particular embodiment of free will no longer retains its previous condition or value. Abstract right, however, does not guarantee any specific condition or value to what is owned. Abstract right accounts for ownership in a way that makes the condition of particular owned things irrelevant. It thus reflects the obvious truth that a particular owned thing remains the property of its owner whatever its condition or value. Although your injuring something that is mine may reduce the satisfaction I derive from it, what was injured nevertheless remains mine. Therein lies the abstractness of abstract right.

Nor does the defendant's causing of the injury constitute a violation of abstract right. The defendant's act, it is true, has impaired the condition or value of the plaintiff's property. But if impairment does not violate abstract right, how can the defendant's having caused the impairment do so? The abstractness of abstract right means that the plaintiff is not entitled to have his property in a certain condition.[45] Because any property's condition is always the result of some cause or other, the cause of the condition cannot, without more, create liability where the condition does not.

One might reply that the defendant is not merely a cause like any other. Although the deleterious effect of the defendant's act may be equal to that of a natural phenomenon such as a bolt of lightning, the defendant is more than a natural phenomenon. The defendant's act is an emanation of a free will; it thus should have a status under the idea of right that a natural phenomenon does not. The fact that the same consequence can be produced either by a free will or by nature does not render operations of free will and of nature juridically equivalent. Indeed, the point of abstract right is to highlight the special significance of the will's freedom by exhibiting the juridical sphere that actualizes it.

This response is insufficient. The centrality of free will to abstract right does not imply that the defendant should be liable for any damage resulting from his acts. The origin of the act in free will means only that conformity to the right is a standard to which the defendant can intelligibly be held. This makes abstract right applicable to the damage that one free will does to the body or the property of another, but it does not make the doing of such damage a per se violation of abstract right. The fact that the defendant is the sort of being whose injurious actions may be considered incompatible with abstract right does not of itself necessitate so considering it.

Takings The second argument for strict liability presents as a "taking" the harmful effect that the defendant's activity has on the plaintiff's moral space.[46] The strength of this stratagem is that takings, properly understood in the context of abstract right, do justify liability. The weakness is that accidental injuries are not takings in this sense. Let us consider each of these points in turn.

Takings justify liability inasmuch as they imply a general denial of the validity of right. A taking is an illegitimate appropriation: the taker attempts to assert dominion over something that is already a physical or proprietary embodiment of another's personality. In acting as if the embodiments of another's personality are available for appropriation, the taker is treating those embodiments as if they were devoid of free will. Thus, the taker signals through his actions that he does not recognize the categorical difference between persons, who have a capacity for rights, and other entities, which lack free will and therefore do not have that capacity. Because free will is the substance of right, and because personality represents the most fundamental condition of the will's freedom, to treat persons as if they were entities lacking free will is to imply that right can have no field of application. Understood in this way, takings are wrongs that constitute general denials of the validity of right.[47] Liability for takings juridically nullifies this denial and thus expresses the law's vindication of the freedom that right actualizes.[48]

Accidental injuries are not, however, properly understood as takings. An appropriator must direct his attention to that which he is purporting to appropriate, so that the act through which he appropriates is an execution of his purpose. One cannot inadvertently place one's will in a thing, because what one does to the thing does not then rank as an expression of one's will with respect to the thing. Injuries are accidental inasmuch as the injurer fails to direct attention to the object he injures. Because accidental injuries are not consequences that the actor intends, their occurrence does not contain an implicit assertion by the defendant of dominion over the harmed object. Thus, accidental harm does not imply a general claim that right has no field of application. In abstract right, therefore, the causing of accidental injury does not rank as a taking.

Fault If strict liability is not the liability regime appropriate to abstract right, what is? Fault, which is made up of intentional and negligent wrongdoing, is the general standard for liability under both the common law and the European civil law. As our discussion of takings indicates, intentional wrongdoing clearly violates abstract right, because the wrongdoer treats the personal and proprietary embodiments of another's free will as still available for appropriation. I wish to propose that negligent conduct can also be understood to violate abstract right.

The negligence standard divides injuries that actors accidentally cause into those for which they are liable and those for which they are not. This division is accomplished in any particular case by assessing the defendant's conduct according to a flexible and indeterminate standard of reasonableness. The standard presupposes that there is a certain level of risk to which the defendant can expose the plaintiff without committing a wrong, even if injury should result. The defendant is liable only for injuries that materialize from risks above that level.

The law's focus on risk ties in to abstract right. Abstract right deals with the doing and suffering of a harm. This doing and suffering is regarded as a unit that starts with the action of the defendant and ends with the effects of that action on the plaintiff. Risk allows us to conceive of the doing and suffering of an accidental harm as the maturation of a single process, since it captures the potential for harm present in the defendant's act that materializes in the plaintiff's injury. Risk is the relational concept that connects the active and passive aspect of injurious conduct, so that what the defendant did and what the plaintiff suffered are not regarded as two discrete happenings. Thus, risk supplies for unintended injuries the unity that, for intentional harms, is found in the identity of the consequence that the actor desires and the victim suffers.

In abstract right, the doing and suffering of injury connects two free wills, the one exercising his or her freedom through the act that harms, the other through the embodiment of free will that is harmed. The operation of free will has, as we have seen,[49] an inherent normative dimension. The defendant's action—and the legal judgments of that action—must be consistent with the abstract freedom implicit in the status of the parties as persons.

Two aspects of the relationship of risk to action are pertinent here. First, risk is an unavoidable concomitant of all action. Although action is the attempt to realize some purpose that the actor sets for himself, it takes place in a world that is not completely within the actor's control. "As the aim posited in the external world," writes Hegel, the action becomes "the prey of external forces."[50] The actor, therefore, cannot be under a duty not to impose risk. Such a duty would deny the possibility of action, and therefore, since a person is the embodiment of that possibility, would be incompatible with the status of the actor as a person. Indeed, it would be contradictory for the victim to claim an immunity from risk. Since both parties are persons, the victim cannot implicitly deny the defendant's personality without denying his own, thus depriving himself of the standing to complain. This is one way of expressing the defect of strict liability: just as the law cannot immunize the plaintiff against all the risks created by another's activity, so it cannot immunize him against the materialization of the risk, since risk is nothing but the possibility of its own materialization.[51]

Second, although risk is a concomitant of action, it can nonetheless be affected by the actor. Through action, actors attempt to work their purposes in the world. Nothing prevents the reduction of the risks engendered by their own actions from being among those purposes. An actor who claims that he can change the world through action (and therefore through the creation of risk), and yet that he cannot affect the risks that attend his action, asserts a convenient but incoherent powerlessness in the exercise of power. The harm into which risk materializes is not alien to the actor who has created the risk, since action by its very nature involves the possibility of unintended consequences. To refuse to mitigate the risk of one's activity is to treat the world as a dumping ground for one's harmful effects, as if it were uninhabited by other persons. Since doing and suffering is here, however, a relationship of free wills, one cannot claim the status of personhood—and thus the prerogatives of free activity—while implicitly denying that status to other free wills.

The division of accidental injuries through the negligence standard of reasonableness reflects these two considerations about risk. On the one hand, the actor is permitted to create risks up to a certain level, because action must inevitably be accompanied by some risk. On the other hand, the creation of risks above a certain level is grounds for liability, because it manifests a failure to respect the persons who are within the ambit of the act's effects. This analysis in terms of risk does not, of course, lead to an apodictically certain benchmark of liability. The function of abstract right, however, is not to reveal specific rules but to exhibit the normative framework to which particular legal determinations concerning doing and suffering must conform. The common law mirrors the necessary indeterminacy of abstract right by reserving the specific assessments of reasonableness to the triers of fact, who apply vague instructions to particular cases.[52]

Unlike intentional wrongs, negligent acts are not denials of the general validity of right. The negligent actor pursues his own purposes without encompassing the plaintiff or the plaintiff's property within his intent. The gist of the complaint against the negligent actor is that he did not regard the plaintiff when he should have, rather than that he did regard the plaintiff when he should not have. The negligent actor does not negate right generally by implicitly asserting that even the embodiments of the personality of others lie available for his appropriation; he merely makes a mistake about the compatibility of a particular act with what is required of interaction among free beings. Far from denying the freedom of others, the negligent actor misapprehends what that freedom implies for his own.[53]

Accordingly, abstract right—the purest rights-oriented approach to private law—demands that the negligence standard rather than strict liability be the norm for interaction. This conclusion reverses the common assumption of contemporary scholarship, where strict liability is identified with the protection of rights[54] and negligence with the maximization of wealth.[55] Construing the negligence standard as a requirement of abstract right has the merit of preserving features of the conceptual structure of private law that contemporary accounts sacrifice. Whereas strict liability ignores the distinction between intentional and negligent injuries by making the suffering of harm decisive regardless of fault and by interpreting the causing of any injury as a taking, abstract right attaches a different juridical significance to intent and negligence by relating them to general and particular negations of right, respectively. Whereas negligence seen as wealth maximization figures in a framework of economic analysis that ignores the distinction between misfeasance and nonfeasance, negligence in abstract right presupposes the conceptual relevance of that distinction. Thus, abstract right, more satisfactorily than either strict liability or wealth maximization, grounds the fundamental distinctions that underlie the lawyer's understanding of private law.

The superiority of fault to strict liability illustrates the general theme that private law, conceived in terms of rights, abstracts from the particularity of advantage. Strict liability protects the condition or the value of the right even though the nature of right in private law is precisely to abstract from immediate guarantees of condition or value. Under strict liability the objects to which the plaintiff is entitled are equated with the level of well-being that accrues to the plaintiff from those objects. Unanswered is the question of why that well-being should restrict the defendant's freedom. Although abstract right, as the intelligible structure of the relationship between free wills, pertains inherently to interaction, strict liability fails to translate the abstractness of right into an interactional norm. Under the fault standard, in contrast, delictual interaction is entirely pervaded by abstract right.

CONCLUSION

Hegel's account of abstract right is the most sustained attempt in Western legal philosophy to capture the distinctive rationality of private law. The special kind of abstraction involved in private law had been described by Aristotle and elaborated by Kant.[56] Hegel, however, driven by his encompassing logical and metaphysical concerns, pressed that abstraction to a radical extreme. He thereby showed how private law can be a coherent system of rights when, and only when, "there is no question of particular interests, of . . . advantage or . . . welfare."[57]

Yet in the resurgence of private law theorizing in the last two decades, Hegel's abstract right has been more or less ignored. On the one hand, the dominant strand of legal scholarship, now represented by economic analysis, has been concerned to torture private law into the maximization of advantage. On the other hand, those who have championed rights have argued against maximization while nonetheless conceiving of private law in terms of advantage. From the standpoint of abstract right, this difference involves only a local controversy about how advantages are to be treated. Neither side recognizes that the conceptual structure of private law abstracts from advantage.

Hegelians have not been entirely without blame for the neglect of abstract right. They know that for Hegel abstractness is a defect not a merit, and that, in Hegel's philosophy of right, abstract right is only the first—and therefore the least satisfactory—phase of right. Consequently, some have been tempted to ignore private law, others to read into it the welfare rights that come from later developments in the dialectic of right.[58] The former fail to notice that, whatever other manifestations of right there are or should be, private law remains the most pervasive example in our legal culture of the immanent rationality of right as Hegel conceived it. The latter stand condemned out of Hegel's own mouth, for Hegel expressly affirmed that private law has obligatory force only inasmuch as it actualizes abstract right.[59]

The centrality of rights in current legal discourse suggests the continuing relevance of Hegel's philosophy of right. Hegel's insistence that "freedom is both the substance of right and its goal, while the system of right is the realm of freedom made actual"[60] provides the basis both for understanding and for criticizing our assumptions about rights. If the contemporary analysis of private law is truly to take rights seriously, it will have to come to terms with abstract right.

NOTES

1. For a similar question, see Peaslee, Multiple Causation and Damage, 47 Harv. L. Rev. 1127, 1139–41 (1934).

2. Berry v. Borough of Sugar Notch, 191 Pa. 345, 43 A. 240 (1899).

3. I do not mean to imply that one could not, with sufficient ingenuity, reach the same result through the calculation of advantages. One could, for instance, argue that although we know ex post that *this* plaintiff benefited on *these* facts, the calculation of advantages should proceed ex ante and should be directed to a

more generalizable rule. Such an approach, however, will not capture the way lawyers think and talk about the situation. Cf. Calabresi, Concerning Cause and the Law of Torts: An Essay for Harry Kalven, Jr., 43 U. Chi. L. Rev. 69, 105 (1975) (noting that the law's language is "alien" to his economic analysis of tort law). (I also suspect that such complex and unverifiable calculations of advantage would only be rationalizations of a result that appeals to lawyers on rights grounds. Economists who treat tort liability as a pricing system for the activity of defendants, for instance, have never satisfactorily explained the entitlement of plaintiffs to the proceeds. But that is another story.)

4. Fontainebleau Hotel Corp. v. Forty-Five Twenty-Five, Inc., 114 So. 2d 357, 359 (Fla. Dist. Ct. App. 1959), cert. denied, 117 So. 2d 842 (Fla. 1960).

5. Id. (emphasis in original). But cf. Prah v. Maretti, 108 Wis. 2d 223, 321 N.W.2d 182 (1982) (use of land must not unreasonably impair another's use or enjoyment); T. H. Critelli Ltd. v. Lincoln Trust & Sav. Co., 20 O.R.2d 81 (H.C. 1978) (same); Nor-Video Servs. Ltd. v. Ontario Hydro, 19 O.R.2d 107 (H.C. 1978) (same).

6. See Boomer v. Atlantic Cement Co., 26 N.Y.2d 219, 257 N.E.2d 870 (1970).

7. See Spur Indus. v. Del E. Webb Dev. Co., 108 Ariz. 178, 494 P.2d 700 (1972).

8. See G. Calabresi, The Costs of Accidents: A Legal and Economic Analysis (1970); R. Posner, Economic Analysis of Law (3d ed. 1986). For reflections on how economic insights should affect the way law is thought about and practiced, see B. Ackerman, Reconstructing American Law (1984).

9. G. Hegel, Philosophy of Right §§ 34–104 (T. Knox trans. 1952) [hereinafter Philosophy of Right].

10. Id. § 37.

11. Id. § 29.

12. Id. § 36 (single quotes in original).

13. Id. § 48R.

14. Id. § 36.

15. Id. § 41.

16. Id. § 36 (emphasis added).

17. Id. §§ 44, 44A.

18. Id. § 49.

19. Id. § 36.

20. The last two examples are taken from J. Bentham, An Introduction to the Principles of Morals and Legislation 293 n.u (J. Burns & H.L.A. Hart eds. 1970).

21. One might think that one respects personality by making personality the end that one tries to promote through one's action in situations of both misfeasance and nonfeasance. Thus, when I allow someone to drown, I am not making that person's personality the object of my action and, so, I am failing to respect it just as surely as when I kill him. This, however, misunderstands the imperative of abstract right in paragraph 36 to "respect others as persons." Philosophy of Right § 36. Hegel does not mean that in abstract right one must make personality one's goal: such a goal would itself be a particular goal, and abstract right abstracts from this particular goal as it abstracts from all particular goals. The absence of the

requirement to make personality the object of one's action is what distinguishes abstract right from morality for Hegel. See id. § 104. Because abstract right abstracts from particular goals, it contains no affirmative obligations—not even an affirmative obligation to promote personality itself. Accordingly, respect for personality in abstract right takes the form of compliance with the negative command: "Do not infringe personality and what personality entails." Id. § 38. The obligation to abstain from infringing personality imposes a limit on what the actor can do without making any particular act obligatory. In abstract right, my actions need only be consistent with the capacity for rights that marks the personality of others. My ignoring someone who is drowning is not inconsistent with his having a capacity for rights; I am merely failing to help him overcome circumstantial impediments to the exercise of that capacity. In contrast, my murdering him would be inconsistent with his having the capacity for rights, since I would be treating him as a thing that was available to my purposes and, thus, not as an embodiment of free will. It is true that someone about to drown is not very well off, and that he will soon be dead and thus without a capacity for rights or for anything else. Abstract right, however, does not require that anybody be alive— let alone some particular individual be alive—only that existing persons' acts conform to the minimally compossible conditions for their interaction as persons.

22. This weasel expression here is meant to postpone, not to avoid, the further requisite specification. My discussion at this point deals only with the infringement on personality as a necessary condition of wrongful interaction in abstract right. I argue in Part IV, section B, that this necessary condition is not a sufficient condition. See infra notes 42–55 and accompanying text.

23. Philosophy of Right § 38.

24. On this difference, see, e.g., Mack, Bad Samaritanism and the Causation of Harm, 9 Phil. & Pub. Aff. 230 (1980).

25. R. Nozick, Anarchy, State, and Utopia, 150–74 (1974).

26. See id. at 178 (adopting Locke's formulation).

27. Id. at 174–82. For a detailed treatment of the difficulties of Nozick's proviso, see Stick, Turning Rawls into Nozick and Back Again, 81 Nw. U.L. Rev. 363, 387–416 (1987).

28. On the difference between market and full compensation, see Nozick, supra note 25, at 63–65, 68.

29. See Kavka, An Internal Critique of Nozick's Entitlement Theory, 63 Pac. Phil. Q. 371 (1982).

30. Cohen, Self-Ownership, World-Ownership, and Equality, in Justice and Equality Here and Now 108, 118–30 (F. Lucash ed. 1986).

31. This claim that private law, construed as abstract right, has a remedial integrity, may strike some as being unduly optimistic. Of course, I cannot argue for it here. The classic difficulty for lawyers has been with expectation damages in contract law. See, e.g., Atiyah, The Theoretical Basis of Contract Law—An English Perspective, 1 Int'l J.L. & Econ. 183 (1981); Fuller & Perdue, The Reliance Interest in Contract Damages, 46 Yale L. J. 52, 57–66 (1936). In my opinion, the coherence of expectation damages has been decisively vindicated in Peter Benson's as

yet unpublished essay *The Executory Contract in Natural Law* (available from the author).

32. Nozick, supra note 25, at 178.

33. Id. at 155–60.

34. Bohlen's formulation. See F. Bohlen, Studies in the Law of Torts 294–95 (1926).

35. This is not to say that the law must treat every advantage the same as every disadvantage, only that there is no initial reason not to do so. Theorists concerned with advantage usually perform further operations on advantages and disadvantages (e.g., maximizing the utility of all) that may in the end yield a reason for treating (most) losses inflicted differently from (most) gains not realized. For an example of such an argument, see Weinrib, The Case for a Duty to Rescue, 90 Yale L. J. 247, 280–86 (1980). Such a difference in the significance of gains and losses, however, is contingent rather than categorical: it applies only to most rather than to all gains and losses because it is only the output of the argument and not something that is initially built into its structure.

36. On the theoretical problems that result when willingness to pay does not coincide with ability to pay, see Weinrib, Utilitarianism, Economics, and Legal Theory, 30 U. Toronto L.J. 307, 315–16, 328–29 (1980).

37. Coase, The Problem of Social Cost, 3 J.L. & Econ. 1, 2 (1960).

38. Id. at 2–13.

39. See, e.g., Posner, supra note 8, at 11–15.

40. B. Ackerman, Private Property and the Constitution 222 (1977).

41. Cf. Powell v. Fall, 5 Q.B.D. 597, 601 (C.A. 1880) (Bramwell, L.J.):

    It is just and reasonable that if a person uses a dangerous machine, he should pay for the damage which it occasions; if the reward which he gains for the use of the machine will not pay for the damage, it is mischievous and ought to be suppressed, for the loss ought not to be borne by the community or the injured person. If the use of the machine is profitable, the owner ought to pay compensation for the damage.

42. Two prominent examples of this standard view must suffice here. Nozick discusses the remedial consequences of transgressing the boundary of the rights that constitute another's moral space. Nozick, supra note 25, at 57–87. He regards any crossing of the boundary as juridically significant. Thus, when he lists the possible remedies for an actual or prospective boundary crossing, id. at 75–76, he assumes that the transgressor must be held at least to strict liability. The fault standard that is basic to all Western legal systems is not even mentioned. In the same vein, Richard Epstein asserts that strict liability is entailed by the notion of property. R. Epstein, Takings: Private Property and the Power of Eminent Domain 96–98 (1985) [hereinafter Epstein, Takings]. For a detailed criticism of Epstein's views, see Weinrib, Causation and Wrongdoing, 63 Chi.-Kent L. Rev. 407, 416–24 (1987). In response to this criticism, Epstein has now abandoned his previous position. See Epstein, Causation—In Context: An Afterword, 63 Chi.-Kent L. Rev. 653, 660 (1987).

43. Epstein, Takings, supra note 42.

44. Philosophy of Right §§ 84–86, 98.

45. We are concerned here only with liability in tort and therefore assume the absence of relevant contractual terms.

46. E.g., Epstein, Takings, supra note 42, at 40.

47. Philosophy of Right § 95.

48. Id. § 98.

49. See supra notes 11–12 and accompanying text.

50. Philosophy of Right § 118.

51. For a fuller statement of this argument, see Weinrib, Liberty, Community, and Corrective Justice, 1 Canadian J.L. & Jurisprudence 3, 10–16 (1988).

52. The paradigm case for the interpretation of negligence from the standpoint of abstract right is Bolton v. Stone, [1951] App. Cas. 850 (H.L.). Lord Reid's opinion in that case is the leading English and Commonwealth formulation of the negligence standard. Lord Reid observes that "[i]n the crowded conditions of modern life even the most careful person cannot avoid creating some risks and accepting others. What a man must not do, and what I think a careful man tries not to do, is to create a risk which is substantial." Id. at 867.

    Lord Reid considers the chance and the seriousness of injury to be appropriate factors in an assessment of reasonableness, but not the difficulty of remedial measures. His approach thus differs from Judge Learned Hand's test in United States v. Carroll Towing Co., 159 F.2d 169 (2d Cir. 1947). See Perry, The Impossibility of General Strict Liability, 1 Canadian J.L. & Jurisprudence 147 169–70 (1988). The Learned Hand test, which involves a comparison of the present discounted value of the risk and the value of the precautions necessary to avoid the risk, treats tort law as a system of involuntary exchange in which the defendant's action is permissible so long as he gains more than the plaintiff loses. The exchanges of abstract right, however, must be voluntary and must involve equal values. See Philosophy of Right §§ 76–77. Accordingly, the Learned Hand test is not an adequate expression of abstract right.

53. See Hegel's discussion of nonmalicious wrong, Philosophy of Right §§ 84–86. Hegel deals with the negation of the particular will in nonmalicious wrong through competing claims on the same thing. He does not expressly deal with the issue of the proper understanding of delictual interaction. My point here is that the distinctions that Hegel draws between general and particular negations of right is applicable to the tort standard as well as to the proprietary and contractual rights with which Hegel is expressly concerned.

54. See Epstein, Takings, supra note 42.

55. Posner, supra note 8, at 147–52.

56. See Weinrib, Aristotle's Forms of Justice, 1 Ratio Juris (forthcoming 1989); Weinrib, Law as a Kantian Idea of Reason, 87 Colum. L. Rev. 472 (1987).

57. Philosophy of Right § 37.

58. See, e.g., Brudner, Hegel and the Crisis of Private Law, 10 Cardozo L. Rev. 949 (1989).

59. Philosophy of Right § 212.

60. Id. § 4.

Part Three

Law, Family, Civil Society and the State

10

Lucinde's Shame: Hegel, Sensuous Woman, and the Law

David Farrell Krell

> *Ethicality turned somewhat pale, and her eyes welled with tears. "But only yesterday I was so virtuous . . . It's all I can do to deal with my own reproofs; why must I hear still more of them from you?"—Friedrich Schlegel[1]*

Hegel wants spirit *alive*. Spirit alive is not only rational (*vernünftig*), not only thinking and willing spirit, but also spirit sentient, sensible, and sensuous (*sich empfindender Geist*). My paper is about *Empfindung*, so essential to life, yet so difficult to control, so mobile and prolific. A tradition as old as that of "spirit" identifies sentience and the sensuous with various figures of woman—as though spirit alive were *of woman*. Hegel's system confronts the following predicament: If woman were purged from the system, spirit would die; remaining within the system, however, woman condemns spirit to a fate worse than death.

In the handwritten notes and the "Addendum" to § 164 of Hegel's *Philosophy of Right* appear two explicit references to Friedrich Schlegel's novel *Lucinde*, first published in 1799.[2] "Lucinde" is the second of three major figures of woman dominating the first part of the first division of "Ethicality" (142–360), treating the family (§§ 158–81) and marriage (§§ 161–69). The first figure is *Venus vaga* (§ 161R), wandering, vagrant, vagabond Venus, whom the Greeks called Pandemian Aphrodite; the third is of course the heroine of Sophocles' *Antigone* (§ 166). The dialectic of marriage and the family turns on the axes of these tree figurines, as it were: the goddess of sensual love and beauty is abandoned for the infinitely free personality of Romantic lover, and Lucinde in turn is abjured for Antigone, at which point the law of woman succumbs to the law of the state.

Allow me to focus on the middle figure, Lucinde, and to ask what it is about her that so unnerved Hegel. For whenever Lucinde is espied in his text, Hegel's irritability and even anxiety or sense of jeopardy wax strong. What has the system to fear from her? Nothing—if we trust Hegel's account of her pitiable position. Everything—if Philippe Lacoue-Labarthe is right to see in her poetry, literature, and aesthetics, the despised parts of the system, which return to haunt the speculative.[3] Taking my cue from Lacoue-Labarthe, I want to ask about those despised parts of literature and life. I shall examine some of the predicates that cling to Lucinde in Hegel's text, comparing them to passages in Schlegel's *Lucinde*. I shall then examine in a shameless way Hegel's Jena lectures on the *pudenda*;[4] and I shall close with some speculations concerning sensuous woman—as though she were one, and as though I had the right to invoke her—senuous woman and the law.

It is all a matter of proper sequence, succession, and consequence: *Folge*. A matter of reversing a natural chronology of events by grace of a spiritual (*geistigen*) anachronism. If nature brings together a particular "this" (male) with a second particular "this" (female), as it must do if the species is to perpetuate itself; and if natural passion causes all the "strings" of one self-consciousness to "reverberate . . . only in this one being, only in possession of this *one contingent* person" (§ 162R); then spirit will have to elevate the accidental conjunction by reversing the order of dependence. Meeting and mating will not *lead to* marriage but will be *consequent upon* marriage and *subsequent to* it. Only in this way will the particularity (*Besonderheit*) and contingency (*Zufalligkeit*) of passionate sensibility (*Empfindung*) dissolve in the universality of bonded spiritual love. Only in this way will the high necessity of spiritual progression to civil society and the State occur.

Yet the stakes are hardly the same for the two "thises" destined to be elevated by the spiritual anachronism of matrimony. Hegel sets the stakes high, infinitely high, for woman, inasmuch as her honor (*Ehre*) is won solely on the field of marriage (*Ehe*). Honor and matrimony (*Ehre und Ehe*) are in fact one for woman: *Eh(r)e*. That becomes clear in otherwise often elliptical notes that Hegel jotted into his copy of *Philosophy of Right*. Let us examine extracts from two sets of these notes, those to §§ 162 and 164. First, those from § 162:

What does the man want, what does the girl [*Madchen*] want?
The girl wants a man; the man wants a woman [*eine Frau*] (§ 162A).

Already the difference in the stakes is clear. Twice the word *Mann* asserts itself, as both the subject and the object of desire.[5] The girl is apparently equal to herself (although even here the self-sufficiency is illusory), whereas as an object of desire she will have to be transmogrified into a woman. How will that happen? Hegel continues:

She loves him. Why? Because he is to become her husband (§ 162A).

It is still the same word, *Mann*, that serves for male, man, and husband—German being the language of thinkers. (When French girls fall in love, as every Heideggerian knows, they always have to speak German!) But to continue:

> [H]e is to make her into a woman [*sie zur Frau machen soll*]. She is to receive from him as man her dignity, value, joy, and happiness as a *wife* {*Ehefrau*}; that is, she is to become woman [*das sie Frau wird*]. Love—she recognizes the basis of her interest in the man; this is preeminently the *girl's sensibility* [*dies vornehmlich die Empfindung des Mädchens*] (§ 162A).

At least two kinds of appropriation are going on here. We are accustomed to one of them—appropriation of the names *girl, woman, wife* as tokens of masculine desire. Yet the second appropriation, albeit every bit as traditional, is more difficult to descry and less calculable in its effects: the first stage of ethicality as a whole—love as the nonmediated substantiality of spirit, the family as a unit of sensibility (*sich empfindende Einheit*) (§ 158)—is in effect surrendered to the maid. Without sensibility, Hegel himself stresses, the life of spirit would be dry and brittle (*sprode*) (§ 33A); indeed, without sensibility in the Kantian sense, the processes of intelligence and cognition would not have their start.[6] However, sensibility and receptivity are appropriated to and by a girl—neither a goddess nor a mortal woman, but a mere maid. Antigone. A girl under arrest. And a case of arrested development. On the one hand, Hegel holds no truck with patriarchy, which makes slaves of its children and even arranges their marriages, as though love were a matter of contract (as it apparently was for Bachelor Kant). Hegel does not want to reproduce the Romish-monkish mistake of vilifying natural vitality and mortifying sensuality as negative in themselves.

On the other hand, sensibility is clearly of woman; better, it is girlish, childish; worse, it readily becomes what novelists call "the sensibility of the flesh."[7] *Empfindung* will thus have to be a passing moment for Hegel and for spirit, if not for Lucinde and Julius. It is no accident that all the predicates of sensibility, the lifeblood of spirit and an essential component of the system, assemble in one place in *Philosophy of Right*: these predicates—naturalness, contingency, accident, particularity, inclination, drive and desire loom at and as the origins of evil (§ 139). The second set of handwritten notes takes up the seducer's sophism,

"Prove That You Love Me Darling," and the stakes for a "Oh Please Don't Make Me Prove It Maid" (§ 164R). Of course, the notes become compelling only if § 164 is viewed as a whole. Permit me, then, the following brief résumé.

Only when solemnization through matrimony takes place, in the presence of the family and community, does natural love receive its spiritual bond. Hegel emphasizes the importance of the antecedence (Vorangehen) of the ceremony; the antecedence reversing the natural sequence of events in such a way that "the sensuous moment pertaining to natural vitality is posited [gesetzt] in its ethical relationship as a consequence and mere accident [Folge und Akzidentalität] (§ 164). True, some moderns take solemnization itself to be accidental and superfluous, an extrinsic formality, a mere civil instance that interrupts the intimacy of the lovers' union. These persons do not accept that the formal ceremony is "the antecedent condition of their mutual and total abandon" (§ 164). (The word rendered by "abandon" is Hingebung, and it will soon return to haunt the spiritual bond). They even believe that love is disunited[8] by such ceremonial intrusion.

Modern, Romantic love is no doubt superior to the "Platonic love" of popular conceit, for it is closely tied up with the essential individualism of modernity and of Protestant Christianity. Nevertheless, Romantic love does raise the "pretension" (§ 162R) of being purer than purity itself. It denies the ethicality of love, rejects "the more elevated inhibition and suppression of the mere physical drive," an inhibition and suppression that occur naturally through "shame" and spiritually through the inculcation of "chastity" and "decency" (§ 163). The natural and sensuous moment is thus to be subordinated or demoted (herabgesetzt) (§ 163); or else all is insolence, impudence, and even impudicity—for we are already talking about Lucinde and her paramour. Impudence (Frechheit) is the very allegory played out so shamelessly by the author of Lucinde, an author possessed of intellect and wit but blind to the speculative nature of love and marriage—which is acknowledged, on the contrary, by the "legislation of all Christian peoples." (§ 164).[9]

Perhaps now we are in the position to talk our way through the handwritten note to the Remark of § 164, and to cite verbatim its Addendum. Sophistry[10]—the seducer's art, as Schlegel admits ("[a] stream of importunities, flatteries, and sophisms flowed from his lips,")[11]—demands sensuous abandon as proof of love before marriage, whereas love believes and spiritual consciousness has faith. The girl, victimized by such sophistry, surrenders her honor (gibt ihre Ehre auf); not so the man. For the man still has another field for his ethical efficacy; for example, in the corporations of the state (§ 255R); not so the girl. For her, ethicality exists essentially in the relation of marriage. Here there is no parity. On the part of the man, senuous abandon is no proof of love and no threat to honor. Love, Hegel notes laconically, can make demands that are different from those of marriage. Love is the substantial unity of spirit in sensibility (§ 158), but also "the most monstrous contradition, one which the intellect cannot resolve" (§ 158A). With love, all is one and undivided, both sensuous and ethical. However, only the supplement of solemnization, the exchange of spoken words and stipulated promises, establishes the relation in such a way that sensuous abandon is not a cause but a consequence. (Indeed, a consequence that is essentially inconsequential for marriage, in which it is effectively suppressed [zurückgedrängt], in order that connubial equanimity not be disturbed by passion) (§ 163A). In agreeing to the marriage, concludes Hegel cryptically, "the girl concedes this too" (§ 164). The note is unclear. Concedes what? Concedes that sensuous abandon will now follow? Or concedes that sensuality is merely a supplement, indeed a bothersome stipulation, to the ethical bond? What does the girl concede in marriage? We do not know, even if Hegel's remarks on the role of the housewife (§ 167A) certainly give us some indication of the concessions involved. What we do know is that at the end of these handwritten notes appears the underlined word *Lucinde*. The juxtaposition of the tile of Schlegel's novel with these notes on a victimized girl (*ein Mädchen*) is nothing short of bizarre, as we shall soon see. But let me now cite and discuss the Addendum to paragrph 164:

> *Addendum.* That the ceremony which sets the seal on the marriage is superfluous, a mere fomality that can be set aside inasmuch as love is what is substantial, and that love even loses some of its value through this solemnization—this has been argued by Friedrich von Schlegel in Lucinde and by an anonymous supporter in a series of letters.[12] Here in senuous abandon [*Hingebung*] is represented as though it were demanded as a proof of the freedom and intense ardor [*Innigkeit*] of love, an argumentation not foreign to seducers. Furthermore, one must note concerning the relation of man and woman that the girl surrenders her honor in sensuous abandon, which is not the case with the man, who has yet another field for his ethical activity [*Tätigkeit*] than the family. The girl is defined essentially only in the relation of marriage; what is called for is that love receive the form of marriage and that the sundry moments of love assume their truly rational relationship to one another (§ 164).

We know that the truly rational relationship enjoined by Hegel is the inversion, not to say perversion, of the natural order, such that sensuous abandon follows matrimony rather than inducing it. Let us now examine more closely the scene of sensibility. The girl's honor (*Ehre*) is at risk; she is being asked to surrender herself, to give herself over to utter abandon and erotic transport (*Hingebung*). The man's honor will not risk in this transaction, inasmuch as he performs his ethical activity (*Tätigkeit*) not only in marriage and the family but also in civil society and the state. *Ehre, Hingebung, Tätigkeit*: let me focus on these three aspects of the scene of *Empfindung*.

Ehre (honor) is ubiquitous in Hegel's *Philosophy of Right*. This is suprising, since it seems to belong more to the bygone era of chivalry, to the Age of Heroes and Patriarchs (§ 71R), or even to the Age of the Oriental Potentates (§§ 348–49, 355), than to the modern world. For the girl, the meaning of honor is exhausted in her resisting *Hingebung* prior to marriage. (Forgetting for the moment that Antigone too is a girl, one who pays her brother the ultimate honor [*die letzte Ehre*] (§ 118R), confronting the state with the stubbornness of a Cassandra.) For a man, honor is more a matter of corporations in the state, or of his class and status in civil society (§§ 244, 253, 255). Even a criminal has his honor (§ 132), and the honor consists in reaping punishment for his deeds (§§ 100R, 120R). Honor is also a matter of rights, thought, and the concepts themselves, inasmuch as all these must "come to honor" (140A, 189A, 211A).

One matter of honor to which Hegel attaches great importance is that of "spiritual production"—for example, in the authorship of books (§ 69R). Such honor is threatened by overt plagiarism and covert scholarly pilfering. Yet no legal code can protect an author from such pilferage, just as no law can protect neophytes from the sophistry of seducers. How well does honor function in the law's stead? Given the fact that we no longer hear about plagiarism in the learned world, one must assume that honor has thoroughly repressed (*verdrängt*) such dishonor. Either that, or we have come to accept that adding a little windfall of one's own to someone else's work, a touch-up here, a touch-up there, suffices for orignality. Ah yes, the precarious honor of all spiritual production, the fragile flowers of spirit! Some two hundred pages before he mentions Schlegel's *Lucinde*, Hegel complains bitterly that "the most wretched book can have a higher [financial] value than the most thoroughly researched book" (§ 64R). That *Lucinde* should outsell *Philosophy of Right*—cruel irony, irony of ironies![13]

Hingebung. Sensuous abandon. The girl's capitulation to the man, in order to attain womanhood. In the "Remark" to § 164, Hegel speaks of abandon as mutual (*gegenseitig*). In § 168 he emphasizes the fact that *unconstrained abandon* ("freie Hingebung") proceeds from the infinitely proper personality of the two sexes bonded or bound in marriage, though never in incest. In another context, as we shall see below, Hegel speaks (only once, as far as I know) of *Hingeben* as the activity of the man; otherwise, such devotion or surrender (*Hingabe*) and sensuous abandon (*Hingebung*) are markedly feminine, or female, or of woman. She gives. One must prevent her from giving up (*aufgeben*) her fragile honor too soon. Such prevention is no doubt a burden and a nuisance. She gives. An infinite invitation to guilt and chagrin. One hears it in Hegel's wry, doleful phrase, *eine Argumentation, die Verführern nicht frend ist*: an argumentation not foreign to seducers. The Voice of Experience. The Voice of Hegel. She gives. For the love of spirit, who can stop her? Useless, Leopold Bloom says. Might as well try and stop the sea. She gives. And it is much more than a mere nuisance. She gives. She? Milly. Or is it Molly? Moly? Useless. She gives, somewhere on that shifting scene of sensibility, somewhere between Act I, Girlhood, and Act II, Womanhood.

In Schlegel's novel too, *Hingebung* is of woman, but of woman with man. "I begged you," remembers Julius, "to abandon yourself for once utterly to furious passion [*der Wut ganz hingeben*], and I implored you to be insatiable."[14] In his "Dithyrambic Fantasy on the Loveliest Situation," which culminates in a childlike ring-around-a-rosy of male-female roles, his (now Lucinde's) role is "the protective vehemence of the man," while her (now Julius's) role is "*die anziehende Hingebung des Weibes*," the inviting abandon of woman—the charming, attractive giving-over that draws the other towards itself.[15] The ultimate oxymoron: a giving-over that draws toward and takes in. Julius accounts it as an "allegory on the consummation of male and female in humanity whole and entire," and he concludes impudently: "A lot lies in this— and what lies there certainly will not rise as quickly as I do when I lie under you." An impudent translation, no doubt, of the more ambiguous German: "*wenn ich Dir unterliege,*"[16] whenever I am inferior to you. *Hingebung* is Julius's happy defeat, his glorious infirmity, his situated inferiority. Hegel would agree at least in this: Julius's "foolhardy enthusiasm," "divine to the point of vulgarity," his identification of *Freiheit und Frechheit* (freedom and impudence) can prevail only "at the cost of manliness itself," *nur auf Unkosten der Männlichkeit selbst.*"[17] She gives, she takes. He gives, he is taken. "She was not a little surprised, although she sensed it all along, that after the surrender [*nach der Hingebung*] he would be more loving and faithful than before. . . . They were altogether devoted and one [*ganz hingegeben und eins*], and yet each was altogether himself, or herself, more than they had ever been. . . ." [18] However, there is one more reference to sensuous abandon, in another text of Hegel's, to which we now in turn in search of *activity*. *Tätigkeit*. Activity. Doing the deed. Or, as Hegel calls it in § 166, "*das Mächtige und Betätigende*," the mighty and the activating. Recall that in Hegel's 1805–06 lectures at Jena on the human genitalia and the mating process, activity is attributed to the bifurcated part (*das Entzweite*), the self-differentiating part: not the testicle, which though twofold is encompassed by the ovaries of the female and "does not emerge into its opposite, does not become for-itself, does not become an active brain [*zum tätigen Gehirne*]."[19] Hegel does not name this bifurcated, self-differentiating, diaphoric/metaphoric organ that moves across space toward its opposite, although he cites its passive homologue in the female: "[A]nd the clitoris in woman is inactive feeling [*das untätige Gefühl*] in general; in contrast to it, we have in the male active feeling [*das tätige Gefühl*], the upswelling heart [*das aufschwellende Herz*]. . . ."[20] "Thus," Hegel can conclude, "the man is the active one [*Der Mann ist also das Tätige*] by the fact that his activity possesses this distinction [*dadurch dass diesen Unterschied seine Tätigkeit hat*]."[21]

The active brain, the upswelling heart, the heart in diastole. Whose heart? And where is it located? The handwritten notes to § 165 invoke the hearts of men. Oddly, the hearts of men—so powerful and all-activating—fall under the spell of another power. Among the exceedingly rare words of poetry that appear in *Philosophy of Right* are some verses extracted from that great epic poem of honor and chivalry, *El Cid*. Try to keep the Lord Cid (Charlton Heston) in your mind's eye as you read these verses; do not allow your concentration to wander and to be drawn in the direction of Doña Elvira (Sophia Loren):

> The mystery is—the power of
> Women over the hearts of us men.
> This mystery hides in them,
> Deeply concealed; the Lord God,
> I believe, cannot plumb such depths.
> [Hegel's marginal note:] (Now you've gone too far!)
> When on that Great Day
> The sins of all are brought to light,
> God will look into women's hearts:
> Either he will find them all
> Culpable, or all equally innocent,
> so interwoven is their heart (§ 165R).

The hearts of us men. *Unsere Männerherzen.* The upswelling hearts of us men, under the power of the tightly woven heart of woman. A heart so close to God that he cannot see it. (*Das nun eben nicht!* objects Hegel, in an effort to restore orthodoxy.) The undifferentiated and undifferentiating heart of woman, as tightly woven as a wreath of rush, closer in its undeveloped unity to the spirit of origins and the origins of spirit than My Lord Cid will ever be.²² For, as long as sensibility prevails, all individuality surrenders, abandons itself, and gives itself over to her. Thus we find ourselves back at *Hingebung.* She gives, she takes. She harbors. She conceives:

> Conception is the contraction of the whole individual into simple self-surrendering unity [*in die einfach sich hingebende Einheit*]; contraction into the representation of the individual; semen [or, the seed: *der Samen*] the simple physical representation—altogether one point, like the name [or, as of the taking-up] and the whole self.—Conception nothing else than the becoming-one of these abstract representations.²³

The simple physical representation, the simple seed, semen, Simple Semen, contracting in self-abandoning unity, the unity that serves as the congenital mark of woman, the fertilized egg in the womb; contracting in spasmodic waves, the foaming waves of Aphrodite and the shuddering waves of *Venus vaga.* She gives. She takes. She harbors. She conceives. The concept. Let us see if the hearts of us men can escape the ties that bond.

The active brain, the upswelling heart, the heart in diastole bring us back one more time to *Hingebung,* giving over, sensuous abandon, surrender, erotic devotion. In the margin of the Jena lectures, just above the paragraph on conception, at the point where woman is designated as the one who conceives, a marginal note about the breast: "Digestion turned to the outside—woman, milk of the breast." Next to this, as marginalia to marginalia, Hegel writes: "The metaphorical surrender [*Hingeben*] of heart and soul to the woman."²⁴

As I confronted the necesity to translate *metaphorisches Hingeben des Herzens und der Seele an das Weib,* I puzzled long and hard. I knew that it should be the woman who gives, that the marginal note should have read: *an dem Weibe, am Weibe, beim Weibe.* Yet Hegel's accusative pointed the finger: he gives, to her, heart and soul; to her upswelling heart and active brain. Or, without the commmas: he gives to her heart and soul, to her upswelling heart and active brain, to her conceiving. However, let me not abandon the margin too quickly, but linger on the breast. For it too, according to Julius, is engorged and magnificently swollen. Lucinde's body, bathed in the glimmer of twilight, is luxuriant—*Die üppige Ausbildung ihres schönen Wuchses*[25]— and the very vision of her goads his love to fury. These are not the breasts of a girl, Schlegel's Julius tells us; this is not the mirror of a maidenly body trembling on the brink of maturity. Her swelling outlines (*die schwellenden Umrisse*), which he is mad to touch, tell him— even if we are untouched by the extraordinary force and heat of her embrace—that Lucinde is not a girl at all.[26] Lucinde is a woman. Some time ago she has had a son, a son who is now dead.[27] Mourning—*die Trauer, le deuil*—marks her past. In addition, she is an accomplished painter. Her brain is active. She is one who produces spiritually, like those who write books or deliver lectures in the university. She thus bears an uncanny resemblance to Hegel. Except perhaps for those swellings—and even in those swellings not altogether different from Hegel. Julius, watching waves of ebon hair flow over the snowfields of those white breasts murmurs, Magnificent woman! Masterly woman! Lordly woman! *Herrliche Frau!*[28] Lucinde—a helpless girl ripe for the blandishments of seduction? Schleiermacher's epistolary hero replies that "a kiss from a woman who has already seen love face-to-face is undeniably more significant and more decisive than a maiden's very best approximation."[29] The Voice of Experience; the Voice of Schleiermacher, here peeping under all the veils that are woven in his name. In the face of Hegel's juxtaposition of the seduction story and Schlegel's *Lucinde*, one must ask: Can Hegel have read Friedrich Schlegel's epochmaking *Lucinde*?

Of course he read it. That is why a third figure has to be conjured once again. A fourteen-year old who accompanies her honor into the tomb, joining her brother and lover in Death. The law of the state seals her tomb with a granite boulder, the granite of spiritual fate, as Nietzsche says. In the same way, her lips are sealed: no further impudence against the substantial spirit of the State. She will contract into simple unity one last time. In the nick of time. No swelling profile. No uxoriousness. For Lucinde's is the law that unsettles every law, deranges all positing, upsets every *Setzen* and all *Gesetze*. Lucinde undercuts religion with sensuous transport; Julius adores her.[30] She undercuts matrimony with what he calls "the elevated lightheadedness of our marriage."[31] Homely ethicality pales before her,[32] and all her wisdom is baffled.[33] She is a spirited woman. She absorbs his activity utterly:

You feel everything whole and infinitely, you allow nothing to be separated off, your being is one and indivisible. That is why you are so serious and so joyful; that is why you take everything to heart and are so careless of it; and that is why you also love me wholely, leaving no part of me to the State, to posterity, or to my men friends. Everything belongs to you.[34]

Seal Lucinde's lips; seal her fate. Useless. Might as well try and stop the sea. In the dark cavern, diastole, upswelling heart, engorgement of the lips with blood and the breast with milk. And Lucinde's words, Lucinde's tears and laughter, Lucinde's give and take. The law of woman, *das Gesetz des Weibes*, will be heralded not by Antigone, the interred adolescent, and not as the law of the ancient gods, as Hegel has it. Hers is the law of the goddess, *Venus vaga*, Lucinde's glory, the contracting waves subterranean power, "eternal law which no one knows from what dawn appeared."[35]

Has Hegel successfully sealed off and fully interiorized the law of woman? Has he forgotten nothing? And would we remember him at all if he claimed to be so perfectly memorious? In the preface to the *Phenomenology of Spirit*, he depicts the moment at which extraneous preoccupation with results, conclusions and generalities *ends* and thinking *begins* not as remembrance but as self-forgetting. Like Lucinde giving himself to Lucinde's snowscape and tropics, the phenomenologist remembers when to give, when to live and let live, when to forget: "to linger with the matter in question and to forget himself in her . . ., abandoning himself to her [*in ihr (der Sache) zu verweilen und sich in ihr zu vergessen, . . . sich ihr (hingeben)].*"[36]

NOTES

1. F. Schlegel, Lucinde, in 2 Werke in Zwei Bänden 5–99, 22 (W. Hecht ed. 1980) [hereinafter Lucinde]. *Lucinde* was first published in 1799 by Heinrich Froelich in Berlin. After completing my paper, I discovered a fine English translation, F. Schlegel, Lucinde and the Fragments (P. Firchow trans. 1971), containing Lucinde, the Athenaeum Fragments, and other writings.

2. G. Hegel, 7 Werke in zwanzig Bänden: Grundlinien der Philosophie des Rechts (E. Moldenhauer & K. Michel eds. 1970). See Lucinde, supra note 1. [Editor's note: Henceforth, all references to *Philosophie des Rechts* will be by section numbers and placed in the text.]

3. Lacoue-Labarthe, L'imprésentable, 21 Poétique 53 (1975). Lacoue-Labarthe discusses Hegel's references to Lucinde in *Philosophy of Right*, but focuses principally on the *Lectures on Aesthetics*. G. Hegel, 13 Werke in zwanzig Bänden:

Ästhetik (E. Moldenhauer & K. Michel eds. 1970). (See the list of these references below.) His thesis concerns the uneasy presence of poetry (and art and literature generally) in Hegel's system of speculative philosophy; it is a thesis that cannot be reduced to a few words of mine here. Suffice it to say that Lacoue-Labarthe's preoccupation is with Hegel's moral accusation of Schlegel's *Lucinde*, an artwork which establishes the "epoch" not of Romantic art proper, but of moral turpitude and dissipation (*Liederlichkeit*)—having, in Hegel's view, nothing to do with music and song. Even though Schlegel's novel marks an epoch in the history of art and literature, it is nonetheless Schiller's more edifying poesy to which Hegel constantly reverts. Unlike Schiller, Schlegel is (as Creon says to his son Haemon) "weaker than woman." Sophocles' Antigone, line 680 (author's translation). Yet, behind the contempt in which Hegel holds Schlegel, Lacoue-Labarthe senses a certain anxiety—indeed, an anxiety for the whole of the speculative system. In the context of *Philosophy of Right*, see especially Part Three of Lacoue-Labarthe's fine essay, L'imprésentable, entitled L'Impudeur: La Voile et la Figure. Lacoue-Labarthe, supra, at 64–75. The clearest and most succinct statement, of his thesis appears in Part Four, La Subornation d'Aphrodite: Poesie et Philosophie, Id. at 78, 85–86. (My warm thanks to Rodolphe Gasché, who first presented me with Lacoue-Labarthe's essay.)

Hegel's references to Friedrich Schlegel in his *Lectures on Aesthetics* and in other works would have to occupy a separate study. In a nutshell, they relate Schlegel's moral lassitude to his poor poetry, bad prose, and contemptible pathos. Thus Hegel's vicious circle! See 13 Werke, supra, at 93–95, 348–49, 382–83, 404–05, 513; 14 Werke, supra, at 116, 180, 305–06, 497.

4. 8 G. Hegel, Gesammelte Werke, Jenaer Systementwürfe III (R. Horstmann ed. 1976).

5. I am of course using the phrase that serves as the title of Judith P. Butler's excellent study, Subjects of Desire: Hegelian Reflections in Twentieth-Century France (1987). Butler concentrates on Hegel's *Phenomenology of Spirit*, especially chapter one, on the ontology of desire and on lordship and bondage. See Krell, Pitch: Genitality/Excrementality from Hegel to Crazy Jane, 12 boundary 113 (1984) (special issue "On Feminine Writing"), which takes its point of departure from a passage in Hegel's remarks on "Observational Reason" in the *Phenomenology*.

6. 8 Hegel, Gesammelte Werke, Jenaer Systementwürfe III, supra note 4, §§ 44–47, 399–402. I have discussed sensibility and intelligence in the context of "interiorizing remembrance" (Erinnerung), in chapter five of On the Verge (forthcoming).

7. Lucinde, supra note 1, at 26.

8. "Disunited" renders the word *veruneinige*. Georg Lasson, editor of an edition of *Philosophy of Right* published in the 1920s, reads it as *verunreinige*, "to pollute," as though the pollution could be due to the altar or the civil registry rather than to the natural order of events. Even Friedrich Schlegel did not dare go so far.

9. A letter written in October 1824 reveals that Hegel never crossed Schlegel's path until that date—and even then the two men did not meet. 3 Briefe von und an Hegel 74 (J. Hoffmeister ed. 1952). Schlegel's conversion to Catholicism and his support of the House of Habsburg against Napoleon no doubt displeased Hegel. 2 Briefe von und an Hegel 283 (J. Hoffmeister ed. 1952); Philosophie des Rechts, supra note 2, § 284. Yet surely it is Schlegel's liaison with Dorothea Veit—taken by virtually every early reader of *Lucinde* to be the heoine-in-real-life of that

scandalous work—that most disturbs him. When Schlegel seduces Dr. Veit's wife, he duplicates the crime committed by Schelling against Schlegel's own brother, August Wilhelm: just as Schelling inveigles himself with Caroline Schlegel, so does Schlegel insinuate himself with Dorothea Veit. Thus, Friedrich Schlegel becomes something of a fratricide, committing the very crime that has been perpetrated against his own flesh. Reason enough to raise Hegel's ire. Yet I must confess that this is all speculation on my part; we are no doubt better advised to seek the reasons within *Lucinde* itself, and in "Lucinde" herself.

10. In his Foreword to Friedrich Wilhelm Hinrichs' Philosophy of Religion, 1 Hegel, supra note 2, at 61; 18 Werke, supra note 2, at 81, Hegel identifies Schlegel as an advocate of everything that is wrong with the times: the accidental and fortuitous quality of subjective feeling and opinion, bound up with the particular "formation of reflection" that betrays the fact that (Schlegel's) spirit is incapable of knowing the truth—an incapacity the ancients called sohpistry. Schlegel's is "worldly wisdom," for he is expert in the contingent, untrue, and temporal: he elevates vanity and the accidents of feeling to the Absolute. Sophistry shares with philosophy the "formation of reflection," yet does so in a merely formal way. And because it rejects the truths of Revelation, Schlegel's sophistry has no other ground to stand on than its own vanity.

11. Lucinde, supra note 1, at 47.

12. F. Schleiermacher, Vertraute Briefe über Friedrich Schlegel's Lucinde (K. Gutzkow ed. 1835) (Intimate Letters on Friedrich Schlegel's Lucinde, first published in 1800). No doubt Schleiermacher is an ally of Schlegel's: "And now we have this work, which stands there like a vision from a future world—God alone knows how far in the future!" Id. at 2. And: "Love must be resurrected, a new life must unify and ensoul its fragmented members, so that it can prevail joyously and freely in the hearts of mankind and in all its works, driving out the lifeless shadows of once vaunted virtues." Id. at 9. How difficult such an alliance is for Schleiermacher becomes clear in the sixth letter, "To Eduard," id. at 90–99, in which the divine advocate tries rather desperately to condemn Wieland's erotic writings while blessing Schlegel's. See id. at 94.

13. With regard to irony, in his review of Carl Wilhelm Ferdinand Solger's Posthumous Writings and Letter, 11 Werke, supra note 2, at 215, 234, 255, Hegel refers to the "most audacious and luxuriant period of irony" in German letters, mentioning by name *Lucinde* and the *Athenaeum Fragments*. He endorses Solger's view that Schlegel's notion of irony is "one-sided" and "dogmatic." Schlegel will not stoop to argumentation, to reasons and grounds. His high perch on "divine impudence" is also therefore "satanic," "diabolical" impudicity. Claiming to straddle the peak of philosophic wisdom, Schlegel never penetrates into the valleys of science. In 1800, when Schlegel offers a course on "transcendental philosophy" at Jena, he runs out of things to say after only six weeks, thus defrauding his listeners. See 2 Briefe von und an Hegel, supra note 12, at 98; 4 Werke, supra note 2, at 420–21.

Though clever and doubtless well-read, Schlegel remains utterly uninitiated in *der denkenden Vernunft*, "thinking reason." Irony is Fichtean subjectivism without the saving grace of Fichte's practical, ethical philosophy: that is the gist of Hegel's judgment on Schlegel in the Lectures on the History of Philosophy. 20 Werke, supra note 2, at 415–17. In the Solger review, 11 Werke, supra note 2, at 256–57, Hegel refers us to his discussion of irony in *Philosophy of Right*,

§ 140, which treats of evil as it appears in modern philosophy itself. See also Philosophie des Rechts, *supra* note 2, § 140A (further discussion of good, evil, hypocrisy, and irony). As significant as the polemic here is for Hegel's critique of Romanticism as a whole, let the following summary suffice: whereas Plato's Socrates ironizes the pretense of the Sophists, he never ironizes the ideas themselves—whereas this is precisely what Schlegel does. See 18 Werke, *supra* note 2, at 460–61. Finally, Solger's own views on tragic irony may well strike us as more radical than Hegel's and as pointing forward to Nietzsche. Precisely for that reason, they resist reduction to a note.

14. *Lucinde*, *supra* note 1, at 10. *Hingegeben*, in id. at 28, 47. *Gegeben*, in id. at 58.

15. *Lucinde*, *supra* note 1, at 16.

16. Id.

17. Id. at 17.

18. Id. at 66–67.

19. 8 Gesammelte Werke, *supra* note 6, at 173–74. See Krell, *supra* note 5, for a more detailed discussion of these materials.

20. 8 Gesammelte Werke, *supra* note 6, at 174.

21. Id.

22. See J. Derrida, Glas 1, 160 (1981).

23. 8 Gesammelte Werke, *supra* note 6, at 175. "Like the name," supposing that *der Nahme* is a curous (mis)spelling of *der Name*, masculine gender, nominative singular; or "as of the taking-up," "as of the assumption," supposing *der Nahme* to be from *nehmen*, "to take," as in the instance *She takes*, feminine gender, genitive singular.

24. Id. at 174.

25. *Lucinde*, *supra* note 1, at 67.

26. Id.

27. Id. at 65.

28. Id. at 66.

29. F. Schleiermacher, *supra* note 12, at 87.

30. *Lucinde*, *supra* note 1, at 10, 15, 29, 71, 81.

31. Id. at 14.

32. Id. at 23.

33. Id. at 28.

34. Id. at 14.

35. Sophocles' Antigone, lines 456–7 (author's translation). These lines are cited by Hegel in both Philosophie des Rechts, *supra* note 2, § 166R and Phemenology of Spirit. See G. Hegel, Phänomenologie des Geistes 311 (J. Hoffmeister ed. 1952).

36. Hegel, Phänomenologie des Geistes, *supra* note 35, at 311.

11

A Reconstruction of Hegel's Theory of Civil Society

Andrew Arato

The Hegel of the *Philosophy of Right* is the representative theorist of civil society. This is the case because of the synthetic character of his work and even more because he was both first and most successful in unfolding the concept of civil society as a theory of a highly differentiated and complex social order.

Running through Hegel's work, however, is a contradiction between systematic philosophy and social theory, expressed politically as the antinomy of étatistic and anti-étatistic positions to be found in the doctrines of both civil society and the state.[1]

Hegel's social theory presents modern society both as a world of alienation, and as an open-ended search for social integration. His philosophical system on the other hand announces that this quest has ended in the modern state, though it is never entirely clear *whether* he meant a possible and desirable state, *or* a not yet existent but necessary state *or* an already existing actual state. But even in the weakest version of this argument where the possible and desirable form of the state is identified with a modernizing and constitutional version of a bureaucratic monarchy, the étatistic implications of Hegel's system building becomes inevitable. Nevertheless, at the same time, Hegel's recurring arguments against monarchical absolutism and revolutionary republicanism revive an anti-étatistic stress on intermediary bodies limiting bureaucratic sovereignty and providing a locus for public freedom. This trend in his thought is compatible only with the repeated, implicit, but nowhere systematized, denial that the search for social integration can end in institutions like "our modern states" that can provide citizens only with "a limited part in the business of the state."[2]

The contradiction runs through Hegel's analysis of civil society and, in particular, in the form of two interrelated questions to be pur-

302 / Law, Family, Civil Society

sued below: First, is *Sittlichkeit* or ethical life only possible as inherited and unquestioned *ethos* to which individual subjects must conform to be consistent with their very identity, or is it possible to think of ethical life in a truly modern form which permits and even requires both its own questioning and criticism as well as a plurality of normatively valued forms of life? Second, is civil society to be conceived as *Sittlichkeit* or *Antisittlichkeit* or as a dynamic combination of "moments"? The two questions are of course deeply related and may indeed be ultimately the same. To answer them we must begin with some of the basic categories of the *Rechtsphilosophie*. As is well known, Hegel differentiated objective spirit [*objektiver Geist*], rationally reconstructed intersubjective structures of meaning ("spirit") embodied in institutions ("objective"), into three dimensions: abstract right, morality, and *Sittlichkeit* (ethical life). The differentiation among them is not so much that of content (though each successive level gets progressively richer than the prior one) but among three levels of moral argumentation. Abstract right represents a form of argument based on dogmatically assumed first principles exemplified in natural rights theories. Morality, a level clearly referring to the Kantian ethics, represents the self-reflection of the solitary moral subject as the proposed foundation for a universalistic practical argumentation. Finally, *Sittlichkeit* represents a form of practical reason that is to raise through self-reflection the normative content and logic of inherited institutions and traditions to a universal level. Only *Sittlichkeit* allows the exploration of normative questions (including "rights" and "morality") through the framework of concrete historically emergent institutions and practices that represent, at least in Hegel's view of the modern world, the institutionalization or actualization of freedom (§§ 4, 142). Ethical life is itself differentiated in a way (entirely unique to Hegel) that combines the two dualities of *oikos/polis* and state/society in the three part framework of family, civil society, and state. Civil society (*bürgerliche Gesellschaft*) is defined in various ways, but most revealingly as ethical life or substance "in its bifurcation (*Entzweiung*) and appearance (*Erscheinung*)" (§ 33).

This definition of civil society can only be understood through a more thorough examination of the notion of *Sittlichkeit*. Charles Taylor is surely on solid foundations in at least one dimension of Hegel's text when he interprets the content of this notion as "the norms . . . of a society . . . sustained by our action, and yet as already there."[3] According to Taylor, "in *Sittlichkeit* there is no gap between what ought to be and what is, between *Sollen* and *Sein*."[4] Hegel's overall scheme indeed repeatedly stresses the total identity of the rational will of the subject with that of laws and institutions (§§ 147, 151, 155), making any clash between particular and universal will, subject and object, and right and duty impossible or at least irrational.[5]

Taylor is less on solid ground, however, when he interprets *Moralität* and *Sittlichkeit* merely in the form of opposition. Modern ethical life, as Hegel unfolds it, is distinguished from all ancient *ethos* because it contains the other two ethical dimensions, rights and universalistic morality, on a higher, institutionalized level. Indeed, institutional space is created for private morality which according to Hegel should not become "matter for positive legislation" (§ 213).

To be sure Taylor reaches only the main strand of Hegel's conception, but not the antinomic whole. Hegel's own definition of *Sittlichkeit* involves a greater stress on its production and reproduction through self-conscious action (§ 142). Yet it remains questionable whether the bases of such action are found in *Sittlichkeit* alone or also in *Moralität*, or at least, for the modern world, in a form of ethical life that has incorporated morality, along with the tension between is and ought. When we say that *Sittlichkeit*, as the norms of a society's public life, is already there, Hegel's authority only takes us so far as to register the institutional existence of the norms in question, possibly in forms of discourse only or also as legitimations and ideologies. Their often "contra-factual" character is noted by Hegel himself in the case of the principles and practice of positive law. Unfortunately, Hegel did not discover that modern society is characterized not only by the conflict of moralities (which he at times seemed to note) but also by the conflict of the normative conceptions of politics itself. Thus, he did not see that a new form of *Sittlichkeit* could be established containing a plurality of forms of life, making consensus possible only on the level of procedures, though such consensus can lead to some shared substantive premises and even a common identity. At the same time, he certainly did admit the possibility of conflict between the institutionalized norm, the actual basis of moral opposition, and the practice of institutions. It is for this reason above all that his thought and the social world he describes is open to immanent critique.

Civil society is the framework par excellence where the tension between is and ought occurs because of the internal division of this institutional sphere. But, as we shall see, this division hardly disappears in Hegel's theory—even in the state sphere which is supposed to be that of reconciliation of all antinomies. Hegel periodically implies that no actually existing state should be stylized as already rational. Nevertheless, the ethical (*sittliche*) substance defined by Hegel in terms of the identity of rational self-reflection and actualized institutions is revealed by Hegel to be as the *"wirkliche Geist einer Familie und eines Volks"* (the actual mind of a family and a nation) (§ 156). The absence of civil society, and the presence of state only as people, are the notable features of this definition of *Sittlichkeit.* Consistently enough in the next paragraph (§ 157), civil society reappears but only as an "abstract" and "external" version of *Sittlichkeit.* Again, in the section on the transition between the family and civil society (§ 181), Hegel speaks of the "disappearance of ethical life" and its reemergence only as a "world of ethical appearance." He goes on to speak of civil society "as a system of ethical life lost in its extremes." (§ 184) (my translation).

Civil society is, thus, a level of *Sittlichkeit* where the oppositions of is and ought, subject and object, right and duty, and even rational and actual would all reappear. But it would not be difficult to argue in this context that this level of *Sittlichkeit* is its veritable antithesis, a *Gegen-* or *Antisittlichkeit.*[6] Indeed, much of Hegel's discussion of civil society emphasizes the disintegration of the supposedly natural form of ethical life, represented by the family in a world of egotism and alienation. Nevertheless, when he speaks of the ethical roots of the state, he speaks of the family and the corporation, the latter "planted in civil society" (§ 255). Here is the real sense of seeking of civil society as the "bifurcation of ethical life," as *both Sittlichkeit* and *Antisittlichkeit,* where the unity of substantial ethical life, according to Hegel's final judgment on civil society, is attained only in appearance.

Hegel's unfolding of the categories of civil society from the system of needs and the system of laws to the police (general authority) and corporations, and even beyond to the estate assembly and public opinion, depicts modern society as a veritable dialectic of *Sittlichkeit* and *Antisittlichkeit.* Only the illusions of system building put an end to this movement in the highly inconsistent depiction of the state as fully realized but no longer naturally given ethical life.

We should stop to consider the great importance of a two-sided understanding of Hegel's concept of civil society. If it was interpreted only as alienation, social integration would have to be conceived exclusively on the levels of family and state. In relation to civil society, then, the prescriptive or critical dimensions of the theory would come to the fore, but a transcendent version of critique[7] would have to take either the form of romantic communalism with face-to-face relations as its telos, or that of étatism whose self-legitimation could take various republican or nationalist forms. If, however, civil society were interpreted exclusively in terms of the forms of social integration that emerge here, the descriptive and tendentially conformist elements of the theory would come forward, and the negative aspects of bourgeois civil society that Hegel was one of the first to thematize would be lost from view. The richness and power of Hegel's social theory lie precisely in his avoiding both a transcendent critique of *civil* society and an apology for *bourgeois* society.

Many interpreters of Hegel see the integration of modern society as a series of mediations between civil society and state. Yet, by phrasing the issue this way, the interpreters become hostage to the étatist dimension in Hegel's thought. Not to accept from the outset that the only important line of thought in Hegel assumes the state as the highest, most complete and universalistic level of social integration allows the issue of mediation to be put differently. On a more abstract level mediation is, as should be clear already, between *Antisittlichkeit* and *Sittlichkeit*. On a more concrete level, however, it involves the distance between *private* and *public*, if we understand the former as the vanishing point at which the social integration of the family is dissolved before the ones characteristic of civil society begin. Thus it is my thesis that the mediation of *Antisittlichkeit* and *Sittlichkeit* culminates in a notion of public life that is only inconsistently identified by Hegel with state authority.[8] After Marx's early critique of Hegel's philosophy of the state, little would have been left of this identification, except for the small detail of the role of étatism in the critiques of the capitalist market economy in the next century and a half,[9] including Marx's own followers. In Hegel's and Marx's work, however, the étatistic trend is in a powerful tension with anti-étatistic options.

As any reader of Hobbes should immediately know, the road to étatism is prepared by the identification of society outside the state with egotistic competition and conflict. If the concrete person is first defined as "a totality of needs and a mixture of natural necessity and arbitrary will (*Willkür*)," we must ascribe this to Hegel's starting point, the system of needs as the first level of civil society. As the argument proceeds through the next levels, "the administration of law" and "general authority and corporation," the concrete person reappears but under new headings: legal person, client of general authority, and association member.[10] Further, it is only on the level of the system of needs, the description of which Hegel derives from political economy,[11] that a radical depiction of civil society as *Antisittlichkeit* is consistently upheld. For example, when Hegel defines civil society as a system of *Sittlichkeit* "split into its extremes and lost," (§ 184) he has in mind a condition where egoistic individualism—one extreme—is integrated by an abstract generality entirely foreign to the will of individuals— the other extreme. Civil society, therefore, involves the creation of a new type of market economy that integrates the "arbitrary wills" of self-interested economic subjects by an objective and "external" process that achieves a universal result unintended and unanticipated by the participants (§§ 187, 199).

In many respects, Hegel's model of integration on the level of the system of needs is similar to Adam Smith's description of the self-regulating market as an invisible hand linking egotism and public welfare. Nevertheless, Hegel's arguments are less economic than sociological. He sees three levels of integration in this context: needs, work, and "estates." Moreover, more than any political economist he understood that social integration must occur outside the system of needs for the market economy itself to be able to function. But unlike early modern political philosophers in the natural law tradition, this level of integration is confined by him neither to the exercise of sovereign power nor to the sphere of the state. In fact, it was conscious opposition to these theoretical traditions that he developed a theory of social integration that constituted one of the founding acts of modern sociology, or at least of the paradigm developed by Durkheim, Parsons, and Habermas among others.

Leaving aside for the moment Hegel's systematics, his theory of social integration moves through the following steps: (1) legal framework (*Rechtspflege*), (2) general authority (*Polizei*), (3) corporation, (4) the (bureaucratic) executive, (5) the estate assembly or legislature, and (6) public opinion. While the first three of these are developed as parts of the theory of civil society, and the second three belong to the theory of the state or rather constitutional law, the line of argumentation turns out to be essentially continuous and dualistic.[12] Indeed, two lines of argumentation can be differentiated, even if Hegel's movement back and forth between them is so constructed as to avoid the appearance of such differentiation. It is this double argument concerning social integration that I would like to concentrate on.

As has been shown, the system of needs in Hegel's theory is itself integrated, but in an "external" (outside of will and consciousness), incomplete (less than fully universalistic), and self-contradictory manner. Integration beyond the system of needs operates according to *two* different logics: the logic of state intervention into society, and the logic of the generation of societal solidarity, collective identity, and public will. Throughout most of the text, the unfolding of the two logics can be clearly differentiated; the series universal estate, police crown, and executive expresses the line of state interventionism while the series estates, corporation, estate assembly, and public opinion follows that of the autonomous generation of solidarity and identity. Only in the "administration of law" is it difficult to separate the two lines of argument. This level represents, in Hegel's exposition, the possibility of the universally, or at least generally, valid resolution of the clash of particulars in civil society. The overcoming of *Gegensit-tlichkeit*, as the division of particular and universal, begins here, but in a form that is capable of generating only a limited collective identity. The legal person identifies with the collective only in the form of abstract obligations. To begin with, Hegel not only recognizes the modern, noneconomic presuppositions of economy in the law of property and contract (§§ 213, 218), but also sees that their implications go far beyond the economy. In particular, the corresponding publication of the legal code, and even more the publicity of legal proceedings, are changes of universal significance and validity that make possible the emergence of a universalistic sense of justice (§§ 215–16, 224).

This argument becomes fully intelligible in the context of Hegel's understanding of the concept of the public (*Öffentlichkeit*) that goes beyond the Roman law dichotomy of public and private. On the one side, Hegel sees a functional relation between modern law and the system of needs, each necessary for the emergence and reproduction of the other. On the other side, he equally insists that the relation between modern law and the system of needs is more than merely functional because it provides for institutionalization of subjective right and objective law which protects the freedom and dignity of individual subjects in a way that can be mutually recognized (§ 217) not by isolated individuals, but by private persons brought together in a public process. To Hegel the achievement of the institutionalization of right as law requires both state action (he strongly prefers statutory codification to precedent-based adjudication) (§ 211), and autonomous cultural processes. Thus, Hegel is neither a legal positivist, a natural law theorist, nor even an historicist. According to him, universal rights having more than just an historically restricted validity do emerge in cultural development and can receive universal recognition only through a process of education (*Bildung*) that has become possible in civil society (§ 209).

Universal rights do not, however, attain objective existence without being posited as law (*gesetzt als Gesetz*) which involves legislation, codification, and administration by public authority (*öffentliche Macht*). Without autonomous cultural processes of right creation, rights cannot acquire their validity and recognition. But without the various necessary acts of the state and its organs neither true determinacy nor systematicity are possible (§§ 211, 216). Only the combination of the two yields obligatory force. Hegel wisely recognizes the possible discrepancy between the two moments,[13] cultural and political, "between the content of the law and the principle of rightness" (§ 212). Yet, within the analysis of law, he can offer only some formal and procedural requirements that should not be violated by legislators and judges, in particular the requirement of publicity and the formal generality of law. Presumably he expects the achievement of a closer fit between the principle of right and positive law regarding substantive legal rules through inputs into law creation via the other institutional mediations of his theory, from the corporation to public opinion.

The complementarity achieved between societal and étatist strategies of social integration cannot be maintained by Hegel beyond his analysis of the administration of law. From this point in his argument on,[14] the two types of strategies become identified with differentiated institutional complexes. The étatist trend in Hegel's thought, anticipating Marx and especially Marxism, is clearly connected to the notion of civil society as *Gegensittlichkeit*, and is rooted in the analysis of the system of needs. The pathological consequences of the system of needs, which include extremes of wealth and poverty, want and luxury, as well as the severe threat to both humanity and the very existence of the class of direct labor, call for measures which allow Hegel to anticipate features of the modern welfare state.[15] In particular, it is the bureaucracy of the modern state (that is, the universal class, the class of civil servants) that is called on to deal with the dysfunctional consequences of the system of needs in two forms.

There is no need to repeat here Marx's brilliant 1843 critique of the pretensions of Hegel's view of the universal estate, pointing out its rather particular interests and status consciousness. Hegel managed to delude himself on this score partly because of the étatist strain in his thought, and partly because he did not see any reason to consider the social antagonism implied by the existence of the "class of direct labor." Not capable of intraclass integration, workers in this view do not seem to be capable of interclass conflict. The dysfunctional consequence of the plight of this class is seen in the existence of an anomic mass, the *Pöbel* whose integration calls for measures that aim at individuals (that is, clients) rather than integrated groups. But with the poorest strata removed from the field of analysis, the idea of the representation of a general interest by the bureaucracy needs to be reconciled only with the interests of the possessing classes.[16]

Hegel's discussion of the civil servants takes place in two sections of his analysis: the system of needs of civil society and the executive of the state. This is of course a wise decision since the bureaucracy is both a social stratum and a state institution.[17] But what Hegel's theoretical

decision initially disguises is that this estate is different from the others
he discusses in two respects. First, it is constituted by the state and not
the societal division of labor. Second, in the state, the bureaucracy
finds its institutional place in the executive, rather than in the estate
assembly. Thus in this context Hegel's argument concerning the fortunate double meaning of the German term *Stände* (§ 303), referring
both to social orders and to a deliberative assembly, does not apply.
By calling the bureaucracy a *Stände*, Hegel misses the opportunity to
discover the second, specifically modern form of stratification whose
constitutive principle is political power, and even more important
disguises the étatistic principle of the form of social integration under
consideration.

The way the bureaucracy is to accomplish the integration of antago-
nistic estates reveals at least some of the consequences. The executive
of the state, the political bureaucracy, has the role of "subsuming
the particular under the universal," and of executing the laws. Hegel
accepts, as we will see in more detail below, the parliamentary assumption that an estate assembly is capable of generating a public and
general will. But he believes that in civil society all the particularisms
will reappear, and that therefore outside the state sphere proper the
bureaucracy must perforce be the executor of universality. The fact,
however, that he feels compelled to admit that the authority of local
communities (*Gemeinden*) and corporations is needed as a "barrier
against the intrusion of subjective caprice into the power entrusted to
a civil servant" (§ 295) shows that Hegel is aware that reality can be
quite different from his idealized depiction. The presentation of the
bureaucracy as an estate of civil society is thus not only a way of
disguising the actual level of state intervention advocated, but also
is a way of deflecting the responsibility for dysfunctional or even
authoritarian intervention from the state to a social group and to the
subjective caprice of its members.

Second, the model of integration through state intervention is further
developed in the theory of general authority or police (*allgemeine
Macht* or *Polizei*). The modern term police does not indicate Hegel's
meaning, because in accordance with earlier absolutist usage the term
police means more here than the prevention of crime, tort, and the
maintenance of public order. But unfortunately Hegel uses the term
general authority in senses not covered by the section on the *Polizei*.
Thus it may be best to list the actual uses of this concept by Hegel: (1)
surveillance (linked to crime and tort) (§ 234); (2) intervention in the
economy in the form of price controls and regulation of major indus-

trial branches (§ 236); (3) public welfare in the form of education (§ 239), charity (id.), public works (§ 245), and founding of colonies (§ 248).

The idea behind Hegel's linking these apparently diverse areas is quite coherent. The police is the state penetrating into civil society to serve the interests of justice and order. As a result the centrifugal and anomic consequences of conflict are diminished but not entirely done away with. Crime for example, does not disappear because of "crime prevention" and the punishment of criminals, but is kept within tolerable limits. Conflict and alienation are not abolished by provisions for social welfare and public education, but the decline of the class of labor to the status of the *Pöbel* (unorganized mass or rabble) can be prevented. In all these cases, and also in the case of price and production controls, the goal Hegel espouses is compensation for the dysfunctional side effects of the new type of market economy.

Nevertheless, Hegel does not claim that, on this level at least, the state produces a thoroughgoing unification of society and the attainment of universality in what amounts to merely a form of "external" imposition and control (§ 249) (my translation). In civil society we encounter the state only in the form of externality, and the metaphor of civil society as "universal family" is entirely misplaced in the theory of the police or general authority. This metaphor belongs instead to the second strand of Hegel's conception of social integration, the societalist strand. This strand runs from the family to the corporation and eventually to the estate assembly and public opinion. Since Hegel considers, incorrectly, the integrating role of the family to be null and void in civil society (e.g., § 238), the corporation is the starting point of the self-integration of civil society.

The function of a corporation, according to Hegel's theory, is primarily socialization and education. The business association in particular is to combine vocational training with training for citizenship. Thus all corporate life, by educating individuals to internalize the common good, helps to overcome the gap between bourgeois and citizen produced by civil society. In the process, solidarities are expected to develop that would affect the very motivation structure of individuals, substituting collective concerns and identifications for egoistic ones. In this context Hegel's problem as he well knew was the same as Rousseau's, namely how to move from the particular to the general, given modern individuality. But his answer is significantly different, because Hegel believes neither that the reality of the modern large scale state could or should be imagined away, nor, consequently, that individuals, entirely egotistical in private life, can attain the general in the political sphere. In his view, generality can be attained only through a series of steps that incorporate something of the public spirit in what is juridically the private sphere.

While the corporation represents a crucial step in the development of the strand of Hegel's thought stressing the self-integration of society, the antinomy of his political position is nevertheless visible in it. Like Montesquieu before him and de Tocqueville after him, Hegel sought an intermediate level of power between individual and state; he feared the powerlessness of atomized subjects and sought to control the potential arbitrariness of the state bureaucracy (§ 295). But on the other hand, in line with his doctrine of the state, he wants to defend a model of socialization that will make the transition to a state-centered patriotism plausible. In this context Hegel's aim is to provide a smooth transition based in everyday life from the *Geist* of the corporation, as the schoolhouse of patriotism, to the *Geist* of the state where patriotism is to achieve its full "universality" (§ 289). Much depends on whether the conception of the state implied here is based on public, parliamentary generation of identity, or bureaucratic-monarchical imposition of unity. But since, as it will be shown, the antinomy is not resolved on the level of the state, the role of the corporation in political education also becomes ambiguous. This in turn affects the conception of the relation of the corporation and the general authority. As Heiman shows, Hegel never could decide between a medievalist doctrine involving corporate independence and legal personality and a Roman law conception stressing state control and oversight.[18]

Whatever the ambiguities of Hegel's corporate doctrine, the different center of gravity here when compared to the concept of the police cannot be overlooked. Both police and corporation are at times identified as the individual's second family. Some of the same functions are assigned to each, for example, education. Further, the different normative justifications produced for each are equally convincing. The corporation is a second family small enough and determinate enough in its purpose to allow genuine participation by its members. These include only a part of the population, however; vis-à-vis its members, the corporation inevitably represents a particular interest vis-à-vis other groups and those not "incorporated." Nevertheless, the corporation is capable of creating internal motivations, and does not depend on external sanctions guaranteeing compliance. On the other hand, the regulation of the police is universalistic and should not allow the formation of particular clusters of interests. The activity of the police,

however, does rely on external sanction, does not involve any participation of those concerned, and does not lead to the formation of autonomous motivation.

As the comparison of police and corporation shows, étatism in
Hegel's thought is not only linked to some kind of political opportun-
ism, but also to the idea of universality, without which no modern
conception of justice is possible. Hegel has good reasons not to make a
definite normative choice between police and corporation, and between
abstract universality and substantial particularity. These moments are
sundered in civil society, and it is Hegel's thesis that they can be
reunited only in the state. It would only be on this level that the
corporation, as the second ethical root of the state (after the family),
would achieve its universality.

This reconstruction of Hegel seeks to replace a stage model that
suggests that the antinomies of civil society are resolved on the supposedly higher level of the state. Instead it is more fruitful to interpret
Hegel's thought as dualistic or antinomic on both levels; and what we
crudely label as "étatistic" and "societalist" trends in his thought
appear in the analysis of *both* civil society and state. Accordingly, the
doctrine of the state itself can be analyzed in terms of these two trends.

In Hegel's conception the police represents the penetration of the
state into civil society. Analogously, the estates assembly represents a
penetration of civil society into the state. The civil society that is
represented in the state through the estate assembly, however, is one
already organized; to Hegel, the presence of an atomized civil society
in the state would be most regrettable. According to the rather free yet
convincing translation of Knox:

> The circles of association in civil society are already communities. To
> picture these communities as once more breaking up into a mere
> conglomeration of individuals as soon they enter the field of politics,
> i.e. the field of the highest concrete universality, is *eo ipso* to hold
> civil and political life apart from one another and as it were to hang
> the latter in air, because its basis could then only be the abstract
> individuality of caprice and opinion. (§ 303).

This conception directly links the estates and corporations of civil
society with the estates assembly. While Hegel at first stresses the link
of the estates to the estate assembly as indicated by the German term
Stände, the more important theoretical foundation of the assembly is
in fact the corporation, the existence of which is the only real evidence
provided for the claim that organization and community are possible

in an otherwise atomized civil society. The deputies of civil society are "the deputies of the various [c]orporations" (§ 303). Earlier, this statement is limited and expanded. Atavistically, the agricultural estate (suddenly meaning only the nobility) is to be directly present, as in the assemblies of the *Ständestaat*. The business estate, on the other hand, is represented by the deputies of associations, communities, and corporations (*Genossenschaften, Gemeinden und Korporationen*) which are all incorporated forms of association. Hegel does not even feel the need to indicate and justify his exclusion of the class of direct labor, which is supposedly totally disorganized, from political life (§ 311). More important than the conformist and conservative elements in his thought, however, are his reasons for recommending his particular version of representative government. According to Hegel's model, civil society, when electing its political deputies, "is not dispersed into atomistic units, collected to perform only a single and temporary act, and kept together for a moment and no longer."[19] Rather, in the process of deliberating and choosing deputies, the associations and assemblies of social life acquire a connection to politics in the same act that politics acquires a foundation in organized social life. It is precisely at this level, at the point of interpenetration of civil society and state, that Hegel rediscovers and integrates the ancient topos of *political* society, without explicitly saying so.

The estate assembly has the role of completing the job begun by the corporation, but at a society-wide level of generality that Hegel, and especially his English translator, often refer to as universality. This job is bringing public affairs, and even more public identity into existence (§ 308). Again, parallel to the doctrine of the corporation, the estate assembly is regarded as a mediating organ, this time between the government (*Regierung*) and the people differentiated as individuals and associations (§ 301). The former is thus prevented from becoming tyrannical, while the latter from becoming a mere aggregate, a mass with an unorganized and therefore according to Hegel dangerous opinion. Of course Hegel does stress the role of the estate assembly in legislation and even constitution making (§ 302). But his main interest throughout is in the constitution of the subject of legislation and even more its proper medium. The category of publicity indicates that only the genuine representatives of the public are legitimately entitled to make the laws. The laws they enact are to be considered legitimate only if the procedures of public deliberation are rigorously followed. Since Hegel insists on genuine and unconstrained discussion and deliberation, he emphatically rejects the *imperative mandate*, the principle of the traditional *Ständestaat*. The assembly must be "a living body in which all members deliberate in common and reciprocally instruct and convince one another" (§ 298 (my translation).

Hegel's vehement insistence on genuine publicity in the legislature (as well as the courts) has other important grounds as well. He wished to promote knowledge of public business in society, as well as to make (however inconsistently) the estate assembly permeable to the influence of public opinion. Like de Tocqueville, Hegel is ambivalent concerning public opinion: Defined as "the formal, subjective freedom of individuals to express their own judgments, opinions and recommendations concerning general affairs whenever collectively manifested," (§ 309) (my translation) public opinion is internally contradictory, and "deserves to be as much respected as despised [geachtet als verachtet]" (§ 316). Respect is due because of a hidden strain of rationality that is buried and inaccessible to public opinion's opinion about itself because of its concrete empirical form of expression. Interpreting public opinion is thus the role of intellectual and political elites (§ 318). To promote the formation of public opinion, Hegel supports extensive freedom of public communication (especially speech and press), and is only slightly worried about its supposedly possible excesses. Indeed, he believes that the genuine publicity of legislative debates has a good chance of transforming public opinion and eliminating its shallow and arbitrary components, making it *harmless* in the process.[20] Nevertheless, it is also implied here that the debates of the estate assembly can transform public opinion precisely to the extent that its essential content and strains of rationality are raised to a higher level. In this sense, not only does the political public of the legislature control public opinion (Hegel's stress), but a prepolitical public sphere plays an important role in the constitution of public life in the political sense.

The concept of public opinion as developed by Hegel is not free of the antinomic structure of his political thought. The étatistic trend in this context is expressed in the concern to control and disempower public opinion, to make it compatible with the management of the state. The societalist trend, on the other hand, involves the raising of public opinion to a higher level of rationality in a parliamentary framework between state and society, itself exposed to the controls of publicity. The étatistic trend views public opinion as ultimately a threat, and the proper relationship to it on the part of political and parliamentary elites is manipulative. The societalist trend views public opinion as the condition of possibility of political public life, and the proper relationship to it on the part of elites would have to be one of public dialogue in which truth would remain an open question to be decided by the more convincing arguments, and would not be the a priori possession of one of the sides. The public sphere of the estate assembly can play its role in the enlightenment and education of public opinion precisely because truth is not known in advance of the debate, but emerges during the process itself, along with the virtues that serve as examples to the larger audience (§ 319). One trend in Hegel's thought implies that in those states where the life of the legislature is genuinely public, the structure of public opinion will itself change: "what is now supposed to be valid gains its validity no longer through force, even less habit and custom, but by insight and argument (*Einsicht und Gründe*)" (§ 315). However at other times the dialogic model of rational political deliberation is restricted to the parliamentary public sphere. In these contexts, the étatistic trend in his thought, supported by the false analogy between the search for scientific truth and the attainment of normative truth in politics, stops Hegel from extending the model to the public sphere as a whole.

Ultimately, the issue here, as well as in Hegel political theory as a whole, is the locus and nature of public freedom. I accept the interpretation according to which Hegel sought to develop a political doctrine in terms of a whole series of mediations that relativize the Roman law distinction between private and public law (§ 316), but with two reservations. First, the mediations are two distinct series. Second, I do not accept the implicit identification of state and public presupposed by the interpretation, or that each succeeding step in Hegel's exposition represents (even in terms of his own argument) an unambiguously higher level of public life than the one before. The two series once again are: (1) civil servants, police, executive, and crown juxtaposed to (2) estates, corporation, estate assembly, and public opinion. The two once again express the antinomic trends in Hegel's thought. Indeed, the very manner in which they mediate the spheres regulated by private and public law is significantly different in each case. The first series involves public law categories taking on private roles. The second, on the other hand, indicates private law entities, developing structures of publicity, and taking on public functions.[21] This pattern is the same as the model of constitutional rights which constitute public law rights of private subjects.[22] Once these two patterns are separated, the meaning of the public sphere in Hegel becomes uncertain. Is its primary paradigm that of public authority or that of public communication? And if he maintains both paradigms, what is to be their relationship?

For Hegel, undoubtedly the highest purpose of public life is the generation of a rational universal identity, which he identifies with the patriotic ethos of the state. What remains unclear is whether the vocation of generating this ethos is assigned to a state sphere dominated by the executive and linked only to the projections of the state into civil society, or to one dominated by an estate assembly drawing on autonomous societal resources like the corporation and public opinion. This issue cannot be decided if the problem of the mediation between private and public realms alone is stressed. Most categories of Hegel's theory of *Sittlichkeit*, beginning with the system of needs, provide such mediations. But it can be decided if the generation of a modern rational collective identity is linked to the concept of public freedom Hegel repeatedly uses in this context, that is to a process that allows the effective participation of individuals in the free shaping and appropriation of the meaning of a "we." Obviously, public freedom is quite a bit more than the kind of freedom available to the agents of the system of needs who cannot participate in the formation of any collective identity whatsoever. But Hegel also registers serious doubts about whether the modern state as such can be the locus of public freedom, doubts that run completely contrary to the étatistic strain in his thought.

Although Hegel nowhere systematizes a conception of the public sphere (*Öffentlichkeit*), the categories of public authority, public freedom, public spirit, public opinion, and publicity play key roles in his work. Let us recall K.-H. Ilting's often repeated thesis that the *Philosophy of Right* seeks above all to synthesize the negative freedom of modern liberalism and the positive freedom of ancient republican thought. The categories of the public sphere represent important ways in which republicanism could be sustained in Hegel's thought after his supposed conservative turn. But even here an essential difference with ancient republicanism should be registered. Instead of restricting the formation of public freedom to a single social level, that is, political society, Hegel works out a modern republican theory in which a whole series of levels have key roles to play, including: the public rights of private persons, the publicity of legal processes, the public life of the corporation, and finally the interaction between public opinion and the public deliberation of the legislature. Not all of these processes have a public political purpose, yet they are the stages of learning leading to the formation of public identity. What is common to all of them is the free public participation of those concerned in the formation of decisions. Of course, the public purpose of the acts of the police, at times identified as general (*allgemeine*) and even public (*öffentliche*) power is beyond doubt for Hegel. The same is true of the acts of the executive, and in a *Rechtsstaat* the crown as well. Yet in these cases, Hegel speaks neither of the formation of public spirit, nor the actualization of public freedom. In fact, it has been noticed that Hegel's most

explicit discussion of public freedom juxtaposes the corporation, belonging to civil society, and the modern state:

> In our modern states [*modernen Staaten*] citizens have only a re-
> stricted part in the general [*allgemeinen*] business of the state; yet it
> is essential to provide men—ethical entities—with activity of general
> character over and above their private business. This general activity
> which the modern state does not always provide is found in the
> corporation (§ 255A (my translation).

In this passage, Hegel not only registers the tension between modern
state and public life, but also identifies a different locus for public
freedom than did classical antiquity. The corporations are in his own
words "the pillars of public freedom (*öfentlichen Freiheit*)."[23] Unfortunately for Hegel the public freedom possible in the corporation, involving relatively high level of participation, cannot be primary in society
as a whole. Z.A. Pelczynski and so many others are surely right when
they argue that Hegel believed that he has proved that "the (modern)
state is the actuality of concrete freedom" (§ 265). While this argument
is in general supported by the greater universality of the estate assembly, this veritable corporation of corporations, over the inevitably
particularistic societal associations, it also disguises the reality of the
modern state as a hierarchy of offices and the monopolistic possessor
of the means of violence as well as a compulsory association. By
reversing the sociologically obvious hierarchy of the modern state, that
is, by making the legislature primary and the executive secondary,
Hegel is constructing a legitimation both in the sense of contra-factually
justifying a structure of authority, and establishing a set of normative
claims open to critique. These critical potentials come into view for
example when the assembly on which the normative surplus of state
is predicated is depicted as its penetration by civil society.

Hegel, as the peerless social theorist of his time, was aware of the
sociology of the modern state. In this respect, we are fortunate to have
Ilting's careful reconstruction of Hegel's turn from an early conception
stressing the freedom of the citizen in the state to one stressing the
freedom of the state.[24] The shift, however, may also have its independent intellectual motivations that were reinforced by Hegel's reaction
to the reactionary Karlsbad decrees. Hegel knew and rejected both
absolutist and revolutionary étatisms as so much of the *Rechtsphilosophie* demonstrates. Is it too farfetched to assume that precisely a reactionary turn in Prussian politics made him realize (as did de Tocqueville
soon after) that features of two supposedly aberrant versions of the

modern state belonged to its ideal type instead? If this were so, the shift to institutions of civil society as the pillars of public freedom would be logical and indispensable, from the point of view of strengthening this dimension in parliamentary institutions of the state. Thus Hegel in his mature text not only restricted the possibility of the citizen's freedom in the state, but also expanded, in Ilting's words, the liberties (*Freiheitsrechte*) of civil society into rights of participation (*Teilnehmerrechte*). The most obvious objection in this reading of Hegel is that he himself did not admit and, for systematic reasons, would have rightly rejected the idea that there could be two unreconciled strands in his thought. I am not particularly concerned with this criticism (which in any case is refuted by Ilting's reconstruction) or with the systematic aims of Hegel's work. I am only interested in rebuilding Hegel's conception around what may only be a subtextual antinomy in his political philosophy, to trace a new theory of civil society back to the institutionally most elaborated conception available from which we can still learn. Thus a more serious objection to my reconstruction would insist, as did the young Marx in 1843, that precisely those dimensions that I bring into special relief represent nonmodern elements in Hegel's thought next to the modernity of his conception of the system of needs on the one side, and the bureaucracy on the other. On this reading, Hegel's corporation is an attempt to save *medieval* corporate doctrine, his estate assembly, the institutions of the *Ständestaat*, his notion of public opinion, the *early bourgeois* public sphere, and perhaps the very idea of public freedom, the institutions of the *ancient* city republics. Accordingly, in looking for the modernity of Hegel's social theory, it would be better to focus on either the critical aspects of his depiction of the capitalist economy (as Lukács does) or his anticipation of the welfare state (as Avineri does).

NOTES

1. In perhaps his greatest work in political theory, the young Marx paid much attention to the link in Hegel between étatism and system building. K. Marx, Critique of Hegel's "Philosophy of Right" (J. O'Malley ed. 1970).

2. G. Hegel, Grundlinien der Philosophie des Rechts, in 6 Werke § 255 addendum (1970). The translation by Knox is not quite right. See G. Hegel, Philosophy of Right (T. Knox 1952). [Editor's note: Henceforth, references to the Knox translation will appear by section number in the text. The author occasionally retranslates the German from the original.]

3. C. Taylor, Hegel 382 (1975).

4. Id. at 376.

5. Hegel cannot accept these identities on traditional, i.e., non-reflective grounds and warns against a merely habitual acceptance of *ethos*. Astonishing, though, was that his certainty that after reflection the existing ethos will turn out to be rational was always unshaken. But what if after the most thorough reflection, the opposite turned out to be the case? In this respect the incomparably greater modernity of Kant's conception of practical philosophy is obvious.

6. Pelczynski, The Hegelian conception of the State, in The State & Civil Society: Studies in Hegel's Political Philosophy (Z. Pelczynski ed. 1984). To be sure, the emphasis of Pelczynski's several articles is on the reemergence of positive social integration *within* civil society.

7. T. Adorno, Cultural Criticism and Society, in Prisms (1982).

8. For an analysis of the historical roots of this inconsistency, and the republican strain in Hegel's thought, see Ilting, The Structure of Hegel's *Philosophy of Right*, in Hegel's Political Philosophy, in Hegel's Political Philosophy: Problems and Perspectives (Z. Pelczynski ed. 1971) [hereinafter Ilting, Structure]; Ilting, Hegel's Philosophy of the State and Marx's Early Critique, in The State & Civil Society: Studies in Hegel's Political Philosophy (Z. Pelczynski ed. 1984).

9. Karl Polanyi's *The Great Transformation* (1944) is both an eloquent analysis and symptom of this étatistic trend.

10. Only for the system of needs can Hegel maintain that in civil society everyone is an end for himself, all others are nothing. Id. § 182A.

11. See S. Avineri, Hegel's Theory of the Modern State (1972); G. Lukács, The Young Hegel (1975).

12. Hegel's political contradiction between étatism and antiétatism is revealed, however, in the order of exposition. While the outline of the argument concerning the state in paragraph 273 moves from the legislature to the executive and finally to the crown as the highest level, see id. § 273, the actual exposition in §§ 275–320 moves from crown to executive and finally to the legislature itself, culminating in the doctrine of public opinion. The legislature is of course civil society in the state!

13. Contrary to Taylor's interpretation of the concept of *Sittlichkeit*, according to which "the end sought by the highest ethics is already realized." Taylor, supra note 3, at 383.

14. And even before, though, we should recognize that part of the system of needs, the section on the estates where the two logics are already visible, at least in part belongs to the later discussion of social rather than system integration.

15. Such is the stress of Avineri in the already cited work. See Avineri, supra note 11.

16. Which is also not always as easy as Marx thought in 1843. Marx of *The Eighteenth Brumaire of Louis Bonaparte* can teach us this lesson as well. See Marx, The Eighteenth Brumaire of Louis Bonaparte, in The Marx-Engels Reader 594 (R. Tucker ed. 2d 1978).

17. Thus Hegel surely does not suffer from the problem mentioned by Luhmann that theorists of the state/society dichotomy are forced, in a preposterous manner, to distribute actual individuals neatly on either side of the societal divide.

18. Heiman, The Sources and Significance of Hegel's Corporate Doctrine, in Hegel's Political Philosophy Problems and Perspectives 125 (Z. Pelczynski ed. 1971).

19. Hegel raises this issue only in his polemic against the democratic, i.e., universal, participation in politics of all members of civil society. On his own terms Hegel has a good argument here to the extent that he wants to include only those already organized. It is not clear why he does not recommend (and even seems to exclude) the organization of all members of civil society in associations, communities, and corporations so that they could also participate in politics and the election of deputies. Further, voting by the unorganized for deputies who are themselves organized (e.g., the English and American political parties even in Hegel's day) would not have the consequence that Hegel feared: namely the appearance of atomized opinion on the political stage. It is another matter, as the debate on the views of Carl Schmitt was to show, that the representation of a democratic electorate in the liberal 19th-century form could be seen as raising the problem at least of "indecision" or "ungovernability." For this to happen, one key component of legislation as understood by Hegel had to lose its power: namely rational, public discussion and deliberation. See C. Schmitt, The Crisis of Parliamentary Democracy (E. Kennedy trans. 1985).

20. While Hegel rightly calls our attention to the volatility and manipulability of public opinion, he is also quite insistent that the essential truths of politics do have this medium for their vehicle. Unfortunately, he also says, however, that the interpretation of these truths is to be the role of political leaders and/or theorists. He considers the following of public opinion, both in life and in science, to be the road to mediocrity. On the other hand, the rather passive acceptance of the views of elites by public opinion is to him unproblematic altogether. Id. § 318.

21. See Heiman, supra note 18, at 129–35. See also Ilting, Structure, supra note 8, at 107 (arguing that "civil society and the state" are in Hegel "two different spheres of *public* life").

22. See J. Habermas, Die Strukturwandel der Öffentlichkeit (1962); G. Jellinek, The Declaration of the Rights of Man and of Citizens (M. Farrow trans. 1979).

23. Quoted by Pelczynski, Political Community and Individual Freedom, supra note 1, at 72 in Knox's translation which I had to revise.

24. Pelczynski, supra note 1, at 76.

12

Rethinking the Hegelian State

Fred Dallmayr

Hegel is not in vogue today. Outside of restricted circles or enclaves, his philosophy is no longer the fulcrum of sustained inquiry—not to mention creative reinterpretation. This view is not limited to Anglo-American analytical philosophy which has for some time regarded Hegel's work as outmoded or conceptually *dépassé*. Of late, even continental thinkers—and those attentive to their writings—have come to share this sentiment. In an age of non- or anti-foundationalism, notions such as "absolute spirit" and "absolute knowledge" are bound to appear as hopelessly obsolete, if not intellectually perverse.[1] A product of holistic speculation, Hegel's opus is seen as the endpoint of a long metaphysical tradition, or as the watershed between the past and the dawning age of post-metaphysics first captured and given voice by Nietzsche.

Nowhere is this presumed obsolescence more evident than in Hegel's theory of law (or "right") and the "state." At a time when a theoretical premium is placed on diversity, contestation, and dispersal, the view of the state as an ethical fabric permeated by *Sittlichkeit* is liable to be regarded as a quaint relic of classicism—if not as the emblem of sinister totalitarian designs. From different (philosophical and political) angles, our age thus seems to seal the longstanding "dissolution" or disintegration of the Hegelian system, a dissolution already witnessed by the first generation of his heirs (including Marx). Yet, perhaps the triumph of posterity is premature. Perhaps, as Heidegger once observed, the problem is not so much the decay or decomposition of Hegel's work, but rather the inability of our time to raise itself to the complexity of his insights.[2]

My point here is not to rekindle a Hegelian orthodoxy (if there is such a thing). Neither philosophically nor politically do I see any

322 / Law, Family, Civil Society

possibility of neglecting—or even adequately bridging—the vast distance separating us from Hegel's epoch. Philosophically, a long string of initiatives—stretching from Nietzsche over pragmatism to the so-called "linguistic turn"—have cast doubt on the prospect of finding secure beginnings of thought, whether in "reason," "consciousness," or "subjectivity." In social and political terms, our age is segregated from Hegel's by the effects of the industrial revolution, the expansion of markets and media networks, and the resulting consolidation and diversification of "civil society." In addition, the rise of large-scale bureaucracy and the succession of two world wars have weakened, if not eroded, confidence in the ethically benign character of the modern nation-state.

By itself, however, historical change does not amount to complete disconfirmation—especially in the case of a (self-styled) "dialectical" philosophy. Thus, the bureaucratization (and militarization) of the contemporary state may belong to those external "positivities" whose constraint is to be set aside or overcome by the dialectical impulse of "spirit"—a shift leaving unaffected the status of *Sittlichkeit* as the basic social bond. Similarly, the demise or implausibility of the civil service as a viable "universal class" does not vitiate the search for open-ended human contacts capable of mitigating individual or collective self-enclosure.

In the following I intend to first sketch or recollect the main features of Hegel's theory of the "state" as they are outlined chiefly in his *Philosophy of Right.*[3] Next, I shall discuss some critical rejoinders to Hegel's conception, from Marx and Nietzsche to Popper and Lyotard. By way of conclusion I shall ponder possible ways of rehabilitating and reinvigorating the notion of *Sittlichkeit* and ethical community in the dramatically changed context of a post-metaphysical and post-"statist" theory of democracy.

HEGEL'S THEORY OF THE "STATE"

The notions of an "ethical state" and of *Sittlichkeit* as concrete social bond are recurrent themes in Hegel's evolving opus—although not always under the same labels or in the same terminological guise. Thus, the emphasis in the early theological writings on popular religious beliefs was meant to invigorate (and purify) community life, in opposition both to the stale "positivity" of established churches and to the abstract rational principles extolled by Enlightenment thought. Without great difficulty, one can discern anticipations of the later critique of empirical customs and historical factuality, on the one hand, and of a purely internalized and nonsocial "morality," on the other.

In the *Phenomenology of Spirit*,[4] human and social life was presented as in the throes of a protracted learning experience leading from immediate "consciousness" over reflective "self-consciousness" to reason (as the consciousness of self-consciousness), and finally to "spirit." The latter term at this point was equated with "ethical actuality" (*sittliche Wirklichkeit*) or with "actual ethical being." Although considered a culmination of the drama of consciousness, spirit or *Sittlichkeit* was said to exhibit its own intrinsic dialectic, namely, a story of conflict and its resolution.

On a first, quasi-natural level, spirit designated the prevailing customs of a people as well as the rules or habits governing family life. These customs were bound to be contested by the emergence of individual freedom and free inquiry, a process leading to the struggle between rational "enlightenment" and pure faith or between immanence and transcendence. Only in a final stage was this struggle subdued or overcome in the mode of self-actualized *Sittlichkeit*—that is, in a fully developed ethical and communal life attesting to the reality of "absolute spirit."

As we know, Hegel's *Phenomenology* was only a prelude or precursor to his later encyclopedic system—into which it was precariously integrated on the level of "subjective spirit," or at the transition point leading from the latter to concrete-objective *Sittlichkeit* and the theory of the state. In the *Philosophy of Right*, ethical life appears as the culminating apex of a complex triptych or triadic sequence embracing as its components "abstract right" (or abstract law), "morality," and *Sittlichkeit*, with the latter domain being subdivided, in turn, into "family," "civil society," and the "state." The entire sequence is said to reflect the development and self-actualization of human freedom and, more particularly, of "free will"—where "will" does not stand in opposition, but rather forms an integral modality of thought or "spirit."

As Hegel writes toward the beginning of his treatise: "The grounding of right or law [*Recht*] resides basically in *spirit*, and its precise location and point of origin is the *will* which is *free*—with the result that freedom is both the substance and goal of right and the legal system is the realm of actualized freedom." According to the same paragraph, free will should not be contrasted to spirit (or *Geist*), for "spirit is thought as such, and man is distinguished from animals by virtue of thinking." But "one should not imagine that man is half thought and half will"; rather, will is only "a special mode of thinking: namely, thought translating itself into existence," or actualizing itself in reality.[5]

Free will in Hegel's account does not coincide with arbitrariness or a purely contingent disposition. On the contrary, for him, freedom always has reference to concrete contexts and thus involves an intermeshing of inside and outside, of ego and alter (or fellow human beings). If one defines freedom as the "ability to do as one pleases," Hegel insists such a view "can only be taken to reveal a complete immaturity of thought." A purely private disposition divorced from all contexts, he notes, is only "will's *abstract* certitude of its freedom; but it is not yet the *truth* of freedom because the latter has not yet found itself as its content and goal, and consequently the subjective side is still other than the objective." Instead of being the will "in its truth," arbitrariness is "the will seen as *contradiction*" (§ 15) (emphasis added).

The triadic sequences alluded to above are predicated on the dialectical movement of thought and will: namely, from a stage of immediacy to a reflective withdrawal from immediacy (and thus a moment of division or *Entzweiung*) to a final reintegration of reflexivity and context on a higher level. Thus, free will taken by itself or "empirically" is the source of abstract right (or law) concerned with objects. By contrast, a reflective will gives rise to the separation of inner and outer worlds and to a sphere of "morality" opposed to external law. The two moments of givenness and reflexivity are finally reconciled in the idea of *Sittlichkeit* which reveals the actuality of freedom.

A similar development occurs inside the field of ethical life itself. The entire dialectic is lucidly explained by Hegel himself, in one of the numerous "additions" to the main text. Free will, he writes, must first give itself some "existence or embodiment" (*Dasein*), and the primary sensual materials of such existence are "things, that is, external objects." Thus "the initial mode of freedom is the one which we know as *property*—the sphere of formal and abstract right" (§§ 33A, 42, 42A, 44, 44A, 45).

However, freedom cannot remain satisfied with the sheer immediacy of existence, and thus proceeds to negate this immediacy in the sphere of morality. At this point, "I am free no longer only regarding immediate things but also in the state of sublated (or superseded) immediacy: which means I am free in myself, in my subjectivity." On this level, everything depends on my intentions and purposes, while externality is irrelevant. Yet internal purposes also demand to be actualized or to be given concrete existence. Consequently, morality, just like purely formal right, now appear as abstractions or abstract moments whose "truth" is *Sittlichkeit* alone—that is, ethical life seen as "the unity of will as a general concept and particular or subjective will" (§ 33A).

In turn, the primary embodiment or existence of ethical life is a natural bond, namely, the family united by "love and feeling." Reflective individualization dissolves this primary bond, and gives rise to "civil society" whose members relate to each other as "independent agents" connected only through the "bond of reciprocal need." Reconciliation and reintegration occurs here on the level of the state—the stage of *Sittlichkeit* and of spirit which "yields the enormous unification of autonomous individuality and universal substantiality." The state thus is "freedom in its most concrete form" (subordinate only to the "absolute truth of world spirit") (§ 33A).

For present purposes, the most important dialectical phase is the transition from civil society to the state—for it is here that particularity and generality first separate and then coalesce again. Hegel is explicit in presenting individual or subjective particularity as the chief acquisition of modernity and as the feature distinguishing modern from ancient political life. As he states (in the section dealing with "morality"):

> The right of the subject's *particularity*—his right to be satisfied or (differently put) the right of subjective freedom—is the pivot and center of the difference between antiquity and modern times. This right in its infinite scope has been articulated in Christianity and been erected into the general governing principle of a new form of civilization (§ 124R).

This aspect is reinforced at a later point in the section on "civil society" in even more dramatic terms. "[T]he creation of civil society," we read there, "is the achievement of the modern age which for the first time has given all the facets of the 'Idea' their due" (§ 182A).

By contrast, the autonomous development of particularity appeared in the ancient world "as the beginning of ethical decay and as the ultimate cause of that world's demise." The reason was that these ancient states were built on "patriarchal and religious grounds," or else on an "intensive but relatively simple *Sittlichkeit*"—in any case, on a "primitive natural intuition." The result was that they could not "withstand the disruption [*Entzweiung*] of this condition and the infinite reflection of self-consciousness," and thus "succumbed to the latter as soon as it arose." For instance, Plato, in his *Republic*, portrayed ethical substance in its "ideal beauty and truth." However, as regards autonomous particularity—which in his day had begun to "invade Greek ethical life," he managed to cope with it only "by opposing to it his purely substantial state," while excluding particularity entirely from the structure of the *Republic* (§§ 185, 185R, 185A).

Returning to the contrast between ancients and moderns, Hegel adds that the notion of "the autonomous and inherently infinite personality of the individual"—which means the "principle of subjective freedom"—could not come into its own in the ethical context of antiquity. Rather, the principle "dawned first inwardly in Christian religion and externally (linked with abstract general rules) in the Roman world" in order to unfold its full potential in modernity (§ 185R).[6]

In the *Philosophy of Right*, modern civil society appears both as an advance over substantial (or unreflective) ethics and as a mode of rupture or diremption requiring further mediation and reconciliation. Basically, civil society is the arena of individual interests and needs, that is, the domain of particularity—although particular, subjective wills remain linked through general rules (but on a purely formal level). As Hegel writes, "the concrete person bent on his (her) particularity as a goal" is one or the first principle of civil society construed as "a totality of wants and a blending of natural necessity and caprice" (§ 182). But due to the reciprocity of wants and their satisfaction, the same society is also governed by "generality" (*Allgemeinheit*) as its second principle.

Generality here means the necessary rules and external constraints imposed on individual satisfaction. In Hegel's words: Although in civil society "everyone regards himself (herself) as supreme end and everything else as nothing or immaterial," yet no one can fully pursue or achieve his (her) ends "except by relating to others"—which bestows on the fabric of reciprocal needs the "form of generality" (or universality). Since particularity is inevitably conditioned by generality, he adds, civil society is "the terrain of mediation allowing free play to every idiosyncracy, every talent, every accident of birth and fortune" (§§ 182A, 199).

Seen from the vantage of necessity or generally binding rules, civil society can also be designated as an "external state," that is, as a state based on need and abstract reasoning (*Not- und Verstandesstaat*). More comprehensively viewed, civil society marks the diremption (*Entzweiung*) of ethical life where the particularity of needs and the generality of rules are granted separate existence and develop in opposite directions. In the (well known) formulation of the *Philosophy of Right*, civil society is "the system of *Sittlichkeit* split and lost into its extremes—which constitutes the abstract moment of the idea's actuality." Since the separate existence of particular needs and general necessity is ultimately illusory, however, Hegel also portrays the divided character of civil society as a mode of "appearance" (*Schein*)—in the sense that both particular wills and generality claim to be something which they truly cannot be—namely, separate. The divided relation "constitutes *Sittlichkeit* as a world of appearance—which is civil society" (Id. §§ 182, 182A, 183, 184, 184A).[7]

Correcting and overcoming this divisiveness is the task of the modern state—whose conceptual novelty Hegel emphasizes both vis-à-vis classical substantial ethics and vis-à-vis atomistic or contractarian construals (tied to the domain of civil society). For Hegel, the state is basically the "idea"—and thus free will or human freedom—on the level of fully reflective (not merely intuitive) actuality. Differently phrased, it is the actuality of freedom where particular self-consciousness is elevated to, and permeated by, *Sittlichkeit* as the common good.

Throughout the *Philosophy of Right*, Hegel takes great pains to differentiate this conception from purely individualistic or contractarian views. As he writes at one point, in the case of *Sittlichkeit*, two views are possible and have traditionally prevailed: "either one starts from ethical substantiality or else one proceeds atomistically and builds on the basis of isolated individuals. The latter view is senseless because it leads only to a juxtaposition, whereas spirit is nothing isolated but rather the unity of the particular and the universal" (§ 156A).

The contrast is underscored in the section on the "state." "If the state is confused with civil society and if its end is seen in the security and protection of property and subjective freedom," Hegel affirms, "then the interest of the individuals as such becomes the end of their association, and it follows that membership in the state is something optional." However, the state's relation to the individual, he continues, is "quite different: since the state is objective spirit, it is only as one of its members that the individual attains objectivity, truth and *Sittlichkeit*. The community as such is the true content and aim (of life)" (§ 258R).

Although in the order of presentation the state follows the discussion of family and society, in actuality public community precedes and renders possible the more limited forms of ethical experience. Neglect of this primacy is the common mistake of contractarian thinkers—including Rousseau, despite the latter's great depth of insight. Although commendably positing thought and the will as the basic "principle of the state," Rousseau erred in treating will only "in the distinct form of isolated, individual will (like later Fichte)," and in regarding universal will "not as the rational essence of will but only as a 'general will' derived from individual wills in deliberate fashion"—that is, in reducing "the union of individuals to a contract" (§ 258R).

While embodying the unity or unification of individuals, the state in Hegel's conception is not simply an undifferentiated collectivity— which would mean a regress to premodern substantiality. As he insists, the actuality of freedom accomplished in the state consists in the fact "that personal individuality and particular interests attain their complete development and recognition as rightful, while simultaneously they blend of their own accord into the common (or universal) interest" (§ 260) and even perceive it as their own. Differently put: actuality of freedom means that the common or universal good does not prevail "without attention to particular interests and particular modes of knowing and willing," or with individuals living only for particular private ends "without simultaneously embracing the common good and effectively pursuing its aims" (§ 260).

While in ancient states particularity was still entirely overshadowed and dominated by community goals, the situation has changed in modernity. The essence of the modern state, Hegel affirms, is "that the universal must be bound up with the complete freedom of particularity and the well-being of individuals"—which means "that the interests of family and civil society must converge in the state just as the commonality of ends cannot be advanced without the knowing and willing participation of particular members whose own rights must be maintained." Thus, in modern states the common or universal good must be furthered "while at the same time subjectivity is fully and vibrantly developed." This consideration leads Hegel to one of the most famous and intellectually most challenging formulations in the *Philosophy of Right*. "The principle of modern states," we read, "has this prodigious power and depth of allowing the principle of subjectivity to unfold completely to the extreme of autonomous personal particularity while at the same time guiding it back into the substantive unity (of the state) and so preserving this unity in the principle of the subjectivity itself" (§§ 260, 260A).

The meshing of particularity and common goal is also the hallmark of a properly designed "internal constitution" of the state—a topic on which I shall be very brief, owing to the dated character of many details. As Hegel notes, only when the two moments (the subjective and the universal) "subsist in their strength can the state be regarded as properly structured and genuinely organized" (§§ 261R, 272, 273, 273R). In large measure, proper structuring involves the differentiation or separation of governmental powers in Montesquieu's sense—though it remains oriented toward the common good (more strongly than occurs in a system of "checks and balances").

According to the text, a constitution is rational "insofar as the state internally differentiates its activity along clear conceptual lines, namely in such a manner that each of its powers represents the totality (of the constitution) by maintaining the other moments operative in its own domain" (§ 272). Differentiation in this case is at odds both with a complete fusion or concentration of powers and with their radical segregation or opposition. As Hegel adds:

> The principle of the separation of powers contains the essential aspect of *difference* and thus of actualized rationality. However, as contrued by abstract reasoning, it signifies (falsely) either the absolute mutual independence of powers or else (one-sidely) a relation of reciprocal negation and restriction. In this view, the principle turns into hostility and into the fear of each power of the evil machinations of the others (§ 272R) (emphasis added).

For Hegel, the crucial feature of the principle is that, though differentiated, the powers mutually corroborate each other and coalesce to uphold the unity of the whole.

Applying the dialectic of particulars and universals to internal constitutional order, he assigns the determination of general or universal rules to the legislative branch, the subsumption of particular cases and situations under these rules to the administrative branch (including the judiciary), and the reintegration of these functions in a higher-mode of subjectivity to the monarchical power. This constitutional arrangement ultimately buttresses Hegel's preference for "constitutional monarchy" as ideal regime or as the regime's most congruent with actualized freedom, a preference predicated on that regime's ability, not only to balance internal powers, but to reconcile and sublate traditional constitutional forms, like monarchy, aristocracy, and democracy. "The development of the state to constitutional monarchy," he states, "is the achievement of the modern world where the substantive idea has gained infinite form. The history of this inner deepening of spirit . . . or the story of this genuine formation of *Sittlichkeit* is the content of general world-history" (§ 273R).[8]

Seen as embodiment of the "Idea," constitutional monarchy forms the apex of Hegel's conception of the state—a conception whose ethical significance he repeatedly emphasizes. Relevant passages to this effect are widely known and are frequently cited as evidence of Hegel's

extreme idealism. Thus, in terms of one of the famous "Additions" to
the text, the state is said to be "the ethical totality, the actualization of
freedom—just as it is the absolute goal of reason that freedom should
be actualized." The state consequently is "spirit-standing-in-the-world
and involved in a process of conscious self-realization." According to
another, even more provocative formulation, the state is part of "the
march of God in the world" and its basis is "the power of reason
actualizing itself as will" (§ 258A).

What is less frequently noted is the undertow of realism in Hegel's
work. Thus, in talking about the "march of God in the world," he
immediately continues that the reference is not to particular empirical
states or particular institutions, but only to the concept of the state. In
the *Philosophy of Right*, he is quite aware of empirical examples
contravening the concept—of the fact that there have been "historically
times and conditions of barbarism" where the state was "merely a
wordly regime of violence, caprice, and passion." These conditions, he
says, are historically attested, but it is a "bland and shallow" view to
equate these examples with the concept (§ 270R).

More generally, Hegel recognizes the frequent coincidence of state
activity with the sheer exercise of domination and violent coercion—
but he refuses to identify the description of empirical-historical conditions with the task of philosophical understanding. In a passage ably
summarizing his views on the matter, he writes that the state

> is no ideal art-work but stands on earth and so in the sphere of
> caprice, accident, and error; bad behavior thus may disfigure it in
> many ways. Yet even the ugliest man, or a criminal, or an invalid or
> cripple is still a living human being; the affirmative moment—life—
> subsists despite these defects, and it is this affirmative factor which is
> our theme here [in the theory of the state] (§ 258A).[9]

RESPONSES TO HEGEL'S THEORY

Hegel's *Philosophy of Right* has met with varied reactions over time,
often provoking lively polemical attacks; given our distance from its
initial composition, the book cannot be properly read and understood
without some attention to its *Wirkungsgeschichte*. On a general philosophical level, critical comments have frequently focused on the presumed priority of idealism over realism, of universal over particular
categories, and of speculative theorizing over practical engagement. In
more specifically political terms, rejoinders have concentrated on the

preponderance of public institutions over private-particular initiatives and of collective unity over individual freedom. Less frequently, concerns have been voiced regarding the fragile and precarious status of public *Sittlichkeit* given the internal momentum of civil society.

On the whole, scholarly debates have tended to revolve around the balance (or imbalance) of the diverse moments encompassed by ethical life. In Charles Taylor's presentation, Hegel's theory of the state was meant to counteract "two great disruptive forces" which imperil modern society and politics:

> The first is the force of private interest, inherent in civil society and in its mode of production, which constantly threatens to overrun all limits, polarize the society between rich and poor, and dissolve the bonds of the state. The second is the diametrically opposed attempt to overcome this and all other divisions by sweeping away all differentiation in the name of the general will and the true society of equals.[10]

The latter attempt, he adds, must, in Hegel's view, issue "in violence and the dictatorship of a revolutionary elite," or in any event in a repressive political regime."[11]

Beyond the issue of proper balancing, more radical critiques have been leveled at the basic design or substance of Hegel's conception. Marx was one of the first to raise such substantive-ontological questions, particularly in his *Critique of Hegel's Philosophy of Right* (and the somewhat later "Introduction" to that study).[12] According to Marx, Hegel's work had failed to implant *Sittlichkeit* concretely in the real life of people, preferring instead to celebrate its abstract-speculative "idea" (as manifest in the state and its bureaucratic institutions). Despite certain rational-progressive features, the proposed public order offered only partial reprieve from past abuses.

Applying "transformational criticism"—a strategy first developed by Feuerbach[13] in religious matter—to the public-political domain, Marx portrayed the Hegelian state ultimately as made of human self-alienation and self-subjugation, a defect which could only be overcome by a return to its social and economic underpinnings. While acknowledging that the "philosophy of right and of the state" had been given "its most logical, profound and complete expression by Hegel," Marx's review urged the extension of critical analysis to the modern state in its concrete operation, that is, to "the *imperfection of the modern state* itself, the degeneracy of its flesh."[14]

Although impressive in its array of abstract categories, what Hegel's work left out of his account was chiefly "the *real man*" (or real human being)—and this only because "the modern state itself leaves the real man out of account or only satisfies the *whole* man in an illusory way."[15] What was needed to correct illusory abstractions, according to Marx, was a radical "humanization" of *Sittlichkeit* through a focus on the actual contradictions of civil society. Only by revolutionizing the latter could state-reason become a universal reason and political rationalization issue in general human emancipation:

> A class must be formed which has *radical chains*, a class in civil society which is not a class of civil society . . . (one) which claims no traditional status but only a human status . . . which is, in short, a total loss of humanity and can only redeem itself by a total redemption of mankind.[16]

Despite its important insights and fertile new vistas, Marx's critique cannot in turn escape critical scrutiny of its premises. In large measure, the use of Feuerbach's method—the turn from ideal speculation to the situation of "real man"—involved mainly a reversal of accents, while leaving the character and meaning of "reality" basically opaque. In some respects, Marx's arguments even reinforced (on a less subtle level) Hegelian assumptions and the premises of modern philosophy as such. This is evident in the stress on "humanization" and on "man" as producer of his material life conditions—an emphasis congruent with modernity's anthropocentric leanings and its infatuation with *homo faber.*

More dramatically, the same continuity surfaces in the treatment of the proletariat as "universal class"—a treatment clearly indebted to the notions of a collective identity (of "objective spirit") and of a teleological movement of mankind.[17] By comparison with Feuerbachian modes of reversal, Nietzsche's attack on Hegelianism was more radical and thoroughgoing—because it aimed at the metaphysical underpinnings of Hegel's thought (and of much of Western thought in general). Turning against the thesis of the progressive actualization of "spirit" or reason, Nietzsche affirmed that history is only "a chaotic pile of rubbish."[18]

The same verdict applied to the modern state and its institutions. As Nietzsche observed, in one of his early "Notes": "But a state has no aim; we alone give it this aim or that;" far from embodying a higher purpose or a common *Sittlichkeit*, the state was merely "[i]ndividual and collective egoisms struggling against each other—an atomic whirl of egoisms."[19] Still more eloquently and zestfully, the same sentiment recurs in the later *Zarathustra*—where the state is portrayed as "the death of peoples" and as "the name of the coldest of all cold monsters."[20] Against the homogenizing and streamlining ambitions of the state, Nietzsche exhorted his readers to "break the windows and leap to freedom"—from the prison of the "new idol": "Only where the state ends, there begins the human being who is not superfluous: there begins the song of necessity, the unique and inimitable tune."[21]

The contest over Hegel's legacy was continued and intensified in our century—sometimes (though not always) in a Nietzschean idiom. On the whole, the dismissal or distrust of public *Sittlichkeit* has been a common feature of theoretical reformulations of the state, both among philosophers and social scientists. Partly under the impact of Nietzsche's attack and partly in response to Marxian initiatives, Max Weber defined the state simply as a means of control—as the (more or less legitimate) locus of the monopoly of force in a given territory.

Efforts in our century to reinvest the state with a substantive purpose or collective identity have almost invariably yielded dismal results. Thus, attempts by right-wing thinkers, like Giovanni Gentile,[22] to enlist Hegel's teachings for autocratic aims have paved the way for, or at least aided and abetted, the rise of fascist regimes—with damaging and even disastrous results for the image of Hegelianism in Western (liberal) countries. Scholarly studies stressing the progressive and emancipatory aspect of Hegel's work—like Marcuse's *Reason and Revolution*[23]— were only partially able to undo the damage and to restore Hegel's credit in the political field.

For many liberal intellectuals in the West, Karl Popper's verdict has become nearly canonical—to the effect that Hegel was an enemy of the "open society,"[24] if not simply a spokesman of Prussian militarism. Among the aspects of Hegel's philosophy allegedly conducive to political closure and even totalitarianism, Popper particularly emphasized the subordination of individuals as particular agents to a higher collectivity and the equation of state-interest (or *raison d'État*) with a common *Sittlichkeit*. In his view, holistic construals of politics were theoretically dubious in reflecting an "essentialist" metaphysics rendered obsolete by modern science. They were as well practically obnoxious in sponsoring violence and the destruction of freedom. "[O]nly democracy," he insisted, "provides an institutional framework that permits reform without violence, and so the use of reason in political matters."[25]

In recent decades, Popper's indictment of political holism (as a mode of closure) has been corroborated by many thinkers otherwise distant from Popperian empiricism. Foremost among these thinkers are contemporary Nietzscheans (or post-Nietzscheans) and especially spokesmen of French "post-structuralism." Although anti-holistic and anti-Hegelian themes are pervasive in post-structuralist literature, I shall focus here for the sake of brevity on the work of Jean-François Lyotard.

More resolutely than other French authors, Lyotard's writings challenge and denounce unitary conceptions of politics, together with such ancillary notions as the intelligibility of historical evolution and the steady unfolding or actualization of reason. As he affirms in *The Postmodern Condition*,[26] the great unifying or universalist schemes of the past have become obsolete in our time—an age marked by the "crisis of narratives," that is, by the erosion of the metaphysical underpinnings of thought and action.

In lieu of comprehensive "metanarratives," what is increasingly coming to the core is the experience of fragmentation, disjunction, and "agonal" contestation—and especially the dispersal of traditional philosophical systems into "clouds of narrative language elements." This experience is bound to reshape profoundly both human knowledge and political practice. "[T]he society of the future," Lyotard writes, "falls less within the province of a Newtonian anthropology [with its unifying assumptions] than a pragmatics of language particles. There are many different language games—a heterogeneity of elements. They only give rise to institutions in patches—logical determinism." In terms of cognitive endeavors, "postmodern" theorizing can no longer be integrated or accommodated in a common framework; rather, it "refines our sensitivity to differences and reinforces our ability to tolerate the incommensurable."[27]

According to *The Postmodern Condition*, the departure from metanarratives means a turn to the "pragmatics" of language or to practical "speech acts"—and away from universal syntactical rules and a shared semantics of meaning. Accentuating the innovative, discontinuous character of pragmatics, Lyotard presents speech acts or utterances basically as "moves" and "counter moves" in a language game—where "move" denotes a combative strategy or challenge. This focus, he writes, "brings us to the first principle underlying our method as a whole: to speak is to fight, in the sense of playing, and speech acts fall within the domain of general agonistics."[28]

These arguments carry over from linguistic behavior into the domain of social and poitical interactions and decisively mark the nature of the "social bond" today. Regarding the latter, the study contrasts contemporary agonistics chiefly with traditional models of integral holism and social harmony—models first inaugurated by the French founders of sociology and later developed and reformulated by functionalist "systems" theory cybernetics. Despite shifts of accent, Lyotard notes, we can discern in this tradition "a common conception of the social: society is a unified totality, a 'unicity.'" This holistic outlook is particularly pronounced in contemporary cybernetic frameworks where all information processes are programmed in advance. Countering these (and related) sociological approaches, the study stresses the central role of language games—in fact, of multiple, hetero- geneous games—in supplying the only remaining "social bond" in a postmodern context. In sharp distinction from unitary schemes, our age is said to witness the "'atomization' of the social into flexible networks of language games," where each speaker or participant is located at particular "nodal points" of competing communication circuits. Instead of being submerged in social harmony, the "atoms" of society are seen as operating at the "crossroads of pragmatic rela- tionships" and involved in perpetual "move[s]" and agonal confronta- tions. "What is needed," Lyotard comments, "if we are to understand social relations in this manner, on whatever scale we choose, is not only a theory of communication, but a theory of games which accepts agonistics as a founding principle."[29]

As presented by Lyotard, linguistic and social agonistics is a radical counterpoint to Hegelian philosophy—which is treated as a pillar of one of the great metanarratives or legitimating stories of modernity: the story of the dialectic of "spirit" and its progressive self-actualiza- tion. Under the auspices of German idealism, philosophy is said to aim at the "unity" of knowledge and understanding, as an antidote to their disintegration into separate disciplines. This task, however, can only be accomplished

in a language game that links the sciences together as moments in the becoming of spirit, in other words, which links them in a rational narration, or rather metanarration. Hegel's *Encyclopedia* (1817–27) attempts to realize this project of totalization (which was already present in Fichte and Schelling in the form of the idea of the System.[30]

According to Lyotard, Hegel's dialectic of spirit is couched in terms of narrative knowledge, as a phenomenology of subjective experience or of the life of subjective spirit; but actually the story can only be told as a metanarrative, from the vantage of a universal subject or "metasubject," that is, from the vantage of absolute spirit. With regard to modes of empirical learning and the structure of cultural and political institutions, it is this metasubject which gives voice "to their common grounding, realizes their implicit goal. It inhabits the speculative University."[31]

Thus, it is only through a transgression of language games, by ascending to the level of a universal subject or metasubject, that Hegel was able to extricate himself from the strife of heterogeneous discourses and perspectives—ultimately, to formulate the vision of a common ethical life in the state. In Lyotard's words:

> German idealism has recourse to a metaprinciple that simultaneously grounds the development of learning, of society, and of the state in the realization of the "life" of a Subject, called "divine Life" by Fichte and "Life of the spirit" by Hegel. In this perspective, knowledge first finds legitimacy within itself, and it is knowledge that is entitled to say what the State and what Society are. But it can only play this role by changing levels . . . that is, by becoming speculative.[32]

As Lyotard adds polemically—in language matching Popperian invectives—speculative or transcendental reasoning is far from innocuous in its effects. On Kantian as well as Nietzschean premises, diverse modes of knowledge and language games are seen to be separated by a gulf or "chasm"; only "the transcendental illusion (that of Hegel) can hope to totalize them into a real unity. But Kant also knew," he continues, "that the price to pay for such an illusion is terror. The nineteenth and twentieth centuries have given us as much terror as we can take."[33]

In Lyotard's view, speculative thought is vitiated not only by its practical consequences but also by its intrinsic dilemmas and deficiencies—faults which are glaringly evident in our time. Turning to developments in postmodern science, the concluding section of the study finds a decisive shift in contemporary scientific inquiry—namely, from uniformity and stability to the search for instabilities, from predictable causal processes to the analysis of discontinuity and indeterminacy. What remains in present-day scientific theory, Lyotard notes, are at best "islands of determinism." In contrast to the harmonious schemes of the past, the accent on conflict and antagonism is today "literally the rule."[34]

All these changes augur ill for speculative or "totalizing" paradigms, including the Hegelian vision of synthesis and historical teleology. After the demise of traditional metanarratives, the only plausible legitimization of knowledge, he insists, is one based on "paralogy," that is, on the transgression and continuous revolutionary mutation of paradigms. To the extent that unity and consensus are still favored by rationalist approaches, their effect is only the consolidation of conformism: "[I]t is now dissension that must be emphasized."[35]

The preference for agonistics over holism is reinforced in one of

Lyotard's more recent studies, appropriately titled *The Consent* (*Le Différend*).[36] Elaborating on the study's title, the author distinguishes sharply between "contest" (*différend*) and judicial "litigation" (*litige*). "In contrast to a litigation," he states, "an agonal contest is a conflict between (at least) two parties which cannot properly be decided due to the absence of a decision rule applicable to both sides of the argument." As he adds, "the title of the book suggests that generally there is no universal rule applicable to diverse modes of discourse"—a circumstance which is traced to the pragmatics of language games and their intrinsic heterogeneity. Just as sentences belonging to diverse rule systems "cannot be translated into each other," so the multiplicity of discourse structures produces interdiscursive conflict or contest—one unable to be settled by a higher authority or tribunal.[37]

Renewing the attack on holism, Lyotard stresses that universal ideas or categories cannot be objects of cognition or knowledge. The thesis affirming the opposite "might be called 'totalitarism'"—a term carrying connotations both of theoretical deception and practical-political oppression. In an "excursus" specifically devoted to Hegel, the study criticizes the notion of a "speculative discourse" involving a steady unfolding of meaning and culminating in a comprehensive or total knowledge. What this notion entails, Lyotard observes, is a privileging of continuity over discontinuity, of cumulative meaning over its dispersal—a privilege which is "undeniable in Hegelian thought" and which ultimately is rooted in the primacy of the "self" or subjectivity (over otherness).[38]

Although acknowledged in the *Phenomenology of Spirit*, plurality of experience, Lyotard points out, is progressively discarded in the course of Hegel's *Encyclopedia*—until at the level of objective and absolute spirit the plural pronoun ("we") is "no longer necessary." This entire ascent, however, is said to be spurious, for the concept of a supreme or absolute discourse is logically untenable. Either this discourse is a discourse like others—in which case it is not supreme— or it is separate from other discourses—in which case it is not comprehensive (by exempting itself from the whole). Hegel's speculative discourse raised the claim of supremacy, but "the principle of an absolute triumph of one discourse over others is senseless."[39]

A NEW VIEW OF THE ETHICAL COMMUNITY

Seen in conjunction, the preceding criticisms or indictments show Hegelianism to be troubled and beleaguered paradigm today. Actually, the reviewed attacks are only examples of broader intellectual currents in our time which jointly and from diverse angles lay siege to Hegel's legacy. In my view, a vindication of some Hegelian themes—and especially the theme of *Sittlichkeit*—cannot proceed without awareness of this situation and without attentiveness to some of the major charges or objections.

As it happens, not all the reviewed forays are equally weighty or damaging. Thus, the Popperian charge of collectivism and totalitarian repression can be readily countered by pointing to the centrality of freedom in Hegel's theory of the state and his insistence on the linkage of objective reason and public *Sittlichkeit* with particular initiatives (a point previously noted).

Similarly, the focus of the young Marx on "humanization" is not only compatible with, but essentially predicated on Hegelian premises, and more generally, premises of the modern philosophy of consciousness—though with a peculiar instrumentalist twist. In Taylor's words, Marx's innovation consisted basically of a "transposition of Hegel's synthesis from *Geist* on to man." But, already in Hegel's thought, *Geist* or spirit could not be actualized or realized without human participation (on both a reflective and practical level).[40]

Thus, what Marx's "transposition" amounted to was the production of synthesis through human design or will power—stripped of, or in abstraction from, its ontological moorings. "Man is one with nature," Taylor comments, "because and to the extent to which he has made it over as his expression. The transformation of human society is not aimed at an eventual recognition of a larger order" [as in Hegel] "but ultimately at the subjugation of nature to a design freely created by man."[41]

More troubling and provocative, in my view, is the Nietzschean and post-Nietzschean indictment. As portrayed by Lyotard, Hegelianism is essentially a totalizing metaphysics in which all forms of otherness or non-identity are ultimately integrated or submerged in the maelstrom of absolute spirit and its progressive self-actualization. Against the homogenizing thrust of this vision, Lyotard—like Nietzsche before him—invokes the power of discord, rupture, and discontinuity. In lieu of the consensual harmony of elements, the accent is shifted to contest, dissensus, and "agonistics." The motives for this shift are not hard to detect. Philosophically, Lyotard's poststructuralism is a rebellion against the "computerization" of holism or synthesis, as propounded by contemporary systems theory and cybernetics. On a social and political level, his arguments militate against global ideologies and against the all-pervasive tentacles of the bureaucratic state.

In his study of Hegel and modern society, Taylor recognizes the relentless dynamic of integration and "homogenization"—but as an antipode or counterpoint to Hegel's deeper ambitions. It is clear today, he writes, that the process of homogenization "has swept away traditional bases of identification, traditional modes of *Sittlichkeit.*" Further, "the resultant vacuum has been largely filled by national identifications which are frequently divisive and destructive."[42]

Although unable to anticipate the full effects of this process, Hegel in his account saw the dismantling of differences as incompatible with a properly constructed ethical and political life. Far from endorsing a bland sameness, he realized that the latter "would undermine all possible bases of *Sittlichkeit*, would reduce society from an articulated unity to an undifferentiated 'heap' which could only be held together by despotic force."[43]

Taylor's comments can, no doubt, be vindicated by reference to Hegelian texts—but only up to a point. Perhaps textual vindication in this case tends to overachieve what it seeks to demonstrate: the integral or systematic unity of meaning. As it seems to me, Hegel's arguments are frequently in danger of jeopardizing their own tensional richness and ambivalence in favor of univocacy. A case in point is the issue of identity. The phrase (articulated in an early text) that spirit means "the identity of identity and difference" seems to privilege identity while truncating the tensional interplay of sameness and otherness. The same privileging seems to be at work in terms like "idea," "spirit," or "reason"—to the extent that these terms are meant also to embrace their counterterms or counterpoints (on the level of full actualization).

This consideration applies with special force to the notion of the "state" and its embodiment in constitutional monarchy. As previously indicated, Hegel's legal and political theory stands in opposition to two antithetical approaches: on the one hand, the mere description of empirical institutions, and, on the other, a moralizing utopianism abstracting from the real world. Wittingly or not, the Hegelian state partakes of a precarious ambivalence. Identified with concrete institutional features, it is liable to merge into empirical factuality or "positivity"; yet, removed from such concreteness, it turns into an abstract category if not a reflective chimera. Readers (and non-readers) of Hegel are amply familiar with this intrinsic tension or dilemma—a dilemma highlighted in the well-known and even notorious phrase that "the rational is the real or actual" (and vice versa).

As it seems to me, what needs to be remembered at this point is the ontological or metaphysical status of Hegel's claim (in contrast to descriptive or moralizing conceptions). The "state" for Hegel is neither simply an external givenness nor an inner-moral principle, but rather the actualization of human *Sittlichkeit* and the culmination of ethical life—through a culmination necessarily embedded in concrete interactions and social life-forms.[44]

If these considerations are correct, then Hegel's conception of the state cannot simply be attached to, or equated with, the modern state and especially the so-called "nation-state." Since his time, the flaws and "imperfections" of the modern-state—the "degeneracy (or putrefaction) of its flesh" (to use Marx's terms)—have become evident in manifold ways. Reduced to an instrument of bureaucratic controls or to a vehicle of chauvinist ambitions, the state has increasingly lost its Hegelian sense, instead approximating the external *Verstandesstaat* or models of collective immediacy (and unfreedom).

While implicit in the "march of God on earth" may be some kind of public *Sittlichkeit*, the latter no longer finds embodiment in statist structures. In this situation, a plausible response may be to retain the impulse of Hegel's dialectic—without clinging to his institutional format. Actually, such a move is quite in keeping with Hegelian motifs. As he observes in the preface to the *Philosophy of Right*, Plato's political thought was an expression of Greek *Sittlichkeit* at that time—but one which was about to be transcended by freer modes of reflexivity. Though often seen as an "empty ideal," he writes, Plato's *Republic* was "in essence nothing but an interpretation of the nature of Greek ethical life"—a life increasingly infiltrated during that period by "a deeper principle which could appear in it directly only as a longing still unfulfilled," and he sought to muffle or subdue it by clinging to a "particular external form of that same Greek *Sittlichkeit*."[45]

These comments do not have to be limited to classical Greek thought, with its focus on ethical "substantiality," but can readily be extended to the teachings of German idealism—a point frankly acknowledged by Hegel in the same preface. "As concerns the individual," he states (in a passage not often taken seriously enough),

> everyone is in any case a child of his time; and so philosophy too is its own time apprehended in thought. It is just as absurd to fancy that a philosophy can transcend its contemporary world as it is to assume that an individual can overleap his own age, or jump over Rhodes.[46]

Taking Hegel at his word, there is clearly a need today to reconsider the issue of public *Sittlichkeit* and, in that context, to "rethink the Hegelian state." As it seems to me, the identification of *Sittlichkeit* with formal state structures is disavowed today by the pervasive instrumentalization of these structures in the hands of bureaucratic, economic, or ethnic elites. At the same time, the format of "constitutional monarchy" has been rendered implausible—if not entirely obsolete—by advances of the democratic spirit or the "deeper principle" of universal participation (although this principle remains to a large extent a "longing—still unfulfilled"). Under these circumstances, and still pursuing Hegelian motifs, the remedy cannot simply be found in a revival of private morality or the invocation of abstract ethical maxims—a move which merely reinforces prevailing divisions or modes of alienation (between private and public spheres, between individual and society).

One of the important legacies of Hegel's philosophy is the stress on the institutionalization of *Sittlichkeit* and especially on the embodiment or "incorporation" of public spirit in a "universal class"—a stress later adapted by Marx on economic premises. Honoring the intent (though not the letter) of this legacy, I see the need for a renewed and more radical adaptation. Under democratic auspices, I believe, embodiment of public spirit can no longer be located in either a bureaucracy or a class, but only in plural and heterogeneous groupings cross-cutting social divisions (or inhabiting the margins of such divisions). In our postmetaphysical or nonfoundational context, such groups cannot constitute unified collectivities pursuing univocal goals. Instead, at best, they represent open-ended and shifting alliances dedicated only to a generic and almost nonpurposive endeavor: the endeavor of healing the cleavages splitting society along racial, economic, and other lines (as well as the cleavage between society and nature).

Examples or approximations of such groupings in our time are fraternal organizations, "rainbow coalitions," base communities, and especially the so-called "new social movements" concerned with such issues as ecology, nuclear disarmament, and the dismantling of discriminatory practices. I realize that these are only fledgling institutions vulnerable to exploitation by particular interests. Perhaps, to strengthen social and public ecumenism, one should think of establishing or reinvigorating cross-cultural communal settings or "ashrams," in the Gandhian sense, where people from different backgrounds could live and work together for a period of time. In Gandhi's description, ashrams are multi-dimensional meeting places bypassing caste, class, and religious barriers. In addition, communal functions or occupations are not distributed in terms of traditional sex or gender roles.[47]

To be sure, notions of this kind seem to collide head-on with "postmodern" accents on fragmentation, discontinuity, and rupture. Clearly, concern with public *Sittlichkeit* does not not concur readily with a Nietzschean "will to power," or, particularly, with Lyotard's celebration of "general agonistic." Yet, the opposition may well be deceptive or misleading. As it seems to me, it is precisely post-metaphysics which militates against complete fragmentation or a self-enclosed particularism. Once foundational premises are dropped (be they located in substances or a generic "subjectivity"), no element of society can be accorded a stable, self-contained status or the character of univocal fixity. These considerations not only cast doubt on every type of integral holism or collectivism, but also equally jeopardize the fixity and enclosure of fragments or particulars.

However, once fixed separateness is abandoned, all elements or participants of society are seen to be involved in complex relationships. These relationships—in mutual assessments and reinterpretations— cannot be confined to the level of conflict or hostility (still wedded to separateness) but must include bonds of sympathy. At this point, democratic theorizing (I believe) gets caught up in Hegel's radical relationism, or in that "bacchantian revel" of thought in which, as the *Phenomenology of Spirit* states: "no member remains sober" and in whose vortex every part that seeks to isolate itself "immediately dissolves."[48]

The same relationism, I would add, can still be invoked as locus of an open-ended public space and thus as emblem of a democratic "social bond." No longer buttressed by stable or univocal state structures, public *Sittlichkeit* today must emerge from concrete human interactions cutting across entrenched cleavages and decentering all forms of self-enclosure. This view accords well with Hegel's *Philosophy of Right*, even in its most elevated and high-spirited expressions. As one of Hegel's personal annotations remarks (paraphrasing a poem by Goethe): "What is holy? That which binds humans together—even if it does so only lightly, like the straw a wreath. What is most holy? That which eternally combines and reconciles spirits, fashioning a genuine bond."[49]

NOTES

1. I do not deny a resurgence of interest in Hegel's work among some philosophers— except to note that many of these efforts remain academic (or removed from ongoing philosophical debates). Most noteworthy in this context are C. Taylor, Hegel (1975); S. Rosen, G. W. F. Hegel: An Introduction to the Science of Wisdom (1974); R. Solomon, In the Spirit of Hegel (1983). Richard Bernstein once observed that Anglo-American analytical philosophy was moving by its own internal momentum to a Hegelian position—an assessment which was probably

too summary or optimistic. See R. Bernstein, Praxis and Action: Contemporary Philosophies of Human Activity 233–38 (1971).

2. 32 M. Heidegger, Hegel's Phänomenologie des Geistes 57 (1980).

3. G. Hegel, Grundlinien der Philosophie des Rechts (J. Hoffmeister ed. 1955).

4. G. Hegel, Phenomenology of Mind (J. Baillie trans. 1964).

5. G. Hegel, Philosophy of Right, §§ 4, 4A, 15 (T. Knox trans. 1967) [hereinafter Philosophy of Right]. For all further references to this work, I have changed the translation slightly for purposes of clarity. [Editor's notes: Section references to the *Philosophy of Right* will henceforth be placed in the text.]

6. As Hegel adds:

> Plato wished to exclude particularity from his state, but this is no help—for exclusion of this kind would contravene the infinite right of the "idea" to allow freedom to the particular. It was first in Christian religion that the right of subjectivity arose, together with the infinity of self-awareness, and while granting this right, the whole order must at the same time retain strength enough to put particularity in harmony with the unity of ethical life.

Id. § 185A.

7. One should note at this point the ambivalent correlation of *Schein* and *Erscheinung* in Hegel's philosophy.

8. Hegel's view of the separation of powers differs from a mechanical system of "checks and balances" in which each power relates to the other only in the mode of competition or hostility. As he states:

> To take the merely negative as a starting-point and to elevate ill will and mistrust to the level of first principle, and then on the basis of this premise slyly to construct dikes whose efficiency in turn necessitates counter-dikes against them—this is characteristic of negative reasoning (*Verstand*) and in sentiment of the outlook of the rabble . . .
> The truth is that the powers are to be distinguished only as moments of the concept. If instead they subsist independently in abstraction from one another, then it is clear as day that two autonomous units cannot constitute a whole but must give rise to strife, whereby either the whole is destroyed or else unity is restored by force.

Id. §§ 272R, 272A.

9. Id.. Compare also Hegel's critique of Haller's empirical-historical treatment of the state, and especially of the latter's contention that domination is part of the "unalterable, eternal ordinance of God." Id. § 258R.

10. C. Taylor, Hegel and Modern Society 131 (1979).

11. Id. In a similar vein, countering charges of an oppressive "statism," Pelczynski observes that, in the view of some critics:

> [a] traditional patriarchial society, a feudal monarchy or a modern collectivist, highly regulated state would all seem happily to fit Hegel's conception of an ethical order. But to think that would be to ignore the peculiar modern dimensions of *Sittlichkeit* represented by abstract right and morality . . . . To count as true *Sittlichkeit* the ethical order in our own epoch must be shot

through with personal rights and spheres of autonomy, and be acceptable to individual conscience. It must (in other words) incorporate the principles of particularity and subjectivity . . . .

Pelczynski, Political Community and Individual Freedom in Hegel's Philosophy of State, in The State and Civil Society: Studies in Hegel's Political Philosophy 55, 69 (Z. Pelczynski ed. 1984). The notion of a balance of universality and particularity is corroborated in S. Avineri, Hegel's Theory of the Modern State 98–109 (1972); A. Vincent, Theories of the State 143 (1987).

12. K. Marx, Critique of Hegel's 'Philosophy of Right' (J. O'Malley ed. 1970) (translations of this reference have been slightly altered).

13. L. Feuerbach, The Essence of Christianity (M. Evans trans. 1957).

14. Marx, supra note 12, at 136–37 (emphasis added).

15. Id. at 137 (emphasis added).

16. Id. at 141–42 (emphasis added). The citations are actually from Marx, A Contribution to the Critique of Hegel's *Philosophy of Right*: Introduction (1843–1844) in Marx, supra note 12, at 129. As O'Malley comments:

In terms reminiscent of Hegel's early doctrine on the simultaneous development of religious and political alienation, Marx declares that the modern political state exists as the religious sphere of human life in opposition to the mundane sphere of civil society; it is the religion of popular life, the heaven of its universality in opposition to the earthly existence of its actuality.

Marx, supra note 12, at li (editor's introduction).

17. Only in a few passages did Marx touch at the roots of modern metaphysics, for example, in the statement: "Hegel's chief mistake consists in the fact that he conceives of the contradiction in appearance as being a unity in essence, i.e. in the Idea; whereas it certainly has something more profound in its essence, namely, an essential contradiction." Marx, supra note 12, at 91.

18. The Portable Nietzsche 39–41 (W. Kauffmann ed. 1968).

19. Id. at 41.

20. Id. at 160.

21. Id. at 162–63.

22. G. Gentile, Genesis and Structure of Society (H. Harris trans. 1966).

23. H. Marcuse, Reason and Revolution (1941).

24. K. Popper, The Open Society and Its Enemies (5th rev. ed. 1966).

25. Id. at 4.

26. J. Lyotard, The Postmodern Condition: A Report on Knowledge (G. Bennington & B. Massumi trans. 1984).

27. Id. at xxiii-xxv.

28. Id. at 9–10, 16 (footnote omitted).

29. Id. at 11–12, 15–17.

30. Id. at 33–34.

31. Id. at 34.

32. Id. at 34–35 (footnote omitted).

33. Id. at 81 (Appendix; translated by R. Durand).

34. Id. at 59.

35. Id. at 61. The linkage of Hegel and "terror" actually occurs in the essay "Answering the Question: What is Postmodernism?" which is attached as an Appendix to the study. Id. at 81. In Lyotard's account, the main example of a contemporary rationalist defense of consensus is Habermas's theory of communicative action. Curiously, despite the distance between the two authors, Habermas also has taken Hegel to task for stressing holism (or the unity of the state) at the expense of particular initiatives or the will of "free and equal persons." See J. Habermas, The Philosophical Discourse of Modernity: Twelve Lectures 39–40 (F. Lawrence trans. 1987).

36. J. Lyotard, Le Différend (1983).

37. Id. at 9–10.

38. Id. at 139–42.

39. Id. at 199.

40. Taylor, supra note 1, at 548.

41. Id. at 550. And Taylor adds that Marx, while acknowledging his debt to Hegel, naturally released all the indignation of the radical Enlightenment at his conception of the state. The Hegelian synthesis is denounced as one achieved in thought only, masking the effective diremption of the real. In the polemic Marx inevitably distorted Hegel, speaking at times as though he was somehow concerned with "abstract thought" alone, and not also the protagonist of another kind of praxis. But the debt is undeniable and comes through Marx's text even when he is not engaged in acknowledging it. Id. at 551.

42. Taylor, supra note 10, at 133.

43. Id. A central political motivation of Lyotard's critique is the memory of Auschwitz, and the impossibility of integrating the latter into an unfolding teleology of meaning. See Lyotard, supra note 36, at 17.

44. The phrase regarding the "identity of identity and difference" occurs particularly in the so-called *Differenzschrift* of 1801. See G. Hegel, Differenz des Fichte'schen und Schelling'schen Systems (G. Lasson ed. 1928). The thesis that "the rational is the real" is formulated in the preface to the *Philosophy of Right* where Hegel elaborates that if

> the idea passes for "only an idea", for a mere fancy or opinion, then philosophy rejects such a view and shows that nothing is actual except the idea. Once this is granted, the important thing is to apprehend in the appearance of the temporal and transient the substance which is immanent and the eternal which is present.

Philosophy of Right, supra note 5, preface at 10.

45. Id.

46. Id. at 11.

47. For Gandhi's description of the ashram at Kochrab, see 2 The Moral and Political Writings of Mahatma Gandhi: Truth and Non-Violence 562–64 (R. Iyer ed.

1986). Akin to ashrams are some forms of *kibbutzim*, particularly if members are gathered from different classes and nationalities. On the whole, the ideas of the so-called "utopian socialists" are in my view not entirely obsolete.

48. Philosophy of Right, supra note 5, § 47.

49. G. Hegel, Grundlinien der Philosophie des Rechts, in 7 Werke 249 (E. Molden-hauer and K. Michel eds. 1970) (The annotation is not contained in Knox's English translation.) For some of the above arguments I am indebted to E. Laclau & C. Mouffe, Hegemony and Socialist Strategy: Towards a Radical Democratic Politics (1985).

13

The Inherent Rationality of the State in Hegel's *Philosophy of Right*

Bernhard Schlink

In Hegel's *Philosophy of Right*, the section on civil society has always been easier to accept than the section on the state.[1] The section on civil society, especially the first part on the system of needs, obviously deals with economic and social reality, while the section on the state often reads, at least to the casual reader, like a strange idealization or even apotheosis of the state. Further, the details of the internal constitution, which Hegel examines, are the details of the constitutional monarchy which has long been outdated. Finally, if according to some modern French and also American social philosophers, our social world is atomized into conflicts and agonal confrontations, then this analysis is a better fit with what Hegel writes about the system of needs than with what he writes about the state.

So, the difference between the two contributions by Andrew Arato[2] and Fred Dallmayr[3] is not surprising. As the titles suggest, Arato finds Hegel's theory of civil society still relevant enough to merit reconstruction; Dallmayr sees Hegel's concept of the state in ruins which can only be arranged into something new, and so he takes every freedom in rethinking the Hegelian state.

But we should not be misled. Whatever the time difference between Hegel's world and ours, and however atomized our social world may be, the state has remained. It is an even stronger presence today than it was in Hegel's time. The state has become the predominant political formation of society the world over. For a long time, the European reality and concept of the state and the American reality and concept of government have been understood as being far apart. Today, the distance of the political system from society that characterizes the concept of the state, as opposed to the concept of government, is regarded as an inherent feature of the American political reality, to no

347

less a degree than in Europe. Many countries in African and Asia try to change their political systems so that they can rid themselves of their tribal or feudal structures and gain the functional and objective quality that, in the evolution of political systems, is ascribed to the modern state. Today, the USSR is trying to reduce the role of the party and its ideology in the political system; the trajectory of *glasnost* and *perestroika* may include a stronger and more autonomous state.

It is true, as Hegel writes and Dallmayr cites, that "[w]hatever happens, every individual is a child of his time; so philosophy too is its own time apprehended in thoughts."[4] But the "own time" referred to is not the decade or the century, but rather the epoch. We are still living in the epoch of the state; the dusk when Hegel's and Minerva's owl spreads its wings has not yet given way to the dawn of a new day.

I

Hegel's *Philosophy of Right* is, as he writes in the preface, "nothing other than the endeavour to apprehend and portray the state as something inherently rational."[5] Hegel does not construct abstract right, the family, or the state, but rather takes all this as given and looks for its inherent rationality. The continued reality of the state poses the question of whether a corresponding search for the inherent rationality of the state is still worthwhile. One can argue that under Stalin, Hitler, and Pol Pot, we have seen so much cruelty and contingency by the state that we can only portray and apprehend the state's inherent irrationality. Or one can argue that the search is still relevant, but that the state's inherent rationality is better apprehended by Marx, Weber, or Popper than by Hegel. I think that Dallmayr, after and with Nietzsche and Lyotard, finds the search itself somewhat passé; at least he judges Hegel's portrayal and apprehension of the state as being outdated by Marx, Weber, and others.

As a constitutional lawyer, I understand the state as something inherently rational. This is neither my personal idiosyncrasy nor my German and European heritage. Research, teaching, and practicing in the field of constitutional law all presuppose the apprehension of the inherent rationality of the state. Without this presupposition we would simply flounder or even drown in a sea of legal discourse. This is especially evident in the field of interpretation. Interpretation is the reconstruction of a hidden rational meaning; interpretation of legal texts lives on the presupposition of their inherent rationality.[6]

As a legal philosopher, I think that Hegel's portrayal and apprehension of the state is easily misunderstood and has been frequently misunderstood, from Marx to Lyotard. Hegel's thought develops step by step, level by level. These steps and levels mark neither an historical process, nor (as much as I like Arthur Jacobson's expression)[7] a *Bildungsroman* of the legal person, nor is it a sequence of idealistic configurations. The development of free will is not the development of an idealistic entity that somehow creates the outer legal world. Rather it is a development of comprehension. The object of this comprehension is the state. Since the state is of course an historic phenomenon, the comprehension has to be aware of the historic quality of the state, that is, recognize how the state has developed over history. But the historically, fully developed state can be comprehended in itself; and this comprehension, step by step, level by level, takes place in the *Philosophy of Right*. What Hegel teaches is that we cannot apprehend property, contract, and wrongdoing, unless we see the formal and abstract quality of these legal concepts. We cannot apprehend morality if not in its opposition to and conflict with abstract right. We cannot comprehend institutions—namely the family, the civil society, and the state—unless we relate them to the conflict between morality and the abstract right. More specifically, we cannot comprehend the state if we do not see it in its relation to the conflicting human tendencies that are present on the one hand in the family and on the other hand in the civil society. I cannot show in detail how well Hegel's philosophy of right reads as a development of the comprehension of the modern state. But I would like to give three examples.

The first example is the concept of property in Hegel's *Philosophy of Right*. Much has been said on this subject during the conference.[8] But first of all, Hegel teaches the following: to comprehend the role that property plays in the modern state, one has to start with its abstract quality. One has to conceive property as a formal relationship between a person, whoever he or she may be, and a thing, whatever it may be. Everything else, the property of the family, the property of communities, restrictions of property, obligations put on property, comes later, has to be portrayed and comprehended later, and needs special justification. This may seem too self-evident to be worked out so carefully by Hegel. But it was not self-evident in Hegel's time. In the first half of the nineteenth century the modern, abstract, and formal concept of property only slowly gained legal recognition[9]. The aristocracy fiercely defended another concept of property, belonging to the preconstitutional feudal political structure. According to this concept some important property was inherently bound to and combined with specific personal qualities; not everybody could own everything, not everything could be owned as such but maybe just in parts and as an aspect of some political title. Against this old concept of property Hegel proposes his new one; only in its abstract quality is property a rational element of the inherently rational modern state.

Another example is Hegel's understanding of the source of law. This too has been an issue during the conference; Jacobson has differentiated between an internal and an external position, the first finding the sources of law inside the legal system, the second finding it outside, and he has identified Hegel with the internal position. Indeed, if Hegel would deal ontologically with the law, one could expect an internal position. On the other hand, if he would deal historically with the law, one could expect an external position. But what Hegel says on this point is neither the one nor the other. In paragraph 273 he emphasizes that "it is absolutely essential that the constitution should not be regarded as something made, even though it has come into being in time."[10] This is a surprisingly modern, almost Kelsian position. It makes sense because Hegel's purpose is comprehension. To comprehend the constitution we have to accept its positivity. Of course it is made, but when and where and how and by whom is a matter of *is* that does not help with the matters of *ought* to be dealt with under the constitution. This exclusion of the question of *pouvoir* constituant, of the power that creates the constitution was of course especially important for the constitutional monarchy with its unsolved and unsolvable antinomy of the monarch's and people's power and legitimacy.[11]

The last example is a negative one. Hegel is not convincing when he is not portraying and comprehending the modern state as it is. I share the view of many Hegel scholars that Hegel is weak when he deals with the corporations.[12] It is hard to see how the corporations could possibly hold together the civil society that Hegel has shown as being so conflict ridden, centrifugal, explosive. It is hard to believe that Hegel should have believed in this capacity of the corporations. He is not convincing here, because he leaves the track of portraying and comprehending the modern state. The corporations, as they appear in the philosophy of right, are something that Hegel simply constructs and postulates. In reality they did not play the role that Hegel ascribes to them.[13] Here, Hegel is normative in an abstract and, by his own standards, negative sense.

II

I think that Arato might agree that the development in Hegel's philosophy of right is a development of comprehension. And so maybe it is a difference more in words than in substance that unlike Arato I cannot find antinomies in Hegel's portrayal and apprehension of the state. I see conflicting needs, interests, and concepts in reality and Hegel trying to portray and apprehend them. I even believe that Hegel has done this with some success. What Arato calls Hegel's antinomies I would prefer to call the antinomies of the modern world.

I would certainly not call antinomous the two different perspectives under which Hegel portrays and apprehends the state in the last two sections of his philosophy of right. In the context of civil society Hegel writes about the external state, the *Not- und Verständesstaat*. On the next step Hegel deals with, let us call it the internal state, that is, the state as the actuality of the ethical idea. It is not the case the external state is the real and the internal state is the ideal, or that we have first the realistic portrayal and then the idealistic apprehension, or that affirmation is followed by critique. Hegel's portrayal and apprehension of the external as well as of the internal state are not affirming and critical. It knows and shows what is necessary and what is accidental, what is legitimate and illegitimate. The difference between the two levels of portrayal and apprehension lies elsewhere.

The state, for Hegel, to be fully apprehended as something inherently rational, cannot be apprehended only in its functions for the civil society. These functions are very important and it is indispensable that they are apprehended; the *Not- und Verständesstaat* has the task of keeping the economy in shape, providing the administration of justice, dealing with law and order and social welfare and even integrating the civil society. But the state as the actuality of the ethical idea is something different, not a function for or of civil society but an institutional environment in which individuals are object and subject of the political decisions and so fully reconciled with community.

This is not, as Arato might see it, a question of *Sittlichkeit* and *Antisittlichkeit*, of the ethical and the anti- or unethical life. The purely functional or instrumental point of view is not unethical in Hegel's terms, is it only ethically limited. As I understand Hegel, even on the level of civil society we have some reconciliation of individual and community. But it is a limited, purely external reconciliation; and this is evidenced by the fact that it cannot be fully successful. The state of the civil society, the *Not- und Verständestaat*, cannot change the fact that "despite an excess of wealth civil society is not rich enough, that is, its own resources are insufficient to check excessive poverty and the creation of penurious rabble."[14] Hegel states that the civil society and with it the *Not- und Verständesstaat* is pushed beyond its own limits, into colonization and imperialism, and he knows that this can be no final solution for the problems of civil society. It can be a solution for this or that particular civil society but not for modern civil society as such, because Hegel sees that the colonies have to become liberated and emancipated at one point and will share the destiny of civil society, namely to be rich but never rich enough.

So the *Not- und Verständesstaat* is in a way stuck with these problems, unable to solve them, and the state as the actuality of the ethical idea does not solve them either. I think this is an important, easily underestimated point. The state does not reconcile the individual with the community by solving the problems of the civil society. Reconciliation by the internal constitution instead means the creation of an institutional environment in which the individual can accept living with the unsolved problems of the civil society. That is the creation or rather the apprehension of the internal constitution as a procedure where the individual is object and subject of the political decisions. Hegel thought the constitutional monarchy provided this procedure. And to his credit one can say that in 1820 in Prussia it was certainly an emancipatory concept. Today we would not agree with him on the merits of constitutional monarchy. But we may agree that apart from the functioning civil society there is a question of participation and emancipation. During this conference Jean Cohen has reminded Bruce Ackerman of the limits of a liberal approach and the necessity of democratic thought. That is exactly what Hegel is dealing with: the limits of the liberal *Not- und Verständesstaat* and the necessity of a different approach to reconcile individual and community.

So the purely functional or instrumental point of view is not unethical but only ethically limited. The state of the benevolent and even the malevolent dictator that guarantees as much functioning economy, social welfare, administration of justice, law and order, and the integration of civil society as possible and which, at the same time falls beyond the level of freedom and emancipation that could be realized, is ethically limited but not unethical. Dallmayr's ashram, by the way, where people live according to their good moral intentions, is in Hegel's terms neither ethical nor unethical but ethically arbitrary and neutral.

The question remains whether Hegel is right in analyzing the state not just under a functional point of view but also under the criterion of realized freedom and emancipation, and whether this has relevance today. Shall we ask ourselves how much freedom is possible, how our political environment can be organized to minimize alienation and to maximize emancipation? Or shall we confine ourselves to a functional or instrumental point of view that comprehends our state only as the *Not- und Verständesstaat?*

Dallmayr has referred to the old reproach regarding totalitarianism that has frequently been leveled against Hegel. The remedy against totalitarianism is often seen as purely functional or instrumental, by that hopefully nonideological understanding of the state and its political institutions. But I think that this is not only deceiving, because there is such a thing as a totalitarianism of functions, but also it misses an essential quality of Hegel's concept of the ethical life and his portrayal and apprehension of the state as something inherently rational. That Hegel proceeds step by step, level by level, is in itself a refusal of totalitarianism. By this Hegel says that the ethical life, that is the fully developed private and public life, cannot be realized in one dimension alone. The ethical life presupposes the acknowledgment of the abstract right and of subjective morality, it takes place in family and civil society, it asks for welfare and law and order and an internal constitution where individuals are object and subject of the political decisions. In contrast to this totalitarianism is essentially one-dimensional.

Is Hegel not in vogue today? At least in Europe he is not regarded as passé as Dallmayr suggests.[15] We should not overestimate the influence of the new wave of French philosophy in Europe. What is more important: our political and legal philosophy, even though it can certainly not limit itself to Hegel, has to go through Hegel. The world has become more complex since Hegel's day and so we need more steps and levels of comprehension, not fewer. The state is still here, more powerful and dangerous than ever, and so the task of portraying and apprehending it as something inherently rational is more important than ever. If we do not fulfill this task we lack the power and the legitimation to criticize, and where necessary to change it.

NOTES

1. See S. Avineri, Hegel's Theory of the Modern State (1972); K. Marx, Critique of Hegel's 'Philosophy of Right' (J. O'Malley ed. 1970) (1843); 2 K. Popper, The Open Society and Its Enemies (1945); M. Riedel, Bürgerliche Gesellschaft und Staat bei Hegel (1970); 2 F. Rosenzweig, Hegel und der Staat (1920); Ilting, Die Struktur der Hegelschen Rechtsphilosophie, in Hegel's Political Philosophy 90–110 (Z. Pelczynski ed. 1971).

2. Arato, A Reconstruction of Hegel's Theory of Civil Society, in this volume.

3. Dallmayr, Rethinking the Hegelian State, in this volume.

4. G. Hegel, Philosophy of Right 11 (T. Knox trans. 1952) [hereinafter Philosophy of Right].

5. Id.

6. See H.-G. Gadamer, Wahrheit und Methode 371–77 (3d ed. 1972).

7. Jacobson, Hegel's Legal Plenum, in this volume.

8. Hegel and Legal Theory Symposium held March 27–29, 1988, at Cardozo School of Law, Yeshiva University.

9. See H. Rittstieg, Eigentum als Verfassungsproblem 191–247 (2d ed. 1976).

10. Philosophy of Right, supra note 4, para. 273.

11. See E.-W. Böckenförde, Der Verfassungstyp der deutschen konstitutionellen Monarchie im 19. Jahrhundert, in Moderne deutsche Verfassungsgeschichte 146–70 (E..-W Bökenförde ed. 2d ed. 1981).

12. See S. Avineri, supra note 1; J. Findlay, Hegel, A re-Examination 321–22 (1958); R. Hoevar, Hegel und der PreuBische Staat 94 (1973); M. Riedel, Tradition und Revolution in Hegel's "Philosophie des Rechts," in Zwischen Tradition und Revolution 170–202 (M Riedel ed. 1982); 2 F. Rosenzweig, supra note 1.

13. See R. Kosselleck, PreuBen zwischen Reform und Revolution 52–77, 116–42, 560–616 (2d ed. 1975).

14. Philosophy of Right, supra note 4, § 245.

15. Among the recent German philosophical literature, see J. Habermas, Moralität und Sittlichkeit, in Moralität und Sittlichkeit 16–37 (W. Kuhlmann ed. 1986); M. Hanisch, Dialektische Logik und Politisches Argument (1981); D. Henrich & R.-P. Horstmann, Hegels Philosophie des Rechts (1982); V. Hösle, Hegels System (1987); G.W.F. Hegel. Vorlesungen über Rechtsphilosophie 1818–1831 (K.-H. Ilting ed 1974); R. Jakobson, H.-G. Gadamer & E. Hollenstein, Das Erbe Hegels (1984); C. Jermann, Anspruch und Leistung von Hegels Rechtsphilosophie (1987); H.-C. Lucas, Hegels Rechtsphilosophie im Zusammenhang der Europäischen Verfassungsgeschichte (O. Pöggeler ed. 1986); J. Ritsert, Das Bellen des toten Hundes (1988); M. Theunissen, Sein und Schein (1980).

Index

Contributors

ANDREW ARATO is Professor of Sociology, Graduate Faculty, New School for Social Research. He is co-author of *Civil Society and Social Theory* published by MIT Press and of the *Young Lukacs and the Origins of Western Marxism* (Seabury Press 1979). He has also co-edited many volumes, including, *The Essential Frankfurt School Reader* (1979) and *Crisis and Reform in Eastern Europe* (1991).

PETER BENSON is Associate Professor of Law at McGill University. He teaches and writes in the areas of contract law, the basis of fundamental rights and freedom, and the philosophy of law.

ROBERT BERNASCONI is the Moss Professor of Philosophy at Memphis State University. He is the author of *The Question of Language in Heidegger's History of Being* (1985) and a number of essays on various aspects of continental philosophy and the history of social thought. He is currently completing two books: *Heidegger in Question* and *Between Levinas and Derrida*.

ALAN BRUDNER is Associate Professor of Law and Political Science at the University of Toronto.

DAVID GRAY CARLSON is Professor of Law at the Benjamin N. Cardozo School of Law, Yeshiva University. He teaches in the areas of commercial law and bankruptcy and is co-editor of *Deconstruction and the Possibility of Justice* to be published by Routledge in 1992. He is currently working on a treatise entitled *Security Interests in Personal Property* to be published by Little Brown & Co.

DRUCILLA CORNELL is Professor of Law at the Benjamin N. Cardozo School of Law, Yeshiva University. She is the author of *Beyond Accomodation* (Routledge 1991) and *The Philosophy of the Limit, Justice and Legal Interpretation* (Routledge 1992) (forthcoming) and co-editor of *Deconstruction and The Possibility of Justice* to be published by Routledge in 1992.

FRED DALLMAYR is the Dee Professor of Government at the University of Notre Dame. He is the author of numerous books, which include *Twilight of Subjectivity* (1981), *Polis and Praxis* (1984), *Language and Politics* (1984), *Critical Encounters* (1987) and *Margins of Political Discourse* (1989).

ARTHUR J. JACOBSON is the Max Freund Professor of Litigation and Advocacy, Benjamin N. Cardozo School of Law, Yeshiva University. He is an editor of "Philosophy, Social Theory and the Rule of Law," a series published by The University of California Press. His work on *Dynamic Jurisprudence* will appear in the series, along with *Weimar Jurisprudence,* a collection of translations of leading works of Weimar legal theory, which he is editing with Bernhard Schlink.

DAVID FARRELL KRELL is Professor and Chair of Philosophy at DePaul University in Chicago. He is the author of *Of Memory, Reminiscence, and Writing On the Verge* (Indiana University Press, 1990), *Intimations of Mortality: Time, Truth, and Finitude in Heidegger's Thinking of Being* (Pennsylvania State University Press, 1986; 2nd ed., 1991), and *Postponements: Woman, Sensuality, and Death in Nietzsche* (Indiana University Press, 1986). He is editor and translator of many books by Martin Heidegger. He is currently at work on a text entitled *Daimon Life: Heidegger and "Lebensphilosophie".*

MICHEL ROSENFELD is Professor of Law at the Benjamin N. Cardozo School of Law, Yeshiva University. He is the author of *Affirmative Action and Justice: A Philosophical and Constitutional Inquiry* (Yale University Press 1991) and the co-editor of *Deconstruction and the Possibility of Justice* to be published by Routledge in 1992. He is an editor of the book series "Philosophy, Social Theory and the Rule of Law" published by the University of California Press, and is currently working on a book entitled *Contract and Justice* for that series.

BERNHARD SCHLINK is Professor of Public Law at the University of Bonn and Justice of the Constitutional Court of the State of Nordrhein-

Westfalen. He is the author of *Absägung im Verfassungsrecht* (1976), *Die Amtshilfe: Ein Beitrag zu eine Lehre von der Gewaltenteilung in der Verwaltung* (1982) and co-author of *Grundrechte* (7th ed. 1991).

PETER G. STILLMAN is Professor of Political Science at Vassar College where he has also taught in an interdisciplinary humanities program. He has published numerous articles and book chapters on Hegel's political philosophy, Marx's political theory and utopian political thought.

CHARLES TAYLOR was for many years Chichele Professor of Social and Political Theory at Oxford. He is now Professor of Political Philosophy at McGill University. He is the author of numerous books including *Hegel* (Cambridge University Press 1975) and *Sources of The Self: The Making of the Modern Identity* (Harvard University Press 1989).

MICHAEL THEUNISSEN is in the philosophy department, Free University of Berlin.

ERNEST J. WEINRIB is Professor of Law and Special Lecturer in Classics at the University of Toronto.